POET-MONKS

POET-MONKS

THE INVENTION OF BUDDHIST POETRY IN LATE MEDIEVAL CHINA

Thomas J. Mazanec

CORNELL EAST ASIA SERIES
AN IMPRINT OF
CORNELL UNIVERSITY PRESS
Ithaca and London

Number 217 in the Cornell East Asia Series

Copyright © 2024 by Cornell University

The text of this book is licensed under a Creative Commons Attribution NonCommercial-NoDerivatives 4.0 International License: https://creativecommons.org/licenses/by-nc-nd/4.0/. To use this book, or parts of this book, in any way not covered by the license, please contact Cornell University Press, Sage House, 512 East State Street, Ithaca, New York 14850. Visit our website at cornellpress.cornell.edu.

First published 2024 by Cornell University Press

Publication of this Open Access monograph has been made possible by generous funding from the The Regents of the University of California, Santa Barbara campus, making it possible to open this publication to the world.

ISBN 9781501773839 (hardcover)
ISBN 9781501773846 (epub)
ISBN 9781501773853 (pdf)

LCCN 2023015812 (print)
LCCN 2023015813 (ebook)

ISBN 9781501778780 (pbk)

Contents

List of Illustrations vii
Acknowledgments ix
List of Abbreviations xiii
Note on Conventions xv

Introduction   1

Part I. History

1. Introducing Poet-Monks: History, Geography, and Sociality   19
2. Inventing Poet-Monks: The First Generation and Their Reception, 760–810   48
3. Becoming Poet-Monks: The Formation of a Tradition, 810–960   82

Part II. Poetics

4. Repetition: Retriplication and Negation   113
5. Incantation: Sonority and Foreignness   143
6. Meditation: Effort and Absorption   185

Conclusion   214

Notes 229
Bibliography 289
Index 317

Illustrations

Maps

1.1.	Poet-monk activity, 720–810.	27
1.2.	Poet-monk activity, 811–874.	29
1.3.	Poet-monk activity, 875–907.	30
1.4.	Poet-monk activity, 908–960.	31

Figures

1.1.	Network graph of poems exchanged between contemporaries in the late medieval period.	39
1.2.	Detail of the network graph in Figure 1.1.	40
1.3.	Detail from P. 3886, verso.	45
4.1.	Bar graph of retriplication in the Tang and Five Dynasties, by fifty-year periods.	118
4.2.	Bar graph of retriplication in the Tang and Five Dynasties, by type.	127
5.1.	Detail from P. 2104, verso.	149
5.2.	Depiction of the arhat Piṇḍola in the style of Guanxiu (11th–12th century).	171

Acknowledgments

In the decade or so that I have been writing this book, I have accrued many debts to teachers, colleagues, friends, and family. The foremost of these is to my PhD advisors, Anna M. Shields and Stephen F. Teiser, who helped me develop a half-formed thought into a research project, then a dissertation, then a book. Paul W. Kroll's tireless mentorship, from my very first classical Chinese course to the present day, has at times been my scholarly lifeblood. I have benefited from the guidance of many other teachers, especially Ping Wang and Antje Richter. I also learned much from Chen Yinchi 陳引馳 and Zhu Gang 朱剛 during my time at Fudan University on a Fulbright fellowship.

Cornell University Press's anonymous reviewers provided important feedback that helped me clarify and hone the arguments presented herein. Fellow poet-monk enthusiast Jason Protass read and commented on an early manuscript, and our ongoing conversations have pushed me to rethink or reframe many aspects of this book. Paul Vierthaler's guidance, direct and indirect, was crucial in helping me gain sufficient facility with Python to carry out some of the macroscopic analysis in what follows. He patiently answered my relentless emails about issues large and small, even as he was busy with his own commitments. Xiaoshan Yang read through the whole manuscript and provided many helpful suggestions. Lucas Bender offered important comments on the first three chapters. All remaining errors are solely my responsibility.

An earlier version of chapter six first appeared in *Asia Major* as "How Poetry Became Meditation in Late-Ninth-Century China." Part of the "Sociality" section of chapter 1 first appeared in the *Journal of Chinese Literature and Culture* as part of "Networks of Exchange Poetry: Notes toward a Dynamic History of Tang Literature." Both of these papers were greatly improved by the insights of editors and anonymous reviewers. I have presented other parts of the research for this book in other venues: the Specialist Lectures in Chinese History and Culture at Hong Kong Polytechnic University (PolyU) in 2018, the "Prospects for the Study of

Dunhuang Manuscripts" conference at Princeton University in 2014, the "Beyond the Tang-Song Transition" panel at the Association for Asian Studies annual conference in 2017, the American Oriental Society's 2012 and 2015 Western Branch meetings, the "Literary Networks" seminar at the American Comparative Literature Association's annual meeting in 2015, and the "Religion, Literature, and Global Humanities" panel of the "Indian and Chinese Religions Compared" Unit for the American Academy of Religion in 2020. My thanks to all who offered feedback at these events, especially Jia Jinhua 賈晉華 at PolyU.

I am also grateful to my institutional home, University of California, Santa Barbara, for its support. As chair of the Department of East Asian Languages and Cultural Studies when I arrived, Katherine Saltzman-Li graciously oriented me to this new environment. Conversations with Xiaorong Li, Dominic Steavu, Peter Sturman, Hangping Xu, Xiaowei Zheng, and Ya Zuo have been especially generative. Sabine Frühstück offered important practical advice at critical moments. Funding from the EALCS Department, the East Asia Center, the Faculty Senate, the Interdisciplinary Humanities Center, and the College of Letters and Science has supported my participation in many of the academic events listed above. Other sources of funding that supported the research for this book include the Fulbright Foundation, the T'ang Studies Society, the Interdisciplinary Humanities Program at Princeton, and the Center for Digital Humanities at Princeton.

The comradeship of colleagues has been essential to the formation of this book. While there are too many to name individually, I would like to single out Heng Du and Peiting C. Li to thank them for our ongoing conversations. David Chai, Yiyi Luo, Qingfeng Nie, Jui-lung Su, and others helped with locating difficult-to-find materials at crucial moments.

I would also like to thank Cornell University Press, especially Cornell East Asia Series acquisitions editor Alexis Siemon for her many helpful suggestions and her clear, speedy correspondence. Thanks are also due to Kendra Mills for preparing the index and to Bill Nelson for producing the maps in chapter 1, based on my models, to comply with Cornell's rigorous standards. The production of the maps and index were supported by a scholarly production grant from the T'ang Studies Society.

The time between filing my dissertation and finishing this book has seen the birth of my two children, the source of much happy chaos in my personal and professional life. None of the writing and revising of this book would have been possible without the support of childcare workers. Thanks to Benyapa Srivala, Emily Nicholson, Heather Walters, Jill

Drewisch, and Allan Fiedkou. When our firstborn was still very young, Daaigumaa 大姑媽 spent a month showing us the ropes of infant care. My in-laws Guoliang Yu 余國亮 and Xiaoan Ge 戈小安, as well as my parents Thomas S. and Sandra J. Mazanec, also stepped up to help with the kids during parts of the COVID-19 pandemic.

My wife Jenny 余捷 has been a constant source of support in ways too numerous to count. My children Rae 余曦 and Tommy 余亮 are the joys of my life. This book is for you.

Abbreviations

ca.	circa
Ch.	Chinese
d.	died
Digital Appendix	https://github.com/tommazanec/poet-monks
fl.	floruit
HJAS	*Harvard Journal of Asiatic Studies*
Hu Dajun	Hu Dajun 胡大浚, ed. and annot. *Guanxiu geshi xinian jianzhu* 貫休歌詩繫年箋注. 3 vols. ZHSJ, 2011.
JAOS	*Journal of the American Oriental Society*
JIABS	*Journal of the International Association for Buddhist Studies*
j.s.	date *jinshi* 進士 degree received
MC	Middle Chinese
Pan Dingwu	Pan Dingwu 潘定武, Zhang Xiaoming 張小明, and Zhu Dayin 朱大銀, ed. and annot. *Qiji shi zhu* 齊己詩注. Hefei: Huangshan shushe, 2014.
QTS	*Quan Tang shi* 全唐詩. Comp. Peng Dingqiu 彭定求 et al. ZHSJ, 1960.
QTSBB	*Quan Tang shi bubian* 全唐詩補編. Comp. Chen Shangjun 陳尚君. ZHSJ, 1992.
QTW	*Quan Tang wen* 全唐文. Comp. Dong Hao 董浩 et al. ZHSJ, 1983.
r.	reigned
SBCK	*Sibu congkan* 四部叢刊. Ed. Zhang Yuanji 張元濟. Shanghai: Shangwu yinshuguan, 1919.
SGSZ	*Song gaoseng zhuan* 宋高僧傳. Comp. Zanning 贊寧. T no. 2061, 50:709a–900.
SHGJ	Shanghai: Shanghai guji chubanshe
SKQS	*Wenyuange Siku quanshu* 四庫全書. Ed. Yang Ne 楊訥 and Li Xiaoming 李曉明. Taipei: Shangwu yinshuguan, 1983–86.
Skt.	Sanskrit

T	*Taishō shinshū daizōkyō* 大正新脩大藏經. Ed. Takakusu Junjirō 高楠順次郎 et al. Tokyo: Taishō Issaikyō Kankōkai, 1924–1935. Online editions at https://cbetaonline.dila.edu.tw/ and https://21dzk.l.u-tokyo.ac.jp/SAT/satdb2015.php.
Wang Xiulin	Wang Xiulin 王秀林, ed. *Qiji shiji jiaozhu* 齊己詩集校注. Beijing: Zhongguo shehui kexue chubanshe, 2011.
Z	*Shinsan Dainihon Zokuzōkyō* 新纂大日本續藏經, ed. Nishi Giyū 西義雄 et al. Tokyo: Kokusho Kankōkai, 1975–1989.
ZHSJ	Beijing: Zhonghua shuju

Note on Conventions

Following sinological convention, Chinese names and terms have been transliterated according to their Mandarin pronunciation in standard Hanyu pinyin, minus tonal diacritics. Middle Chinese pronunciations, indicated with "MC," follow William Baxter and Laurent Sagart's reconstruction as reproduced in Kroll's *Student's Dictionary*, with one modification: rising tone (*shangsheng* 上聲) and departing tone (*qusheng* 去聲) are rendered not with the letters *X* and *H* at the end of a word but with caron and grave diacritics over the main vowel (*dzyǎng* and *khjò* instead of *dzyangX* and *khjoH*). This is meant to make them more legible to readers familiar with pinyin. Rhyme patterns, when relevant to the analysis of a poem, are indicated with capital letters to the right of the poem's English translation, with off-rhymes (same finals, different tones) indicated with an asterisk. Japanese transliterations follow the modified Hepburn system. Chinese characters have been converted to their full, complex forms. Asian names are given with the surname first, except for modern scholars who publish in Western languages and put their given name before their surname. I transliterate modern sinophone scholars' names according to their preferred styles ("Hsiao Li-hua," not "Xiao Lihua," for 蕭麗華), defaulting to Hanyu pinyin if unable to determine their preference.

Premodern Chinese works are cited by *juan* 卷 number and page number, separated by a dot, in modern critical editions when available. Tang writings also reference the standard compendia, *Quan Tang shi* and *Quan Tang wen*, for the reader's convenience. Thus: "Zhu, *Bai Juyi ji jianjiao*, 21.1445–49; *QTS* 444.4978." Buddhist scriptures are referred to by their serial number within the Taishō canon, followed by volume, colon, page number, and register. So a quote from the *Great Wisdom Śāstra* (Ch.: *Da zhidu lun* 大智度論, Skt.: *Mahāprajñāpāramitā śāstra*), which is the 1509th text in the Taishō canon, located on the third register of page 259 in volume 25, is cited as "*T* no. 1509, 25:259c." Dunhuang manuscripts are listed with the standard abbreviations for their collection names followed by a dot and their index number: "S" for the British Library's Stein collection, "P" for the Bibliothèque nationale's Pelliot chinois collection, "Dx" for the Dunhuang collection at the Institute of Oriental Manuscripts of the Russian Academy of Sciences, and "BD" for the Beijing Dunhuang collection of China's National Library.

Historical figures are listed with their characters and dates at first appearance, then only by transliteration afterward. In translations, I generally refer to people by their most well-known name, even if the source text uses an alternate name ("Guanxiu" instead of "Chanyue"), unless the alternate name has particular significance in the passage. Dates of Tang poets generally follow Zhou Xunchu's *Tangshi dacidian*, which builds on Fu Xuancong's *Tang caizi zhuan jiaojian*; dates of early and early-medieval writers follow Knechtges and Chang's *Ancient and Early Medieval Chinese Literature*. Bureaucratic titles follow Hucker's *Dictionary of Official Titles*. Identification of flora and fauna follow Kroll's *Student's Dictionary*.

POET-MONKS

Introduction

On a cool spring morning, sometime in the 920s or 930s, the Buddhist monk Qiji 齊己 (864-937?) decided to compose a poem. Spring seemed to invite a response. An orphan taken in by a monastery when he was seven, Qiji had had a knack for poetry since his youth, composing verses with a bamboo stick from the backs of the cows he herded. Now, six decades later, after he had witnessed the world's collapse in his prime years, his heroes' deaths soon thereafter, and his own conscription into bureaucratic service near his childhood home, the practice of poetry still captivated him. Words into lines, lines into couplets, couplets into poems. It was all right there, just out of reach, embedded in the scene before him. He began to compose aloud, reciting as he went so that he might remember his poem later when he got back to brush and ink.

Stirred by a Whim in Mid-Spring 中春感興
Qiji

Spring wind day after day
    and rain from time to time.
A winter power subtly
    declines with the warmth.

The single breath, unspeaking,
    contains true forms;
Where then could the ten thousand spirits
    thank its impartiality?
Poetry (penetrates the order of things)
    can be gathered while walking;
The Way (in tune with Heaven's workings)
    can be glimpsed while sitting.
So it should be the Right Man who
    upholds creation,
Driving all the hidden subtleties
    into his forge.

春風日日雨時時，
寒力潛從暖勢衰。
一氣不言含有象，
萬靈何處謝無私。
詩通物理行堪掇，
道合天機坐可窺。
應是正人持造化，
盡驅幽細入爐錘。¹

The resulting poem was not just a description of the scene before Qiji but also an articulation once more of his thoughts on the world, poetry, Buddhism, and their relationship.² The world, he claimed, is a diverse yet interconnected, constantly changing whole. Phenomena are composed of forms (images, shapes—*xiang* 象 in its cosmic sense) that emerge out of an ultimate reality—an underlying pattern (*li* 理) known as the "single breath" (*yiqi* 一氣) to Daoists, also called "suchness" (Ch. *zhenru* 真如, Skt. *tathātā*) by Buddhists. This reality cannot be fully identified with any single thing, but every single thing partakes of it.

According to Qiji, there are two ways to access this hidden cosmic order—poetry and religion. The Way (Dao 道) is the transcendent principle of reality in each of the three major religious traditions at the time—Buddhism, Daoism, and Confucian classicism (Ru 儒). It is what we pursue in religion. Whether gathering verses while on a walk or mentally merging with the Way while seated in meditation, the Right Man (*zhengren* 正人) sees phenomena and, what is more, sees through them. He glimpses ultimate reality through the mundane, for ultimate and mundane are perfectly interfused. The Right Man engages with the world in order to understand its process of unceasing creation and add it to his own work. He puts it into his "forge" (*luchui* 爐錘)—a figure for the poet's representation of reality, which mirrors nature's endless transformative power, that can be traced back to the Daoist classic *Zhuangzi* 莊子.[3] The Right Man venerates and perpetuates the ongoing process of making and shaping the cosmos. "The Right Man," like "the Way," is a term that transcends divisions: it refers to Buddhist saints, Confucian sages, and Daoist sylphs alike. To Qiji, this Right Man is both the poet and the monk. He is, above all, the one in whom these two callings meet. He is the poet-monk.[4]

Qiji was not alone in making such bold claims. His understanding of the relationship between poetry and religion was shared by other Buddhist monks of the time. It reflected their vision of a fundamental unity between the two great cultural traditions they inherited, Buddhism and Confucian classicism.[5] Most people at this time understood poetry to fall under the domain of Confucian literati, while meditation, incantation, and other spiritual practices fell under the domain of religious professionals, such as Buddhist monks. These monks sought to break this dichotomy. Qiji's contemporary Qichan 棲蟾 claimed, "Poetry is meditation for Confucians" 詩為儒者禪.[6] Guanxiu 貫休 (832–913), an older monk much admired by Qiji, equated Confucian and Buddhist senses of the divine when he wrote that "Yao's heaven is Brahma's heaven" 堯天即梵天.[7] Qiji himself, in many of his own poems as well as in his guide to writing poetry, used the technical jargon of Buddhism to describe the practice of poetry.[8] These statements were radical. They proposed nothing less than a tonsuring of the classical literary tradition.

The men who made these claims, known as poet-monks (*shiseng* 詩僧), worked toward unifying Buddhist and literary practices. The monks who wrote at the peak of this tradition, especially Guanxiu and Qiji, created something called "Buddhist poetry" in its fullest sense— elite verbal art that was understood to accomplish the same ends as Buddhism. By tracing the emergence and growth of a self-conscious tradition of poet-monks, this book makes three critical interventions in the fields of Chinese literature, religious studies, and comparative literature. First, it highlights the crucial role played by Buddhism in the history of Chinese poetry, despite its relative neglect by traditional and modern scholars. Second, it demonstrates that, in the realm of poetry, the period surrounding the collapse of the Tang dynasty (860–960) was one of innovation and possibility, not of stagnation and decadence. Third, it argues that the intersection of religion and literature is best understood at the level of practice, not at the level of belief, worldview, or scripture—concepts that stem from modern, Protestant assumptions about what religion is. In short, this book shows how the poet-monks were the inventors of Chinese Buddhist poetry for their time.

On Chinese Buddhist Poetry

Buddhism occupies a paradoxical place in histories of Chinese literature. It has been considered its pinnacle, its nadir, and its marginalia. On the one hand, popular translations in the West see in premodern Chinese poetry a Zen-like, environmentalist spirituality that could articulate an alternative to the modern, capitalist world that we live in, and Sinophone scholars of the early twentieth century saw precedents to their own vernacular literary movement in the colloquial verses of Hanshan 寒山, Wang Fanzhi 王梵志, and the anonymous Buddhist preachers of Dunhuang.[9] To both of these groups, Buddhist poetry is central to understanding Chinese poetic history. On the other hand, many of the traditional critics of imperial China who shaped the canon saw Buddhist poetry as immature, clumsy, stinking of the tasteless vegetarian food that monks live on—or worse. The influential critic Wang Fuzhi 王夫之 (1619–1692), for example, listed "the monkish" 似衲子者 as one of four types of bad poetry, and his contemporary Shu Wei 舒位 went so far as to say that, in poetry, "the flavor of meditation is like that of a shit stick" 禪味如是乾屎橛.[10] Many others said that monks' poetry had a "stench of vegetables and bamboo shoots" 蔬筍氣.[11] Buddhist poetry may be a minor curiosity, or it may be an affront to good taste.

Modern critics, however, usually do not think of Buddhist poetry as the pinnacle or the nadir of the tradition; they do not think of it at all. The most widely taught anthologies and textbooks of classical Chinese poetry, in multiple languages, routinely feature few or no poems by Buddhist monks.[12] General histories of Tang poetry rarely feature more than passing references to poet-monks.[13] From a purely statistical point of view, the works of at least Guanxiu, Qiji, and Jiaoran 皎然 (720?–797?) deserve greater attention: their corpora are the seventh-, eighth-, and fourteenth-largest of all Tang poets.[14] Even literary histories devoted to the period of 860–960 (the focus of this book), in which Guanxiu and Qiji appear to be by far the most productive poets, give short shrift to Buddhism.[15] To these critics, Buddhist poetry is marginal to Chinese poetic history.

All three of these views miss a much more complicated, much more interesting story. Buddhist poetry was not a given in Chinese literary culture, nor was it an outlier. Rather, Chinese Buddhist poetry was a thing—a discursive tradition—that had to be invented and reinvented at different times.[16] In the course of each invention, it adapted to the needs of new communities. Buddhism and poetry inspired, influenced, accommodated, clashed, and merged in multiple ways under the direction of numerous actors. These negotiations, and the literary works they produced, run straight through the heart of both the Buddhist and the poetic canons. The stories of Buddhism's intersection with the Chinese poetic tradition have typically been explored in more specialized studies rather than macroscopic overviews of literary history. Yet Buddhism fundamentally shaped many of the tradition's most celebrated writers as well as many poetic genres and norms of literary criticism. Similarly, the Chinese poetic tradition shaped Buddhist scriptures, writings, and nonliterary practices.[17] The aim of this book is to tell the story of one invention of Chinese Buddhist poetry. It does so by recounting the emergence of the Buddhist poet-monk as a new kind of literary actor in the latter half of the Tang and its aftermath (760–960 CE) and describing the ways that these monks created their own idea of Chinese Buddhist poetry.

This is not to say that the late medieval poet-monks were the only ones who found continuities between poetry and Buddhism. Buddhism entered China sometime around the year 65 CE, and it began to take hold among the literati about two hundred years later.[18] This is roughly the same stretch of time in which elite poetry (*shi* 詩) developed into the independent art form we recognize today.[19] In many ways, Chinese Buddhism and poetry can be seen as twins. Both grew out of a hybrid of foreign and indigenous influences in the late Han and developed into prominent features of literati culture. And, like twins separated at birth, it seems fated that their paths would one day cross.

And so they did, as Buddhism and poetry alike flourished in the third and fourth centuries. Prior to the Late Tang period, monks like Zhi Dun 支遁 (314–366) and Huiyuan 慧遠 (337–417) wrote well-regarded poems, while literati poets like Sun Chuo 孫綽 (ca. 310–397) and Xie Lingyun 謝靈運 (385–433) studied and performed Buddhist rituals with prominent monks.[20] Monks continued to compose poetry through the end of the early medieval period and into the first half of the Tang. Huixiu 惠休 (mid-fifth cent.), Baoyue 寶月 (fl. 483–493), and others wrote in the elegant, ornate style that dominated courtly literary circles in their time.[21] These early monastic writers were not called "poet-monks"—that term was invented in the mid-eighth century to describe the monks at the center of this study—but later generations saw them retrospectively as such. Well after the time period covered by this book, monks like Daoqian 道潛 (1043-1106) and Juefan Huihong 覺範惠洪 (1071-1128) maintained close associations with famed literati and exchanged worthy poems with them.[22] Monks, to be clear, were not the sole proprietors of Buddhist-inflected poetry. Literati could also write powerful poetry that drew on Buddhist ideas and images, and some considered themselves devout lay Buddhists whose literary works could help propagate and perpetuate Buddhist institutions. Each of these groups—monks during the late fourth century, late fifth century, and turn of the twelfth century, and literati at various times—articulated their visions of Buddhist poetry in response to their own circumstances, and each did so in ways that were distinct from the poet-monks of the Late Tang.

To take just one example, the Buddhist-inflected poetry of the fourth-century monk Zhi Dun uses the language of "arcane studies" (*xuanxue* 玄學) that was popular in his time, a kind of metaphysical discourse that drew on Daoism and Buddhism.[23] As such, he was not known as a poet-monk but rather as one who practiced "pure conversation" (*qingtan* 清談), an elite art that emphasized the display of wit, erudition, character evaluation, and philosophic digression.[24] His literary works use a vocabulary markedly different from that of the late medieval poet-monks, written in a higher, more opaque register. When his poems allude to Buddhist scriptures and practices, they do so at greater philosophic remove than our poet-monks. Zhi Dun may have understood there to be a deep harmony between Buddhism and poetry (as mediated by the prevailing intellectual discourse of his day), but he did not boldly assert their practical unity. His own idea of Buddhist poetry, if he had one that was distinct from the poetry of the arcane, was quite different from that of the late medieval poet-monks. The same could be said of Huiyuan's landscape verse or Huihong's "lettered Chan" (*wenzi chan* 文字禪).[25] Zhi Dun's Buddhistic verse was an invention for his own time. The poet-monks' was one for theirs.

On Literary History

Taking Buddhist poetry seriously, and understanding the necessity of its continual reinvention, forces us to rethink aspects of how we tell medieval Chinese literary history. Instead of the canonical narrative, which presents a neat arc of development that peaks with the High Tang in the mid-eighth century and declines in the ninth and tenth, we see instead various aesthetic paradigms wax and wane in different periods and at different rates. The paradigm of Buddhist poetry, as understood by the poet-monks, crests around the turn of tenth century, when several major poet-monks lived through the collapse of the Tang dynasty and the subsequent rise of regional kingdoms.

This period, also known as the End of Tang (*Tangmo* 唐末) and Five Dynasties and Ten Kingdoms (*Wudai shiguo* 五代十國), is commonly seen as a low point in the history of Chinese poetry. This view is deeply entrenched, having been reiterated thousands of times since the twelfth century, when Wu Ke 吳可 declared that "the poetry by men from the End of the Tang is weightless, frivolous" 唐末人詩輕佻, and Lu You 陸游 (1125–1210) said that "looking at writings from the Late Tang / makes one want to burn his writing brush" 乃觀晚唐作，令人欲焚筆.[26] In modern times, scholars frequently characterize this period as moribund, "the last ebbs of a mighty wave, the lingering echoes of a great sound" 洪波之末流，大聲之餘響.[27]

This attitude of dismissal is prevalent in anglophone scholarship as well. Most anthologies of poetry translations contain few or no poems from this period.[28] The *Columbia History of Chinese Literature* gives passing reference to the last few decades of the Tang (one and a half pages out of forty on the Tang) and avoids the poetry of the Five Dynasties period entirely.[29] In *The Late Tang*, Stephen Owen characterized the poetry written between 860 and 1020 as follows:

> There is much poetry after 860 that is worthy of consideration. It is easy to read the poetry of this later period with an eye to the momentous events that were occurring, but the vast majority of poems composed during this period simply carry on the kinds of poetry created in the period encompassed by our study [827–860]. It was a poetry that may have been traumatically ossified. If we wish to uncover the relation between the history of poetry and the larger sense of "history," we may find it not in changes in poetry but in poetry's refusal to change, in its fine couplets, its absorption in pleasures both poetic and sensual. . . . This same poetry may have continued mimetically in the provinces during the Five Dynasties; but the society in which the poetry was first created was dead, bodies left rotting in the ditches and fields.[30]

Owen describes this period as static—there is no major change in poetry between the mid-ninth and early-eleventh century. While he concedes that there is some poetry of value from this period, he qualifies this by characterizing it as unoriginal and decadent. He underlines his judgment with a striking metaphor in the last quoted sentence, conjuring the image of poetry from this period as a ghost that lived on after its body (the society that produced it) had begun to decompose. In the book's conclusion, he elaborates on the reasons why this is a low point for poetry: "With the deaths of Du Mu, Li Shangyin, and Wen Tingyun, an era had ended. . . . There were no more strong poetic personalities to leave a lasting mark on the poetry of the next millennium."[31] However, as I hope to show in the following chapters, poet-monks like Guanxiu and Qiji were indeed strong poetic personalities who attempted to accomplish new things, even if later critics, due to a combination of changing sociopolitical forces, dismissed their achievements.[32] This critical view, it should be clear, is not unique to Owen: he is only the most prominent articulator in English of the consensus. Many other examples could be adduced in scholarship on Tang poetry written in many languages.[33] While there exist studies of this period that avoid the narrative of decline, they are few.[34]

The denigration of the end of the Tang and Five Dynasties in literary history is based on long-held biases built on an assumed correlation between the political and the literary. An inferior sociopolitical realm necessarily leads to inferior works of literature. Lateness is always characterized by formalism, decadence, sensuality, superstition, escapism, and imitation. Precisely the same criticisms have been made about the poetry of Late Antiquity in the West (third through seventh centuries). The problem, in Late Tang China as in Western Late Antiquity, is that critics impose the standards of earlier or later periods (such as classical unity or modern innovation) and condemn poets for failing to achieve something they never set out to do.[35] If instead we seek out contemporaneous ideas of the poetic, such as those found in the poetry manuals (*shige* 詩格) that were popular in late medieval China, we can begin to understand the era on its own terms, noticing subtler developments in poetics. Instead of privileging biographical testimony to history or lyrical expression of personal feelings, we can focus instead on the juxtaposition of parallel imagery, on the patterning of rhymes and tones, on the adaptation of generic conventions, on the repetition of key words and phrases, and on systems of figuration.[36] One aim of this book is to revive interest in this period and demonstrate how it is crucial to a fuller account of literary history.[37]

By literary history, I mean something more than a historicist understanding of literature. Literary history aims to account for the changing system of relations among texts; between texts, people, and the world; and among the critical, social, political, intellectual, and material conditions that shape the production of texts.[38] To this end, it requires both macro- and microscopic analysis of the late medieval literary scene, both of which may be found in this book. Some may be put off by my occasional references to digitally assisted analysis. This book is, admittedly, a hybrid—mainly a work of classic literary criticism but one that is framed by computational inquiries. It takes this approach not to make any methodological point but instead to use whatever resources are currently available to describe the poet-monks' literary world in as clear and accurate a manner as possible.[39] Digital tools, if used with care, may reveal aspects of this world that would have been invisible to earlier generations (and future researchers will no doubt apply new tools to reveal aspects that I have overlooked).[40] Nevertheless, my main interest lies at the level of the individual poem, and the reader will find plenty of close readings in what follows. The macroscope is a means of situating a work. The microscope is a means of understanding it. Literary history needs both.

At the same time, this book is not intended to be a comprehensive literary history of late medieval China. It is a study of one strand in the complex web that constitutes the literary at this time, namely the sense of Buddhist poetry advocated by poet-monks. I focus mainly on *shi*-poetry (elite, classical verse) and related genres like song-style poetry (*gexing* 歌行 and *yuefu* 樂府). I therefore set aside the rise of song lyrics (*ci* 詞) and the significant changes in didactic Buddhist verse (*gāthā* or *ji* 偈) except when they help us understand developments related to Buddhist *shi*.[41] Likewise, since I am concerned with the poetry of Buddhist monks—men who lived in same-sex communities, devoted themselves to religious pursuits, shaved their heads, wore distinctive robes, and ideally remained celibate and refrained from consuming meat and alcohol—I do not attempt to account for lay Buddhist poets like Bai Juyi 白居易 (772-846), Sikong Tu 司空圖 (837-908), or the legendary Hanshan, except insofar as they shine light on the poet-monks.[42] Similarly, other important literary actors of this time with varying attitudes toward Buddhist practices, such as Pi Rixiu 皮日休 (834?-883?), Lu Guimeng 陸龜蒙 (d. 881?), Wei Zhuang 韋莊 (836-910), Zheng Gu 鄭谷 (851?-910?), Luo Yin 羅隱 (833-910), Han Wo 韓偓 (844-923), Li Pin 李頻 (d. 876), Fang Gan 方干 (d. 885?), Chen Tao 陳陶 (803?-879?),

and Wu Rong 吳融 (d. 903), appear only as minor characters tangential to the story of the poet-monks.

Poet-monks are Buddhist monks who wrote poetry and understood themselves to be participants in elite literary circles. The poet-monk category was created in the mid-eighth century to describe a specific kind of literary actor. Due to the nature of our sources, it is impossible to say how many poet-monks were active from the mid-eighth through the mid-tenth centuries. If we define the term very narrowly, as only those who are explicitly called a "poet-monk" in extant sources, it refers to twenty individuals. If we expand our definition a little to include those monks for whom some elite poetic writings and biographical information has survived, it refers to forty-eight individuals. These forty-eight people are the main focus of this study, with a particular emphasis on the two with the largest extant poetry collections, Guanxiu and Qiji. But it is important to remember that in the late medieval period the term "poet-monk" likely referred to many more people whose works have not survived or who are addressed only by generic titles such as "a monk" (*seng* 僧), "a clergyman" (*daoren* 道人), "a meditation master" (*chanshi* 禪師), or "the reverend" (*shangren* 上人). For a sense of how many more, I will point to the fact that in the comprehensive compendium of Tang poetry compiled in the early eighteenth century, *Quan Tang shi* 全唐詩, there are 115 monks to whom are attributed forty-six fascicles (*juan* 卷) of poetry, occupying about 5 percent of the entire corpus.[43] This number does not account for the monks whose enormous literary outputs are now mostly lost but were mentioned in historical sources, such as the thirty-fascicle collection of Zhenguan 真觀 (538–611), the ten-fascicle collection of Guanxiu's disciple Tanyu 曇域, or the ten- and twenty-fascicle collections of the otherwise-unknown Guangbai 光白.[44] Most poet-monks embarked on a monastic career at a very early age (seven or eight years old), though some converted later in life. Most would have learned to read and write in a monastery, trained on the Confucian classics as well as Buddhist texts.[45] All poet-monks, by definition, positioned themselves as participating in the broader Tang literary world.

My main goal in this book is to understand the poetry of two monks in particular, Guanxiu and Qiji—how they reflected broader trends in literary and religious history as well as how they helped shaped these pathways. That is, I am not attempting a prosopographical study of poet-monks—such a study would be impossible, because Guanxiu, Qiji, and Jiaoran are the only poet-monks whose extant corpora are larger than five hundred poems (and Jiaoran, having lived and written over a century before the other two, reflects very different aesthetic, religious, and political trends). Nonetheless, we do occasionally find some of Guanxiu and Qiji's ideas on poetic and religious practice in the small surviving corpora of other monks, and I suspect that if more monastic poetry had survived from Guanxiu and Qiji's era, we would find still more evidence. However, barring the sudden excavation of the collections of monks like those listed above, such broader hypotheses will remain speculative.

Finally, because I am interested in articulating Guanxiu's, Qiji's, and other poet-monks' sense of Buddhist poetry, I look at only a small selection of the thousands of poems they wrote, namely those that have implications for what it means to be a practicing poet-monk. The poet-monks, like their literati counterparts, wrote many poems on objects, on history, on events, on landscapes, on parting, on frontier wars, on sensual beauty, on official corruption, and on a variety of social occasions.[46] Extant sources suggest that there was, at this point in history, no substantial difference in subject matter addressed by monastic and literati poetry. Seemingly taboo subjects to monks, such as drunkenness and eroticism, could be broached by writing on conventional, preexisting poetic themes or by critiquing them even as one described them in lavish detail.[47] However, I have set aside most poems that do not touch on monastic and related aesthetic issues. My concern in this book—the ideas of the poet-monk and Buddhist poetry—are the most fundamental to understanding these writers. The concept of the poet-monk set the terms by which they were understood in literary society, and Buddhist poetry was the goal that many of them hoped to achieve in their literary works. Without a solid grasp of these concepts, we may continue to think that this period has little to contribute to literary history.

On Religion and Literature

By focusing on poet-monks' concepts of Buddhist poetry, this book is situated somewhere between the fields of religious and literary studies. Religion and literature are both concepts that elude easy definition. They have meant many things to many people at many times, and there are a myriad ways they can relate to one another. For this book, the working definition of "religion" is "traditions of practices that mediate the relationship between human and supramundane realms." The word "tradition" here is meant to assert some kind of continuity across time, even if that involves continuous adaptation to new environments. Religions, in this definition, are mainly characterized by practices, which I define further below. It is important to remember, however, that these practices are moderated (but not fully determined) by scriptures, doctrines, and formal institutions, including the material and human resources that constitute and perpetuate these things. Like Adam Yuet Chau, I understand religious traditions "as complex, dynamic, ever-changing clusters of institutions, practitioners and consumers, knowledge and practices, sociopolitical relations and hierarchies, fully amenable to innovations, inventions, and reinventions all the time."[48] My main concern in this book is one religious system, Tang Buddhism, and I mainly use the term "Buddhist" to describe the activities of the poet-monks in this book. However, I occasionally use the term "religious" to signal the broader comparative implications of my analyses.

I define "literature" broadly as "patterned language," drawing on the root meaning of the Chinese term *wen* 文. What constitutes patterning, and who gets to decide what is patterned or not, changes with community and with time. With this simple sociohistorical definition, I aim to avoid creating strong dichotomies between "documentary" and "literary" (or "aesthetic") since in the Tang, many "documentary" genres—such as entombed inscriptions (*muzhiming* 墓誌銘), memorials to the throne (*biao* 表), prayer texts (*jiwen* 祭文), and letters (*shu* 書)—were appreciated for their literary qualities.[49] My main concern in this book, however, is narrower: the *shi*-poem and related genres like song-style poems (*gexing* and *yuefu*). For convenience, I refer to these simply as "poetry" or "elite verse" throughout this book, despite the fact that many other genres of verse flourished at this time, such as the inscription (*ming* 銘), the praise-poem (*zan* 讚), and the rhapsody (*fu* 賦).[50] Elite poetry was just one type among several, but it was the one most closely associated with literariness. At this time, *shi* was mainly divided into "recent-style" (*jinti* 近體) and "old-style" (*guti* 古體). Recent-style *shi* (also called "regulated verse," *lüshi* 律詩), was usually written with five or seven characters per line and four or eight lines per poem (but could be much longer in *pailü* 排律 form) and had metrical and rhyming constraints based on tones. The form lent itself to intricate craft, but it could be used for all kinds of purposes. Old-style *shi*, which included song-style poetry, had looser metrical and rhyming requirements. During our period of study, new-style heptameter was the most commonly used form, but the poet-monks wrote in other forms as well—Guanxiu, in particular, seems to have been fond of old-style poetry.

I hope that this book can contribute to the field of religion and literature in anglophone academia, despite that field's narrow focus on

Abrahamic religions and the assumptions that stem from them.⁵¹ My study, in contrast to much anglophone scholarship on religion and literature, understands religion as a set of practices. To be precise, by "practices" I mean consciously patterned movements of the body that are regarded as significant or efficacious within a field. Linguistic habits, especially in their performative aspect, may fall under this category. Practices involve bodily movements and poses that retain traces of the larger structures and histories in which they are embedded.⁵² The practices of poet-monks are the actions they may have actually performed—exchanged poems, recited words, read texts, uttered phrases, sat in certain postures, concentrated in certain ways, and visualized certain things. These are to be understood as *actions*, actions that helped structure the feelings, beliefs, and discourses around them. The poetic and Buddhist traditions shaped the horizons of poet-monks' thoughts and practices, but the monks were also active participants, in possession of bodies, who shaped and changed the traditions they inherited.

The idea of religion as a set of practices offers a robust framework for this study of poet-monks. Most importantly, it is conceptually closer than "worldview" or "belief" to the way the poet-monks would have seen Buddhism. After all, the things we might call religions in medieval China—Buddhism, Daoism, Confucianism, popular ritual systems—stress *practices* oriented toward the self, the world, and the transcendent. In the Tang dynasty, we might define "religion" as a set of practices that facilitate the pursuit of the Dao, often guided by institutionalized scriptures and authorities. For elites, religious pursuits are rhetorically opposed to official pursuits. As Robert Campany has noted, the widely used metaphor of the Dao 道 (path) implies that religion is something meant to be walked more than believed.⁵³ The works of the poet-monks, as we have already seen in Qiji's poem, testify to this. However, to my knowledge, there is no full-length study of Chinese Buddhist poetry that takes the implications of this concept seriously and none that explicitly theorizes its approach as such. Recently, some of the anachronisms and generalities of previous scholarship on Chinese Buddhist poetry have begun to fade away.⁵⁴ My book aims to build on these trends to describe the historically specific practices of the poet-monks and their implications for the study of Chinese and comparative literature.

Beyond the poet-monks' own conceptual world, religion as practice offers a better framework for the comparative analysis of religious poetry in general. It is conceptually closer not just to medieval Chinese concepts of the religious but also to early uses of the term "religion" in the West, which stressed ritual duties.[55] Empirical studies done by cognitive scientists have begun to demonstrate the importance of action (practice) to the formation of thought (belief).[56] By thinking of religion and literature as practices that change and overlap at different points in history, we make room for comparative analysis beyond these practices' places of origins. There already exist a number of compelling studies of the relationship between specific, historically situated literary and religious practices on a small scale, though these are not usually considered part of the field of religion and literature.[57] A practice-based theory of religion and literature could bring the insights from these studies together for comparison in a way that does not reinscribe the hegemony of the modern West. The vision of Buddhist poetry proposed by the poet-monks of late medieval China can help us find our way there.

Overview

This book is composed of two parts, "History" and "Poetics." The first traces the formation of the poet-monk as a position one could occupy in the late medieval literary world, while the second describes the idea of Buddhist poetry that the most accomplished poet-monks put forth. Chapter 1 offers a macroscopic outline of the development of the poet-monk tradition, from the first use of this term in the eighth century to the culmination of this tradition in the tenth. It situates the poet-monks in their historic, geographic, and social contexts, using a variety of digital tools (GIS and network analysis) to give a sense of where they fit in the late medieval literary world. Next, I trace the development of the idea of the poet-monk in literary discourse. Chapter 2 shows how the very term "poet-monk" was invented in the second half of the eighth century to marginalize the people it named. Despite the complexity of the attitudes held by the first generation of poet-monks, elite literati and monastics alike wrote about them in conventional terms as hermetic bonzes or would-be literati, giving them narrow berth in the literary discourse of the time. It was only later that poet-monks established their own self-conscious literary tradition that allowed them greater flexibility. Chapter 3 describes how these later poet-monks, especially those around the turn of the tenth century, reclaimed the term "poet-monk" and used it to position themselves as advocates of the fundamental harmony between poetic and religious practices.

The second half of the book examines precisely how the poet-monks infused their literary works with three Buddhist practices. Chapter 4 identifies the poet-monks' unusual fondness for verbal repetition—such as the repetition of a single character three times in a row, or "retriplication"—and its relationship to the discourse of negation in Buddhist logic, which also showed a propensity for such abnormal phrasings. Chapter 5 demonstrates the ways the ritual recitation of spells and scriptures (incantation) was both a topic of and resource for the monks' poetry. In particular, attention to the spiritual power of sonority and foreignness—the root principles of incantation—helped them articulate a new vision for Chinese Buddhist poetry. Chapter 6 describes the process by which Qiji became the first to assert the fundamental unity of poetry and meditation. By drawing on the literary discourses of painstaking composition (kuyin 苦吟) and spirit-roaming as well as the Buddhist practice of finding liberation in the contemplation of the mundane world, he was able to assert that poetry and meditation were nothing more than two gates to the same goal. The conclusion explains why these poet-monks' new idea of Chinese Buddhist poetry never took hold and how they faded to become footnotes in Chinese literary history, before a final meditation on what we can learn from their approach to religion and literature.

Part I

History

CHAPTER 1

Introducing Poet-Monks
History, Geography, and Sociality

Shiseng ("poet-monk"), like any word, has a history. It emerged at a specific time and place. It is the result of myriad historical, political, and cultural forces that coalesced in southeastern China in the mid-eighth century, and its meaning shifted significantly over the following two centuries. It is best not to take it as a stable, transcendent category of literary actor.[1] Rather, it was a tool used for both the marginalization and self-justification of Buddhist monastics living during the eighth, ninth, and tenth centuries who took the writing of poetry very seriously. The first three chapters of this book describe exactly what happened to this term, "poet-monk," from the Mid-Tang to the Five Dynasties period, or roughly 760–960. They focus on who was using the term, to whom the term was being applied, where the people using it were located, and what assumptions were implied by these uses of the term. They trace the changing answers to these questions over time.

In this first chapter I provide a macroscopic overview of the concept of the poet-monk, from its invention in the mid-eighth century through its peak in the tenth. I outline the historic, geographic, and social evidence for the emergence, growth, and prominence of the poet-monk as a distinct type of literary actor over the course of two centuries. Important parts of this chapter rely on digital analyses of data distilled from historical sources. These quantitative and visual arguments, balanced by close readings of selected sources, are meant to orient the reader to the dynamic literary landscape of late medieval China and the poet-monks' place in it. Specifically, I show that the term "poet-monk" was invented in southeastern China in the 760s or 770s to describe a specific community of monks. Only later, as these monks' fame spread, did this term become more broadly applicable to any Buddhist monk who wrote *shi*-poetry. I also demonstrate that poet-monks were not isolated from mainstream literary communities but were central to networks of literary connection, especially in the late-ninth and early-tenth centuries.

This bird's-eye view of the poet-monks' place in history, geography, and sociality forces us to rethink the literary history of late medieval China. Against the traditional narrative of decline, I posit that what we see is the waxing of new aesthetic paradigms largely thanks to the works of poet-monks. They are emblems not of decline but of growth. The later poet-monks actively developed historic, geographic, social, and aesthetic trends begun by their predecessors at the height of the Tang dynasty—trends explored in subsequent chapters of this book.

History

The first surviving use of the term "poet-monk" comes from a poem written around 775 by the monk Jiaoran, on the occasion of the departure of another monk, Shaowei 少微.

Replying to "Parting with Shaowei, Poet-monk of Xiangyang" (In the poem, I respond to the significance of the venerable monk's dream of going home) 酬別襄陽詩僧少微 (詩中答上人歸夢之意)

Jiaoran

Why are there dreams to bear witness to the mind?
Let me explain your repeated dreams of going home.
For words, you carry in mind the books of Qin,
In poetry, you study the men of Chu.[2]
Orchids blossom the colors upon your robes,
Willows bend toward the spring in your hand.
We shall surely meet again after this parting:
My body is a floating cloud.[3]

證心何有夢，
示說夢歸頻。
文字齋秦本，
詩騷學楚人。
蘭開衣上色，
柳向手中春。
別後須相見，
浮雲是我身。[4]

This poem offers many clues to the earliest layers of the term "poet-monk." First, it implies that Jiaoran's poem is a response to an unknown earlier author. This means, at the very least, that the title of this poem is not the first use of the word "poet-monk." The original poem to which it is responding, written by a third party, must precede it. Second, the term "poet-monk" is used as an identifying label. Paired with Shaowei's place of origin, it serves as an index for locating the monk socially and geographically. Other writings attest to the fact that Shaowei was indeed well-connected to literati circles. Records of his exchanges with nine prominent literati survive, and there is also indirect evidence of an exchange with twenty-seven prominent officials at the capital.[5] Shaowei is not just a monk but more specifically a poet-monk, someone with the necessary learning to participate in literary exchanges, who is well-versed in the classics (line 3) and can write in the style of the *Songs of Chu* (line 4). Nonetheless, Shaowei's status as a poet is subordinated to his status as a monk: in classical Chinese, modifier comes before modified, so *shi* ("poet") modifies *seng* ("monk"). He is mainly a monk but one who has some training in poetry. "Poet-monk" is here a social label much like a literatus's official title: it places the monk in elite society.

Although the earliest use of the term "poet-monk" is now lost to us, we can reasonably guess that it came not long before this poem, sometime in the 760s or 770s. Why it should emerge at this time and place is the result of multiple historical factors. By the eighth century CE, Buddhism was firmly entrenched in Chinese life. Having first come to the central plains via northwestern merchants and monks at the beginning of the common era, it had been promoted and suppressed, patronized and demonized by centuries of rulers. Buddhists of the eighth century were roughly as far separated from Buddhism's appearance as we are from Thomas Aquinas. In the intervening seven and a half centuries, Buddhist monasteries had become part of the landscape, and monks part of the social structure. According to the official histories of the

Tang, in the years 713–755 there were about 126,100 Buddhist clergy; and in the 840s, about 360,000. This amounts to around 15–18 monks per 1,000 households for the former period and 73 per 1,000 households for the latter.[6] By comparison, the United States reported about 429,000 clergy members in the year 2010, or fewer than 4 per 1,000 households.[7] So, relative to its population, the High Tang had around four to five times as many Buddhist clergy as the United States of 2010 had of all clergy members, of any tradition, sect, or denomination; and the Late Tang had about eighteen times as many. Monks were abundant, far beyond anything a twenty-first-century American would be used to.

From very early on, Chinese Buddhist monks had written poetry. As mentioned in the introduction, many early medieval monks were known for their literary talent, and some, like Zhi Dun and Baoyue, became major figures in elite literary circles. Monks like Huiyuan and his disciples are often credited with helping to establish the tradition of landscape poetry.[8] However, it was not until the latter half of the eighth century that the poet-monk emerged as a distinct literary figure. Before this period, there existed poems by monks (*sengshi* 僧詩) but never poet-monks (*shiseng*).

There are several historical causes for this emergence. Many previous scholars have drawn a neat line of connection between the rise of the "Chan" lineages in the eighth century and the emergence of poet-monks.[9] Such scholars point out that certain versions of Chan emphasized everyday experience and the ordinary mind (*pingchang xin* 平常心) as the locus of enlightenment.[10] While the emergence of Chan certainly contributed to the rise of poet-monks, it was only one factor among many. In fact, many of the early poet-monks were initially trained in Vinaya (*lü* 律), not Chan, Buddhism—a variety that was particularly amenable to the scholastic mind.[11] This should not be surprising: classic Vinaya rulebooks did allow for the reading and writing of poetry as a form of "external studies" (*waixue* 外學) for as many as two to four hours per day.[12] The deeply learned monk Shenqing 神清 (d. ca. 814), for example, received extensive training in Vinaya and wrote a lengthy justification of external studies in erudite prose, quoting from Confucian and Buddhist classics, in his *North Mountain Record* (*Beishan lu* 北山錄).[13] Shenqing's essays reveal how doctrinal tensions between Buddhist and literary pursuits—such as the injunction not to engage in "ornate speech" (*qiyu* 綺語, Skt. *saṃbhina-pralāpa*)—could be eased by appealing to Indic precedent and to the practicality of education in the social sphere.[14] As will be noted in chapter two, many of the first generation of poet-monks, trained early on in Vinaya and later exposed to Chan practices, drew from multiple religious traditions to justify their literary activities. There is no necessary reason why poet-monks should appear only after the development of Chan lineages.

Though developments in Buddhist doctrine and practice may have been one contributing factor, the political context of the late eighth century was another. The poet-monks emerged just as the disastrous An Lushan Rebellion of 755–763 had concluded. This was one of the most fatal conflicts in human history, sending millions to their graves and nearly toppling the world's most powerful empire.[15] The chaos of the rebellion forced many Tang elites to move to the prosperous region south of the eastern end of the Yangtze River known as Jiangnan 江南. After order was restored, the Tang instituted a system of military governorships (*jiedushi* 節度使) that cycled major political figures to positions outside of the capital, leading to a general decentralization of power. The fleeing literati and the military governors, combined with eastern Jiangnan's wealth as a riverside trading center, meant that it was in place to become an alternate cultural center.[16] Many of the most important literati of the Mid-Tang spent at least some time here, often rubbing shoulders with Buddhist monks.

The Buddhist community at Jiangnan was already well established by the time these elites fled there. Buddhism rose to prominence in this region early on thanks to the loyal patronage of the court official Wang Dao 王導 (276–339) at Jiankang 建康 (modern Nanjing) in the first half of the fourth century and of local gentry at western Jiangnan in the latter half of the fourth century.[17] Buddhism became popular among the elite, its proponents holding debates with those interested in arcane studies (*xuanxue*), its practitioners developing new creeds and rituals. It was during this time that the monk Huiyuan established a major Buddhist center on Mount Lu 廬山, called Donglin monastery 東林寺, where a fellowship of 123 lay and monastic practitioners met to devote themselves to meditation and veneration of Amitābha Buddha. Known as the White Lotus Society 白蓮社, it is notable for including artistic luminaries such as the painter-calligrapher Zong Bing 宗炳 (375–443) and the soon-to-be famous poet Xie Lingyun, and therefore it became a touchstone for later intermixing between Buddhist monks, Daoist priests, and literati.[18] Qiji, for example, named his poetry collection *The White Lotus Collection* (*Bailian ji* 白蓮集) after this community. The Jiangnan region proved to be one of the most innovative and resilient loci for medieval Chinese Buddhism, and it would persist as such for centuries to come. This reached a crescendo in the Tang dynasty. According to one scholar's estimates, 22 percent of eminent monks in the first half of the Tang and 51 percent of those in the second half came from the Jiangnan region.[19]

Daoism too prospered there. Mount Lu, for example, received renewed Daoist attention after Emperor Xuanzong ordered a shrine built there in 731 to the Perfected Lord of Inspection 採訪真君 following a dream in which this lord promised five hundred years of prosperity to the region.[20] The famed Daoist poet-priest Wu Yun 吳筠 (d. 778), like many literati, spent his post-rebellion years in Jiangnan, even participating at one point in writing linked poetry with Yan Zhenqing and Jiaoran, despite his personal aversion to Buddhism.[21] This confluence of religious and cultural prosperity, along with growing political decentralization, created the right conditions for the emergence of a robust poet-monk movement. In fact, we can trace the prominence of early poet-monks to their many ties to the capital-derived elites who served in the area.

The An Lushan Rebellion of the 750s and 760s also prompted a "crisis in culture," leading to renewed attention to the importance of literature (*wen*) to the health of the Tang polity.[22] The elites' response to the rebellion was to invest further in literature. To be clear, the crisis was not about faith in literature's ability to save the state or in the existence of cosmological patterns (*wen*) but rather about how to restore literature's maximal efficacy.[23] In an effort to rejuvenate such culture, imperial patronage of literary activity grew in the post-rebellion period, as seen in the increased importance given to the Hanlin Academy and to the civil service examinations.[24] While some extremists—such as Han Yu 韓愈 (768–824) and other *guwen* reformers—sought to define "literature" in so narrow a way as to exclude Buddhists, most took a more moderate, inclusive position.[25] This general promotion of literature was another factor that created the conditions for the poet-monks' emergence during this time period.[26]

Another major factor in the poet-monks' rise was the increasingly stringent educational requirements for monks instituted in the eighth century.[27] When the Tang was restored after the Zhou interregnum of 685–705, Emperor Zhongzong instituted clerical examinations for monks. These were meant to ensure that those who registered with the government as members of the Buddhist church were actually qualified as religious professionals (and to curb the power of the Buddhist clergy who had supported the now-toppled Zhou 周). In 773, under Emperor

Taizong, thought to be "the most devout of all the Tang rulers," these tests were expanded to more closely resemble the civil examinations, requiring monks to memorize and explain in writing core Buddhist scriptures.[28] Such high standards led to improved monastic education in the eighth century and beyond. It was in this context that the Hongzhou lineage, with its significant reinterpretations of canonical sūtras, emerged. Some have described this as the Buddhist parallel to the Confucian "crisis in culture" following the An Lushan Rebellion: a "deep interiorization" of core teachings and texts that sought to revive their relevance to contemporary issues and central concerns.[29] As we will see, many of the Late Tang poet-monks had connections to the Hongzhou lineage, even if it is best not to think of them as members of a closed school. High educational standards and reinterpretations of the classics facilitated the emergence of highly literate poet-monks.

Yet another factor in the poet-monks' rise was the dominance of a mainstream poetry aesthetic in the mid-eighth century, one that was associated with Wang Wei 王維 (700–761), a devout Buddhist himself.[30] This aesthetic stressed close attention to landscapes, relatively simple vocabulary, occasionally difficult syntax, and surprising insights. Its ruminative qualities were particularly amenable to the poetically inclined Buddhist monks of Jiangnan who presented themselves as experts in mental cultivation living in mountain monasteries. This aesthetic, which stressed insight over ornament and allusion, reclusion over service, and craft over novelty, created space for poets who were understood to be disengaged from political affairs in the capital.

In short, the convergence of many different changes led to the right conditions for the emergence of poet-monks in Jiangnan in the late eighth century. These were not limited to innovations in Chan Buddhism but included historical, political, geographic, institutional, and aesthetic factors as well. The migration of elite poets to the southeast in the post-rebellion period was an especially important factor. Further attention to geography will help clarify the growth of the poet-monk as a distinct literary actor beyond the first Jiangnan community.

Geography

The An Lushan Rebellion marks a crucial turning point in nearly every facet of Chinese history. After the rebellion, as many elites migrated south, the center of the Tang literary world also shifted southward, and developments in the technical and literary representation of geography led to significant changes in the collective spatial imaginary.³¹ Political historians see this as the beginning of a turn toward localization that would be fully realized in the Song dynasty, though recently excavated evidence suggests that this turn only began in earnest after the Huang Chao Rebellion of the 880s.³² Either way, it is clear that the latter half of the Tang dynasty and its aftermath marked a period of great change in cultural geography. The growth of the poet-monk phenomenon should be seen against this background.

To map the collective growth of poet-monks, I have made systematic lists of where the poet-monks lived over the course of two and a half centuries (720–960). The poet-monks mapped here are the forty-eight for whom some *shi*-poetry and some biographical information survives. My data come from the chronological history of Tang literature by Fu Xuancong and his collaborators, which is based on a combination of historical records (biographies, epitaphs, lists of examination graduates, etc.) and information embedded in exchange poems (prefaces, official titles, settings).³³ Fu and his team of researchers used this information to triangulate exactly where a given poet was located at a particular time. I have used Fu's chronology to quantify the number of years poet-monks spent in different places and have visualized these on maps of the Tang empire and the polities of the tenth century.³⁴ Such visualizations highlight otherwise invisible geographic trends that, when combined with careful analysis of selected primary sources, provide a general history of poet-monks' development—a history that will unfold in greater detail in the following chapters.

Geographic data suggest that the history of late medieval poet-monks can be divided into four periods that very roughly correspond to the traditional periodization of late medieval literary history: 1) High and Mid-Tang 盛中唐, 720–810; 2) Late Tang 晚唐, 811–874; 3) End of Tang 唐末, 875–907; and 4) Five Dynasties and Ten Kingdoms 五代十國, 908–960.³⁵ Although the periods are similar to those of traditional literary history, the poet-monks present a narrative arc quite different from the normal story of Tang literature. Rather than a gradual decline from the glories of mid-eighth century, there is a growth that culminates in an explosion of innovation and creativity during those periods that previous scholars have assumed to be stagnant.

The first period is illustrated by map 1.1, which focuses on the early development of the poet-monk tradition, 720–810. Poet-monk activity is heavily concentrated in the eastern Jiangnan region, especially in the Suzhou-Hangzhou area. This corroborates early written accounts of the

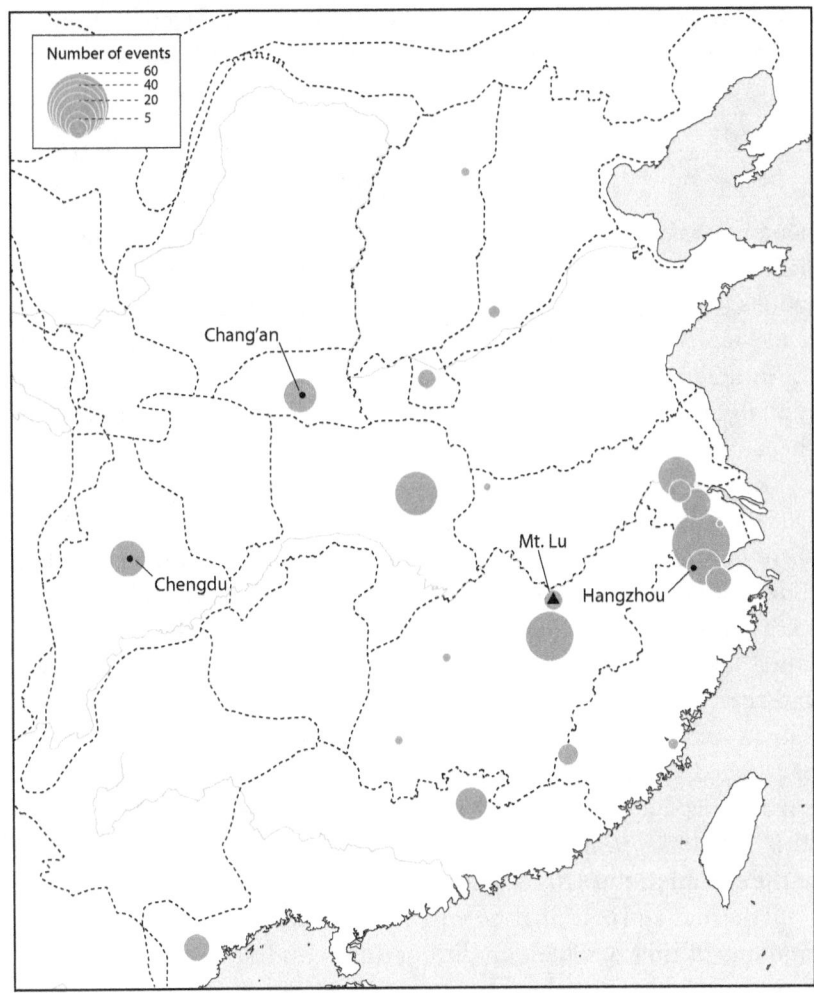

Map 1.1. Poet-monk activity, 720–810. This map shows the total number of years spent by poet-monks at various places. Larger circles correspond to more years of poet-monk activity in a given place. For example, if Lingche spent the years 770–771 in Guiji, this is measured as two years of poet-monk activity there. If both Lingche and Huguo spent the years 770–771 in Guiji, this counts as four years of poet-monk activity there. Data for all poet-monk activity may be found in the Digital Appendix. Map of Tang dynasty circuits adapted from Harvard WorldMap. This period covers 296 events concerning twelve poet-monks. Here the poet-monks are concentrated in the southeast, around Hangzhou.

development of poet-monks, found in sources such as the *Record of Conversations* (*Yinhua lu* 因話錄) by Zhao Lin 趙璘 (*j.s.* 834):

> There are many famous monks in Jiangnan. Since the Zhenyuan and Yuanhe eras [785–821], there have been Qingjiang and Qingzhou

[i.e., Jiaoran] in Yuezhou, and Qianjun and Qianfu in Wuzhou. They were known at the time as the "Two Qings of Guiji" and the "Two Qians of Dongyang."[36]

江南多名僧。貞元、元和以來，越州有清江、清晝，婺州有乾俊、乾輔，時謂之「會稽二清」，「東陽二乾」。

Jiangnan was home to the first community of poet-monks, who included Jiaoran, Lingyi 靈一 (727–766), and Lingche 靈徹 (746?–816). The poet-monks were originally a local group concentrated in the southeast. They made occasional pilgrimages to holy mountains—such as Mount Lu 廬山, located in the western end of Jiangnan—and a few journeys to the capital, but mostly they remained in a single region. We will look at them in more detail in chapter 2.

The second period, illustrated by map 1.2, covers the years 811–874. During this time, poet-monks spread throughout the empire. While there is still a great deal of activity in the poet-monks' birthplace (Suzhou-Hangzhou), it has become far more diffuse. This is due first to the fame of the original poet-monks spreading beyond their original home, leading to opportunities for some monks to travel to the capital, and then to the term's definition expanding to refer to other monks. Jiaoran may have been the first to achieve great fame, as the emperor dispatched an official to collect and publish his poetry in 792.[37] Jiaoran and his fellow poet-monk Lingyi are also noted in Li Zhao's 李肇 (fl. 806–820) *Supplement to the History of Our State* 國史補, likely composed at the capital in the 810s or 820s.[38]

In the map and in textual records, we see that more monks spent greater amounts of time at Chang'an during this period, sponsored by wealthy patrons, including the emperor himself. The poet-monk began to achieve cultural acceptance in the middle of the ninth century and therefore can be seen in the highest echelons of literary society. Guangxuan 廣宣 (early ninth century), a southwestern monk who served three emperors at court and exchanged poems with Bai Juyi and Yuan Zhen 元稹 (779–831), is one example of a poet-monk who achieved such recognition.[39] So did Zhixuan 知玄 (811–883), another southwestern monk who traveled to the capital, participated in religious debates at court, and exchanged verses with poets such as Li Shangyin 李商隱 (ca. 813–858).[40] Buddhist monks had served at court before, but most did not write poetry that has come down to us, and none were referred to as poet-monks.[41]

Mount Lu, which had long been home to thriving religious communities, became a new hub for poet-monks, one that would continue to

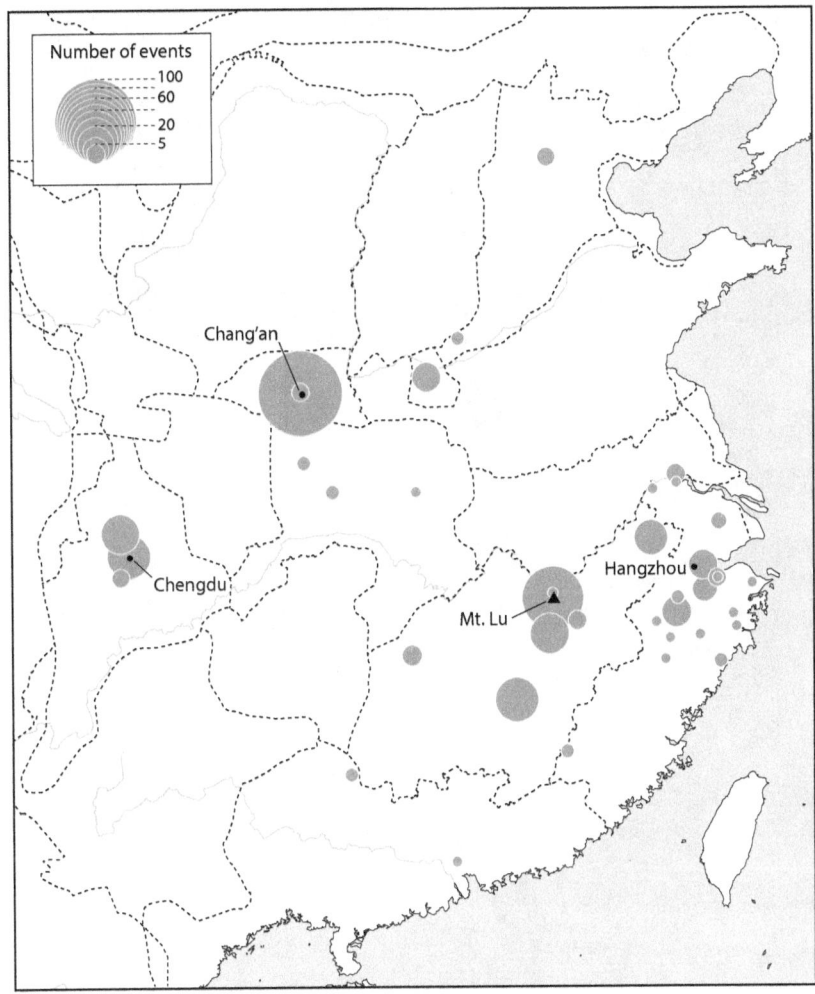

Map 1.2. Poet-monk activity, 811–874. This period covers 378 events concerning twenty-five poet-monks. Here poet-monks are becoming more prominent in the capital region of Chang'an.

develop in the decades ahead. Hongzhou began to attract a fair share of poet-monks, having established itself as an important Buddhist town in the 780s thanks to the presence of the renowned master Mazu Daoyi 馬祖道一 (709–788).[42] And from Chengdu, a secondary cultural center frequented by the powerful people at the capital, came indigenous poet-monks such as Guangxuan and Zhixuan. Despite being nearly twelve hundred miles (nineteen hundred kilometers) from the homes of the first monks who claimed this title, Chengdu had a number of men who saw themselves as working in the same poetic tradition.

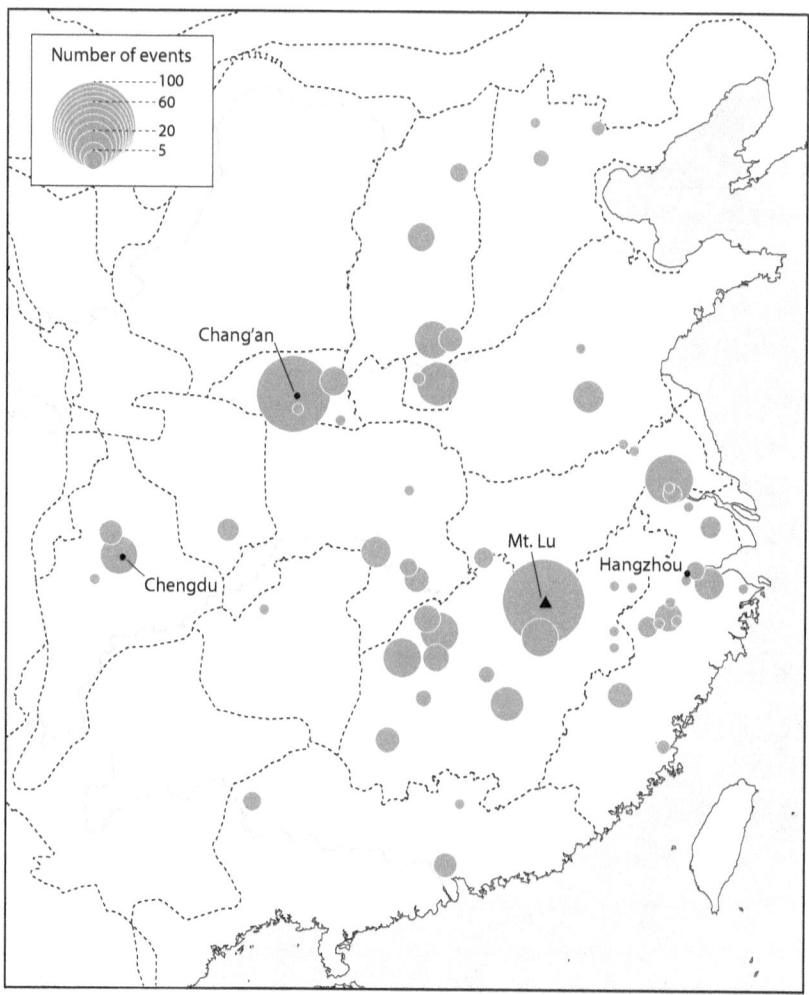

Map 1.3. Poet-monk activity, 875–907. This period covers 554 events concerning twenty-six poet-monks. Here is evidence that many poet-monks fled urban centers to escape the destruction of the Huang Chao Rebellion.

During this era, poet-monks were no longer oddities but instead a part of the literary scene.

The Huang Chao Rebellion and its aftermath mark another moment of intense change, as seen in map 1.3 (875–907). Leading up to this time, Huang Chao's troops rampaged through Jiangnan and up to the capital region, leaving smoldering wreckage in their wake. They would eventually set fire to Chang'an, the cultural center of the Chinese world.[43] In response, poet-monks fled from urban monasteries to safer regions,

INTRODUCING POET-MONKS 31

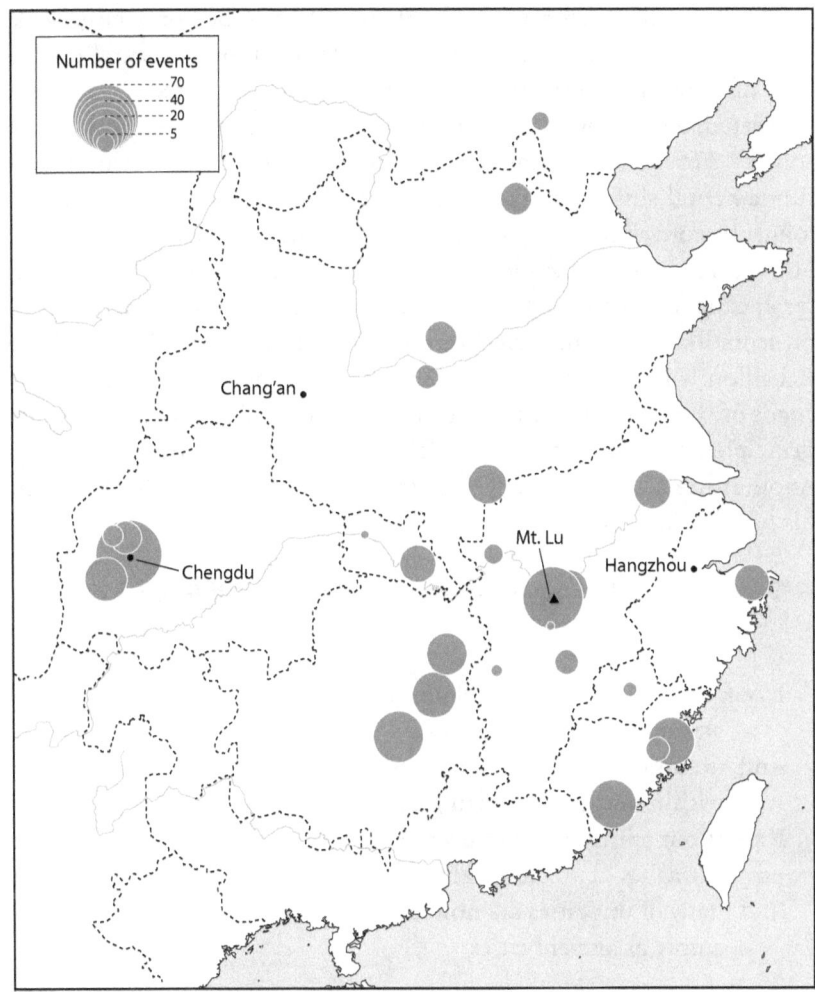

Map 1.4. Poet-monk activity, 908–960. Map of the Five Dynasties and Ten Kingdoms adapted from Harvard WorldMap. This period covers 558 events concerning twenty-four poet-monks. Here the poet-monks are stabilized in regional capitals (such as Chengdu and Hangzhou) and sacred mountains (such as Mount Lu).

such as the Buddhist monasteries located in the south and on sacred mountains like Mount Lu and Mount Heng 衡山.[44] Indeed, at this time the poet-monk Xiumu 修睦 (d. 918) became Saṃgha Rectifier 僧正 of Hongzhou and used his official appointment to make nearby Mount Lu into an important grounds for poet-monk activity in the waning years of the Tang. Nearly every important poet-monk of the period lived there at one point during the late ninth century.[45]

Moreover, the very act of the Huang Chao Rebellion's large-scale butchery of the capital elites left a void at the Tang's cultural center. Tens of thousands of the most powerful and well-educated literati were murdered, and many of the survivors fled for the relative safety of the south.[46] Among the educated, there was widespread recognition that a fundamental shift had taken place, that the cultural sphere could no longer be conceived as a unified whole. Evidence for this shift abounds. For example, the anonymous philosophical text *Wunengzi* 無能子 (Master Incapable), which advocates for a return to quietist naturalism, presents itself as being written in direct response to the Huang Chao Rebellion.[47] Its preface implies that the only logical response to the chaos of the period is a kind of primitivism rooted in classically Daoist principles, since civilization has failed to bring anything but tragedy. Another literatus, Pei Yue 裴說 (late ninth and early tenth cent.), put his feelings into a quatrain:

Taking Backroads to My Hometown during the Chaos 亂中偷路入故鄉
                                                                    Pei Yue

I look with sorrow on the villains' fires
    arising from their beacons
And, unnoticed, find the next stop
    within my grief-stricken gaze.
Half of our entire state has been rendered
    the ashes of a fallen state;
And many of our cities are now as
    empty as ancient cities.

愁看賊火起諸烽，
偷得餘程悵望中。
一國半爲亡國燼，
數城俱作古城空。[48]

As the chaos of the Huang Chao Rebellion raged on, Pei Yue saw civilization crumbling before his very eyes, manifested at the levels of state and city. Wei Zhuang, writing about the ruination visited upon Jiangnan in the 880s, described the fracturing thus: "Having a land, having a family—both are dreams, / And those who were dragons, who were tigers have become nothing" 有國有家皆是夢，爲龍爲虎亦成空.[49] Sikong Tu made the universal personal, writing of the fallen world's effect on his own life in one of his counterintuitive or "mad" quatrains.

Mad Inscriptions: 2 of 2 狂題二首（其二）
                              Sikong Tu

Know that it's hard to preserve one's life
    in an era of chaos;
Delight not at heaven's sunlight
    and the chrysanthemums' bloom.
I've always been itinerant
    in this life, long or short—
The yellow flowers help
    to speed the whitening of my head.

須知世亂身難保，
莫喜天晴菊併開。
長短此身長是客，
黃花更助白頭催。[50]

In the midst of troubled times, the speaker can take no delight in the joys of nature, for its very exuberance seems to mock him. The chrysanthemums, normally thought to extend one's life, ironically bring on signs of aging in the speaker. Further examples of such laments could be produced ad infinitum.[51] To the educated Chinese of the late ninth and early tenth centuries, the idea of a unified world was no longer tenable.

But this destruction also presented a rare opportunity for cultural reinvention. As civilization was threatened, it became plastic, moldable. A space opened up for relatively minor or marginalized figures—such as poet-monks—to grow and attempt to reshape literature in their own image. And they seized this opportunity. Even though the poet-monks had become familiar figures in literary society by the mid-ninth century, it was not until this period of instability that we really see rapid growth in their numbers—of the 184 poets in *Quan Tang shi* who were active during this period, 23 (13 percent) were Buddhist monks, compared to the Tang up to 880, in which 40 of about 2,400 active poets were monks (>2 percent).[52] This may be due to their relative move upward when the top rung of the ladder (i.e., the capital elite) was lopped off. Although the elites may not simply have been physically eliminated, the destruction of the capital and the displacement of tens of thousands of the most powerful people would certainly have shaken the foundations of elite culture.[53] This, combined with the existence of a strong poet-monk figurehead like Guanxiu, may have been enough to encourage rapid growth among poet-monks.

In the fourth period (map 1.4), which corresponds to the Five Dynasties and Ten Kingdoms following the End of Tang (907–960), the poet-monks resettled in the newly stabilized regional kingdoms that had emerged. Traditional historiography sees this period as one of transition and chaos, but it did not always appear so to the people who lived through it. The people of the first half of the tenth century did not know that there would be a series of Five Dynasties and Ten Kingdoms that would end with the establishment of the Song in 960 and its consolidation of power in 974. In fact, many of the literary elites (both religious and nonreligious) had great hopes for the regional rulers, that they might enact a cultural renaissance that would reunite the fractured empire.[54]

One example of this was the kingdom of Shu 蜀 in the first few decades of the tenth century. Its founder Wang Jian 王建 (847–918) has been judged unfavorably by history. He was, after all, illiterate and left his kingdom to an incompetent son. But he succeeded in attracting many of the most important poets, Buddhists, and Daoists to his court as he began to break away from the Tang. Wei Zhuang, Du Guangting 杜光庭 (850–933), and Guanxiu all threw their lots in with Wang Jian and were handsomely rewarded for it.[55] The other prolific poet-monk of the tenth century, Qiji, also set out to go to Shu to meet Guanxiu and his disciple Tanyu but was waylaid by the ruler of Jingnan 荆南, who forced the monk to become Saṃgha Rectifier of his newly established kingdom—an appointment that Qiji occasionally spoke of as imprisonment.[56] All of these men bet their lives on the belief that Shu was poised to become the next Chang'an, the hub of civilization as they knew it. Although Shu's plans began to fall apart in the 920s, these poets were not entirely wrong: Chengdu contained the most advanced printing technology and would soon produce the literary collection that would elevate the burgeoning genre of *ci* (song lyric) poetry—the *Collection among the Flowers* (*Huajian ji* 花間集).[57] In similar ways, other poet-monks saw the kingdoms of Jingnan, Chu 楚, Min 閩, and the Southern Tang 南唐 as the bastions of civilization after the fall of the Tang. Many of these new kings were aspiring emperors, competing to produce the next world-conquering empire.[58] One of the ways to strengthen a claim to legitimacy was to draw in leading poets, artists, and religious leaders through promises of patronage. These rulers drew on prominent Buddhists' cultural capital in different ways. Chengdu and Hangzhou attracted highly regarded monks displaced from the capital, while the smaller southern cities—such as Hongzhou and Fuzhou—promoted locally renowned clerics in an attempt to match these efforts.[59] Thus, many of the poet-monks were drawn to these regional kingdoms.

The other trend during this period was for poet-monks to relocate to religious centers—such as Mount Lu, Mount Heng, and Hongzhou—where they could keep the ruling powers at arm's length. As we have seen, this trend had already emerged in the mid-ninth century and gained traction during the fall of the Tang. Though such sites often relied on the patronage of political rulers for support, they also provided an alternative power structure that was based on religious merit. Remote from urban centers and relatively inaccessible due to their elevation, such mountains were spared much of the violence of the Huang Chao Rebellion and its aftermath. Buddhist monasteries in these areas made a concerted effort in the ninth and tenth centuries to establish strong relationships with local rulers and patrons.[60] Such relationships benefited both parties: the monasteries would receive financial and political support from their patrons, while the patrons would accrue merit and legitimacy by sponsoring Buddhist activities. Thus, places like Mount Lu, Mount Heng, and Hongzhou served as alternative hubs for poet-monks after the collapse of the Tang.

So the big picture that emerges from looking at the geographical distribution of poet-monks from 720 to 960 is a development in four stages: 1) birth in Jiangnan, 720–810; 2) spread to the capital, 811–874; 3) growth and dispersal across the empire, 875–907; and 4) consolidation in new cultural centers, 907–960. These four stages correlate closely with some of the large-scale historical developments we know about late medieval China. 1) The poet-monks emerged out of an area that was rich in both Buddhist and literary culture just as power began to decentralize because of political changes following the An Lushan Rebellion. 2) Poet-monks gained recognition across the empire and began to drift to the capital as peace was restored and elites returned to their home region. With the notable exception of Wuzong in 840–845, the emperors and nobles of this period were generous patrons of Buddhism, attracting poet-monks to the capital. 3) The Huang Chao Rebellion caused thousands to flee urban centers and left a void at the cultural center, creating the space for poet-monks to develop further and gain traction in literary society. 4) As some regional rulers attempted to establish their own universal dynasties (or at least fully autonomous kingdoms), they attracted numerous monks and literati in an effort to assert their own religious and cultural legitimacy. Some poet-monks were wooed by these promises of lavish donations, while others retreated to sacred mountains such as

Mount Lu and Mount Heng. These four stages ought to be understood not as distinct periods but as general trends that waxed and waned, overlapping with one another. Geographical analysis of poet-monks' movements provides a rough outline of their historical development, one that can be supplemented with a large-scale analysis of their exchange poetry.

Sociality

It is tempting to think of Buddhist monastics as somehow separate from the rest of society.[61] By its very nature, monasticism claims to cut itself off from the dusty world of mundane life, and Chinese Buddhists were no exception in some of their rhetorical claims. Despite these ideals, Buddhists were never truly separate from the realm of everyday life. Buddhist temples and monasteries required the patronage of wealthy, powerful donors to survive and in turn offered to create and accumulate good merit on behalf of the state or other patrons. Monks from elite families often continued to be considered part of the family.[62] Buddhism was as much a means by which to engage the world as a means by which to escape it.

One way to calculate the extent to which Buddhist monks were involved in the literary world is to look at their connections in exchange poetry. By "exchange poetry," I mean any poem that is explicitly addressed to another person. These may be written on actual social occasions such as meetings, feasts, or partings. They may be written at a distance and sent to their addressee along with a letter. Each of these establishes a literary connection. In all of what follows, I do not suppose that exchange poetry correlates precisely with actual social connections. Rather, I take exchange poetry to represent imagined connections—a collective dream of literary relations that serves as an index of how poets sought to position themselves in the literary world.

Table 1.1 lists the forty poets from the period of 830–960 with at least sixty exchange poems to their name and calculates the percentage targeted to Buddhist monks. The first thing to notice is that no poet addressed a majority of his works to members of the clergy. Even the most prolific and well-known poet-monks—Qiji, Guanxiu, and Wuke 無可 (early ninth century)—wrote large numbers of poems to laypersons, most of whom were literati of one sort or another. This is remarkable, considering the situation in later times. The Song poet-monk Hongzhi Zhengjue 宏智正覺 (1091–1157), for example, sent 80 percent of his exchange poems to other monks.[63] This is about double the rate of the poet at the top of the Late Tang list, Qiji (see table 1.1). The reason for the relatively large number of poems addressed to literati in the Late Tang is related to poetry's social function. Exchange poetry was put to a variety of purposes other than the merely aesthetic: it could be used for flattering superiors, flaunting one's education, or establishing a connection with a literary hero as easily as for thanking a friend.[64] By the mid-ninth century, poet-monks were closely integrated into mainstream literary culture. In the Song, by contrast, the writing of social *shi*-poetry had become routinized in monastic institutions, leading to far more exchanges exclusively between monks.[65]

Table 1.1 Number of exchange poems addressed to clergy, ranked by percentage.

RANK	POET		EXCHANGES	BUDDHIST MONKS	PCT.
1	**Qiji**	齊己	505	192	38%
2	Li Dong	李洞	126	41	33%
3	Zhou He	周賀	78	24	31%
4	Zhang Qiao	張喬	86	26	30%
5	Cao Song	曹松	69	19	28%
6	**Guanxiu**	貫休	410	112	27%
7	Wu Rong	吳融	77	21	27%
8	Jia Dao	賈島	320	74	23%
9	Li Xianyong	李咸用	109	25	23%
10	**Wuke**	無可	87	16	18%
11	Xue Neng	薛能	98	17	17%
12	Zheng Gu	鄭谷	142	22	15%
13	Zhang Hu	張祜	194	30	15%
14	Liu Deren	劉得仁	104	16	15%
15	Yao He	姚合	330	50	15%
16	Ma Dai	馬戴	106	16	15%
17	Bao Rong	鮑溶	101	15	15%
18	Xiang Si	項斯	61	9	15%
19	Zhu Qingyu	朱慶餘	131	19	15%
20	Li Zhong	李中	179	24	13%
21	Du Xunhe	杜荀鶴	214	28	13%
22	Shi Jianwu	施肩吾	77	10	13%
23	Fang Gan	方干	246	31	13%
24	Zhang Pin	張蠙	61	7	11%
25	Xu Hun	許渾	715	80	11%
26	Xu Tang	許棠	78	7	9%
27	Zhao Gu	趙嘏	169	14	8%
28	Han Wo	韓偓	90	7	8%
29	Li Pin	李頻	145	11	8%
30	Xu Yin	徐夤	69	5	7%

(continued)

Table 1.1 (continued)

RANK	POET		EXCHANGES	BUDDHIST MONKS	PCT.
31	Wei Zhuang	韋莊	111	8	7%
32	Huang Tao	黃滔	130	8	6%
33	Wen Tingyun	溫庭筠	133	8	6%
34	Pi Rixiu	皮日休	264	13	5%
35	Lu Guimeng	陸龜蒙	256	10	4%
36	Du Mu	杜牧	194	7	4%
37	Li Shangyin	李商隱	203	7	3%
38	Xu Xuan	徐鉉	220	6	3%
39	Luo Yin	羅隱	227	6	3%
40	Li Qunyu	李群玉	123	3	2%

Note: Includes poets with at least sixty exchange poems to their name. Poet-monks are in **boldface**.

Nevertheless, the monks Qiji, Guanxiu, and Wuke occupy the first, sixth, and tenth positions on this list. They were more likely to have written a poem addressed to another monk than most other major poets of their day. Two of the other poets who rank high on the list, Zhou He 周賀 (mid-ninth cent., third) and Jia Dao 賈島 (779-843, eighth), spent large portions of their lives as monks. Li Dong (second) grew up poor and spent the majority of his life living in reclusion near Buddhist monasteries. Despite their pragmatic connections to the world of officialdom, poet-monks such as Qiji, Guanxiu, and Wuke, as well as ex-monks such as Zhou He and Jia Dao, maintained close ties to the Buddhist community and represented those ties in their literary works. Non-monastic poets were expected to represent their connections to Buddhists in their works, too In my database, 1,457 of the 10,869 poetic exchanges from this period are addressed to monks (13.4%). This overall percentage is roughly the same as the average in any given writer's corpus of exchanges: the median and mean of the numbers listed in table 1.1 are both about 14%. Even those literati who showed no particular affection for Buddhist teachings have some poems addressed to monks. The standard set of poetic topics in the Tang included poems written to Buddhists, at Buddhist sites, and on Buddhist themes. The very minimum an educated person could do was write a few poems to local monks when visiting a monastery in a new town or a mountain retreat.[66]

We can go further and look at these connections more systematically, as a network. To this end, I have created a database of 10,869 poems exchanged between 2,413 individuals during 830-960.[67] When we visualize this data as a network graph, people appear as dots ("nodes") and the poems connecting them as lines ("edges"). Greater quantities of poems exchanged bring individuals closer together in the graph. The overall shape of the network gives us an intuitive sense of the centrality of Buddhist poet-monks in the literary world of the ninth and tenth centuries (see figures 1.1 and 1.2).

The amount of black in the graph suggests the relative centrality of Buddhist monks to the network. The two large, black nodes at the top

Figure 1.1 Network graph of poems exchanged between contemporaries in the late medieval period. Buddhist monks are shaded black. Nodes have been filtered by degree (≥2) and sized according to betweenness centrality (on which see below). Several small clusters of fewer than five actors, disconnected from the central hub, have been removed. Produced in Gephi version 0.9.6, using the ForceAtlas2 attraction-repulsion layout. For the full graph and related data, see "1–2 Network Data, Graphs" in the Digital Appendix.

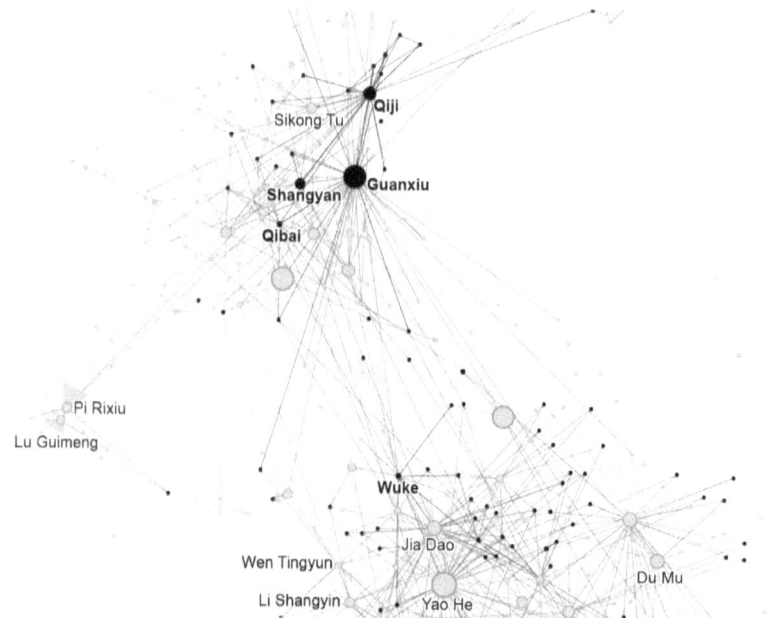

Figure 1.2 Detail of the network graph in Figure 1.1. Note the centrality of Buddhist monks (shaded black).

of the main cluster are Guanxiu and Qiji. Near them is the court monk Qibai 棲白, and on the bottom are Wuke and erstwhile monk Zhou He.

Visualizations, while intuitive, are not very precise. To better understand Buddhist monks' importance to the network, we must analyze the data with algorithms developed by network scientists. The most important metric for our purposes—the place of monks in the network—is centrality. Measures of centrality attempt to answer questions about which node is the most important in the network. There are many different ways of doing this, but the one best suited to the exchange poetry data set is betweenness. This metric answers the question "If one randomly selects two nodes in a network, what is the likelihood that a third node will lie on the shortest path between them?" This would give us the betweenness ranking of the third node. Betweenness centrality identifies actors who have the most connections, often in the most complex portions of the network. To put it simply, if there is evidence that a poet is connected to many other actors who are also well-connected, then that poet must be integral to the network.[68] Recent research has shown that, even if there are significant gaps in our historical records (up to 60 percent of data missing), most centrality metrics will remain accurate.⁶⁹ Doing the calculations on the network of late medieval exchange poetry (table 1.2) reveals that Buddhist monks are three of the sixteen most "between" poets, and five of the top thirty-five.⁷⁰ This is significant, since this is around 1.4–2x higher than the statistical average would predict.⁷¹

The high ranks of Qiji and Guanxiu should come as no surprise. They were widely regarded in their own time as among the greatest poets of the era. They also have some of the largest surviving collections of any Tang poets. But the appearance of Shangyan 尚顏 (830?–930?), in sixteenth place, is unexpected. Only thirty-four of his poems survive,

Table 1.2 Betweenness centrality rankings of major late medieval poets.

RANK	POET	BETWEENNESS CENTRALITY
1	Yao He 姚合	3,467
2	Wu Rong 吳融	2,999
3	Li Qunyu 李群玉	2,806
4	**Guanxiu 貫休**	2,543
5	Fang Gan 方干	2,384
6	Xu Hun 許渾	1,819
7	Du Mu 杜牧	1,694
8	Li Pin 李頻	1,363
9	Zhang Hu 張祜	1,241
10	Yin Yaofan 殷堯藩	1,234
11	Luo Yin 羅隱	1,224
12	**Qiji 齊己**	1,206
13	Jia Dao 賈島	1,182
14	Zheng Gu 鄭谷	115
15	Lu Guimeng 陸龜蒙	105
16	**Shangyan 尚顏**	103
17	Duan Chengshi 段成式	100
18	Li Shangyin 李商隱	90
19	Pi Rixiu 皮日休	88
27	Wen Tingyun 溫庭筠	42
31	**Qibai 棲白**	37
32	Han Wo 韓偓	34
33	Li Deyu 李德裕	32
34	**Wuke 無可**	31

Note: The top nineteen plus several other well-known poets have been included, and Buddhist monks have been bolded. Betweenness centrality figures (normally somewhere between 0 and 1) have been multiplied by 10,000 to make the numbers more legible. For all betweenness centrality rankings, see "1-3 Betweenness Centrality" in the Digital Appendix.

compared to about eight hundred in Qiji's collected works. His fourteen extant exchanges put him far down on our list in terms of quantity, sixty-second overall. By contrast, the other poets with high betweenness centrality have many more exchanges, ranking high on the list in terms of overall quantity of exchanges: Yao He 姚合 (775?–855?, sixth), Wu Rong (thirty-fifth), Li Qunyu 李群玉 (808?–862, seventeenth), and Guanxiu (fourth). Shangyan appears central in the network because his fourteen surviving exchange poems connect him with some of the most important figures of his day, such as Qiji, Zheng Gu, Wu Rong, Fang Gan, and Lu Guimeng, all of whom were themselves well-connected. He also lived nearly to the age of one hundred, so his connections span several generations of poets.

The geographic spread of poet-monks that we saw in the maps above is directly related to their literary connections. Early writings about the first generation of poet-monks in the late-eighth century (not represented in the network graphs) attest to the importance of networks to their ascendancy. Jiaoran, Lingyi, and Lingche were well-known to such eminent literati as Wei Yingwu 韋應物 (737–792?), Qian Qi 錢起 (710?–782?), Dugu Ji 獨孤及 (725–777), Quan Deyu 權德輿 (758–815), Gu Kuang, and the Huangfu 皇甫 brothers, Ran 冉 (717?–770?) and Zeng 曾 (d. 785), among many others. Liu Yuxi 劉禹錫 (772–842), in his 833 preface to Lingche's collected poetry, summarized the monk's ascent in the literary world in precisely these terms:

> He studied how to write poetry under Yan Wei (j.s. 757) when the latter came to Yue, and he gradually earned a reputation. When Yan Wei passed away, he went to Wuxing and traveled with the elder poet-monk Jiaoran and discussed the arts with him a great deal. Jiaoran wrote a letter of recommendation for him to the poet Gentleman Attendant Bao Ji (d. 792), who was very pleased to receive him. He also wrote a letter to Gentleman Attendant Li Shu (d. 834). At this time, everyone said that Bao Ji and Li Shu were the great literary stylists. Consequently, the Venerable Lingche's reputation was bolstered by these three gentlemen, like a cloud grabbing hold of the winds, his branch and leaves lush and flourishing.[72]

從越客嚴維學為詩，遂籍籍有聞。維卒，乃抵吳興，與長老詩僧皎然遊，講藝益至。皎然以書薦於詞人包侍郎佶，包得之大喜。又以書致於李侍郎紓。是時以文章風韻主盟於世者曰包、李。以是上人之名由三公而揚，如雲得風，柯葉張王。

Similarly, later poet-monks used their connections to move beyond their home region and into the upper echelons of the literary world. Qibai appears well-connected in the network data. This is due to his long life lived between the southeast (home to the major poet-monks) and Chang'an (the cultural and political center of the empire until its destruction in 885). Based at Jianfu monastery 薦福寺 in the capital, he served as an "inner offerer" (*neigongfeng* 內供奉)—a kind of court ritual specialist—for Emperor Xuanzong 宣宗 (r. 846–859).[73] One of his exchange poems is addressed to Wuzhen 悟真, a monk who arrived in 850 as part of a mission from the Return to Allegiance Army (Guiyijun 歸義軍) in the far west, which had recently gained independence from the Tibetan empire. This poem survives in two manuscripts unearthed from the cache at Dunhuang in the early twentieth century (see figure 1.3).[74] All throughout the poem, Qibai describes Wuzhen as being between things.

Respectfully Given to Dharma Master Zhen of Hexi 奉贈河西真法師

Qibai

I know that you, master, have come
    from far-away Dunhuang,
You've perfected the skills and practices
    of both Buddhists and Confucians.
You look like Falan,
    hurrying to the capital,[75]
And you discussed Bowang,
    presenting a new map.[76]
I've heard that at the Pass and in Long
    it's always spring,[77]
And it's said that by the Yellow and Huang rivers
    the flora never withers.[78]
How much land separates
    your prefecture from India?
Can you see the Himālayas
    as you look to the west?

知師遠自燉煌至，
藝行兼通釋與儒。
還似法蘭趣上國，
仍論博望獻新圖。

已聞關隴春長在，
更說河湟草不枯。
郡去五天多少地，
西瞻得見雪山無。[79]

Qibai's poem emphasizes Wuzhen as a traveler across geographical and social boundaries. He is from a faraway land (lines 1, 7) about which Qibai seems to have only secondhand information: the weather is always warm, and the vegetation never fades (lines 5–6). Both of these, as anyone who has traveled to Gansu can attest, are not entirely accurate. Wuzhen is compared to a foreign missionary to China and to a Chinese emissary to the Xiongnu (lines 3–4): he is both Chinese and Central Asian. He is said to be skilled in the practices of both Buddhism and Confucian classicism (line 2). Qibai concludes by imagining Wuzhen peering out over the Himālayas, past China, and to the birthplace of Buddhism in Lumbinī (line 8). Qibai's sense of geography may be shaky (the Qinghai-Tibetan plateau separates the Himālayas from Dunhuang by over six hundred miles), but his poem on Wuzhen as a boundary-crosser was well-received. Wuzhen and his disciples preserved Qibai's poem and copied it onto multiple manuscripts. Here Qibai, poet-monk of the capital and ritual specialist at Xuanzong's court, acts as the eminent writer lending some of his cultural capital to a lesser-known figure.

During the third period of the poet-monks' history (875–907), social and geographic mobility was crucial to an individual's survival. Guanxiu, whose life straddles the third and fourth periods, is a case in point. His fame as a poet became widespread only when he won a poetry contest at the age of twenty-six, on the occasion of a Daoist priest's parting:

> The venerable monk's name as a poet made no waves at first. Then, talented men of Southern Chu [Hongzhou] competed to bid farewell to Master Xuanyuan Ji on his way to Mount Luofu with their poetry. The total came to more than a hundred pieces. When Guanxiu recited his piece, everyone else stopped writing.
>
> 初，上人詩名未振，時南楚才人競以詩送軒轅先生歸羅浮山，計百余首矣，上人因吟一章，群公於是息筆。[80]

Later, Guanxiu used poetry to ingratiate himself with rising political leaders like Qian Liu 錢鏐 (852–932) and Wang Jian as well as with acclaimed poets like Wei Zhuang and Luo Yin. As political stability crumbled in the last years of the Tang and regional rulers began to

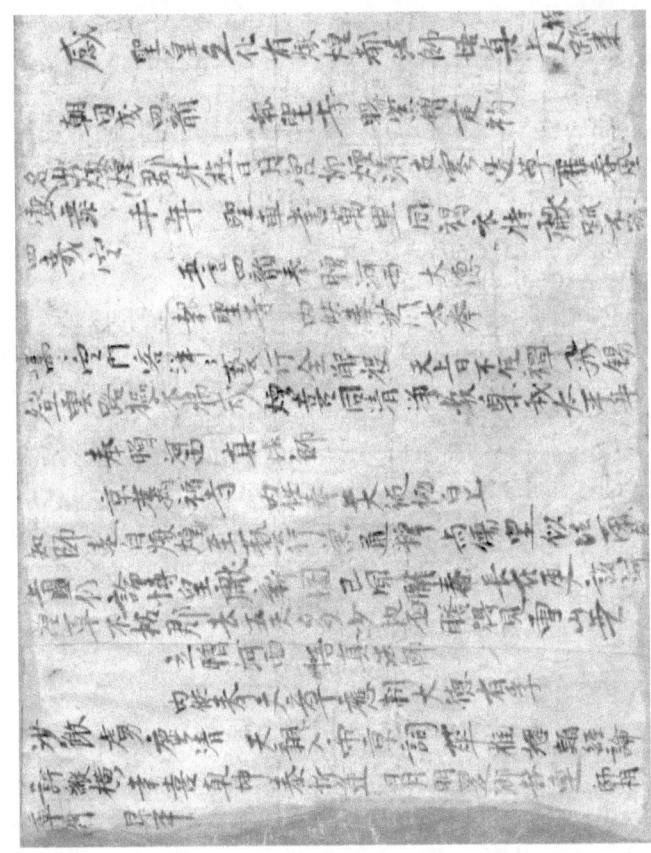

Figure 1.3 P. 3886, verso. Contains exchange poetry between the western monk Wuzhen and the capital-based monk Qibai during the mid-ninth century. A note on the recto side dates the manuscript to 960. Having been copied a century after the initial exchange, this suggests that these poems were cherished by Wuzhen's local community and passed on multiple times.

assert their independence from the central court, poets and monks alike traveled throughout the ruins of the empire to find safety. By roaming widely and exchanging poems with powerful elites, Guanxiu and other poet-monks were able to become some of the most prominent poets of their generation. They were especially well-connected, serving as the brokers that tied disparate groups of poets and monks together.

Poet-monks were not inward-looking, hermetic bonzes but central actors in literary society.[81] In demonstrating this, my network analysis of exchange poems shows that the poet-monks, especially those who lived around the fall of the Tang, should not be regarded as minor actors in literary history. They are an integral part of it.[82] Any history of medieval Chinese literature that minimizes their role risks overlooking major developments in the poetic tradition. In the late ninth century, as the Huang Chao Rebellion plunged the world into chaos, Buddhist monks' mobility became an asset. Their itinerant lifestyle prepared them to travel to the regional cultural centers that sought to establish new polities. Through their travels, they were able to bridge disparate communities and thereby became some of the most well-connected poets of their day.

In the latter half of the Tang dynasty, poet-monks constituted a thriving literary tradition that only continued to grow as the dynasty fell apart and disunity took over. They emerged as the result not only of changes in Buddhist doctrine but also of changes in politics, education, aesthetics, and human geography. Large-scale geographic and social data suggest that the poet-monks developed in four distinct stages: 1) birth in Jiangnan, 720–810; 2) spread to the capital, 811–874; 3) growth and dispersal across the empire, 875–907; and 4) consolidation in new cultural centers, 908–960. Throughout this process of development, poet-monks became more and more integral to literary networks as their mobility ensured that they would serve as hubs between different groups. A close examination of textual sources, as we saw briefly in this chapter and will explore in greater detail in the next two, confirms this macroscopic analysis. Over the course of these two centuries, the poet-monks' place in the literary world fundamentally changed.

Recognizing the centrality of poet-monks to this world should make us reexamine literary history. The end of the Tang and its subsequent period of division is not to be defined by its decadence and ossified, backward gaze. Rather, as this macroscopic picture suggests, and as we will see in detail in subsequent chapters, it is a period of growth, of revival. We will see how, at the turn of the tenth century, the tradition of poet-monks was reaching its apex, developing ideas, attitudes, discourses, and poetic techniques that began with their predecessors in the late eighth century. They are the culmination of a tradition, not its epigones.

CHAPTER 2

Inventing Poet-Monks
The First Generation and Their Reception, 760–810

When the first generation of poet-monks emerged in the mid-eighth century, they acted as the inventors of Chinese Buddhist poetry for their time. Buddhist monks were recognized actors in Tang society—a kind of secondary elite—but not full participants in the world of mainstream, Confucian classicism. They were noticeably different from non-monastics in what they did and in how they looked.[1] Yet poet-monks took up one practice of the literati, the writing of poetry. Elite poetry (*shi*), after all, was an outgrowth of the *Book of Odes* (*Shijing* 詩經), one of the core Confucian classics, and it remained the province of the self-identified inheritors of this tradition. The presence of poet-monks, with their marked difference from normal literary actors, forced the literati to ponder how to accommodate them, to consider how these monks might fit into their world without fully being part of it.

In this chapter, I describe the creation of a discursive space for poet-monks and the poet-monks' accommodation to it. This space was produced mostly through occasional literary documents written by literati that drew on monastic sources, so it is best to think of it as the joint creation of both literati and monastic actors. In what follows, I focus on three of the most prominent monks from this first generation—Lingyi, Jiaoran, and Lingche 靈澈 (746?–816)—and their immediate reception. I show how the literati discourse, combined with at least the passive acceptance of poet-monks themselves, kept poet-monks on the margins of mainstream literary society. This eventually led to the word "poet-monk" becoming a term of disparagement among certain circles in the early eighth century, when the first history of poet-monks was written.

The Founder: Lingyi

Most premodern accounts agree that the original poet-monk was a man named Lingyi, who spent his entire life in Jiangnan.[2] Though there is no record of him being called a "poet-monk" during his lifetime, the discourse around monks writing poetry shifts with him, and he would retrospectively be known as the first poet-monk.

This discourse was a restrictive one. While it often spoke admiringly of monks' poetry, it also placed their poetry in a separate category, produced by men who did not partake of the same social world as mainstream poets. Two written accounts of Lingyi's life and work established these norms for describing poet-monks. One is a biographical pagoda inscription written shortly after Lingyi's death by the acclaimed literatus Dugu Ji 獨孤及 (725–777) called "Inscription for the Pagoda of the Former Vinaya Master Lingyi of Qingyun Monastery in Yangzhou of the Tang (with preface)" 唐故揚州慶雲寺律師一公塔銘並序.[3] The second is a contemporaneous poetry anthology compiled around 788 by Gao Zhongwu 高仲武 called *Collection of Ministerial Spirit from the Restoration* 中興間氣集.[4] Together, these works made Lingyi famous as one who devoted himself to both poetic and Buddhist practices. They laid the foundation for the creation of the label "poet-monk," which was invented to describe Lingyi and the circle of monks associated with him.

Dugu Ji is a curious figure to write the first biographical text on a poet-monk. He is best remembered to history as an advocate of "reviving antiquity" (*fugu* 復古) and classicism in the post-Rebellion period, but he was not purely a conservative Confucian.[5] When he took the civil service exams in 754, he chose Daoist texts as his field and on other occasions advocated Buddhism to his friends.[6] Dugu Ji's interest in Buddhism was not that of a zealous practitioner but of a curious outsider who sought to reconcile it to the classical tradition that he held so dear.

In the pagoda inscription, Dugu Ji describes Lingyi's use of poetry as instrumental, a means of spreading Buddhist teachings. In summarizing

Lingyi's life, he writes, "Lingyi strictly upheld the Vinaya canon, and as he introduced them to the jewel of the dharma he showed others his literary learning in order to seduce their worldly intellects" 嚴持律藏，將紹法寶，示人文學，以誘世智. Lingyi displayed his erudition not for his own sake but as a way to appeal to those with minds mired in nonreligious matters. Poetry was not a distraction, impediment, or supplement to the Buddhist goal of propagating the dharma but rather a means of achieving it.

We should note that Lingyi is identified here as a master of Vinaya, a variety of Buddhism with growing prominence in the Jiangnan region in the late eighth century thanks to increased local patronage following the An Lushan Rebellion.[7] Other sources tell us that Lingyi studied with Fashen 法慎 (669–751), a Vinaya monk known for his acceptance of both Tiantai and Chan practices, for his reconciliation of Buddhist teachings with Confucian conduct, and for his dedication to the written word.[8] Such an openness would clear the ground for monastics to engage in all kinds of literary activity. Lingyi's devotion to poetry may be considered an application of Fashen's logic. Fashen and Lingyi were open to external studies (*waixue*) as something that could supplement or assist Buddhist learning.

Throughout the "Inscription," Dugu Ji places a hierarchy on Lingyi's activities: Buddhism first, poetry second. He underlines this point by emphasizing the severity of Lingyi's monastic vows. Dugu Ji describes how the monk gave away an enormous inheritance he had received from wealthy ancestors, and how he avoided traveling to the homes of laypeople so that he could better maintain his purity. Lingyi, he says, abandoned his body "as if getting rid of snot and spit" 如棄涕唾. Monastic law was his north star, and he never wavered from its guiding light: "He paid no heed to teachers or students, and left behind form and emptiness alike. Even if violent winds covered the mountains, his proper wisdom would never move, or if a great wave blocked the sun, his buoy would naturally keep him safe" 師資兩忘，空色皆遣。暴風偃山，而正智不動；巨浪沃日，而浮囊自安。[9] Even when Dugu Ji describes Lingyi's natural gift as a writer, he states that Lingyi's aims were religious. Lingyi was passionate for poetry but kept his ultimate goal in mind.

> Whenever Lingyi had a break from meditation and recitation, he would engage in the business of writing poetry, entering into uninterrupted thought, filled with soaring inspiration. Lingyi was able to piece together the leftover rhymes of Pan Yue and Ruan Ji, as well as the fragmentary writings of Jiang Yan and Xie Lingyun.

Undoubtedly, he fit in with literary types and went along with the ink of Confucians. Then he would nimbly direct them down the path of study.

每禪誦之隙，輒賦詩歌事，思入無間，興含飛動。潘、阮之遺韻，江、謝之闕文，公能綴之。蓋將吻合詞林，與儒墨同其波流，然後循循善誘，指以學路。

Buddhist practice was Lingyi's work, and poetry his leisure. He devoted every spare moment to the latter activity, entering into a meditative-like trance whenever he composed. Lingyi's verse could vie with the best of the literati, but they were written so that he could have access to the elite and get a chance to draw them in to Buddhism.

We may be tempted to see this as an act of disparagement: if Lingyi were a true poet, he would write poetry for its own sake, not to serve some other goal. But we must remember that Dugu Ji did not himself understand literature in purely aesthetic terms. The literary mainstream at this time, which included Dugu Ji, assumed literature's instrumental use as a force of moral and political suasion. By describing Lingyi's poetry as serving some higher goal, Dugu Ji praises it. Lingyi shares the same attitude toward literature as mainstream Confucian poets. The tools are the same. Only the objects they build are different.

While Dugu Ji lauds Lingyi's noble spirit, it is not Lingyi's explicitly religious verse that he selects for praise but rather his landscape poetry. Dugu Ji places Lingyi in the company of the early medieval canon of landscape poets: Ruan Ji, Pan Yue, Jiang Yan, and Xie Lingyun. In other parts of the essay, Dugu Ji stresses Lingyi's connection to nature: "Being near to green hills and facing fine vistas, he made the ridge pines and gully stones his monastery, and the wind in the bamboos and the frost in the moonlight his chamber" 鄰青山，對佳境，以嶺鬆澗石為梵宇，竹風月露為丈室. Lingyi, in his life and his work, is particularly sensitive to the natural world around him, and this sensitivity would make him a talented poet.

By emphasizing Lingyi's connection to nature and his distance from human sociality, Dugu Ji pegs Lingyi as one who lives "beyond the dust" (*chenwai* 塵外) or, to use the more widespread term at the time, "outside the lines" (*fangwai* 方外). These terms were used to describe anyone who did not abide by the rules of conventional society, especially recluses and religious professionals. The *locus classicus* is a passage in chapter 6 of the *Zhuangzi*, in which Confucius's disciple Zigong observes two people making merry at their friend's grave. When Zigong reports back to the master this blatant violation of ritual propriety, Confucius replies in ambivalent terms:

> These are men who roam outside the lines. I, on the other hand, do my roaming inside the lines. The twain can never meet. It was vulgar of me to send you to mourn for such a person. For the previous while, he had been chumming around as a human with the Fashioner of Things, and now he roams in the single vital energy of Heaven and Earth.[10]

> 彼，遊方之外者也；而丘，遊方之內者也。內外不相及，而丘使汝往弔之，丘則陋矣。彼方且與造物者為人，而遊乎天地之一氣。

Those outside the lines do not adhere to the same values or rules as those in the conventional world. Having disconnected from social norms, they are able to connect with the impersonal forces of nature. They are the opposite of scholar-officials, who are adept at living morally within the lines. The two have adapted to different circumstances: the scholar-official to life as it is normally lived, the one outside the lines to the world in its absolute essence. By describing Lingyi as one who lives "outside the lines," Dugu Ji finds a place for him in mainstream discourse.[11] Like the modern "outsider artist," there is a label that can make sense of his nonconformity. He is one of those who adheres to a higher set of rules: a curiosity, one who is in touch with the Way of Heaven. The term "outside the lines" would be picked up by later literati in their discussions of poet-monks: within twenty years Yu Di 于頔 (d. 818) would use it to describe Jiaoran and Quan Deyu 權德輿 (758–815) to describe Lingche.

Reclusion was a common theme of medieval Chinese literary writings; hence, by the Tang, the iconography of reclusion was abundant. Recluses came in different types, with different tropes used to describe them. Scholar-officials, when demoted to the provinces, could try to maintain their dignity by claiming they were recluses of the "Moral Hero" type, who disengaged from society during times of political corruption.[12] Others could dress themselves in the verbiage of Tao Qian 陶潛 (365–427), who famously quit his official position in favor of a pastoral retirement that allowed him freedom and contentment.[13] Here, Dugu Ji describes Lingyi using the iconography of the "Perfect Man" type of recluse: "he is above and beyond any and all human standards; he identifies himself with nothing less than the universe" and is closely associated with the wilderness.[14] While describing someone in this way is by no means pejorative (just the opposite, in fact), it is limiting. It establishes Lingyi as someone quite different from a normal literatus. Such a man is to be admired but not emulated.

The other major work to establish Lingyi's reputation paints a similar picture. This is the anthology compiled around 788 by Gao Zhongwu, *Collection of Ministerial Spirit from the Restoration*. Inclusion in this anthology is a landmark moment for the development of the poet-monk as an actor in literary society. It helped put poet-monks on the map. At the same time, Gao's introductory remarks on Lingyi make it clear that he regards the monk as an oddity, one who transcended the normal limitations of monks who wrote poetry: "Since the Qi and Liang dynasties, there have been many religious professionals skilled at literature, but rare are those who have entered its stream. Lingyi has expertise in attention and detail and has often exchanged poems with the literati—how could he not be mighty?" 自齊梁以來，道人工文者多矣，罕有入其流者。一公乃能刻意精妙，與士大夫更唱迭和，不其偉歟。[15] By saying that Lingyi "exchanged poems with the literati," Gao Zhongwu posits "literati" (*shidaifu* 士大夫) as a separate category from "religious professionals" (*daoren* 道人). This fact may seem obvious, but it is worth stressing. Lingyi and his interlocutors are not all subsumed under a unified category of "poet"; instead, he is distinct from the others because he inhabits a different place in society (Buddhist monk, not imperial bureaucrat). The phrase "enter the stream" (*ruliu* 入流) was frequently used to describe those who embarked on a career of civil service, and Gao adopted it here to describe Lingyi's acceptance into literary society. He implies that the literary world is closely associated with the official bureaucracy. This reinforces the idea that Lingyi, as a monk, remains outside of it in some fundamental sense.

Gao's selection of Lingyi's poems reinforces his reputation as one who lives outside the lines. Gao includes four poems on standard topics of elite verse: parting, reclusion, mountain climbing, and visiting a religious site. The first two of these are filled with allusions to the literary canon, proving Lingyi's participation in the poetic mainstream. The other Lingyi poems included in Gao's anthology emphasize the serenity of mountain landscapes. These draw on the what Stephen Owen has called the "poetic orthodoxy" of the post–An Lushan Rebellion period: simple descriptions of scenery that belie complex relations between them.[16] One of these poems, on spending the night at a Daoist abbey, uses such descriptive couplets to quash any hint of a religious rivalry with his hosts.

Staying at Lingdong Abbey 宿靈洞觀

Lingyi

Lodging in a stone chamber,[17]
A transcendent happily receives me.[18]
A blossom spring, separated from the water, I see;
A grotto palace, having passed through mountains, I encounter.
A well burbles up from the ground before the stairs,
And clouds emerge from the peaks beyond my door.
I naturally enter into concentration at midnight—
It is not that I shall subdue dragons.[19]

石室因投宿，
仙翁幸見容。
花原隔水見，
洞府過山逢。
泉涌塔前地，
雲生戶外峰。
中宵自入定，
非是欲降龍。[20]

Lingyi, following the conventions of social poetry, adopts the language of his hosts in the first half of the poem. The abbey is a stone chamber where spirits reside, and the priest is a Daoist deity (lines 1–2). The mountains contain the grotto palaces that house the highest gods as well as a "blossom spring" that echoes the "Peach Blossom Spring" 桃花源 utopia described several centuries prior by Tao Qian. Lingyi's poem follows mainstream convention even in its phrasing. The twisted syntax of lines 3–4 was widely used in the mid-eighth century. Line 3 finds a close echo in a poem by Lingyi's associate Huangfu Ran 皇甫冉 (717?–770?), a poet Gao Zhongwu held in especially high regard: "Humans' smoke, separated from the water, I see" 人煙隔水見.[21] The landscape description continues in the third couplet—which Gao Zhongwu singles out for praise in his anthology—where Lingyi balances perspective (well below, clouds above), physical phases (liquid water, gaseous clouds), architecture (stairs, door), and distance (nearby ground, far-off peaks). In this, Lingyi's descriptions resemble those of other poetic masters of the mid-eighth century.

What distinguishes Lingyi's poem from his contemporaries' is the final couplet, in which he plays with the religious commitments that readers would have attributed to Lingyi. This Buddhist monk will not be tested in the same way as the Buddha, who needed to use his powers to subdue the dragon by capturing it in his alms bowl (line 8), even though the calmness of mind afforded by Buddhist meditation would allow it. Instead, Lingyi finds the environment amenable to Buddhist practice, slipping into a deep meditative trance as he contemplates the scenery at midnight (line 7)—he is praising both the serenity of the natural setting and the accommodations of his Daoist host. Lingyi may be a Buddhist monk, but he experiences the world as a poet, and this attention to the physical landscape resolves any religious tension into serene insight.

Gao Zhongwu's anthology confirms Lingyi's reputation as it was established in Dugu Ji's "Inscription," but it hints at deeper complexities. Lingyi was a successful crossover artist. He was primarily a Buddhist monk whose main goal was to explain and propagate Buddhist doctrines, but he wrote great poetry as a means of achieving this goal. As a poet, he excelled at landscape descriptions and was stamped with the approval of famous literati poets. His poems conformed to the mainstream aesthetic of the time, but they also played on his unique religious status. He did not see himself only as a Buddhist monk but as a poet too. Dugu Ji's "Inscription" and Gao Zhongwu's *Collection* set the expectations for generations of poet-monks to come. Literati often admired the writings of poet-monks but nevertheless kept them at a distance. They regarded poet-monks' monastic identity as inseparable from their poetry. These monks existed outside the lines of conventional society, and their poetry was the spectacular result of an alien world coming into contact with the literati's own.

The Figurehead: Jiaoran

Jiaoran is the most prominent poet-monk in Chinese literary history. From the late-eighth century to today, his reputation has overshadowed that of his friend Lingyi. Like Lingyi, Jiaoran was initially trained in the Vinaya tradition but had an insatiable curiosity that led him to study many traditions of self-cultivation. There is evidence that he was familiar with Tiantai, esoteric, Huayan, and Madhyamika teachings as well as several of the emerging lineages of Chan and even Daoism.[22] Later in life he became close to Mazu Daoyi and other leaders of Chan Buddhism that developed in Hongzhou during the eighth and ninth centuries, but it would be a mistake to see him as an exclusive member of this or any school. Mazu and his followers promoted the view that "the ordinary mind is the way" (*pingchang xin shi dao* 平常心是道), and, as Jia Jinhua and

Nicholas Morrow Williams have shown, there are certainly many places in Jiaoran's works that accord with these teachings.[23] However, many of these passages are not specific to this style of Buddhism but are instead part of general Mahāyāna teachings of the mid-Tang.[24] Others appear to fit better with other varieties of Buddhism, such as Madhyamaka.[25] Jiaoran was a capacious intellectual capable of changing his mind and adapting to different rhetorical circumstances. The religious traditions he so fervently pursued over the course of his life were to him repertoires of vocabulary, doctrines, thoughts, and practices more than creeds.[26]

Jiaoran partook of the same Jiangnan literary culture as Lingyi, exchanging and composing his works with the major literati in the area. One of those was the famed calligrapher Yan Zhenqing 顏真卿 (709–784), who, following noble service during the An Lushan Rebellion in the 760s and a brief demotion on account of his unyielding character, came to Huzhou 湖州 to serve as prefect in early 773. There he enlisted Jiaoran and a host of scholars to help him complete his massive rime dictionary, *Mirror of Sources for the Sea of Rimes* 韻海鏡源, now lost. He found in Jiaoran a companion in the literary arts, and much of their exchange poetry has survived, including group compositions of "linked verses" (*lianju* 聯句). While describing Jiaoran in a stele inscription for Miaoxi Monastery in 774, Yan Zhenqing compares him favorably with two other monks: "Regarding the *bhadanta*-monks of Mount Zhu at the time, Jiaoran was a craftsman in literary writing, while Huida and Lingye tasted of meditating and chanting" 時杼山大德僧皎然工於文什，惠達靈曄味於禪誦.[27] While all three of the monks mentioned were literate, Jiaoran distinguished himself by his artisan-like skill (*gong* 工) in belletristic writing.[28] In this comment, we see again an assumed distinction between literary and religious practices, as established in Dugu Ji's comments about Lingyi. Engaging in meditation and chanting sacred texts are nonliterary practices that produce flavors that may leak into poetry and distort its taste. Jiaoran, by contrast, is able to keep his activities cordoned off into separate spheres. He has skill in multiple traditions and can adjust his approach depending on the rhetorical situation.

Throughout his writings, Jiaoran did not hold a single, consistent attitude toward the relationship between his literary and religious pursuits. His views ran the gamut from poetry being a negative sign of his imperfection to it being an unparalleled good, drawing on the language of the Confucian classics as well as the Buddhist scriptures. In his critical writings, Jiaoran described poetry in almost mystical terms, claiming that it gave one access to the divine order of reality.

From "Preface to *Poetic Paradigms*" 詩式總序
Jiaoran

Poetry is the finest fruit of all wonder, the purest flowering of the Six Confucian Classics: though not the product of the sages, it is equal to the sages in its wonder. Heaven and earth, sun and moon, the profound depths of the first transformations, the subtle darkness of ghosts and spirits—if you seek these with intense thought, the ten thousand images will not be able to hide the perfection of their handiwork. When it comes to creating effects, one must be intrepid in giving reign to thought and willing to overcome difficulty in finalizing form. What I draw upon comes from within me, but what I attain is like a manifestation of the gods. When it comes to creating lines that soar above the rest in their heavenly truth—ones that vie with the fashioned world itself—this can be comprehended with the mind but is hard to describe with words: one who is not a *creator* cannot understand it.

夫詩者，衆妙之華實，六經之菁英。雖非聖功，妙均於聖。彼天地日月，元化之淵奧，鬼神之微冥。精思一搜，萬象不能藏其巧。其作用也，放意須險，定局須難。雖取繇我裏，而得若神表。至如天眞挺拔之句，與造化爭??，可以意會，難以言狀，非作者不能知也。[29]

To Jiaoran here, a great writer is a sub-creator: one whose art imitates, parallels, or even competes with the macrocosm.[30] The poet's work mirrors that of the "Fashioner of Things" 造物者, the impersonal force that shapes the phenomenal world. The poet carefully investigates the workings of the world in its fullness and creates lines that, though human in origin, appear to be divine. The poet is one who sees reality in all its fullness. Indeed, the term translated here as "creator," *zuozhe* 作者, harkens back to the words of the "Record of Music" (*Yueji* 樂記) from the classic *Book of Rites* (*Liji* 禮記).

Therefore, those who understand the inherent condition of rites and music are capable of creating. Those who are familiar with the ornamental patterns of rites and music are capable of transmitting. The creators are known as sagely, and the transmitters are known as bright. The bright and the sagely are other words for transmitting and creating.[31]

故知禮樂之情者，能作；識禮樂之文者，能述。作者之謂聖；述者之謂明。明、聖者，述、作之謂也。

A creator grasps the very nature of the two pillars of Chinese civilization: the rites of the state cult and the music that brings people under its righteous influence.[32] His arts conform to the patterns of proper civilization. He is a sage. This religious notion of poetry as sub-creation is thoroughly Confucian. It was based in the classics and was used by many poets who showed no fondness for Buddhism, such as Han Yu.[33] Jiaoran wrote compellingly of poetry's power from a non-Buddhist perspective.

Elsewhere, Jiaoran wrote about poetry as a complement to his Buddhist practice. We see this most clearly in a few of his late poems written to Yu Di, an ascendant official who, at the height of his reputation in 792, would write the preface to Jiaoran's collected works commissioned by the central court.[34] About a year prior, in a poem written in 791 to Yu Di, Jiaoran states that "the Great Way is no burden" 大道無負荷, that is, that religious service does not impair one from pursuing other activities. He later elaborates this thought:

> The expansive air of this western mountain[35]
> Coalesces to reside in the gentleman's breast.
> Reflections in the deep autumn water
> Are useful for nourishing a person's mind.
> Phenomena are like ducks and seagulls:
> They soar around, fond of the clear and profound.[36]

> 盤薄西山氣，
> 貯在君子衿。
> 澄澹秋水影，
> 用為宇人心。
> 群物如鳧鷖，
> 遊翶愛清深。

These lines make increasingly audacious claims about the relationship between the landscape and the cultivation of one's mind. Mountain air enters the poet's body and becomes part of him, but also phenomena actually assist in the process of mental cultivation. What is more, phenomena do not just assist in this process but also partake of the "clear and profound" nature of ultimate reality. Jiaoran applies to his poetry the Buddhist view that the ordinary world and ultimate reality are inseparable. He states this same view even more directly in another poem:

"Replying to Editor Yu's 'On a Winter Night'" 答俞校書冬夜

Jiaoran

In the still of the night, I concentrate on meditation,
And this realm of emptiness is serene and remote.
You, Zizhen, are an official in the ranks of transcendents,
Fond of me like Zong Bing.[37]
Through my whole stay, I am met with secluded majesty:
My body is purified, and my troubles are gone.
Your new sounds different from "Pitched Chu,"
And fine lines resembling "Singing in Ying"—[38]
When you gave me these, my emotions were stirred,
And, chanting low, I forgot the night growing long.
Moonglow dispersing over the jasper-blue water
Instructs you in the realms of meditation.
True contemplation resides in the distant unseen,
While floating thoughts lodge in forms and shadows.
I attain a mind as remote as the Fourbright Mountains:
What need is there to climb peaks and ridges?
Poetic feelings depend on the creation of effects;[39]
For empty nature, only stillness and silence will do.
If we hope to meet again in the woods,
I'll expect you to set aside your paperwork.

夜閑禪用精，
空界亦清迥。
子真仙曹吏，
好我如宗炳。
一宿覿幽勝，
形清煩慮屏。
新聲殊激楚，
麗句同歌郢。
遺此感予懷，
沈吟忘夕永。
月彩散瑤碧，
示君禪中境。
真思在杳冥，
浮念寄形影。
遙得四明心，

何須蹈岑嶺。
詩情聊作用,
空性惟寂靜。
若許林下期,
看君辭簿領。⁴⁰

The landscape is itself transcendent in this poem. It has a therapeutic effect, bringing the speaker's mind and body to order (lines 5–6). As he becomes absorbed in the scene, unaware of time passing, he focuses on a single feature—moonlight on the water—that illustrates what it is like to be in a meditative trance (lines 11–12). The physical realm blurs into the contemplative realm. His mind becomes a mountain range—remote, imposing, unshakeable—allowing him to leave the physical mountains behind (lines 15–16).⁴¹ The speaker states the logic behind these claims in lines 17–18, in which putting one's feelings into poetry and emptying one's nature are placed in parallel. While both are types of mental cultivation, their processes are precisely opposite: poetry requires a person's active intervention, but the realization of ultimate emptiness requires a complete halting of activity. Poetry is craft. Insight is stillness. Yet both emerge out of a serious encounter with a majestic landscape.

In other works, Jiaoran described poetry's relation to religious insight in more ambivalent terms. In the year 788, Jiaoran exchanged verses with the famed literatus Wei Yingwu 韋應物 (737–792?), who was visiting from his post in the neighboring town of Suzhou. In his poem, Wei Yingwu makes passing reference to Jiaoran's parallel fame in religious and literary spheres, writing: "Your fame as a poet makes waves for naught, / For your religious mind has long been settled" 詩名徒自振, 道心長晏如.⁴² This is a light pun. "Makes waves" (zhen 振) refers primarily to the way Jiaoran's poetry has been circulating in literary circles but secondarily to a potential mental disturbance (a mind "shaking"). Jiaoran wrote a response to Wei Yingwu in a more serious tone. He opens with praise for Wei Yingwu as a poet and an official, then turns back to himself in the second half. Jiaoran describes in greater detail the disparity between his religious and literary practices that Wei Yingwu had joked about:

From "Replying to Vice Director Wei Yingwu of Suzhou" 答蘇州韋應物郎中

Jiaoran

You should pity this son of the meditative clan,
Alone in the woods, with no plans;

Whose traces have been trampled by the world's treasures
But whose mind has attained the essence within the Way;
Who has gotten rid of the burden of words
And avoids being unsettled by external things;
Whose writing robe is piled with drifting dust
And whose inkstone has sprouted bits of moss.
I regret that I still don't know you, dear gentleman—
You have passed along the gem in your hand in vain.[43]
How can it possibly coerce my nature?
My first wishes go against goodwill.
I'll make no Simurgh tunes,
But add to your Yunhe pipings,[44]
Chanting them as I face the meditation grounds,
Which nevertheless shame me before the sound of deep pines.

應憐禪家子，
林下寂無營。
跡躡世上華，
心得道中精。
脫略文字累，
免爲外物攖。
書衣流埃積，
硯石駮蘚生。
恨未識君子，
空傳手中瓊。
安可誘我性，
始願慾素誠。
爲無鸞鷟音，
繼公雲和笙。
吟之向禪藪，
反愧幽松聲。[45]

Jiaoran begins by contrasting Buddhist activities and worldly ones, with poetry being an example of the latter. Jiaoran is so absorbed in religious self-cultivation, achieving a state of inner equanimity beyond language (lines 17-20), that he lets his writing materials gather dust (lines 21-22). But by the end of the poem, Jiaoran renounces this dichotomy, humbly declaring that he will build on Wei Yingwu's poems (rather than attempt to make his own lofty "simurgh tunes"), chanting them in his monastery and thereby breaking the stillness symbolized by the sound of the pines in the wind (lines 27-30). In a single poem,

Jiaoran moves between the views that poetry does and does not impede Buddhist practice.[46]

A similar ambivalence crops up in Jiaoran's letters to the literati Quan Deyu and Li Shu 李紓 (731–792). In both letters, written ten years apart (Li's in 780 and Quan's in 790), he describes his impulse to write poetry as neither good nor bad but simply as part of his fundamental nature.[47] As the letter to Quan Deyu puts it: "I, one poor in virtue, am of little reputation. Though I have extinguished all thought, I stubbornly linger on the path of poetry in order to satisfy my inherent nature. Surely this is due to a slight stirring of the remaining dust that I've not yet extinguished: how could there be any greed in this?" 貧道隳名之人，萬慮都盡，強留詩道，以樂性情。蓋絲瞥起餘塵未泯，豈有健羨於其間哉. Jiaoran describes his literary activities as the result of karmic traces lingering from previous lifetimes. They are signs of the imperfection of his religious practice—unshakeable dust. At the same time, they are part of his fundamental nature, and therefore they are not a sign of lust for fame.[48]

In his letter to Li Shu, Jiaoran does not resort to karmic traces to explain his desire to write poetry but instead stresses the separation between his religious and literary activities in other ways:

> It's been over ten years since we last saw each other by the Lake. You, sir, have been honored as a noble of the region, while my traces have remained in the forest of emptiness. We are different in our leaving and staying, and our sound and dust have not touched one another: all of this is reasonable. After we parted, I considered myself to be one whose years are many and whose will is firm, scant in fame but close to the Way, who reveres only the gates of emptiness. Although I've had some visitors, I've never met anyone who understands me. I once jokingly wrote a verse on myself:
>
>> Happily meditating, my mind seems to drift off—
>> There's nothing that comes between me and the Way.
>> I laugh and sing in my solitary enlightenment:
>> Who says you get crazier in old age?
>
> ... As for the writing of literature, I compose the odd piece when I'm not working to master my mind. My intention is to satisfy my inherent nature and find joy in the clouds and springs: how could there be any greed in this?

自湖上一辭，十有餘載。公貴爲方伯，畫跡在空林。出處殊疎，音塵不接，蓋理然也。畫從辭後，自謂年多志固，名疎道親，惟慕空門。若有所詣，然未曾遇知已。嘗戲爲一章自詠曰：

樂禪心似蕩，
吾道不相妨。
獨悟歌還笑，
誰言老更狂。

......又畫於文章，理心之外，或有所作，意在適情性、樂雲泉，亦何能苦健羨於其間哉？

Literary writing is something Jiaoran does when not "working to master [his] mind," or meditating. It is not a fundamental part of his religious practice. He further stresses this contrast between religious and literary pursuits in the way he describes the parallel paths taken by Li Shu and himself. Whereas Li Shu the literatus achieved fame for his work as an officer of the Tang government, Jiaoran the monk has focused on growing nearer to the Way in his seclusion.[49] Jiaoran has adopted the terms of his addressee: the literatus is a Confucian who roams within the lines, and the Buddhist monk is a recluse who roams outside the lines.

There is no evidence, then, that Jiaoran advocated for poetry writing as a means of practicing Buddhist cultivation, as some have claimed. He did not even consistently state that poetry and religion were in fundamental accord. Rather, Jiaoran took a variety of positions that he articulated in different circumstances. Sometimes, as in his letters, he described literary writings as a supplement to religious activity, one that had neutral or negative connotations. It was part of his fundamental nature, some karmic residue carried over from a previous life. At other times, Jiaoran did advance a genuinely religious understanding of poetry. But when he did so, it was either fully Confucian, as in the theory of sub-creation found in the "Preface to the *Poetic Paradigms*," or else it made poetry and religion into parallel and slightly antithetical pursuits, as found in "Replying to Editor Yu." There both literary and Buddhist activities are responses to careful observation of natural landscapes, but poetry is an active intervention, whereas meditation is a calming dissolution. His hesitancy to equate poetry with any religious tradition or practice is best summed up in one of his remarks from Poetic Paradigms: "If Confucians were to venerate it, they would call it the crown of the Six Classics; if Daoists were to value it, they would say it resides at the Gate of All Wonders; if Buddhists were to worship it, they would say it penetrates the secrets of the King of Emptiness" 尊之於儒，則冠六經之首；貴之於道，則居眾妙之門；崇之于釋，則徹空王之奧.⁵⁰ This kind of capacious versatility is one of Jiaoran's strengths as a writer and theorist of poetry. Taking all of the evidence together, it becomes clear that Jiaoran held at least three distinct views on the relationship between religion and literature that he articulated in different rhetorical contexts, and this complexity mirrors his eclectic, situation-dependent, ever-evolving personality.

The Framework: Lingche

There is a disparity between the self-descriptions of the early poet-monks and how the literati perceived them. In the example of Jiaoran, one of the few poet-monks who has a large surviving corpus of writing, we see a diversity of views toward Buddhism, literature, and their points of connection. When we compare Jiaoran's inner complexity to literati writings about him and other monks, we see how they simplified things. Poet-monks are either Buddhist teachers who use poetry to grab the attention of the literati, or they are detached recluses who roam outside the lines of the conventional world. Later generations would associate them with Chan, despite the fact that many were trained in Vinaya and other forms of Buddhism.

This disparity between personal complexity and others' simplification is especially apparent in the example of Lingche, a younger member of the early poet-monk community. Lingche was by all accounts an accomplished writer. He is said to have written two thousand poems during his lifetime, many of them exchanges with important literati. He may also be the author of the preface to *Baolin zhuan* 寶林傳, an important lineage record of the early Chan tradition probably compiled in 801.⁵¹ However, very little of his work now survives—only sixteen poems and a handful of fragmentary couplets—so it is difficult to get a sense of him from his writings. Instead, we must rely on two contemporaneous documents that present him in very different ways. The first is a recommendation letter that Jiaoran wrote for Lingche, sent to Bao Ji in 781; and the second is an essay written by Quan Deyu on the occasion of Lingche's departure from Mount Lu in 788.

Jiaoran met Lingche in 780, when the latter made a short journey, eighty-five miles, from Yuezhou 越州 to Huzhou. The two must have gotten along well. Jiaoran wrote at least six poems to Lingche over the next year and a half and later recommended him to several of his literati friends.[52] Jiaoran's recommendation letter to Bao Ji stresses Lingche's versatility.[53] He praises Lingche's writing for being "neither inferior to the hands of antiquity nor overly dependent on the ancients" 不下古手，不傍古人, then quotes from twelve of Lingche's poems, which cover topics as diverse as Daoist temples, Buddhist monks, replies to literati, holiday nostalgia, and mountain reclusion—excerpts carefully chosen to show the range of his writing abilities. Jiaoran concludes his letter by describing how Lingche could contribute to literary circles:

> Everything written by this monk is marvelous. Reading just a single piece makes me want to abandon brush and ink.[54] I bow before the Vice Censor in Chief in hope of his judgment and magnanimity: will you promote or ignore him? Currently, because of things happening in the empire, none of the great worthies who diligently serve the ruler are eager to meet with him. This only shows how I, an old fool, am out of step of with the times.
>
> Nevertheless, Lingche's grasp on the mind and well-established integrity are unattainable by most, and his religious practice and meditative wisdom would not be put to shame by Dao'an or Huiyuan.[55] He once wrote a twenty-one-fascicle *Origins of the Vinaya School*, which was praised by dark-robed Buddhist monks.[56] He will tirelessly provide answers during abstruse discussions of religious truth, and he will help boost your spirits while at leisure among the moon and wind.

> 此僧諸作皆妙。獨此一篇，使晝見欲棄筆硯。伏惟中丞高鑒宏量，其進諸乎，其捨諸乎？方今天下有故，大賢勤王，輒以非急干請視聽，亦昭愚老不達時也。然上人秉心立節，不可多得；其道行定慧，無慙安、遠。嘗著《律宗引源》二十一卷，爲緇流所歸。至於元言道理，應接靡滯，風月之間，亦足以助君子高興也。

Jiaoran's letter stresses Lingche's ability to contribute to the well-being of a patron in a variety of situations. He is a good companion to have around whether you are staying in to discuss religious doctrine or whether you are going out to write poetry in the wilds. He is a writer so skilled that he makes Jiaoran want to retire. At the same time, his mental and moral cultivation are beyond compare. He has composed powerfully on all the standard topics of elite verse, and he has written a well-respected Buddhist text. He is equally skilled as a poet and as a monk. Jiaoran presents Lingche as one who is just as complicated and talented as himself. The letter implies Jiaoran's complex self-understanding as a poet-monk, and it hints at the literati's ability to appreciate that complexity under the right conditions. A good poet-monk could be useful in a variety of circumstances; he was not just an aloof, morally pure recluse.

Jiaoran's letter was effective. It introduced Lingche into the major literary circles in the southeast, including Quan Deyu's community at Mount Lu in the late 780s. On one occasion, in which Lingche was making the roughly four-hundred-mile journey east to Wozhou, Quan wrote an essay commemorating their parting. This essay, written by a literatus for other literati, marginalizes Lingche's poetry even as it defends its merit.

Essay on Seeing off the Venerable Lingche Back to Wozhou from Mount Lu
送靈澈上人廬山迴歸沃州序

Quan Deyu

In the past, Huiyuan of Lushan (334–416) and Baoyue of Zhongshan broadened the grounds of their minds with literature and used it to guide their juniors. This enabled their students to follow their natural inclinations and become enlightened through language: is this not one tributary of the profound principle of Buddhism? The Elder of Wuxing, Jiaoran, collects the finest flowers of the six arts and the leaders of those outside the lines. Among those who have gone into his room is the Venerable Lingche of Wozhou.

The venerable monk's mind has an abstruse connection to emptiness, yet he has put traces of it into words. For this reason, his language is unassuming and does not appear to leave behind the normal realm of the senses, but in fact all the careful contemplation of scholars couldn't reach its end. His transformations are like a resonance among the wind and pines, or ice and jade knocking against one another, or gold and sapphire buried beneath storied peaks a thousand fathoms high. At first the eyes of the high and the low dare not look at them. Only after thinking them over three times do they hide themselves among their calm, natural ease. So when you look upon his face or cast an eye upon his words, you understand his mind: that it is calm independent of the calming of the senses.

How much more so, then, at the mountains and rivers of Guiji, which has had such unsurpassed beauty since antiquity that a great many recluses of the Eastern Jin dynasty hid away there! In summer, during the fifth month, the venerable monk will go back there from Mount Lu. I know that he'll grab his monastic robe, ride a light skiff, navigate the mirror-like waters, and attain exquisite couplets in the stillness. And then, once he enters deeply into empty silence and washes away his ten thousand thoughts, he'll turn toward the scenery and its waves of grain. I admire him and suspect that he won't get a chance to return, so I sigh over this bird who has dared to leave the flock!

昔廬山遠公、鍾山約公，皆以文章廣心地，用贊後學，俾學者乘理以諧，因言而悟，得非玄津之一派乎？吳興長老晝公，掇六藝之清英，首冠方外，入其室者，有沃州靈澈上人。上人心冥空無，而迹寄文字，故語甚夷易，如不出常境；而諸生思慮，終不可至。其變也，如風松相韻，冰玉相叩，層峰千仞，下有金碧。聾瞽夫之目，初不敢眡；三復則淡然天和，晦於其中。故覩其容，覽其詞者，知其心，不待境靜而靜。況會稽山水，自古絕勝，東晉逸民多遺身於此。夏五月，上人自鑪峰言旋，復於是邦。予知夫拂方袍，坐輕舟，泝沿鏡中，靜得佳句，然後深入空寂，萬慮洗然，則嚮之景物，又其秭秭也。鄙人方景慕企尚之不暇，烏敢以離群爲歎。[57]

Quan's essay begins by firmly placing Lingche in the category of "poet-monk." It connects him to Huiyuan and Baoyue, two monks who wrote poetry in the early medieval period, and to his eminent contemporary Jiaoran. All of these monks, Quan says, use poetry as an instrument for teaching and guiding. Lingche belongs to a contemporary community of literate monks that is rooted in the fourth century, one that views poetry strategically.

Quan Deyu stresses Lingche's difference from Confucian literati. He roams "outside the lines"—a recluse who has a deep connection to the natural landscape and is characterized by his calm purity. Quan's self-deprecating comment, that "all the contemplation of scholars couldn't reach the end" of Lingche's words, praises the monk while at the same time boxing him in. His unassuming appearance belies hidden depths that cannot be understood with ordinary thought. In the closing image, as Lingche disappears into a beautiful vista to compose poetry, he "grabs his monastic robes" and "washes away his ten thousand thoughts." That is, he remains a monk with all distinguishing physical features and mental habits of a monk.

Quan Deyu's description of Lingche is similar to Dugu Ji's description of Lingyi. They admire these monks and write about them in positive terms. However, they keep the poet-monks at a distance from themselves even as they praise them. The monks are visitors from another, inscrutable realm who descend to our social world, act in a different manner, adopt poetry-writing to serve different goals, and then disappear. They can never be fully integrated into the mainstream, elite world of the literati. They are not, in fact, poets, but monks or poet-monks.

Lingche went on to have a storied career. After his time in the southeast, he traveled to the capital around the turn of the ninth century and found favor as high up as the imperial court. However, he ran afoul of other court Buddhists for unknown reasons. They spoke ill of him, and he was sent into exile in the far south. In 805, when a general amnesty was issued, Lingche returned to the southeast to live out his remaining years. He died in 816 at the age of seventy, surrounded by disciples, entombed in a pagoda built in his honor.

Jiaoran's and Quan Deyu's presentations of Lingche are striking in their differences. Jiaoran, as one poet-monk writing about another, stresses Lingche's versatility. He sees Lingche as a kindred spirit, one with the same inner complexity as himself. Quan Deyu, by contrast, admires Lingche as an inscrutable, otherworldly figure. Even as Quan praises Lingche, he does not admit him into the world of mainstream poetry. This shows a fundamental distinction between how the early generation of poet-monks saw themselves versus how the literati saw them. The literati seem surprised to find Buddhist monks who could write good poetry. So, when they created discursive space for these poet-monks, it was as recluses who roamed outside the lines—those whose transcendent values were incompatible with the mundane world. The poet-monks did not necessarily see themselves this way. To be sure, they could themselves adopt these terms for their own benefit, advancing through literary society through an act of self-exoticization. But, at least in Jiaoran's letter, they could also portray themselves as versatile utility players, code switchers who could move between different social spheres with ease. Some literati may even have valued this alternate portrayal—Jiaoran's letter, after all, was written with his readers' expectations in mind and thus implies that some literati valued this versatility. Yet, despite this complexity, the more limiting, mainstream literati discourse would win out, and poet-monks would be understood as strange, fundamentally contradictory creatures for generations to come.

Their Fate

Moving into the ninth century, we find that the fame of Jiaoran and Lingche spread beyond Jiangnan, and with it the term "poet-monk." It is likely that the imperially commissioned edition of Jiaoran's works, published in 792, had a wide readership among capital elites. For instance, the *Supplement to the History of Our State* 國史補, written at the capital sometime in the 810s or 820s by Li Zhao 李肇, mentions this edition of Jiaoran's works and praises Lingyi and Jiaoran as the foremost "literary monks" (*wenseng* 文僧—a synonym for "poet-monk").[58] Jiaoran's works, which mention the term "poet-monk" and embody the best qualities of its associated community, would have helped make this term familiar to a broader audience. Lingche's presence at the capital at the turn of the ninth century also surely reinforced the prominence of poet-monks. Even if he left after being slandered by other monks, he clearly made an impression and helped bolster the idea that there existed monks with a strong proclivity for writing poetry.

Nevertheless, the term "poet-monk" took on negative connotations, at least to certain members of the literary and monastic elite in the early ninth century. To this group of people, Buddhist monks should be devoted to the dharma, not to literary greatness. *Shi*-poetry, in a fundamental sense, belonged to the Confucians. We see this most clearly in a series of poems and essays written on the monk Wenchang's 文暢 departures from the capital in the first years of the ninth century.[59] The most famous of these is an essay written by Han Yu in 803 at the request of Liu Zongyuan 柳宗元 (773–819). Han Yu describes with some puzzlement how "the Buddhist master Wenchang enjoys literature" 浮屠師文暢喜文章 and collects poems from eminent literati. "Having seen the [Confucian] virtues of lord-vassal and father-son relations, and the richness of our cultural activities, his mind yearns for them, yet he is bound by his dharma and cannot join us" 彼見吾君臣父子之懿，文物事為之盛，其心有慕焉，拘其法而未能入.[60] Setting aside Han Yu's boldly anti-Buddhist attitude, we should notice the close association between Confucian virtues and "cultural activities" (*wenwu shiwei* 文物事為), here manifested in the hundreds of parting poems that Wenchang has collected. Buddhism, by contrast, appears only as the chains shackling him from encountering superior, Confucian truths. Han Yu repeats this idea in the poem he wrote for Wenchang on another occasion, where he puts the words into Wenchang's mouth:

> I've already reached the roots of Buddhism
> But only roughly understand the crux of things.
> These fetters bend my true self
> So I'm preparing axle-caps with thoughts of going far away.
>
> . . .
>
> Again I listen to understand the Great Way:
> Which path can restore my branded face and cut-off feet?
>
> 已窮佛根源，
> 粗識事輗軏。
> 攣拘屈吾真，
> 戒轄思遠發。
>
> . . .
>
> 又聞識大道，
> 何路補剠刖。[61]

Monastic regulations are fetters breaking his body, equivalent in their effect to the mutilating punishments reserved for prisoners. Wenchang, according to Han Yu, longs for a miraculous transformation by hearing the "Great Way" of Confucian learning.

While other literati did not see Buddhism in quite such negative terms as Han Yu, they nonetheless made the same assumption: poetry grew out of the indigenous classics and therefore is most closely associated with the Confucian tradition. In Lü Wen's 呂溫 poem for Wenchang, he asserts this more subtly. The poem is filled with well-crafted allusions to Buddhist doctrine, but it nevertheless concludes by emphasizing the difference between the monk and the literati poets: "Now, as we're about to diverge, / We here naturally have feelings" 今日臨岐別，吾徒自有情.[62] Many literati recognized that the Buddhist monastic ideal is to empty out or transcend emotions.[63] In contrast to this ideal, which Wenchang is politely described as embodying, the group of literati become emotional on witnessing his departure. Poetry, after all, fundamentally "stems from the emotions" (yuan qing 緣情), according to one common view at the time.[64] Their physical divergence highlights an emotional divergence. Poets weep; monks do not.

Liu Zongyuan, who was generally sympathetic toward Buddhism, also wrote an essay on parting with Wenchang.[65] Liu takes a lighter approach, appealing to historical precedent for monks writing poetry while in the company of famous literati. Nevertheless, in his framing of this history, Liu makes it clear that poetry is most closely associated with Confucians.

> In the past, leading monks were fond of traveling with worthy literati. Since the Jin and Song [266–479], there have been Zhi Dun, Dao'an, Dharma Master Huiyuan, and Venerable Huixiu. Their travel companions included Xie An, Wang Xizhi, Xi Zuochi, Xie Lingyun, and Bao Zhao. All of them were choice men of their eras. In this way, the dharma stamp of the True Vehicle was used together with the Confucian canon, and people understood them to be models. Now there is Wenchang, who was born knowing the origins of the Way, whose good roots were planted in a previous lifetime, who has such a deep fondness for dharma phrases that he forgets the flavor of sweet dew, and who has served the Way in the south for about thirty years.
>
> 昔之桑門上首，好與賢士大夫遊，晉宋以來，有道林、道安、遠法師、休上人，其所與遊，則謝安石、王逸少、習鑿齒、謝靈運、鮑照之徒，皆時之選。由是真乘法印，與儒典並用，而人知嚮方。今有釋文暢者，道源生知，善根宿植，深嗜法語，忘甘露之味，服道江表，蓋三十年。[66]

The Buddhist dharma stamp and the Confucian canon are separate things, even if they can be applied simultaneously when monks and literati work together. As Liu Zongyuan turns to the present day, where he serves as the literatus and Wenchang as the monk, he praises Wenchang for his Buddhist virtues, not his skills in the traditional Confucian arts. When Liu does mention Wenchang's way with words, it is as "dharma phrases" (*fayu* 法語), a specifically Buddhist term for religious utterances. In this way he depicts literati as the experts in poetry, and Buddhist monks as the experts in religious matters.

Liu Zongyuan's views on poet-monks seem to have taken a hostile turn in the following decade, as suggested by a parting essay written for a different monk, Fangji 方及, in the year 815.

> Of the drifters of our era, those who study literature but are incapable of excellence borrow the look of Buddhists to gain esteem, and those who study Buddhism but are incapable of integrity give themselves over to literary fashions to let loose. For this reason, all who become literary Buddhists are indulgent and disorderly,

and the world tolerates it, not punishing them. At present, Master Fangji alone is not like this.

代之游民，學文章不能秀發者，則假浮屠之形以爲高。其學浮屠不能愿愨者，則又託文章之流以爲放。以故爲文章浮屠，率皆縱誕亂雜，世亦寬而不誅。今有方及師者獨不然。[67]

"Literary Buddhists" (*wenzhang futu* 文章浮屠), another term equivalent to "poet-monks," come in two varieties: bad poets who become fake monks, and bad monks who become fake poets. It is possible that Liu Zongyuan refers here to the original group of Jiangnan poet-monks: Fangji himself was from Jiangnan and likely had connections to Jiaoran's circle.[68] He may also be referring to Wenchang, if there is any shred of truth behind Han Yu's depiction of him as a monk yearning to live as a Confucian poet. Whatever the case may be, it seems that Liu Zongyuan looked upon most monks who wrote poetry with disdain. A monk who is genuinely committed to both his religious and literary practices, such as Fangji, is rare and somehow transcends the category of poet-monk.

Writing around the same time as Liu Zongyuan, the erudite monk Shenqing held an ambivalent attitude toward monks writing literature. As mentioned in chapter 1, Shenqing was a strong advocate for Buddhist monks studying the Confucian classics, justifying Confucianism as a useful guide for this-worldly affairs in contrast to Buddhism's otherworldly orientation.[69] At the same time, he understands that, in the process of reading Confucian classics, one must not abandon Buddhism. To Shenqing, moderation is key, a point he illustrates by comparing learning to cuisine (balancing flavors) and music (harmonizing). In contrast, those who go to the extremes of refusing education or of too obsessively pursuing it deserve harsh criticism:

> There have at times been those who don't study. They are deaf and blind in the mind, confident in their own idiocy like pigs or sheep, crooked and cliquish. When they look upon the arts of knowledge, they laugh at them as foolish. They regard writing to be as excessive as Mount Heng or Mount Tai, not thinking it important. The former sages would have regarded them as a herd of sheep monks, so shallow they were![70] And then there are the madmen. They abandon our teachings and revel through old books, gliding about and offending people, like pigs carrying mud on their backs, averse to cleanliness, such as Huilin and Huixiu of the Song.

但時有不學者，心智聾瞽，恃其頑薄，如豕如羊，很戾朋從。
視於智藝，狎而笑之，以為著文字，過比夫衡岱，未云重也。
先聖以為群羊僧，不甚然乎！復有狂狷之夫，棄乎本教，聊覽
墳素，遊衍內侮，若豕負塗，潔則忌之，如宋慧琳、慧休之流
也。[71]

The example of Huilin and Huixiu here is significant. Both were well-known poets during the Liu-Song dynasty (420–479) who consorted with the literati to the detriment of their monastic communities, as Shenqing goes on to explain. While he does not explicitly compare Huilin and Huixiu to the recent group of Jiangnan poet-monks, others did, as we have just seen in Liu Zongyuan's essay for Wenchang.[72] To Shenqing, poet-monks, with their flouting of typical monastic rules, are madmen. He continues his criticism before providing his own vision of what role poetry should play in a monastic life:

> Now, those who become Buddhists not for the sake of the Way but only for the sake of Confucian learning are but laypeople who have cut their hair off—how could they really last? In the past, when Daobao of the Jin was about to take the tonsure, he wrote a poem that reads: "I now understand that a ten-thousand-mile river, / Begins with a cup-floating trickle."[73] The intention is truly immediate, and those with discernment are moved by its words and strive to apply them. This is called doing literature. [Buddhist monks] should wear rice-patty robes and use clay vessels, make others wear and hold them, and calmly do nothing.[74] Only after this may they, taking the sūtras and vinaya as their plumb line, use literature as an embellishment.

> 今為釋，不以道而但以儒學聞，彼蓋斷髮一俗人耳，其可令得
> 終久乎？昔晉道寶臨剃髮，為詩曰：「方知萬里水，初發濫觴
> 源。」真翛然之道意也，識者感其言而勵進，是曰為文。夫稻
> 畦為衣，陶土為器，使人服而執之，澹然無為，然後以經律為
> 繩墨，以文章為潤色。[75]

From the quoted Daobao couplet, Shenqing's criteria for good monastic poetry is clear. Monastic poetry is simple, easily understood, and conveys feelings uniquely associated with Buddhist monasticism, such as the vast significance of a religious commitment. A monk should be guided by monastic regulations and formed by standard Buddhist practices, engaging in literature only with the goal of making Buddhist things more appealing to outsiders. Poetry must be subordinated to monasticism.

A little over a decade later, the great poet and lay Buddhist Bai Juyi held a similar attitude about monks' literary activity. Bai had traveled to Jiangnan twice around this time (822–824 in Hangzhou, 825–826 in Suzhou). When he arrived back in Chang'an after his second stint in Jiangnan, he wrote a poem for a monk who was particularly skilled in literature, Daozong 道宗. In the process of evaluating the monk's work, Bai's preface debates the worthiness of the first community of poet-monks and finds their religious commitment lacking.

> I began to understand that the Venerable Daozong's works were written for the sake of doctrine, for the sake of the Dharma, for the sake of *upāya*-wisdom, and for the sake of liberation, but not merely for the sake of poetry. Those who understood the Venerable One spoke of him this way, but I fear that those who don't understand the Venerable One would consider him to be a disciple of Huguo, Fazhen, Lingyi, and Jiaoran. Thus I write twenty lines of poetry to explain this.
>
> 予始知上人之文為義作，為法作，為方便智作，為解脫性作，不為詩而作也。知上人者云爾，恐不知上人者，謂為護國、法振、靈一、皎然之徒與？故予題二十句以解之。[76]

Bai Juyi praises Daozong for subordinating his literary activity to the propagation of the Dharma. Although some fools—namely, "those who don't understand the Venerable One"—associate Daozong with the poet-monks, those who truly get him (like Bai) understand that this is not right. As an exemplary monk, Daozong writes for the sake of lofty Buddhist ideals, not for the sake of poetry. To Bai Juyi, the earlier poet-monks were mere aesthetes masquerading as monks, and Daozong should not be considered part of their lineage. Poetry, then, should not be considered an end in itself but rather a form of *upāya*, an adaptive pedagogical tool. Like a raft, it must be abandoned once you have crossed the river. Otherwise it will weigh you down.

Just as in Liu Zongyuan's and Shenqing's essays, the poet-monk is a person of ill repute. To praise Fangji, Liu Zongyuan claims that he cannot be contained by that term. To praise Daobao, Shenqing contrasts him with poet-monk precursors such as Huixiu and Huilin. Likewise, in order to praise Daozong, Bai Juyi distinguishes him from the original poet-monks. Literary and monastic elites cannot hold these monks in high regard if they still fall under the label of "poet-monk." A poet-monk is never a real poet. Either he does not have sufficient literary skill to truly enter the stream of the literary world, or he overindulges in frivolous verbiage, or he uses poetry as a tool to spread Buddhist wisdom, or he completely transcends the category of "poet-monk." In none of these cases can a poet-monk really be a poet in the same way that a literatus is one.

Bai Juyi further clarifies his position in the poem accompanying this preface, praising the instrumentality of Daozong's verses.

Ten Rhymes Inscribed for the Venerable Daozong 題道宗上人十韻

Bai Juyi

The Tathāgata spoke *gāthā*-hymns,
The bodhisattvas composed doctrine-discussions.[77]
For this reason, Vinaya Master Daozong
Uses poetry to do the Buddha's work.[78]
No deviation or disparity from the One Sound,[79]
There is a definite order to his quatrains.
He wants to serve the very best
And in all cases understands the meaning of non-duality.
Pure and clean, [his poems are] imbued with the forms of precepts;
Relaxed and light, they carry the flavor of meditation.
At ease, they give free rein to language,
Dim and distant, they leave behind words.
To the sides, they reach scholars of neighboring states,
Above, they touch kings, dukes, and nobles.
First they draw you in with poetic lines,
Then they bring you to Buddhist wisdom.
Many people love the master's lines,
But only I understand the master's intent.
It's not like the Venerable Huixiu's,
Whose many thoughts of clouds in the blue were in vain.[80]

如來說偈讚，
菩薩著論議。
是故宗律師，
以詩爲佛事。
一音無差別，
四句有詮次。
欲使第一流，
皆知不二義。

精潔霑戒體，
閑淡藏禪味。
從容恣語言，
縹緲離文字。
旁延邦國彥，
上達王公貴。
先以詩句牽，
後令入佛智。
人多愛師句，
我獨知師意。
不似休上人，
空多碧雲思。

Just as in the preface, Bai Juyi praises Daozong for his poetry as a way to understand Buddhism. Although lines 3-6 seem to hint at an equation between the two, it is clearly the religious practices that are given primacy. After all, Daozong "uses poetry to do the Buddha's work," not the other way around: the Buddha's work is the end goal. There is historical precedent for writing this kind of poetry: the Buddha and the bodhisattvas used verse to expound their teachings (lines 1-2). Though later generations would say that the flavor of meditation is antithetical to true poetry, Bai praises it here (lines 9-10). Daozong's poems dazzle with the wonders of finely crafted language, but their ultimate goal is to leave language behind (lines 11-12). In this he is superior to Huixiu, the monk whose work on the grief of separation was immortalized by Jiang Yan's imitation in the *Wenxuan* (lines 19-20). Huixiu, as we have seen, was the chief antecedent of the Mid-Tang poet-monks, and like his successors he is said to have invested too much effort into poetry written for its own sake—indulging in his emotions, going so far as to laicize when given the chance—and not for the sake of teaching Buddhist doctrine and practice.

By praising Daozong's verse on these terms, Bai Juyi is creating a distinction between literati and monastic poetry. This distinction was commonly made by literati sympathetic to Buddhism, as we have seen in descriptions of Lingyi, Jiaoran, and Lingche. Understood positively, monastic poetry follows a track parallel to literati poetry. Both aim at instructing and transforming (*jiaohua* 教化) their audiences, but, whereas literati do so toward Confucian goals, Buddhist monks do so toward Buddhist goals. Understood negatively, monastic verse is considered little more than a highbrow counterpart to Buddhist didactic songs, perhaps not even rising to the level of "poetry"—a criticism we see elsewhere embedded in the debates over the term "*gāthā*" (*ji*).[81] Though different in intent, both praise and blame of monastic verse at this time share a logical premise: a monk's writing should always be motivated by proselytism. This is the simplest way of reconciling Buddhist and literary practice. It declares that monastic writing is different in kind from literati writing—even if this difference is praised by sympathetic readers and writers.

The first comprehensive history of poet-monks was attempted a few years later, in 833 by Liu Yuxi 劉禹錫 (772–842). The occasion for this history was the preface to a definitive edition of the poetic works of Lingche, titled "Notes on Venerable Lingche's Literary Collection" 澈上人文集紀.[82] This was written a full seventeen years after Lingche's death, at the bequest of his disciples. Liu was a prominent literatus who had crossed paths with Lingche as a child. His preface acts as a transitional document in our history of poet-monks. By the 830s, the term "poet-monk" had already broadened significantly in geographic and semantic scope, used to refer to monks who were not part of the initial circle. Liu Yuxi's essay opens with a nod to the past, then proceeds to Lingche's precocious childhood and youth, careful to note his expertise in both literary and religious practices.

> There is a long history of monks skilled at poetry. The Venerable Huixiu composed the "Sorrows of Parting," and Dharma Master Huiyue wept for Minister Fan.[83] Both of them were favorably praised by talented literati of the time. Thereafter many such monks came one after another in succession.
>
> The Venerable Lingche was born in Guiji, originally of the Tang clan. He had an acute curiosity, was obsessed with learning, and could not bear to be ordinary. When he took leave of his father and brother to become a renunciant, he took the name Lingche, and was styled Yuancheng. He upheld the sūtras and śāstras but loved verse with his whole mind.... He gained access to talented men through his writing, and he persuaded the eminent men of court with his understanding of meditation. His unrestrained discussions were very refined, and his light conversation was full of diverse flavors.[84]

釋子工為詩尚矣。休上人賦《別怨》，約法師哭範尚書，咸為當時才士之所傾歎。厥後比比有之。上人生於會稽，本湯氏子。聰察嗜學，不肯為凡夫。因辭父兄出家，號靈澈，字源澄。雖受經論，一心好篇章……以文章接才子，以禪理說高人，風議甚雅，談笑多味。

Liu Yuxi's account of Lingche's life is literary, rather than religious, in nature. It describes his early love of learning and, in the elided section (translated in chapter 1), his connections to famous literati. At the same time, Liu does not downplay Lingche's religious activity. In fact, the two sides are put in parallel to each other: others are drawn to him for both his writing and his understanding of meditation. Lingche's appeal is his complexity. The capital elites find him fascinating because his conversation is full of "diverse flavors" 多味. That is to say, he can talk about both literary and religious matters with authority. Here he echoes Jiaoran's description of Lingche's versatility. Literati are curious about Lingche and other poet-monks. They marveled at these strange creatures who seemed to be able to speak out of both sides of their mouths.[85]

Liu goes on to describe his personal connection to Lingche and his commission in 833 to write a preface for Lingche's works, which have been pared down from two thousand to three hundred by his disciple Xiufeng 秀峰. He concludes with an evaluation of the phenomenon of poet-monks, now seen in retrospect, some seventy years after their first emergence.

> So I offer my evaluation: What the world calls "poet-monks" mostly come from southeast of the Great River. Lingyi traced the source, then Huguo came after him. Qingjiang stirred up the wave, and Fazhen flowed along after him. They played their unique rhymes which made it into men's ears for a moment, but they weren't the tones of grand music. Only Jiaoran of Wuxing was able to master all forms of poetry. After Jiaoran, Lingche succeeded him. For example, his poem "Lotuses at Yuanxin Monastery" says: "Sūtras come to White Horse Monastery / A monk arrives in Redcrow year."[86] And "In Exile in Tingzhou" says: "Green flies act as mourners / On yellow ears are sent letters home."[87] These can be said to be the territory of a *creator*—why consider him to be prominent only among the world of poet-monks?

> 因為評曰：世之言詩僧多出江左。靈一導其源，護國襲之。清江揚其波，法振沿之。如么弦孤韻，瞥入人耳，非大樂之音。獨吳興晝公能備眾體。晝公後澈公承之。 至如《芙蓉園新寺》詩云：「經來白馬寺，僧到赤烏年。」《謫汀州》云：「青蠅為吊客，黃耳寄家書。」可為入作者閫域，豈特雄於詩僧間邪？

The poet-monks, Liu tells us, are a relatively recent and a local phenomenon. Though they had distant roots in canonical writers like Huixiu, it was Lingyi who led the way for the monks of the eighth century. He "traced the source," drew out and channeled the headwaters, and became the start of a new tradition. Lingyi, like Lingche and all the other poet-monks mentioned here, is from the Jiangnan region and spent the majority of his life there. The water metaphors continue, as the other poet-monks contribute to the flow, but all stay within their own stream. That is, the poet-monks mentioned here are isolated geographically, socially, and literarily. Moreover, they are a flash flood: strong and sudden but quick to ebb away. Their songs "made it into men's ears for a moment, but they weren't the tones of grand music." If we had only these men, the poet-monks would be little more than a fad.

Jiaoran was a rare exception. Unlike the other poet-monks, who floated along in their own stream, he was "able to master all forms of poetry." Jiaoran was the first poet-monk who is worth listening to as a poet in his own right, not just as a curious hybrid of poet and monk. He deserves this respect because he exhibited a thorough knowledge of literary genres and literary history. To Liu Yuxi, a "poet-monk" is a monk who plays at poetry—primarily defined according to his nonliterary identity. The scholar-official, by contrast, is an "unmarked" writer whose social status is not made visible. Only Jiaoran is able to transcend his markedness, due to a versatility that demonstrates a thorough knowledge of the literary tradition. And Lingche is the only one who inherits his mantle. The very last lines of the preface state directly what Liu had been hinting at all along: he is more than a run-of-the-mill versifier; he is a *creator*. Just as in Jiaoran's critical preface, the use of the term "creator" has Confucian connotations. It implies that Lingche is a full participant in the production of Chinese civilization according to its classicist norms. He surpasses the other poet-monks: he participates in mainstream literati culture.

To Liu Yuxi, as to Liu Zongyuan and Bai Juyi, "poet-monk" was hardly a flattering term. It was a social label used mainly by the literati to classify a group of monks from the Jiangnan region who tried their hands at poetry. The classically trained official was the unmarked literatus, free to be defined by his literary ability. The poet-monk, in contrast, had to be defined and named by his social role, being a religious professional. Their songs failed to enter the great stream of the classical tradition. What is implied by such remarks is that poetry itself was seen as essentially a literati activity and thus the poet-monk as a curious newcomer, a religious play-acting at being a writer. Jiaoran and Lingche are the exceptions that prove the rule. They are chimeras, composed of both Buddhist and writerly parts. They are monks, but they are also *creators*—idealized practitioners of classical rites and songs who could sway the minds of the people.

A monk who indulged in the writing of frivolous poetry was not living up to his duties. Idealized monks like Fangji and Daozong used their literary skills to pique the literati's interest in Buddhism but made sure never to end the conversation there. True poets like Lingche transcend their status as a poet-monk. Nevertheless, these writings reveal that the idea of the "poet-monk" was spreading beyond Jiangnan and into the capital region, even if it was not a title that one should claim proudly.

When the first community of poet-monks appeared in mid-eighth-century Jiangnan, they were understood to be an unusual phenomenon: Buddhist monks who could write elite poetry well. Until then, poetry had mainly been seen as the province of mainstream literati who carried on the classical tradition. Faced with the works of men like Lingyi, Jiaoran, and Lingche, the literati placed them in the category of otherworldly recluses, those who roamed outside the lines and felt a deep affinity with the nonhuman landscape. At the same time, the poet-monks did not always portray themselves in these terms. They were intellectually complicated people who found a multitude of ways to reconcile their twin pursuits of religion and literature. When presenting themselves to the literati, they stressed their versatility. But when the literati received them, they stressed their remove from worldly concerns.

As the poet-monks' fame penetrated elite circles at the capital in the early ninth century, later literati saw them as creatures of contradiction. A "poet-monk" was a paradox. Poetry was so closely associated with classicism (Ru) and classical culture (*wen*) that it seemed odd to blend it with Buddhism. Although classicist literati had their own ideas about poetry's morally transformative power, these were fully separate from Buddhism. Poet-monks tried to bring these two spheres together, and, in at least some people's eyes, they failed. Poet-monks became either so obsessed with poetry that they lost their religious integrity, or so devoted to religion that they lost the insight of a poet. Bad monks became fake poets, and bad poets became fake monks. On those occasions that literati praised the poetry of Buddhist monks, it was by saying that they transcended the category of poet-monk. It was almost as if, in becoming good poets, they could no longer be good monks.

This discourse on the first community of poet-monks would shape literati understanding of them for generations to come. As we move beyond the early ninth century and into that period known as the Late Tang, we begin to see larger numbers of people referred to as poet-monks, often put into the same box. Many of these people had no direct connection to the initial community in Jiangnan. The definition of "poet-monk" expanded, and "poet-monk" became a general term for any monk who wrote poetry, and their position in literary society would crystallize into a full-fledged literary tradition.

CHAPTER 3

Becoming Poet-Monks
The Formation of a Tradition, 810–960

In the ninth century, the fame of Jiaoran and Lingche spread beyond Jiangnan, and with it the idea of the poet-monk. Monks skilled in poetry began to come to the capital, Chang'an, in increasing numbers. Chang'an functioned as the cultural as well as the political center of the Tang. The corridor between Chang'an and the secondary capital Luoyang was home to an overwhelming majority of elite families, including those of poets and their patrons.[1] Though the emperors could be fickle in their support of Buddhism, the capital provided ample opportunities for the enterprising poet-monk.

By the 820s, references to poet-monks became generalized, applicable to any Buddhist monastic who attempted to write poetry. As noted in chapter 2, in the early part of the ninth century the term "poet-monk" could carry negative connotations, but later on the sharp edge of this term wore down, and poet-monk gradually became a role one could play and eventually a recognized type of literary actor. In the late ninth century, once the idea of the poet-monk had been well-established, literati and monks alike began to construct a full tradition for it. Writings about poet-monks referred not just to distant precursors from the early medieval period but also lineages and communities from the recent past. Guanxiu and Qiji frequently used the term "poet-monk" to describe themselves and their close associates. In so doing, they took a term that once had been used to limit their role in literary society and reappropriated it to describe those with a new vision for poetry, one that would merge literary with Buddhist practice.

A Role

In the first decades of the ninth century, around the time that the first community of poet-monks had begun to achieve widespread fame, a young monk named Wuben 無本 (779–843) came from the distant northeast to the capital region with scrolls of his own poetry in tow. His work caught the attention of the powerful literatus Han Yu, and the two maintained a correspondence in verse for a time. He would spend most of his life in the capital region, living and exchanging poems with Yao He and his own younger cousin Wuke. Though he enjoyed the company of the era's most important poets, Wuben was never content to lead a monastic life and around 812 decided to laicize so that he could take the imperial exams. He failed, remaining discontent for many years, until finally being directly appointed to a minor post in the Sichuan backwater of Changjiang in Suizhou 遂州長江 in the year 837, at the age of fifty-seven. He died just six years later. He is better known to history by his secular name, Jia Dao.[2]

Jia Dao came to be seen as the paragon of an aesthetic called *kuyin*, meaning "bitter intoning" or "painstaking composition." We can think of *kuyin* as the medieval Chinese equivalent of the starving artist: the image of the poet as one toiling away in poverty, spending days or weeks crafting the perfectly balanced parallel couplet. It stressed labor and precision over spontaneous inspiration or erudition. As Stephen Owen has noted, the *kuyin* aesthetic implies that anyone can become a poet, if only they put in the effort. This included non-literati, such as monks and women.[3] Such an aesthetic also stressed a total absorption in craft, a kind of trance-like state that could be comparable to meditation. In this way, it appealed to the poet-monks of the late medieval period, theoretically giving them special access to the fundamentals of poetic practice. And Jia Dao, as the embodiment of *kuyin*, became a model of the true poet.[4]

Due to his early life as a monk, there is a strand of criticism that regards Jia Dao himself as a poet-monk.[5] However, there is no evidence that he was ever called a poet-monk during his lifetime or for several centuries after.[6] Scholarship that has identified him as a poet-monk is based entirely on stereotypes and speculation. Jia Dao's importance in the history of poet-monks is not in his early identity as a monk but rather in his popularization of the *kuyin* aesthetic (explored in detail in chapter 6).

Nevertheless, we do find in Jia Dao's circle one of the earliest uses of "poet-monk" that clearly refers to someone who was not a member of Jiaoran and Lingyi's original community. Jia Dao's cousin Wuke once wrote a poem titled "Sent to a Poet-Monk" 贈詩僧.[7] Their mutual friend Yao He in turn described Wuke with this word in the opening of his poem "Sent to the Venerable Wuke" 寄無可上人, showing how the term had changed since the Mid-Tang: "Of the monasteries within the capital's twelve gates, / Only the poet-monk's monastery is secluded" 十二門中寺，詩僧寺獨幽."[8] It is noteworthy that a capital-based poet used this term to refer to a capital-based monk during the second quarter of the ninth century without making an explicit reference to Jiaoran's circle.[9] Wuke, moreover, was from the northeast, so he could claim no direct continuity with the Jiangnan monks. This is a sign that that the term had begun to lose its specificity: it no longer necessarily invokes the Jiangnan monks of the late eighth century. Lingche, the youngest of the first community of poet-monks, died in 816, at least a decade prior to the period under discussion. Their generation had passed, and a new crop of poet-monks sprang up with no direct connection to their predecessors.

Moving ahead to the mid-ninth century, we see the broader sense of "poet-monk" very clearly in an exchange poem written by Xu Hun 許渾 (788–860). He writes to a monk and a self-styled recluse, both of whom he describes in stereotyped terms.

Sent to the Venerable Zhongyi of Tianxiang Monastery and Recluse Sun of Fuchun 寄天鄉寺仲儀上人富春孫處士[10]

Xu Hun

Poet-monks' and old fishermen's
Sentiments meet across a thousand miles.
Clouds bring Goosegate's snow,[11]
The water connects to the fishing bank's winds.
Your minds look beyond honor and shame,
Your names hang between true and false.
At year's end, I too will head back
To fields east of the limpid Luo.

詩僧與釣翁，
千里兩情通。

雲帶雁門雪，
水連漁浦風。
心期榮辱外，
名掛是非中。
歲晚亦歸去，
田園清洛東。

In the first couplet, Xu Hun refers to his recipients as "poet-monks" and "fishermen," two types of people who have withdrawn from political society in favor of a quiet life near the river.[12] The fisherman as righteous recluse has a long history, going back at least to the story of Lü Shang 呂尚 being discovered by King Wen of Zhou 周文王 (trad. r. 1099–1050 BCE) and being appointed minister soon after, in the *Records of the Grand Historian* (*Shiji* 史記).[13] Poet-monks are said to have sentiments similar to such fishermen. From the rest of the poem, it is clear that this refers to a delight in the beauty of the natural world. The poet-monk, at least in Xu Hun's eyes, is once again the stock figure of one who lives outside the lines. Drawing on the discourse of predecessors like Dugu Ji and Quan Deyu, Xu Hun makes the poet-monk into a generic type of person one could encounter near the mountains and rivers. Other poems from the latter half of the ninth century confirm that poet-monks were firmly entrenched as part of the repertoire of stock figures in reclusion poetry.[14] "Poet-monk" refers not to the Lingyi-Jiaoran circle but rather to any Buddhist recluse who composes poetry. Poet-monks are not individuals; they are archetypes.

As Yao He, Xu Hun, and others solidified the image of poet-monks as recluses who lived outside the lines of mundane life, there were also an increasingly large number of poet-monks honored at the capital, often by the emperor himself. Conventional Buddhist history describes the mid-ninth century as one of persecution and anti-Buddhist sentiment, thanks to the well-known suppression of foreign religions in 842–845.[15] But the reality of official attitudes toward Buddhism at this time was more complicated. The purges of this period did not mean a complete elimination of Buddhists at the capital but rather a withdrawal of support for many practices associated with fringe monks.[16] There were good economic reasons for laicizing unregistered monks and limiting the amount of wealth individual monks could own.[17] Moreover, it is important to keep in mind that the reason a purge was seen as necessary was precisely *because* the Buddhist church was so popular and powerful. One decree limited the number of slaves that could be owned by monastics: monks were permitted one male slave and nuns two female slaves.[18] Although the persecution did become quite intense by 845, it did not last long. After the death of the Emperor Wuzong 武宗 in 846, his successor, Emperor Xuanzong 宣宗 (r. 846–859), was an ardent supporter of Buddhism and quickly reversed his predecessor's policies, ushering in a new age of prosperity. The number of monasteries in the capital increased fivefold, and hundreds more were built at the prefectural level and in the towns where the military governors were based.[19] When Buddhism came back, it was as strong as ever, still tightly woven into the fabric of elite society. Thus, we should not see 845 as a watershed point marking a sudden, fundamental change in the history of the relationship between Buddhism and literature. Rather, the spread of the idea of the poet-monk from Jiangnan to the capital and the rest of the empire should be seen as a slow and evolving.[20]

In fact, several poet-monks became court ritual specialists ("inner offerers" 內供奉) just before or after the suppressions of the 840s.[21] Guangxuan, a poet-monk from the southeast, came to the capital in 814 and lived there until he passed away some time in the late 820s or early 830s. Of his seventeen surviving poems, fourteen (82 percent) were written in response to prompts from the emperor, and exchange poems suggest his familiarity with major literati such as Han Yu, Bai Juyi, and Liu Yuxi. Guangxuan himself seems to have understood Buddhists and Confucians as operating in distinct but complementary realms. In one linked verse written with the court literatus Li Yi 李益 (748–829), Guangxuan wrote that "though Confucian and Buddhist work may be different, / The meanings of their literary works often match" 儒釋事雖殊，文章意多偶.[22] Guangxuan is relying on poet-monks' increased presence to affirm their normalization in literary life, even as their professional lives remain drastically different from those of literati.

On another occasion, when both Li Yi and Guangxuan served at the court of Muzong (821–824), Li Yi tied Guangxuan to the same poet-monk heritage we have seen before as he praised his literary skills.

Given to Master Guangxuan 贈宣大師

Li Yi

Throughout the land, only this *śrāmaṇera*
    understands poetry—[23]
Everyone says he's better than
    Master Huixiu.
The day you were summoned back

>   was under the previous emperor's order,
> And the time you entered the inner palace
>   was when our current Highness ascended as a dragon.[24]
> I see the moon, remembering when I came
>   to stay at your monastery in the pines,
> I follow the flowers and think of making
>   plans for us to meet at my creek in the apricots.[25]
> Having discussed how the Buddha ground
>   is sought in the mind's ground,[26]
> I say only that constant intoning
>   is steadfast upholding.[27]

一國沙彌獨解詩，
人人道勝惠林師。
先皇詔下徵還日，
今上龍飛入內時。
看月憶來松寺宿，
尋花思作杏溪期。
因論佛地求心地，
祇說常吟是住持。[28]

This poem relies on a different set of assumptions than those in the days of Lingyi, Jiaoran, and Lingche. Emperors and famous literati desired to be close to poet-monks (lines 3–4, 6), who could be tied to established precedents (line 2). The grandiose claims of the poem's opening and concluding couplets are best read as witty embellishments rather than as serious claims. In the last two lines, in particular, we see the speaker carrying a common Mahāyānist Buddhist claim to its logical conclusion. If enlightenment must be sought by probing the mind (because the realization of one's inherent buddha-nature is precisely enlightenment), then frequently composing poetry to convey the thoughts and feelings produced by the mind is a form of religious devotion. While it is possible that Li Yi was making a serious claim (one that shares some similarities with claims examined in chapter 6), there is no evidence that he was a devout lay Buddhist, so it is unlikely that he put this theory into practice. It seems instead that he was wittily extending the logic of a discussion he had had with Guangxuan to justify their shared love of poetry. Nevertheless, the very possibility of making such a claim depends on Guangxuan's presence at the courts of two emperors, a sign of poet-monks' increasing visibility in the literary world.

Besides Guangxuan, there were the court monks Zhixuan and Qibai mentioned in chapter 1. Another example from this period is Yuanfu 元孚. Though few details of his life have survived, scattered evidence suggests that Yuanfu came from the Jiangnan region and was based in Xuanzhou 宣州 in the 830s. He later moved to the capital and was appointed as an inner offerer by Xuanzong. The poet Chen Tao, an aloof Daoist practitioner who wrote innovative song-style verse, once wrote a poem to Yuanfu teeming with religious and political references.[29]

Sent to Clergyman Yuanfu 寄元孚道人

Chen Tao

Versifying traveler from Indic eaves[30]
Who's hung orchids from his waist for thirty years,[31]
You have long ridden a blue-cloud horse[32]
And sometimes cracked a Hanlin whip.[33]
You once roamed the Five Marchmounts,
Auspicious mist trailing from your golden robes.
High have you climbed with hands of Lord Paulownia,
To the left have you leaned with the shoulders of a simurgh.[34]
You wept jade in the autumn rain
And clasped stars before the spring wind.
Your horizontal yoke carries Hongyan,[35]
Leaning on an armrest, you see Guangxuan.
Lately you've awakened from Huaxu,[36]
A lonely cloud sleeping at a stone wall.
When this dragon descended, it started to attain *gāthā*s;
Now that this tortoise has aged, it nests in a lotus.[37]
Without a literary monk in the inner palace,
Who could draw out the *zouyu*?[38]
For this, I beseech the waters of Chu
And mourn Qu Yuan with a rivulet of tears.

梵宇章句客，
佩蘭三十年。
長乘碧雲馬，
時策翰林鞭。
曩事五嶽遊，
金衣曳祥煙。
高攀桐君手，
左倚鸞鷟肩。

哭玉秋雨中，
摘星春風前。
橫輈截洪偃，
憑几見廣宣。
爾來瘖華胥，
石壁孤雲眠。
龍降始得偈，
龜老方巢蓮。
內殿無文僧，
騶虞誰能牽。
因之問楚水，
吊屈幾潺湲。[39]

The florid references in this poem, meant to flatter, leap from the political to the religious and back in a dizzying array. Most intriguing are the Buddhist references. The monks to whom Chen Tao compares Yuanfu were both highly literate and closely connected to the central court (lines 11–12). Guangxuan, the more recent of the two, lived at the capital and presented poems at court in the early ninth century. Hongyan, the more distant one, was so renowned for his literary skills that Xiao Gang 蕭綱 (r. 550–551), poet-emperor of the Liang dynasty, is said to have commanded him to laicize and become one of his ministers. Hongyan was able to refuse only because of his extraordinary willpower.[40] Chen Tao establishes precedents for court Buddhists with extraordinary literary skills and puts Yuanfu in their company. Most cleverly, Chen alludes to the mythical *zouyu* of the *Book of Odes*, a sort of freegan beast that will eat only the meat of animals that have died of natural causes (lines 15–16). His implicit claim is that a "literary monk" would be the most qualified to lead the auspicious *zouyu* into the world. Such a monk, well versed in the classics, could recognize the creature and, being a vegetarian himself, would share a similar spirit. Through this allusion, Chen Tao playfully makes Buddhists to be necessary elements of an orthodox court.

As we can see in the poems by Yao He, Xu Hun, and Chen Tao, and in the examples of Wuke, Yuanfu, and Guangxuan, the poet-monk became a more well-known figure throughout the middle of the ninth century. He was no longer confined to Jiangnan but made inroads at the capital. Jia Dao and his cousin Wuke were the two most important figures of this period, capital-dwellers who romanticized their lack of success and became paragons of the *kuyin* aesthetic. Although Jia Dao was not, strictly speaking, a poet-monk, his ideal of total absorption in the crafting of couplets became a model for future poet-monks. This helped create a fertile ground for poet-monks during the restoration of Buddhism in the late 840s and 850s. During this period, poet-monks such as Yuanfu would delight the emperors by presenting their works at court, and literati like Chen Tao would praise them in bombastic terms. Poet-monks were spreading throughout the empire, and the best were celebrated at the capital by the emperor himself.

A Position

At the end of the Tang dynasty, as the capital was crushed by Huang Chao's troops, the idea of the poet-monk reached its fullest flowering (the third period, according to the analysis in chapter 1). It had become an established position in the literary world, one best typified by Shangyan. A monk born to the powerful Xue 薛 clan in the 830s, Shangyan was blessed with longevity, reaching nearly a hundred years of age before dying in the 920s. Not as seemingly prolific or idiosyncratic as his contemporary Guanxiu, he was nonetheless highly regarded in literary society, exchanging poetry with the major writers of his day. As noted in chapter 1, he was one of the most central actors in the network of Late Tang exchange poetry, despite the survival of only thirty-four of his poems. In addition to his exchange poetry, the existence of two prefaces written by literati for his works testify to the high regard afforded to Shangyan.

The first preface, written in May of 900 by the southern bureaucrat Yan Rao 顏蕘, opens by connecting Shangyan to his distant cousin, the famed poet-statesman Xue Neng 薛能 (817?–881).[41] According to Yan Rao, the latter praised his Buddhist relative in startling terms.

From "Preface to the Venerable Shangyan's Literary Collection"
顏上人集序

Yan Rao

Shangyan was surnamed Xue and styled Maosheng. In his youth, he was skilled at pentametric poetry, which he had a natural talent for, far surpassing his more famous contemporaries. Though the literati never spoke the name of Xue Neng—my fellow graduate of the examinations and the former military commander of Xuzhou—his fame in poetry was among the greatest in the empire, for there was nothing in them to decry. Shangyan was the only other person who deserved to be regarded as exceptional. Whenever

Xue Neng would recite Shangyan's startling verses, he would say: "Though I am not happy that Shangyan is a monk, it is good to have a poet-monk in our branch of the family, that it may increase the glory of the Xue clan." By nature Shangyan was upright and calm, shunning the company of others, and his fine reputation was self-evident. Famous nobles and great men vied to get to know him.

顏公姓薛氏，字茂聖。少工為五言詩，天賦其才，迥超名輩。甍同年文人故許州節度使尚書薛公字大拙，以文人不言其名，擅詩名於天下，無所與讓。唯於顏公，許待優異。每吟其警句，常曰：「吾不喜顏為僧，嘉有詩僧為吾枝派，以增薛氏之榮耳。」性端靜寡合，而價譽自彰。名公鉅人，爭識其面。[42]

Yan Rao begins his preface by establishing the reputation of Shangyan's relative Xue Neng and then transfers that reputation to Shangyan himself. Xue Neng's poems, apparently perfect in execution, dominate the literary world. Though he himself is not well-known, his works are respected. Yan then proceeds to show how Shangyan is his cousin's equal in poetry.

Most surprising is the way Xue Neng reportedly praises Shangyan for being a poet-monk who can bring honor to the Xue clan. Though Xue Neng is decidedly averse to Buddhism, he is not averse to poet-monks, who are highly regarded. Xue Neng sees the "poet" half of the term "poet-monk" as dominant and revels in Shangyan's literary reputation. Poetry, after all, was still associated with the mainstream, classical tradition. What is new here, compared to the early ninth century, is that Xue Neng implies that being a poet-monk was a legitimate path to literary success. The "poet-monk" was a familiar enough figure by this time that it was seen as one of several options for gaining a reputation in the cultural sphere. While it may not have been Xue Neng's favorite path, he grudgingly accepted it as a real one that Shangyan could take.[43]

Xue Neng, as depicted here, is a long way from the neutral-to-negative opinion of poet-monks held in the early ninth century by Liu Zongyuan and Liu Yuxi, who regarded most monks' verse as something inferior to that of the literati. The contrast with Bai Juyi's position, as sketched in the preface to his poem on Daoxuan discussed in chapter 2, is even more instructive. Bai too sees poet-monks as primarily poets but stresses that this is not the role that they are supposed to fill. A good Buddhist should use poetry to serve the dharma, regard it as a form of *upāya* that may be used to draw in the literati. Xue Neng, by contrast, sees poet-monks as legitimate participants in literate society. More than fifty years after Liu Yuxi, Liu Zongyuan, and Bai Juyi, the poet-monk has become celebrated as a real poet.

In the preface's conclusion, where we would normally find a summary evaluation of the writer's works, Yan Rao declares his admiration for Shangyan as both a poet and as a person. He seems to become sympathetic to Buddhism because of his relationship with Shangyan.

> Now I attach my preface for the master to the beginning of his poetry collection. In all, there are some four hundred poems in five- and seven-character meter, which can be considered the light of Confucians and Buddhists.[44] I have been around with the master for nearly ten years. Though at first I looked up to him as an outstanding poet, now I anticipate a meeting with him outside of the lines. I am not ashamed to speak of our close friendship. But if we are talking about the master's practicing what he taught, this is something that his disciples will naturally revere and not something that a foolish Confucian could dare to understand.

> 今且掇師之序於詩集之前，其五言、七字詩凡四百篇，以為儒釋之光。余與師周旋殆將十稔，始仰師為詩家之傑，今與師為方外之期，契分知心，言之無愧，若師本教之行，自為其徒所宗，則非愚儒之所敢知也。

Shangyan is not just a poet who happens to have been a monk but rather a poet-monk, one whose works are the culmination of both Buddhist and Confucian traditions. Though Buddhism and poetry (as the province of the Confucians) remain distinct, we find here increasing confidence in their ability to be harmonized in the figure of the poet-monk. Moreover, Yan Rao regards Shangyan as one who upholds the value of practicing what you preach, which, despite Yan's humble denial, is something that Confucians and Buddhists alike can appreciate. When Yan Rao brings up the status of being "outside the lines" of the everyday world (*fangwai*), it is not to exoticize Shangyan. Rather, Yan Rao hopes to join him there, calling his own people foolish by comparison. Although the superiority of Confucian classicism is still implied, Yan Rao boldly declares that he is "not ashamed" to speak of his friendship with the monk since he is such a morally and culturally upright figure. Shangyan is admirable precisely because he can synthesize two distinct traditions.

The other surviving preface to Shangyan's works, written by one Li Tong 李詷 (dates unknown), praises the poet-monk in similarly

Confucian terms. Written in a highly ornamental style, Li's preface praises Shangyan's verse as superior to this world but also part of it.

From "Preface to the Venerable Shangyan's Literary Collection" 顏上人集序

Li Tong

The poetry written by the eminent and virtuous monk Shangyan does not enter into the world of voice, physical traits, gain and loss, sorrow and joy, regret and delight. He simply draws on pure and quiet landscapes to create these few hundred poems. Their sound is pure and harmonious, their breath strong and penetrating. Their mystery goes beyond the imageless; their emptiness contains nonaction. They are cold, as if suspended in the air; they echo without being knocked.[45] Indeed, his achievements are so exquisite that one cannot grab hold of them without praising them. Indeed, his intentions are so profound that one cannot speak of them without complimenting them....

Often I ride into the hills and search caves to find culture and hunt down Confucian works.[46] Looking upon the works of the master, I understand that they are unique, and writing a preface to them is not enough. I hold up the master's beauty as an ideal for future generations to aim for.

釋門高德顏公尚為詩，不入聲相得失哀樂怨歡，直以清寂景構成數百篇。其音清以和，其氣剛以達。妙出無象，虛涵不為。冷然若懸，未扣而響。信其功之妙也，不可得而稱矣。信其旨之深也，不可舉而言矣。......調常蒐文獵儒，乘邱索穴，睹師之作，異而序之不足。舉師之美，為後人宗旨也。[47]

In the first part of this evaluation, Li Tong describes Shangyan's work as existing beyond the everyday world: his poems transcend sense and emotion, presenting the landscape in a neutral manner. Their images hang suspended, objectively, in midair, to be examined from any angle. Unlike the poet of Lu Ji's "Rhapsody on Literature" 文賦, who knocks the void in search of a tone, Shangyan's poems sound without being touched. The vaguely Buddhist terminology Li Tong uses at first seems to put Shangyan's work at a distance, similar to Dugu Ji's epitaph for Lingyi and Quan Deyu's essay on Lingche. But at the end of the preface Li uses terminology that would be less exotic to the elite. He describes his search for "culture" (*wen*) and "Confucian works" (*ru*) in the wilderness, a scout hoping to find the sort of unrecognized talent so consistently lauded in the ancient classics. Oddly enough, it is a Buddhist monk he finds at the end of his search for an exemplar of the Confucian arts. Like Yan Rao, Li Tong marvels at Shangyan's excellence and calls on the literati to imitate him. Although a Buddhist, he can Confucian with the best of them.[48]

Poet-monks in this period were accepted as part of literary society, albeit on the literati's terms. Unlike earlier periods, there was the background assumption that monks could make good poets and that a poet-monk was one kind of poet among others. They received praise from literati with few of the qualifications reserved for Lingyi and Lingche, even if the basis of such praise was their connections to literati and their knowledge of the classical tradition. In the wake of the Huang Chao Rebellion, poet-monks had spread out across the land and filled in the void left by the capital elite. Or, to look at it from another angle: in the late ninth century, more monks had started writing elite verse in an attempt to integrate themselves with high literary society. Due to the upheavals caused by Huang Chao and other rebels, the literary world could no longer be seen as a unified whole, with its center in Chang'an. This destabilization meant that the formerly peripheral zones and actors could attempt to reconstitute the world around themselves, create new cultural spheres. Poet-monks, as one type of peripheral figure, did just that. Thus, as their place in literary society became more secure in the following decades, a need arose to articulate a tradition of poet-monks.

A Tradition

As the poet-monk became a definite position in literary society over the course of the ninth century, more and more monks could be found all over the empire writing many varieties of poetry. Poet-monks clustered in the new regional centers of power, gathering once again after a period of scattering in the late ninth century. As poet-monk became a respectable position in literary society, more monks claimed the title. Absolute numbers, though small, suggest this growth.[49] Indirect records of monks skilled in poetry also appear to increase at this time.[50] The resulting anxiety of abundance led to the need to sort out the varieties of poet-monks, discover lines of affinity, judge the superiority or inferiority of individual poets, and forge ties between recent practitioners and their early predecessors. In short, it was necessary to establish a tradition.

The language of lineage would have been familiar to an educated person in the Tang from at least three distinct sources: 1) the mainstream culture's genealogical charts that facilitated ancestor veneration,

2) religious and intellectual traditions' view of the transmission of teachings from master to disciple, and 3) the dominant theory of literary genre that saw later forms as growing out of one of a handful of classics.[51] By the Late Tang, all of these sources had been around for centuries and were part of the intellectual repertoire of anyone literate enough to write a poem or preface. Indeed, attempts to establish a poet-monk tradition were already present in Liu Yuxi's 833 preface to the works of Lingche. He found distant precursors in the fifth century (Huixiu and Huiyue), a source for the contemporary movement (Lingyi), a few lesser successors (Huguo, Qingjiang, and Fazhen), and an orthodox lineage of transmission (from Lingyi to Jiaoran to Lingche).

Although Liu Yuxi's preface contained some of the same rhetorical moves as a tradition-establishing document, Liu still saw the poet-monks as mainly a local phenomenon tied to eastern Jiangnan. In the late ninth century, we find broader attempts to rein in the expanding tradition, to weed out the inferior specimens and select only the finest blossoms. Artistic proliferation creates a need for lineages and canons. Zheng Gu, an important literati poet of the time and an associate of Qiji and other poet-monks, draws directly on the language of Buddhist lineages to discuss the poet-monk tradition in a poem sent to Wenxiu 文秀.[52]

Sent to the Poet-Monk Wenxiu 寄題詩僧秀公

Zheng Gu

Lingyi's mind was transmitted to
    Qingsai's mind,
And after Wuke's intoning
    came Huaichu's intoning.[53]
In recent years, comrades
    on the proper way are few—
I look up only to my master
    for the depth of what he grasps.
Unceasing in your pursuit of lovely lines,
    you have no days of rest.
For old mountains to retire to,
    you have Donglin.
For this cold cleric, this lowly official,
    is happy to have fallen from worldly honor:
Many thanks for grabbing your bamboo cane
    and seeking me out sometimes.

靈一心傳清塞心,
可公吟後楚公吟。
近來雅道相親少,
唯仰吾師所得深。
好句未停無暇日,
舊山歸老有東林。
冷曹孤宦甘寥落,
多謝攜筇數訪尋。[54]

The first line of this poem mirrors the language of "mind-to-mind transmission" 以心傳心 that was popularized by the *Platform Sūtra of the Sixth Patriarch* 六祖壇經.[55] The famous story about Hongren 洪忍 passing on his dharma to Huineng 惠能 is precisely about orthodox transmission and the fact that a shared mind overrides all else. Huineng's rival, Shenxiu 神秀, is said to have been the favored student, and Huineng himself was supposedly illiterate. The master did not make the obvious choice but opted instead for the disciple with the same mind. Similarly, Zheng Gu emphasizes mental affinity above all, drawing lines of connection between poet-monks who never met or knew each other. Lingyi died in 762, over fifty years before the recipient of his mind, Zhou He, was born. Wuke and Huaichu lived at opposite ends of the ninth century in different parts of the empire, the former around Chang'an and the latter at Mount Baizhao 白兆山 (in modern Hebei province). There was no direct, literal transmission between these monks, but Zheng Gu suggests that they, as poet-monks, have the same mind, a mind of which Wenxiu partakes.

The sense of a poet-monk tradition is further emphasized in the third couplet of the poem. Line 5, describing Wenxiu's obsessive pursuit of good couplets, calls to mind the dogged work ethic of the *kuyin* aesthetic, an aesthetic strongly associated with Jia Dao, his monk-cousin Wuke, and other poets of the mid-ninth century with ties to Buddhism. Line 6 suggests that Wenxiu plans to spend his later years at Donglin Monastery on Mount Lu. As the geographical analysis in chapter 1 has shown, Mount Lu was one of the lasting hubs for poet-monk activity from the Mid-Tang up through the Five Dynasties. Donglin, moreover, was one of Mount Lu's most famous monasteries, and it was where Huiyuan was said to have established the White Lotus Society in 402 and where other poet-monks of the late medieval period, such as Shangyan, Qiji, and Xiumu, spent much of their lives. Zheng Gu is suggesting that Wenxiu will fit in at Donglin, that he will be able to commune with like-minded monks of both the past and the present. He could be among those who, like him, would be potential candidates for receiving the transmission of the great poet-monks' minds.

Several decades after Zheng Gu's poem, discussion of lineage transmission remained vibrant. Most of these lineages, as constructed at the turn of the tenth century, coalesce around Guanxiu. Guanxiu's large collection of idiosyncratic poems, accomplishments in painting and calligraphy, and sharp wit made him one of the most influential artists of his age. His works were collected and published at least twice, each with its own preface. We will look at the second one, written by his disciple Tanyu, in the next section. Here the focus is on the first preface, written on January 7, 900, by the eminent literatus Wu Rong, which praises Guanxiu almost exclusively as a poet.[56] Ever since the works of Li He 李賀 (790–816) became popular in the early ninth century, Wu Rong complains, poets have been derivative, copying Li's overly intricate style.[57] By contrast, Guanxiu, whose "skill is divine and cleverness remarkable, being extremely good at songs and poems" 機神穎秀，雅善歌詩, takes up the tradition of praise and critique. This evaluation is clear from both the frame of his argument and the terms by which he praises Guanxiu. Wu Rong begins his preface by discussing poetry's "twofold Way" 二道: that it should "call the good good" and "the wicked wicked" 善善惡惡. This alludes to the long, classical tradition that the goal of poetry is moral suasion.[58] All ornament, all aesthetics must serve this goal, or else society risks falling into decline. Guanxiu's work upholds this ideal.

> Most of the writings of the Venerable Guanxiu are superior in their grasp of truth and are capable of producing new ideas. His words always take hold of scenes and objects from the edges of unformed Nature, but their real aim is always to merge with the Way. Since Li Bai and Bai Juyi have passed away, who else but this venerable monk could inherit their praiseworthiness?
>
> 上人之作，多以理勝，復能創新意，其語往往得景物於混茫自然之際，然其旨歸，必合於道。太白、樂天既歿，可嗣其美者，非上人而誰？

Wu Rong emphasizes how Guanxiu uses his extraordinary abilities in the service of a noble goal. His poems aim to merge with the Way, which here refers not to the transcendent principle of the Daoists or Buddhists, but to the Way of poetry that can be traced back to the canonical *Book of Odes*: moral transformation of the people. In previous generations, this

Way was upheld by Li Bai and Bai Juyi, who were able to use poetry to assign praise and blame.[59] Now this Way has been passed on to Guanxiu. Though Wu Rong's preface does not establish its own, separate lineage of poet-monks like Zheng Gu's poem, it ennobles the idea of the poet-monk by placing Guanxiu in a literary lineage. A poet-monk is seen as the true inheritor of the orthodox Way of poetry.

Within the next few decades, Guanxiu became the cornerstone of the new generation's conception of the poet-monk tradition. In 938, Sun Guangxian 孫光憲 (d. 968)—one of the most accomplished literati of the mid-tenth century—wrote a preface to the works of Qiji in which he evaluates his subject in terms of an established poet-monk tradition. This may be surprising, since Sun's anecdote collection *Beimeng suoyan* 北夢瑣言 carries a sustained, open hostility toward Buddhists.[60] But since poet-monks had already become a literary tradition in their own right, he could compartmentalize them from the frauds that he saw in the rest of the saṃgha. By this point in the tenth century, there was a stable set of references for the poet-monk tradition on which Sun could draw, without any need to lay out an entire lineage again.

> If we are talking about poet-monks from the Tang onward, meditation master Guanxiu perfected the blending of bone and breath: his poem-worlds and ideas were outstanding and unique, impossible to match. As for Jiaoran and Lingyi, they raced down the path of poetry in the company of meditators, neither too near nor too far from them. South of the Great River and North of the Han, among those black-robed monks who are karmically connected to feeling, there are none who do not aspire to their vivid poetics.[61] Had they not brilliantly manifested the Refined Way, how could they enjoy such a grand reputation?[62]

> 議者以唐來詩僧，惟貫休禪師骨氣混成，境意卓異，殆難儔敵。至於皎然、靈一，將與禪者並驅於風騷之途，不近不遠也。江之南，漢之北，緇侶業緣情者，靡不希其聲彩，自非雅道昭著，安能享茲大名。[63]

There is here, as in Liu Yuxi's preface to Lingche's works, a sense of development. The earliest poet-monks—Jiaoran and Lingyi—are said to pursue their literary and religious practices in parallel. While their works are "brilliant" examples of poetic practice and have brought them much fame, they are mainly appreciated by their fellow monks, especially those who have a karmic affinity for poetry. The rhetorical brilliance here is in blending the Buddhist technical term "karmic connection" (*yeyuan* 業緣) with the standard description of poetry as something "connected to feelings" (*yuanqing* 緣情). It is not the literati, the ultimately authoritative judges of poetry, who have given their poems a grand reception but rather cloistered monastics with a penchant for poetry. Nevertheless, Jiaoran and Lingyi are said to maintain a safe, middling distance from their monastic brethren. Their two vocations in poetry and monasticism never cross, neither in conflict nor in integration. Just as Lingche was full of "diverse flavors," able to talk out of both sides of his mouth but never to fully integrate his two vocations, so are Jiaoran and Lingyi living multiple lives. But instead of being praised by the literati for their versatility, they are implicitly faulted for a kind of shallowness.

Guanxiu marks a turning point. Only he was able to fully integrate his Buddhist and poetic practices. In doing so, he brought together "bone and breath"—a poem's structure and its energy—to create masterworks full of unique "poem-worlds and ideas." The key words here, *jing* 境 and *yi* 意, are two of the most crucial in medieval poetics. *Jing*, literally a "realm," refers to the reality that exists within a poem. It is assumed to be continuous with the external world that we perceive—*jing* was also used to designate perceptual objects in Buddhist philosophical analysis, and to Jiaoran the poem-world had to be "grasped" (*qu* 取) from the sensory realm.[64] *Yi*, literally "mentation," could refer to the thoughts, feelings, and intentions of a poem's author or speaker, to the corresponding thoughts and feelings produced in its audience, and to its higher or allegorical significance.[65] The two sometimes formed a pair in medieval poetics. The poetry manual attributed to Wang Changling 王昌齡 (d. 756?) enumerates that there may be "poem-worlds of objects" (*wujing* 物境), "poem-worlds of feeling" (*qingjing* 情境), and "poem-worlds of ideas" (*yijing* 意境).[66] The *Poetry Manual of the Literary Grove* (*Wenyuan shige* 文苑詩格) attributed to Bai Juyi, for example, describes how poems may use the poem-world to enter an idea, or an idea to enter a poem-world, and each is subject to different kinds of errors.[67] The creation of unique poem-worlds and ideas requires mental training—the kind of heightened perceptual awareness that Buddhists claimed could be honed through meditation and scripture recitation.[68] Although Sun Guangxian nowhere endorses Buddhism wholesale, he does implicitly recognize that the meditative practice of a poet-monk can heighten one's perception, the basis on which poetry is built. In this way, Sun portrays Guanxiu as the culmination of a distinct tradition with its own developmental arc, one that had been building since the late eighth century.

Li Xianyong, likely writing a few decades prior to Sun Guangxian, also regarded Guanxiu as the key figure in a later lineage of poet-monks. Li, a skilled writer of *yuefu* in his own right, posits Guanxiu as the channel connecting the monk Xiumu to the mainstream literary tradition of song-style poetry.

Reading a Compilation of the Venerable Xiumu's Songs 讀修睦上人歌篇

Li Xianyong

Li Bai's passed,
Li He's dead.
Chen Tao and you, Zhao Mu,
    sought to succeed them.[69]
You must know that this generation
    does not lack for *Sao*-poets,[70]
But for heirs to Guanxiu,
There is Xiumu alone.
Lord Mu, Lord Mu,
    truly you are formidable—
When you speak to others
    you shrink from nothing!
Your talent is like the morning mist,
    charming and new;
Your uprightness like the bend-slack flower,
    pointing out flatterers.[71]
Your thoughts teem, teem
    with the workings of the fashioned world;
Your brush drips, drips
    with the marrow of literature.
For thirty years, the bright moon
    and the clear breeze
Have been chased by you
    like a slave.
I urge you to rest—
Be not so rash!
The world has long thought
    the rare to be precious.
Tall coral shelves
    and brushes of five-colored clouds
Are things so small they need not
    vex your thoughts of writing.

李白亡，
李賀死，
陳陶趙睦尋相次。
須知代不乏騷人，
貫休之後，
惟修睦而已矣。
睦公睦公真可畏，
開口向人無所忌。
才似煙霞生則媚，
直如屈軼佞則指。
意下紛紛造化機，
筆頭滴滴文章髓。
明月清風三十年，
被君驅使如奴婢。
勸君休，
莫容易，
世俗由來稀則貴。
珊瑚高架五雲毫，
小小不須煩藻思。[72]

Li Xianyong traces an orthodox transmission of song-style poetry in literary society as a whole, not just in the world of poet-monks. In the lineage of song-style poetry outlined by Li Xianyong, Li Bai was the paragon of the form, and Li He took the reins from the earlier poet. Both were bold writers with a penchant for fantastical imagery and unconventional rhythms, the sort of qualities best displayed in mixed-meter songs. But with the two Lis gone from this earth, the true line of inheritance is uncertain. In lines 2-4 of this poem, Li Xianyong tries to establish his own: Chen Tao to Guanxiu to Xiumu. Chen Tao, the only non-Buddhist, lived for many years at Hongzhou, a thriving center for innovations in Buddhist doctrine in the ninth century, and exchanged poems with Cai Jing 蔡京 (a laicized poet-monk) and Guanxiu. What Li Xianyong implies in his lines is that the poet-monks are the true inheritors of the song-style tradition.[73] The rest of the poem confirms this. Xiumu is praised in terms we normally find reserved for brash, otherworldly poets like Li Bai: he is "formidable" (line 5), "holds back nothing" (line 6), overflowing with ideas (lines 9-10), and "rash" (line 13). Xiumu is admired for his restless energy—a quality that is antithetical to the stereotype of the monk as a meditative bonze—but is in perfect alignment with the aesthetic of madness associated with Guanxiu and other monks who practiced calligraphy during the latter half of the Tang.⁷⁴ Significantly, Li Xianyong implies that poet-monks are taking over the *yuefu* that had previously been considered a literati tradition.⁷⁵ Here, as in Wu Rong's preface to Guanxiu's works, the poet-monks are the keepers of poetry.

These tenth-century poems make it clear that "poet-monk" had become a label for a social position in the literary world, and it is around this position that writers sought to invent a tradition. Poet-monks moved from being peripheral figures—either mere curiosities or souls in parallel—to players in the sphere of poetry. With this development came a need to establish lines of orthodox poet-monks who passed on the tradition over generations. At the same time, it also meant that it was necessary to find precursors to the poet-monks in earlier centuries. In some cases, their precursors were not monks at all but instead major poets of the mainstream tradition, like Li Bai, Li He, and Bai Juyi. Poet-monks had their own tradition and could become the inheritors of others'.

An Identity

It was not just the literati who needed to make sense of the proliferating poet-monks. As we reach the end of the Tang and enter the Five Dynasties era, we find an increasingly acute sense of self-awareness among the poet-monks themselves. "Poet-monk" was becoming an insider's term, reclaimed from its early, marginalizing connotations. It went from being etic to emic. Poet-monks became more active participants in shaping the idea of the poet-monk. They created an identity that they could inhabit.

The self-creation of a poet-monk tradition parallels developments in Buddhism more broadly. It was during the same time—the early- and mid-tenth century—that elaborate Chan genealogies and the related literary genres of "lamp-transmission records" (*chuandeng lu* 傳燈錄) and "records of sayings" (*yulu* 語錄) emerged. Although earlier records of Chan lineages exist, the more systematic ones that represent the emergence of a full-fledged Buddhist sub-tradition came later.⁷⁶ The *Transmission of the Baolin Monastery* (*Baolin zhuan* 寶林傳) was likely compiled in 801, the *Patriarch's Hall Collection* (*Zutang ji* 祖堂集) was compiled in 952, the first notes that would later form the basis of the *Record of Yunmen* (*Yunmen guanglu* 雲門廣錄) were likely starting to take shape as a collection in the mid-tenth century, and *Jingde Lamp Transmission Records* (*Jingde chuandenglu*) was completed in 1004.⁷⁷ The creation of such records, much recent scholarship has argued, is coextensive with the creation of Chan itself as a distinct school of Buddhism.⁷⁸

Among Guanxiu's many poems on reading—which include topics as diverse as the *Lisao*, Du Fu, Jia Dao, Meng Jiao 孟郊 (751–814), Liu Deren 劉得仁 (mid-ninth cent.), Gu Kuang, and Yao He—we find one on the work of two earlier poet-monks, Jiaoran and Zhou He (the latter referred to by his style name, Nanqing). The very fact of placing these two names together in the title of his poem is an argument for their continuity. The two poets lived in different times and places and wrote in very different styles. Jiaoran, who lived in eastern Jiangnan in the late eighth century, was a jack of all trades, while Zhou He, who lived in the capital corridor in the first half of the ninth, specialized in regulated verse. The only thing that connects these two poets is their shared experience as poet-monks and the fact that both can be seen as precursors to Guanxiu himself.

Looking over the Poetry Collections of Jiaoran and Nanqing 覽皎然集南卿集

Guanxiu

Though you do not match each other in learning
You are both the same in purity.
Loftier than Baoyue's moon—
Who could shoot your carved bow?
Your utmost vision touched Yao He;
Your craftsmanship agrees with the Duke of Lu.⁷⁹
So you're worthy of deep admiration
And will share in purest airs for a thousand ages.

學力不相敵，
清還髣髴同。
高於寶月月，
誰得射雕弓。
至鑒逢姚監，
良工遇魯公。
如斯深可羨，
千古共清風。⁸⁰

Following the norms of Late Tang poems addressed to two people, Guanxiu addresses his subjects in multiple ways. In the opening and closing couplets, Jiaoran and Zhou He are addressed together. Both are worthy of admiration (line 7), and both can be characterized by their purity (lines 2 and 8), a fitting praise since both lived in reclusion for long stretches of time, and both have the character meaning "pure" in their dharma names (Jiaoran is Qingzhou 清晝, or "Pure Daylight," and Zhou He is Qingsai 清塞, or "Purity Bastion").[81] Nonetheless, Guanxiu recognizes their differences: Jiaoran's learning is greater than Zhou He's, as evidenced by his writings on poetics. This makes him putting them together even bolder. Though they are different kinds of poets, they are both poet-monks and precursors to Guanxiu.

In the middle couplets, Guanxiu puts his subjects in parallel with each other. In couplet 3, he describes Zhou He in the first line and Jiaoran in the second. Zhou He was a close friend of Yao He and Jia Dao, known for their embodiment of the *kuyin* aesthetic, while Jiaoran exchanged poems with Yan Zhenqing, the Duke of Lu, who praised Jiaoran for his literary craftsmanship.[82] Couplet 2 does not display the same strongly antithetical structure as couplet 3. Here we see the construction of the poet-monk tradition as expressed in a single idea over two lines. Baoyue, the monk whose *yuefu* were collected in a popular sixth-century anthology, is drawn in to the tradition. Though none of Baoyue's surviving poems touch on Buddhist thought or practice in any way, he is claimed as a poet-monk. Line 3 is a dense entanglement of wordplay: "lofty" (*gao* 高) is used in the sense of both physical height and unreachable purity, and "moon" refers both to Baoyue's description of the moon in his poem "Traveling's Hard" 行路難 and to Baoyue himself, whose name literally means "Precious Moon." This playful punning calls attention to the line to stress the continuity of the poet-monk tradition over four hundred years, from Baoyue to Jiaoran to Zhou He to Guanxiu.[83] Guanxiu takes up the idea of the poet-monk and claims it as his own. What had once been a term of derision he makes a badge of honor.

Not long after Guanxiu's death, his disciple Tanyu gathered his writings and, surely frustrated with the way Wu Rong's essay strayed far from its subject, wrote his own preface to Guanxiu's collection.[84] This second preface tells us much more about Guanxiu's life and also something about his relationship with other monks. It opens with a description of some of Guanxiu's religious training. As a child, he set out to memorize a thousand characters of the *Lotus Sūtra* per day, until he could recite the entire text from memory within a month. After his full ordination at twenty, he spent three years studying the *Awakening of Mahāyāna Faith* 大乘起信論, attributed to Aśvagoṣa.[85] All through this time, he was friends with a neighboring monk named Chumo 處默, with whom he recited the scriptures and wrote poems. As Tanyu tells us, "Whenever they would get a break from their intense religious cultivation, they would exchange matching poems with each other" 每於精修之暇，更相唱和. Chumo regarded Guanxiu highly, saying, "He holds an unbridled talent and harbors the way of the Self-So" 抱不羈之才，懷自然之道. Guanxiu was clearly admired by his fellow monks for these talents. His early lectures on the *Awakening of Mahāyāna Faith* attracted listeners hundreds of miles away. When he reached Shu in his later years, "a meditation chamber was built especially for him, and he was invited to be the supervisory monk" 特修禪宇，懇請住持, presumably because of the respect he commanded among his fellow monastics. When he died, "there was no one among the literati or commoners in the city who did not grieve" 在城士庶無不悲傷. Tanyu emphasizes Guanxiu's importance to the monastic community, just as Wu Rong stressed his literary significance. But Tanyu's depiction of Guanxiu, unlike Wu Rong's, is multidimensional: he holds up his master's achievements in both religious and literary realms as the basis for his widespread acclaim. In highlighting Guanxiu's artistic gift, coupled with his devotion to the practice of Buddhism, Tanyu makes him into an ideal model of the poet-monk that others may emulate.

A generation younger than Guanxiu, Qiji inherited a more fully developed concept of the poet-monk, one with a strong sense of its own history and continuity. In fact, Qiji had at the ready an entire repertoire of poet-monk references, culled from previous literati and monks. In a poem of encouragement to Wenxiu—whom we saw earlier praised by Li Xianyong in Confucian terms—he harkens back to "the time of Jiaoran and Lingyi" 皎然靈一時 and is delighted that Wenxiu carries on their tradition.[86] In a poem looking toward the Great River from his dwelling on Mount Lu, he alludes to a poet-monk precursor mentioned in Liu Yuxi's preface, declaring, "I'd like to take off to the Southern Dynasties / When Huixiu was among the poet-monks" 欲向南朝去，詩僧有惠休.[87] Qiji sees himself as a poet-monk, the inheritor of a well-defined literary tradition. In his writing, he reinforces that tradition and strives to embody it.

After the death of Guanxiu in early 913, Qiji seems to have become the most prominent and prolific poet-monk in the land.[88] The *Song Biographies of Eminent Monks*, for example, describes a tenth-century monk named Zongyuan 宗淵, originally from the northeast, who traveled first to Mount Lu to study with a meditation master, then to the kingdom of

Jingnan 荊南 to study poetry with Qiji.[89] Given Qiji's many connections, and the large percentage of his exchange corpus with fellow monks, it is likely that Zongyuan was not the only one to have done so. Sometime in the 920s or 930s, Qiji heard of another rogue monk composing poetry in the north. Qiji seemed genuinely surprised that a poet-monk could have escaped his notice and sent him the following poem.

Sent to Qinggu of Xuzhou 寄許州清古
Qiji

A Confucian scholar from the north says
There's an intoning monk at Xu,
Leaning his body all day long
On the top floor of a pagoda in the clear autumn.
Though words are grasped by relying on the sensory world,
Their truth is manifested only when entering nonbeing.
I dare hope we can see more of each other,
As this weak, frail one is old and cannot best you.

北來儒士說，
許下有吟僧。
白日身長倚，
清秋塔上層。
言雖依景得，
理要入無徵。
敢望多相示，
孱微老不勝。[90]

Qiji, serving as Saṃgha Rectifier in the kingdom of Jingnan, plays the role of the elder statesman. His poem acts as an invitation to Qinggu, that the latter might join the larger community of poet-monks. The self-deprecation of line 8 is a standard humble remark that one would write to a stranger, suggesting that the two are not well acquainted. But he wants to know Qinggu better, engage with him not through roaming Confucians but rather by engaging the person directly.

Qiji also writes about Qinggu's poetry in novel terms, ones that provide a glimpse into Qiji's conception of a Buddhist poetics. Even if we suppose that this poem is merely Qiji politely complimenting a junior poet-monk's work, the terms by which it does so make certain assumptions about poetry. Qiji posits a dichotomy between two levels of reality: 1) the mundane, associated with the visible world, which can be grasped by a poet so long as he uses sufficiently honest language; and 2) the ultimate, associated with truth or principle (*li* 理), which can only be made clear after it enters into nonbeing. The mundane and the ultimate are held in tension: they are considered to be fundamental opposites, yet the everyday world can serve as a doorway to ultimate realization. A gap stretches out between the two, but a momentary encounter with the physical landscape as an independent, objective reality can sometimes act as a catapult launching one over the yawning abyss and into enlightenment.

Qiji's poetic theory here is reminiscent of some of his contemporaries' theories of enlightenment. The concept of two levels of truth was fundamental in Mahāyāna Buddhism, and the doctrine of the "perfect interfusion" (*yuanrong* 圓融) of principle and phenomenon became particularly prominent in the Tang. This doctrine was articulated most systematically by monks associated with Huayan 華嚴 teachings, such as Dushun 杜順 (557-640) and Fazang 法藏 (643-712), who sought to articulate the experience of being enlightened, but it was also well known to those belonging to Chan lineages of the ninth and tenth centuries.[91] Perfect interfusion was articulated in the *Awakening of Mahāyāna Faith* (which Guanxiu preached on) and was espoused by several monks associated with the Buddhist communities that we know Qiji interacted with, such as Lingyou 靈祐 (771-853), patriarch of the Wei-Yang lineage 溈仰宗, and the monk Weijin 惟勁, who lived at Mount Heng 衡山 around the same time as Qiji in 899.[92] The doctrine stressed that ultimate truth pervaded the mundane world. Mazu Daoyi, patriarch of the Hongzhou lineage that Guanxiu and Qiji were familiar with, is said to have put it in a particularly direct way. The "dharmas" he speaks of are the constitutive features of the mundane world, and "suchness" (Ch.: *zhenru*, Skt.: *tathātā*) is the state of ultimate reality. The two, he declares, are inseparable.

> All dharmas are Buddhadharmas, and all dharmas are liberation. Liberation is identical with suchness. All dharmas never leave suchness. Whether walking, standing, sitting, or lying down, everything is always an inconceivable function of suchness. The scriptures say that the Buddha is in each and every place.

> 一切法皆是佛法。諸法即是解脫。解脫者即是真如。諸法不出於真如。行住坐臥。悉是不思議用。不待時節。經云。在在處處。則為有佛。[93]

Profane activities are sacred. The limited is limitless. There is nothing off-limits. Indeed, many Late Tang monks took these pronouncements as encouragement to "play on the borders of language."[94] In his poem to Qinggu, Qiji applies the theory of perfect interfusion to literary composition, thereby reconceiving the possibilities of poetry. From remote antiquity, poetry was the tool by which the literati praised or critiqued the state, but Qiji, as a poet-monk, appropriates it for Buddhist soteriological ends. At the same time, Buddhist insight into reality can be used for poetic ends. Literary practice becomes religious practice, and vice versa.

Guanxiu and Qiji can be understood as the culmination of a concept and a social position that had been developing for over two centuries. They were monks who were not only conversant in both Buddhist and poetic discourses but also able to integrate the two into a coherent practice. Their peers saw them as leading lights of the literary world—poets whose clear ideas and poem-worlds were shaped by heightened sensory perception gained in meditation, monks whose insight into non-duality was aided by their poetic parallelisms. They portrayed themselves as mere iterations of precursors like Huixiu and Baoyue, but they were in fact something completely different. Whereas those earlier monks slipped in and out of standard poetic personae with little trace of their monastic identities, Guanxiu and Qiji sought a full harmonization of their religious and poetic practices. The ways in which they did this will be explored in detail, but for now it is enough to note that they both shaped and were shaped by a poet-monk tradition that grew out of the original community centered around Lingyi, Jiaoran, and Lingche. From the mid-eighth to the mid-tenth century, the poet-monk changed in geographic, social, and cultural position. What began as a local Jiangnan curiosity gradually spread to the capital region, scattered across the empire, then settled down in a variety of local power centers. Along the way, the literati grew to understand poet-monks as participants in their own classical, Confucian tradition, in which poetry was the highest art.

A variety of factors contributed to these developments. In the eighth century, the decentralization of power following the An Lushan Rebellion, combined with Jiangnan's rich cultural and Buddhist heritages, provided a healthy environment for the poet-monks' infancy. In the early ninth century, emperors' and capital elites' patronage of Buddhism brought more poet-monks to Chang'an and other urban centers, where they eventually grew to be an established part of literary society. In the last years of the Tang, the incredible destruction wrought by Huang Chao's armies left a void at the cultural center, creating the space for a diversity of voices to grow, including the voices of the poet-monks. From this time through the middle of the tenth century, sacred peaks' (like Mount Lu's and Mount Heng's) relative isolation from battle, along with their monasteries' connections with local rulers, made them attractive to many poet-monks. Some of the more famous poet-monks, such as Guanxiu and Qiji, found refuge in the capitals of the newly established regional kingdoms. The kings and would-be emperors, like their Tang predecessors about a century prior, lavished these poet-monks with honors in an attempt to lure them to their kingdoms and establish themselves as cultured, legitimate rulers.

Such political, geographical, and social realities created the conditions under which a self-conscious, self-sufficient poet-monk tradition could flourish, a tradition that did not see itself as inferior or wayward but rather as the fullest embodiment of high cultural values, whether those values came from Buddhist scriptures, Confucian classics, or any other source. As we have seen, over the course of about two hundred years, poet-monks went from being a local curiosity of the Jiangnan region to an established part of literary society. Their story is integral to the literary history of medieval China. The significance of their chapter in literary history is related to how they sought to combine literary and religious practices. To understand these innovations, we must begin to look at the kinds of techniques they used in their verses. We must turn from history to poetics.

Part II

Poetics

Chapter 4

Repetition
Retriplication and Negation

The preceding chapters have focused on the social history of poet-monks. By examining a range of sources using various methods, we have seen how the term "poet-monk" refers to a specific literary tradition that emerged in late eighth-century Jiangnan and gradually came to play an important role in literary society across the entire Chinese realm. As travelers between regions, between groups, between discourses, they were among the most well-connected poets of their day. Simultaneously, at the turn of the tenth century, as the Tang empire crumbled, they began to articulate a new vision of poetry. Their dual vocations as monks and poets were not only reconcilable but also complementary.

Turning from history to poetics, this section shows how a widespread, self-conscious poet-monk tradition shaped literary practice and how the poet-monks' works were different from their contemporaries'. This chapter and the next two identify three distinct features of their poetry as well as precedents for them in religious and literary practices. By paying close attention to the patterning of these poems, as found in their formal qualities, allusions, and metadiscursive lines about poetry, and tracing these findings back to practical guides (poetry manuals, sūtra commentaries, etc.) and the works of past poets, these chapters investigate the works of the poet-monks from the inside out.

The three distinct features of the poet-monks' works are 1) their propensity for repeating characters, especially negation particles; 2) their attention to the numinous powers of sonority and foreignness, which are related to the practice of chanting spells and scriptures; and 3) their claims that poetry, like meditation, requires a stillness and absorptive attention that is achieved through great effort. Each of these, we will see, derives at least in part from a specifically Buddhist practice that would have been well known to late medieval poet-monks like Guanxiu and Qiji.

This chapter looks at the poet-monks' propensity for repetition in their poems: what exactly they are doing with repetition, how it functions in their poems, and what sorts of discourses and practices might have led them to use such a technique. The poet-monks drew on the Buddhist discourse of apophasis—understanding concepts via negation—when they used repetition. By repurposing a rhetorical feature of scholastic discourse for poetic ends, they infused their verses with mesmerizing rhythms and puzzling phrases rarely seen among their non-monastic peers.

Retriplication

The most conspicuous stylistic feature of the extant body of work by late medieval poet-monks is repetition. In line after line, verse after verse, poem after poem, the poet-monks often deploy the same characters multiple times in obviously patterned ways, far more than many of their contemporaries. The third poem in Guanxiu's collected works, "Song of Bright Spring" 陽春曲, ends by repeating a character three times in a row, a technique that I call "retriplication." This is unusual in Chinese because, in standard uses of the language, reduplication (doubling) is usually the outer limit of repeating a single character. In his "Song of Bright Spring," Guanxiu goes one step further. Bemoaning the destruction wrought by the Huang Chao Rebellion as it swept through his home region of Jiangnan in the spring of 880, he builds to an emotional fever pitch that reaches its apex in the moment of retriplication.

Song of Bright Spring (Written East of the River, 880) 陽春曲
（江東廣明初作）

Guanxiu

With mouth, do not imitate
    Ruan Sizong,[1]

Who, not speaking of right and wrong,
    denied the impartial.

With hands, we need resemble
    the likes of Zhu Yun,
Whose heroic, balustrade-breaking spirit
    would endure till now.[2]
If boys would tie their hair
    and serve their lords and parents,
They must imitate the former worthies'
    great resolve.

An array of ministers in prosperous times—
    Fang and Du,[3]
Lord Wei, Lord Yao,
    and Commander Song,[4]
Have fully ascended to that sylphic
    heaven above and idle in their palace.
Oh, would they not leave the Emperor on High
    and sink to this sunken earth?
Or could they stand to see us graylife
    suffer suffer suffer?[5]

為口莫學阮嗣宗，	A
不言是非非至公。	A
為手須似朱雲輩，	B
折檻英風至今在。	B
男兒結髮事君親，	-
須斅前賢多慷慨。	B
歷數雍熙房與杜，	C
魏公姚公宋開府。	C
盡向天上仙宮閑處坐，	-
何不卻辭上帝下下土，	C
忍見蒼生苦苦苦。	C[6]

This is a *yuefu* of witness, set in July 880 as rebel forces swept through Wuzhou and forced Guanxiu to flee his home to the neighboring town of Piling 毗陵.[7] The ultimate cause of the Huang Chao Rebellion's violence, Guanxiu declares, is the self-interest of local ministers. They are too much like the bookish Ruan Ji (lines 1–2) and not enough like the bold Zhu Yun, who spoke truth to power even as armed guards dragged him from the emperor (lines 3–4). The critique of the decadent present age continues until the last three lines, at which point the tone of the poem shifts. The meter changes to unusual nine-character lines, and the speaker's thoughts turn heavenward, where he imagines the good ministers idling in transcendent palaces and implores them to descend messianically (lines 9–10). This obsession with other worlds is widespread in Guanxiu's poetic corpus, and here it sets up a contrast with the disaster spreading in the wake of Huang Chao's rebellion.[8] The suffering seen by Guanxiu, that the gods in heaven cannot bear to see, is intensified with the retriplication of *ku* 苦 (bitterness, pain). Guanxiu takes the normal method of intensifying an adjective—reduplication—and intensifies it further. The people do not just *ku* or *ku ku*; they *ku ku ku*.

Guanxiu used retriplication to grab his audience's attention. Such an effect depends on the fact that retriplication is a relatively rare phenomenon in the Late Tang, one that had not become a standard trope in mainstream poetry. A systematic analysis of all uses of retriplication prior to the Song dynasty confirms the phenomenon's rarity. In the entire corpus, there are only 117 instances of retriplication in 96 poems by 50 known authors and several unknown authors—a small fraction of the over 60,000 surviving poems from the pre-Song period.[9] Of these, the vast majority come from the Tang (106 poems, 90.6 percent) and a majority from the Late Tang (59 poems, 50.4 percent).

This systematic analysis also shows that Buddhist monks are disproportionally represented. In *Quan Tang shi*, for example, only 109 of the approximately 2,200 named poets are Buddhist monks (5 percent), but 53 of the 117 instances of retriplication (45.2 percent) come from the hands of monks, nearly as many as the 56 instances from non-monastics (47.9 percent).[10] In addition to Guanxiu and Qiji, retriplication is used by other poet-monks, their precursor Baozhi 寶志 (d. 514), the Japanese pilgrim Kūkai 空海 (774–835), and the anonymous lyricists of didactic Buddhist songs. Retriplication appears to be unusually favored by Buddhists. This tendency is even stronger than these statistics suggest: three of the "unknown" uses of retriplication come from Dunhuang manuscripts, which means that they were likely copied and definitely stored at a Buddhist holy site; and twelve of the lay uses come from well-known lay Buddhists Bai Juyi and Sikong Tu. If we recalculate to include these fifteen instances, Buddhists would account for a full 68 of the 117 examples of retriplicatives (58.1 percent) found in our extant records.

The trends are even more striking when we consider time as well. The usage of retriplication precisely mirrors the development of poetry written by Buddhist monks (figure 4.1). This rare literary technique was used occasionally in pre-Tang poems but only appears regularly in high literary writings at the time when the label "poet-monk" also emerged. Retriplication would later be most widely used by poet-monks at the height of their development (Guanxiu, Qiji, Xiumu, etc.) and some of the literati they were in contact with (Sikong Tu, Bai Juyi).[11] In short, retriplication became associated with Buddhist monks. The reasons for this association will become clear as we delve deeper into the literary and religious resources that these poet-monks, especially Guanxiu, drew on.

Retriplication is a variation of reduplication, the repetition of a character twice in a row. Reduplication has been an integral part of Chinese from its very genesis. As in most languages, the doubling of a syllable in Chinese alters its meaning in a variety of ways. In Sinitic languages, "total reduplication"—the repetition of a single character—usually creates a sense of intensification or vividness.[12] Reduplicatives can be found throughout the earliest layers of the Chinese literary tradition, especially the *Book of Odes* (*Shijing*). Its rhythm, usually created by the repetition of characters in a steady four-beat meter and a host of resonances across lines and stanzas, would later become strongly associated with an elite, formal style. The kinds of reduplication used in the *Book of Odes* can be found in much of the poetry before the medieval period. As such, it was one part of a poetic repertoire that would be shared by virtually all poets of the classical Chinese tradition, from the earliest times up to the present day.

Indeed, there is evidence that repetition was at the forefront of poets' minds in the late medieval period. Repetition was especially common in the old-style poetry (*guti shi*) that drew on songs and in popular verse written in many forms.[13] Poetry manuals throughout the Tang mention various types of repetition, either as faults or models. Early in the Tang, Cui Rong 崔融 (653–706), for example, called the repetition of characters with the same tones "inharmonious" 不調 and "an enormous fault" 巨病.[14] Shangguan Yi 上官儀 (ca. 608–664), in *Ornamental Rafters of Brush and Tablet* (*Bizha hualiang* 筆札華梁), describes various ways of crafting parallel couplets, including reduplicative parallelism (*lianmian dui* 聯綿對), alliterative binom parallelism (*shuangsheng dui* 雙聲對), rhyming binom parallelism (*dieyun dui* 疊韻對), and a kind of parallelism known as "double drafting" (*shuangni* 雙擬), which is based on the repetition of

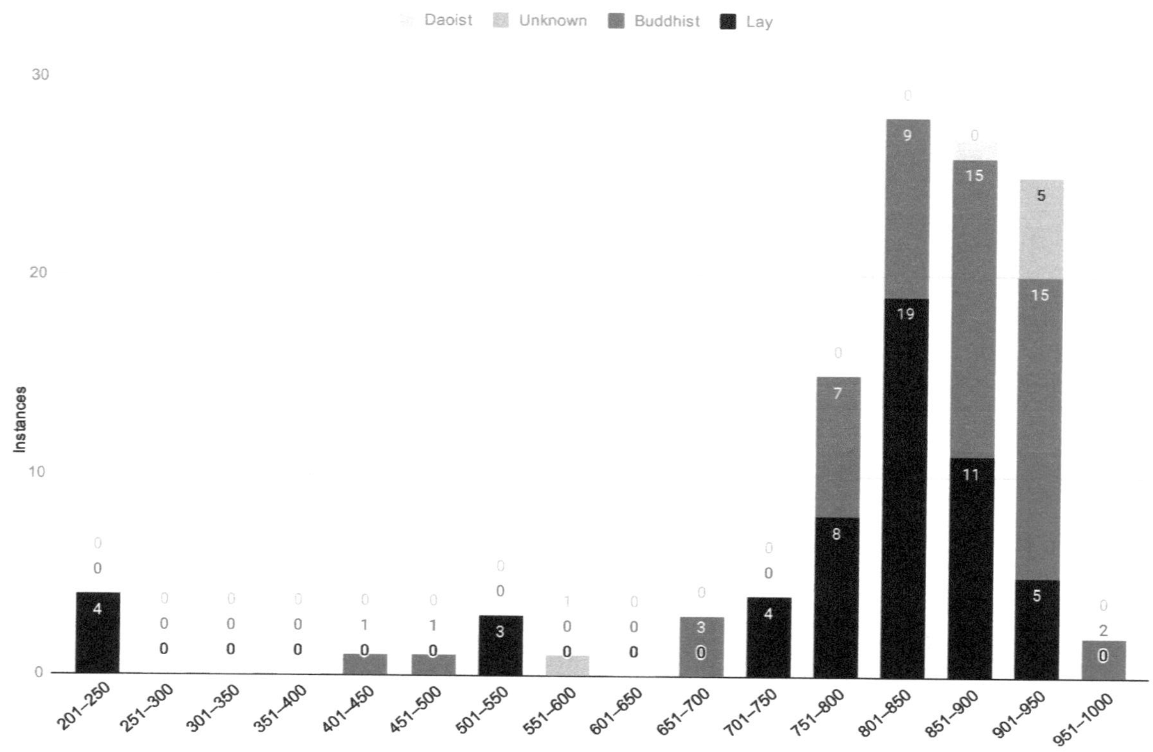

Figure 4.1. Bar graph of retriplication in the Tang and Five Dynasties, by fifty-year periods. Poems that cannot be dated with precision are assigned the year in which their author was forty-five years old. Dunhuang poems follow their rough dating in the standard catalogs, and those manuscripts dated only to a century are assigned the middle of that century (for example, "ninth century" becomes "850" in this chart). Retriplication is used most frequently in the ninth and tenth centuries, the period of the poet-monks' flourishing.

a character at least twice in different parts of a single line (e.g., as the first and third character of a line, or the second and fourth).[15]

Qiji seized on "double drafting" and developed it into its own technique in his poetry manual *Exemplary Models of Poetry* (*Fengsao zhige*). Qiji lists it as the twenty-sixth of poetry's forty "gates" (*men* 門) and illustrates it with a couplet from a poem by Liu Deren: "You sit, darkening eyes and darkening mind / While flowers bloom and flowers fall" 瞑目瞑心坐, 花開花落時.[16] Although the technique was first listed in the literatus Shangguan Yi's manual, and examples are abundant in the *Book of Odes*, it seems that by the late ninth century, it had become associated with Buddhism.[17] As modern scholar Duan Shuangxi has pointed out, the "AXAY" pattern is very frequently used in Buddhist scriptures (and, later, Chan writings) for emphasis or comparison.[18] If we look for all occurrences of this technique in *Quan Tang shi*, we will indeed find that Buddhist monks are more likely than non-monks to use "double drafting." There are 7,009 occurrences of double drafting, in a total corpus of 2,571,562 characters, for a ratio of 2.7 instances for every 1,000 characters. Of the twenty Buddhist monks with significant surviving collections (corpora of at least 500 characters), twelve have a ratio above this average. Qiji's ratio is about one and a half times the average (3.9 per 1,000 characters), and Guanxiu's and Lingche's close to three times the average (7.6 and 7.7, respectively).[19]

Another tenth-century manual on poetic composition, this one by the monk Shenyu 神彧, lists repetition as the fourth of five ways of "proceeding from topics" (*poti* 破題).[20] In this manual, repeating an important character or set of characters is invoked not simply as a means of grabbing the reader's attention but more specifically as an important way to set up the main topic of a poem.

> Four: Sticking to the topic. In proceeding from a topic, a character is repeated in the first or second line of the couplet. A poem by Guanxiu reads:
>
>> Successful (*deli*) but not yet aided (*deli*),
>> The summer fades away again as I intone with pain.[21]
>
> Here he sticks to the same two characters in a single line. Next, a poem by Fang Gan reads:
>
>> Though not yet effective in the task I am set upon (*zhi*),
>> Still I intone with pain to (*zhi*) this day.[22]

Here he sticks to the same character in the first and second lines. Next, a poem on "Seeing off a Monk" reads:

One (*yi*) patchrobe and one (*yi*) tin-ringed staff;
You wear out your entire (*yi*) self, treating it lightly.²³

Here it sticks to the same character three times in the first and second lines. Next, an "Old Poem" reads:

Marching marching and marching marching,
From you have I been parted in life.²⁴

Here it sticks to the same character four times in a single line. Next, a poem on "Parting with a Friend" reads:

We parted in years past,
and today part again.

Let us make today's parting
the same as that past parting.²⁵

Here it sticks to the character "part" (*bie* 別) four times and the character "past" (*xi* 昔) twice in two lines.

四曰粘題，破題上下二句重用其字是也。禪月詩：「得力未得力，苦吟夏又殘。」此乃一句內粘二字也。方干詩：「至業未得力，至今猶苦吟。」此乃上下共粘二字也。《送僧》詩：「一衲與一錫，一身索索輕。」此乃上下共粘三字也。《古詩》：「行行重行行，與君生別離。」此乃一句粘四字也。《別友人》詩：「昔年相別今又別，今別還將昔別同。」此乃兩句粘四「別」字，又粘二「今」、二「昔」字。

According to Shenyu, the repeated characters emphasize their importance to the poem. This is most obvious in the final example, in which the character for "part" is used four times in the opening couplet of a parting poem. The Guanxiu example plays on two meanings of *deli* 得力 (literally "attain strength"): 1) being effective or successful and 2) receiving help. Guanxiu is doubly praising the poem's recipient: not only has he become a minister and a well-known poet, he has also done so without receiving any special favors. Fang Gan's couplet sets up a poem about the practice of writing verse despite not "reaching" (*zhi* 至) his goal of passing the examinations and serving the imperial bureaucracy. The couplet on the monk uses "one" (*yi* 一) to establish a theme of unity that contrasts sharply with the theme of separation. In each case, the repeated character is a crucial part of the poem that works with the topic to establish the main purpose of the work. Repetition, to Shenyu, makes the theme.

Shenyu's manual demonstrates that the repetition of a character is explicitly stated as one way of approaching the act of poetic composition. Many late medieval poets took great pains to perfect every detail of their verses, and the patterns of repeated characters are one detail mentioned in this manual. Whether such patterns were lifted up as models to follow or condemned as mistakes to be avoided, their very presence in medieval guides to writing poetry means that they were regarded as important factors to consider. Moreover, Shenyu's manual explaining the benefits of repetition comes out of the poet-monk milieu. Not only is Shenyu himself a monk, his first example quotes the paradigmatic poet-monk Guanxiu, his first two examples use the phrase *kuyin*, and his third example describes monastic tools and a disregard for the toll taken on the physical body (a hallmark of *kuyin* discourse).[26] As a whole, the manual quotes five of Guanxiu's couplets and two of Qiji's, and it copies the idea of poetry's ten "forces" (*shi* 勢) from Qiji's manual. Although we cannot date Shenyu's manual with precision, it is clear that he was familiar with the works of Guanxiu and Qiji, and it is possible that he had some sort of connection to them. By the late medieval period, the repetition of individual characters was a known poetic technique, discussed explicitly in writings on poetics and associated with the works of poet-monks. Retriplication was only a more extreme version of this same phenomenon.

Types

Retriplication, though striking when it appears, was not a widespread poetic technique. There are only 117 instances of it in the entire corpus of poetry prior to the Song dynasty. But it was unusually favored by poet-monks, and its uses fall into certain patterns. I have classified retriplication into three types based on how they function in a poem: *simple*, *complex*, and *anadiplotic*.

Guanxiu's "Song of Bright Spring," examined above, is an instance of what I call *simple retriplication*. It takes the same logic of classic reduplication and extends it: if doubling an adjective makes it twice as intense, then tripling it makes it three times as intense. In the late medieval period, simple retriplication was relatively rare and therefore arresting. This technique is powerful precisely because of its simplicity. To repeat a single word is to not use a variety of other words. When a character is relatively common, like *ku*, its repetition implies that the author has reached the limits of language. It is as if Guanxiu has thrown up his hands, removed all clever artifice, and is giving it to us in plain language. The people suffer. There is no other way to put it. Simple retriplication appeals to its reader directly, like an actor breaking the fourth wall.

But in Guanxiu's "Song of Bright Spring" there is another type of repetition. This is the use of a single character in two different senses back to back. In line 10, the speaker implores the righteous ministers to *xia xia tu* 下下土, "sink to this sunken earth." The first *xia*, pronounced in Middle Chinese with a departing tone (MC: *hàe*), functions as a verb meaning "to descend." The second *xia*, pronounced with a rising tone (MC: *hăe*), is an adjective describing *tu* ("earth") as "below" or "lower." Although the same character is used twice in a row, it is pronounced in two different ways and serves two distinct grammatical functions. This can happen even when a character's pronunciation does not change. In line 2 of "Song of Bright Spring," the poet Ruan Ji is described as one who "not speaking of right and wrong, denied the impartial" (*buyan shifei . fei zhigong* 不言是非.非至公). Here the negating character *fei* 非 falls across the caesura, which I indicate with a dot in the parenthetical transcription. The line is composed of two clauses describing Ruan Ji: the first four characters tell us what he did ("not speak of right and wrong"), while the last three characters give us a moral evaluation (he is not worthy of imitation because he "denied the impartial"). The first *fei* belongs to the nominal compound *shifei* of the first clause, meaning "right and wrong," "affirming and denying," or "true and false." The second *fei* is a verb of negation that takes as its object the substantive adjective *zhigong* ("the impartial"). Although the character is used in two different senses, its phonic properties are identical. To a reader who would have encountered the poem in its written form, it looks like classic reduplication, though it does not intensify in the same way. Rather, it makes the reader pause, linger over the line an extra moment to pick apart the grammar, run through the words again to make sure it makes sense. The reader must mentally repeat it.

When this kind of repetition is applied to three characters, I call it *complex retriplication*. This sort of retriplication, sometimes very difficult to parse, usually results from linking together two phrases which share a common character. The interpretive difficulties of complex retriplication would be resolved in an oral cantillation—a performer might pause at the caesura, or stress the repeated characters in different ways—but it would still produce an unusual sonic effect. An easily understood example can be found in one of Qiji's poems on the ceaseless march of time.

Song of Sun after Sun 日日曲
Qiji

Sun after sun, the sun rises east,
Sun after sun, the sun sets west.
Though you have the face of a divine transcendent,[27]
Still you must become rotted bones.
Floating clouds disperse and reappear;
Sweetgrass dies and springs forth again.
I know not what the ancients of
     a thousand, ten thousand years ago
Buried facing the green hills
     have turned into.

日日日東上，
日日日西沒。
任是神仙容，
也須成朽骨。
浮雲滅復生，
芳草死還出。
不知千古萬古人，
葬向青山為底物。[28]

The retriplication of the character *ri* 日, meaning both "sun" and "day," sets forth the theme of time's unhalting flow from the very start of the poem. The same pattern appears in both lines of the opening couplet: the reduplicated *ri* ("day after day" or "every day") functioning adverbially, then a single *ri* ("the sun") that acts as the subject of the sentence, followed by an adverbial direction ("in the east/west") and a verb ("rises/sets"). Once again, the repeated word is split by a caesura: *ri ri . ri dong shang* 日日.日東上 (line 1). The retriplication reinforces a more general theme of natural repetition: the unending cycle of nature, in which clouds and fragrant plants disintegrate and regenerate (lines 5–6). Time is an ocean, pounding ceaselessly against the shore of humankind, wearing down even the youthful faces of Daoist adepts into rotted skulls (lines 3–4). But the poem ends with a hint at rebirth. The ancients do not remain buried deep beneath grave mounds; according to the logic of karmic retribution, they could have become anything by now (lines 7–8).

Complex retriplication is often used in this way, to emphasize temporal length. Another example, found in one of Guanxiu's poems on a ruined monastery, stresses the speaker's continual, lonesome wanderings: "Going and going, going but never getting: / Sitting alone—what kin have I?" 行行行未得，孤坐更誰親。[29] However, complex retriplication is sometimes more difficult to parse. Guanxiu opens the eighth poem of his famous "Mountain-Dwelling" series 山居詩 with the line, "Mind upon mind the mind does not abide in Xiyi" 心心心不住希夷, meaning that one's thoughts cannot remain permanently in ineffable, ultimate reality.[30] The way he says this, however, violates the norms of regulated verse. A reader must parse the line with pauses after the second and fifth characters (心心.心不住.希夷) to make sense of the line, even though convention dictates that the strong caesura should come after the fourth character. Through this unusual syntax, Guanxiu forces the reader to mentally concentrate, reread the line, parse it correctly, and thereby experience the kind of mental frustration described in the line itself. To one who heard this poem performed aloud, the audience member would hear either an unusual rhythm (2-3-2) or would be left hanging in anticipation after the fourth character, experiencing a kind of enjambment. Complex retriplication is disruptive. It makes the reader or listener lend greater attention to the grammar and rhythm of a given line.

The third type of retriplication is *anadiplotic retriplication*. Anadiplosis (*dingzhen* 頂真) refers to a character or phrase used at the end of one line and the beginning of the next. Although the Chinese term *dingzhen* was coined in the thirteenth century, the technique is as old as the poetic tradition itself, appearing in early layers of the *Book of Odes* as a way to create connections between stanzas.[31] Anadiplotic retriplication differs from complex retriplication in both its form and function. Formally, the characters are separated by a line break, a much stronger pause than a caesura. Due to this formal difference, anadiplotic repetition does not force the reader to pause and parse but rather creates resonances between lines, reinforcing a poem's structure by strengthening its sense of sequence. In one of Guanxiu's poems on an old *yuefu* theme, he employs anadiplotic retriplication to underscore its concluding theme of interconnection.

After "Ballad of the Bitter Cold" 擬苦寒行
Guanxiu

North wind, north wind,
Ah, how harsh and noxious!

Snaps a strong man's mind,
Shrinks the Goldbird's feet.[32]
Frozen clouds so turbid turbid
They keep a blanket of snow
    from falling.

Its sounds curl 'round withered mulberries
And trunks in the desert frontier.[33]
The Yellow River is completely
Solid all the way to sea.
The Single Breath is fettered:
The myriad things are formless.[34]
Only before my courtyard are
    fir and pine tree branches,
Branch after branch alive.

北風北風,	-
職何嚴毒。	A
摧壯士心,	-
縮金烏足。	A
凍雲矗矗,	-
礙雪一片下不得。	A
聲繞枯桑,	-
根在沙塞。	B
黃河徹底,	-
頑直到海。	B
一氣搏束,	A
萬物無態。	B
唯有吾庭前杉松樹枝,	-
枝枝健在。	B[35]

The retriplication appears across the break between lines 13 and 14, echoing the repetitions of the poem's opening. "North wind" (line 1) and "turbid" (line 5) intensify with their doubling, emphasizing the harsh climate of the northern frontier. As the speaker mentally breaks down (line 3) in a land of dead trunks and withered mulberries (lines 7-8), he is everywhere surrounded by the indifference of the landscape, be it the whiteness of clouds and snow (lines 5-6) or the Yellow River that has frozen solid all the way to the sea (lines 9-10). The harsh north punishes with no relief. Even the original energy of the cosmos is constrained, unable to take on its myriad forms. Yet there is hope. After an abstract reflection, the speaker turns back to the landscape to see, instead of desolation, signs of life. The branches of firs and pines are robust, crisscrossing and reaching over the break between lines 13–14. Their vitality is so powerful it even manifests itself in the poem's formal features as anadiplotic retriplication.

Though all retriplication looks basically the same on the page, it is actually used in three distinct ways. Simple retriplication builds on the intensifying function of reduplication without interrupting the rhythm of the poem. It functions as a single linguistic unit. The other two varieties, on the other hand, are split by the pauses of caesurae and lines. Complex retriplication, which uses the same character in at least two different ways, encourages the reader or listener to halt and parse the line. This interruption works in tension with the incantatory nature of repetition, thereby creating a very unusual reading experience. Anadiplotic retriplication, on the other hand, creates a connection across lines or stanzas, highlighting a poem's formal structure and often hinting at themes of unity.

Of these three types of retriplication, anadiplotic is the most common. It appears first—in the poem "I Watered My Horse by the Great Wall Caves" 飲馬長城窟行 by Chen Lin 陳琳 (160?–217)—and is by far the most frequently used, 69 of the total 117 instances (59 percent).[36] It draws on the long-established technique of anadiplosis, and, interrupted by a strong pause, it is the least intrusive type of retriplication. Simple and complex retriplication are much more arresting by comparison, and they are unusually favored by poet-monks (see figure 4.2). Whereas Buddhists wrote about a third of anadiplotic retriplicatives (31.9 percent), their verses account for the majority of simple (58.3 percent) and complex (70.8 percent). This means that poet-monks not only used retriplication in disproportionate numbers, but when they did, they favored its most conspicuous types.

Retriplication, especially in its simple and complex varieties, was a violation of poetic norms and would have been striking to a Tang poet's audience. By deviating from standard uses of poetic language, these techniques have a roughening effect, arresting readers or listeners in their mental tracks and forcing them to pay closer attention. This effect is most obvious in complex retriplication, in which a poem's underlying

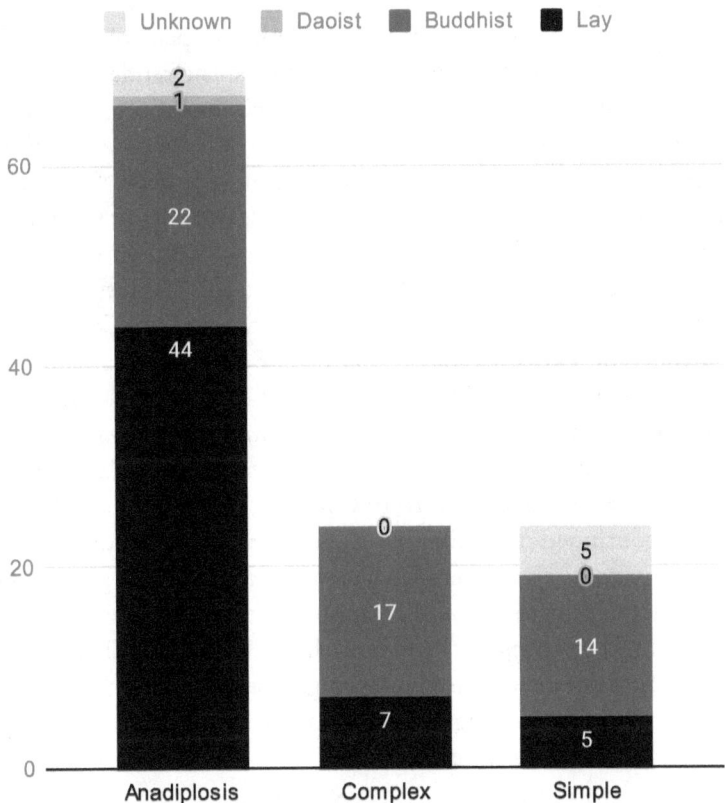

Figure 4.2. Bar graph of retriplication in the Tang and Five Dynasties, by type. Poet-monks favor using the most conspicuous forms of retriplication, complex and simple.

rhythm reads against the sound on the surface (the aural connection of repeated syllables), but it is also apparent in any of the techniques mentioned above. By intensifying, creating connections, or breaking apart rhythmic structures, they create a qualitatively different experience of a poem. In both theory and practice, the repetition of characters was one of the most prominent features of poetry written by Buddhist monks in the late medieval period. It created new rhythms that would have been especially noticeable in the context of oral recitation or public inscription, rhythms that owed much to Buddhist modes of discourse.

Negation

One of the clearest sources of the poet-monks' propensity for repetition is the apophatic tradition of thought, that is, the tendency to articulate truth statements through negation. This has roots in both Buddhist and Daoist philosophic writings. Many of the core teachings of Chinese Buddhism—such as *anātman* ("no-self," Ch. *wuwo* 無我), *nirvāna* ("extinguishment," Ch. *niepan* 涅槃 or *mie* 滅), and *śūnyata* ("emptiness," Ch. *kong* 空)—are in fact denials of other things. Daoism too has since chapter 1 of the *Daodejing* 道德經 proclaimed the inability of language to capture its highest ideal: "The way that can be considered a way is not a constant way; / the name that can be considered a name is not a constant name" 道可道非常道，名可名非常名. Apophatic contemplation techniques were important to pre-imperial and early Han self-cultivation practices associated with Daoist classics.[37] Later developments in Daoism, from the third-century "arcane studies" (*xuanxue*) onward, continued to build on these ideas. This made for happy moments of convergence between the two systems of thought, ones that proponents of synthesis would draw on for centuries.[38]

Guanxiu, something of a syncretist himself, drew on this apophatic tradition in a poem addressed to spring, repeating the character *wu* 無 ("no," "not have," "nothing") four times in a single line to contemplate the power of the natural world.

Spring 春
Guanxiu

Self-coming, self-going,
  you move the Vast Furnace,[39]
No-shape, no-self,
  nowhere no.
Without expending much strength
  to send the geese back,
You exhaust your energy
  on coloring the flowers.
Your lush verdancy is always
  cherished by wealthy households;
Your heavy warmth is what truly
  spurs on governors' brushes.
Don't be surprised when we meet
  if I'm just sleeping in,

> For mine own mind does not
>> abide in flourishing and fading.

自來自去動洪爐，
無象無私無處無。
迴雁不多消氣力，
染花應最費工夫。
溟濛偏被豪家惜，
濃暖深為政筆驅。
莫訝相逢只添睡，
伊余心不在榮枯。⁴⁰

The opening couplet of this poem, using the "double drafting" technique mentioned earlier (*zi* 自 appears in positions 1 and 3 of line 1), portrays spring as both a self-reliant mover of all things and an ultimately empty reality. The unreality of the natural world is driven home especially hard with the intense quadruple negation of line 2. A strong caesura after the fourth character establishes a contrast between the two hemistiches. On the one hand, nature is "nowhere no" 無處無, not nothing anywhere, for it teems with life. On the other, it lacks both "shape" 象 and "self-interest" 私: it has no substance whatsoever. That is, the world is both abundant and nonexistent—a perfectly logical stance if one takes the Buddhist idea of the interfusion of the two truths (mundane and ultimate) seriously. He slowly builds to a contrast between the productivity of others (lines 5-6) in light of spring's abundance (lines 3-4) and his own apparent laziness (line 7). The speaker reconciles this contrast by appealing to the Buddhist ideal of a steadfast mind: though he appears to be lazy, sleeping half the day, he is actually practicing no-mind, non-attachment to the vicissitudes of the world (lines 7-8). In spring, where others see life, the speaker sees only the inseparability of life and death. Spring's vitality will ultimately turn again to winter's destruction, so he focuses instead on the mind, which transcends the cycle of life and death (*saṃsāra*). He is responding, but to the world's ultimate reality—its impermanence, its negation.

To a person of the Tang, one important source of Buddhist apophasis was the *Heart Sūtra*. This text first became popular in the rendition of Xuanzang 玄奘 (602-664) known as *Mohe bore boluomiduo xinjing* 摩訶般若波羅蜜多心經 (*Mahā-prajñā-paramitā Heart Sūtra*).⁴¹ Evidence from Dunhuang, from commentaries, and from miracle tales attest to the frequency with which it was copied and memorized for spiritual benefits in the Tang.⁴² The poet Bai Juyi once wrote that "for seeing mental objects as empty and relying on the wisdom of the Buddha, nothing is better than the *Prajñā-paramitā Heart Sūtra*" 空法塵，依佛智，莫過於般若波羅蜜多心經.⁴³ The scripture's translator Xuanzang himself recited it to ward off demons, and Dunhuang colophons record that people copied it for a wide variety of reasons—such as to cure rheumatism, to accumulate merit for a deceased father, and to counteract the demerit accrued by killing a lamb and two ewes.⁴⁴ Guanxiu once recommended fellow poet-monk Qiyi 棲一 recite it to cure some scarring in his eye.⁴⁵

The *Heart Sūtra* was well-known in the Tang because it pithily summarizes many of the key doctrines of the prajñāparamitā scriptures. The middle portion of this brief scripture contains an extended apophatic reflection on the nature of emptiness.

> Śāriputra, all dharmas have the mark of emptiness. They are non-originated, non-extinct, non-defiled, non-pure, non-decreasing, non-increasing. Therefore in emptiness there is no form, no sensation, no concept, conditioning force, or consciousness; no eye, ear, nose, tongue, body, or mind; no form, sound, smell, taste, touch-object, or mind-object; no eye-realm and so on up to no realm of consciousness; no non-intelligence and no destruction of non-intelligence and so on up to no old-age-and-death and no destruction of old-age-and-death. There is no suffering, arising of suffering, extinction, or path; no knowledge and no attainment.

> 舍利子。是諸法空相。不生不滅。不垢不淨不增不減。是故空中。無色。無受想行識。無眼耳鼻舌身意。無色聲香味觸法。無眼界。乃至無意識界。無無明。亦無無明盡。乃至無老死。亦無老死盡。無苦集滅道。無智亦無得。⁴⁶

Emptiness here is defined by what it is not. The negating terms *bu* 不 and *wu* 無 account for 21 of the 82 characters in this passage, or more than one-quarter of the total. Even more negations are implied—the "no" before the series of body parts and sensations applies to all the words in each list, and the two other lists are abbreviated. Much like nature in the second line of Guanxiu's poem "Spring," the concept of emptiness cannot be approached with conventional language. It can only be reached via the *via negativa*.

The roots of Buddhist apophatic discourse run much deeper and wider than the *Heart Sūtra*. The early scriptures portray the Buddha as trying to quash irrelevant speculations (Skt. *avyākṛta*) by refusing to discuss them. Among these we find questions about the eternality of the world and the existence of the Buddha after entering into nirvāna.⁴⁷ The set of questions posed to the Buddha, which he refused to answer, took the form of *catuṣkoṭi*, or "four alternative positions" (Ch. *siju* 四句). These four possible positions, according to this logical structure, are:

1) A (*you* 有),
2) not-A (*wu* 無),
3) both A and not-A (*yi you yi wu* 亦有亦無),
4) neither A nor not-A (*fei you fei wu* 非有非無).

In plain English, we could render these as *yes*, *no*, *both*, and *neither*.⁴⁸ The Buddha, resolute in his silence on whether or not he would exist after death, denied all of them:

I have not declared that a Tathāgatha exists after death;
I have not declared that a Tathāgatha does not exist after death;
I have not declared that a Tathāgatha both exists and does not exist after death;
I have not declared that a Tathāgatha neither exists nor does not exist after death.⁴⁹
如來終，如來不終，如來終不終，如來亦非終亦非不終。

Later Buddhist thinkers would find the four positions a useful framework for thinking through other matters. Most famously, Nāgārjuna (second–third cent. CE) drew on this technique to elaborate his "Middle Way," which extended the logic of no-self to all phenomena, asserting that they are empty of fixed, eternal essence. This doctrine of emptiness would become foundational to the Mahāyāna schools that thrived in East Asia. Nāgārjuna, like the Buddha of the *Āgamas*, used the four positions of the *catuṣkoṭi* only to deny them. Unlike the Buddha, he did not do this out of commitment to silence but instead in order to elaborate his own positions that could not be contained by the categories of mundane thought.⁵⁰ Nonetheless, he puts forth his doctrine using the same logical categories.

Poet-monks would have encountered the *catuṣkoṭi* in their monastic training, as it appears in many of the most popular sūtras of the time as well as commentaries on them.⁵¹ At least one, Shenyu, used the same framework to describe poetry. In one section of his poetry manual (*Shige* 詩格), titled "On the Chin Couplet" 論頷聯, he analyzes the relationship between surface-level and symbolic meaning in the second couplet of a regulated octave, describing the four ways they can succeed or fail:

> Regulated poetry has chin couplets, which are also called "Tying to the Topic" because they are the most fully tied to the idea of a work.[52] The idea reaches in four ways: 1) the line reaches, but the idea does not, 2) the idea reaches, but the line does not, 3) the idea and the line both reach, and 4) neither the idea nor the line reach.
> From the poem "Mid-Autumn Moon":
>
> > The single wheel's full tonight,
> > Where is there not its clear light?[53]
>
> Here the line reaches but the idea does not. Next, from the poem "On a Fan":
>
> > When sweat streams and soaks backs,
> >   he exerts his power.
> > When the air cools in mid-autumn,
> >   he turns his heart away.[54]
>
> Here the idea reaches, but the line does not. Next, from the poem "On a Willow":
>
> > In the temple of the beauty of Witch Mountain,
> >   the base holds rain.
> > Before the home of Song Yu,
> >   the slanting light brings a breeze.[55]
>
> Here the idea and the line both reach. Next, from the poem "New Year's Eve":
>
> > In tall pines whirl rain and snow.
> > A whole room is covered by incense and lamp.[56]
>
> Here neither the idea nor the line reach.[57]

詩有頷聯，亦名束題，束盡一篇之意。其意有四到：一曰句到意不到，二曰意到句不到，三曰意句俱到，四曰意句俱不到。《中秋月》詩：「此夜一輪滿，清光何處無。」是句到意不到也。《詠扇》詩：「汗流浹背曾施力，氣爽中秋便負心。」是意到句不到也。《詠柳》詩：「巫娥廟裏低含雨，宋玉宅前斜帶風。」是意句俱到也。《除夜》詩：「高松飄雨雪，一室掩香燈。」是意句俱不到也。

This passage distinguishes between a literal meaning (referred to as "the line," *ju* 句) and symbolic meaning (referred to as "the idea," *yi* 意), a distinction elsewhere called "inner and outer meanings" (*neiwai yi* 內外意).[58] A poem in which the idea reaches but the line does not, then, is one that conveys its symbolic sense in a compelling manner but appears uninspired on the surface. In the couplet from "On a Fan" given above, the symbolic meaning is clear—the fan is a figure for a scorned lover—but the surface meaning stumbles along (why would a man turn his heart against a literal fan?). The other couplets illustrate their positions in similar ways. But my focus here is the structure of Shenyu's description, not the content of it. It takes two terms in an oppositional pair (line and meaning) and outlines their possible relations in the same way as a classic Buddhist logician's *yes, no, both*, and *neither*.[59] We thus see here at least one very specific way that a poet-monk adopted a Buddhist practice to conceptualize a poetic one.

In translated scriptures, the practice of fourfold negation, combined with the Indic tendency toward systematic lists, naturally leads to a curious and repetitious sort of vocabulary when rendered into classical Chinese. For example, the *Mahāparinirvāna Sūtra* describes the Buddha's nirvāna as follows:

> Not something and not nothing, not created and not uncreated, not defiled and not undefiled, not formed and not formless, not named and not nameless, not attributeful and not attributeless, not existing and not existenceless, not substantial and not substanceless, not cause and not effect, not dependent and not independent, not bright and not dark, not manifest and not unmanifest, not constant and not inconstant, not ceasing and not ceaseless, not beginning and not ending, not past or present or future, not composed of aggregates and not aggregateless, not sensate and not insensate, not cognate and not incognate, not subject to the twelve phases of dependent origination and not free from the twelve phases of dependent origination.[60]

> 非有非無，非有爲非無爲，非有漏非無漏，非色非不色，非名非不名，非相非不相，非有非不有，非物非不物，非因非果，非待非不待，非明非闇，非出非不出，非常非不常，非斷非不斷，非始非終，非過去非未來非現在，非陰非不陰，非入非不入，非界非不界，非十二因緣非不十二因緣。

The list proceeds systematically through the attributes of existence and denies them and their opposites. Each clause begins with the propositional negative *fei* 非 ("it is not the case that," likely translating the Sanskrit verb *nāsti*), to which is frequently added the negative adverb *bu* 不 or the negating verb *wu* 無 (both likely translating the Sanskrit prefix *a-/an-*) to indicate the second half of the paired attributes. The formal effect of the text is noteworthy. The structure *"fei X fei bu X"* becomes a refrain and creates a rhythm that overwhelms the passage. In the end, the brute force of the formula's repetition is as much the point to be made as anything concerning epistemology.

It is precisely this formula, found in many other Buddhist scriptures as well, which Guanxiu deploys in the opening of one of his few poems explicitly on Buddhist doctrine.[61]

Gāthās on the Nature of the Way: 2 of 3 道情偈三首（其二）

Guanxiu

Not formed, not empty,
    and not un-empty:
Within emptiness is true form—
    it is not clean and clear.
How enviable was Great Lu,
    the firewood hauler,[62]
Who grabbed a morel pearl
    within the bellows![63]

非色非空非不空，
空中真色不玲瓏。
可憐盧大擔柴者，
拾得驪珠橐籥中。[64]

The first couplet of this poem uses highly controlled language in an attempt to describe Buddhist ontology. Four out of seven characters in the first line are negatives. The first two lines use only eight unique characters, and *fei* 非, *se* 色, *kong* 空, and *bu* 不 account for over two-thirds of the characters used therein (ten of fourteen). Despite this limited vocabulary, the poem still manages to fit the metrical requirements for well-formed regulated verse. At the same time, this restricted use of language alerts us to the fact that we are looking at didactic religious verse (*gāthā*), not the typical high *shi*-poetry that Guanxiu usually writes. Both *se* and *kong*, after all, are technical Buddhist terms, and the patterns of negation are taken directly from the scriptures. The alliterative binom at the conclusion of line 2, *linglong* 玲瓏, opens the door to a less restrained use of language, and we find a normal range of vocabulary in the final couplet. This leads us to the story of Huineng, the illiterate laborer who achieved sainthood by writing a poem. The "morel pearl" is a pearl hidden beneath the chin of a morel (i.e., black) dragon. Although it originally came from a parable in the *Zhuangzi*, by Guanxiu's time it was commonly used in Buddhist texts to refer to universal buddha-nature (the pearl), which is difficult to realize from within the dangers of saṃsāra (the morel dragon).[65] In this way, Guanxiu's *gāthā* balances apophatic and kataphatic approaches: the first couplet describes buddha-nature negatively, using abstract terms, while the second couplet describes it positively, using concrete terms. At the same time, both couplets underscore the interpenetration of *saṃsāra* and *nirvāṇa*. buddha-nature is both un-empty and not, has no form and a true form in couplet 1. In couplet 2, the morel pearl that Huineng found is within "the bellows" (*tuoyue* 橐籥) of heaven and earth, a kenning that harkens back to the *Zhuangzi* and reminds the educated reader of the world's simultaneous productivity and emptiness. Repetition here is a literary technique for underscoring the poem's religious aims: describing indescribable reality.

These repetitive, multilayered negations in philosophical texts perhaps reach their peak with Guanding's 灌頂 (561–632) sub-commentary to the *Mahāparinirvāṇa Sūtra*. Guanding was to the Tiantai patriarch Zhiyi 智顗 (538–597) what Plato was to Socrates: a disciple who reportedly transcribed his master's teachings and fundamentally shaped the way later generations saw the master.[66] His works were well known in Chinese Buddhist circles of the late ninth century, and Guanxiu in particular had traveled to both Mount Tiantai and Mount Wutai, which were the main homes to the legacies of Zhiyi and Guanding at the time.[67] In his *Mahāparinirvāṇa* sub-commentary, Guanding addresses the ontology of the Buddha's *vajra* body 金剛身, seeking to explain how "the true body and the false body are formed interdependently" 是身非身因緣相成.[68] To do this, he attempts to catalog all possible positions toward "true" and "false" one could take, providing an expansive elaboration of the *catuṣkoṭi*. This catalog identifies "simple" 單, "repeated" 複, and "complete" 具足 forms of the fourfold schema. A full study of Guanding's categories would be beyond the scope of this book, but one example might help convey how this form of argumentation could have influenced literary style in Buddhist circles. In the "repeated" form of negation, Guanding essentially squares the original *catuskoti*. That is, he takes the positions A, not-A, both A and not-A, and neither A nor not-A, and fills in the variable A with the positions of the *catuskoti*. This gives us sixteen possible negatives:

1) To false "false";
2) to false "not false";
3) to false "both false and not false";
4) to false "neither false nor not false."

5) To not false "false";
6) to not false "not false";
7) to not false "both false and not false";
8) to not false "neither false nor not false."

9) To both false and not false "false";
10) to both false and not false "not false";
11) to both false and not false "both false and not false";
12) to both false and not false "neither false nor not false."

13) To neither false nor not false "false";
14) to neither false nor not false "not false";
15) to neither false nor not false "both false and not false";
16) to neither false nor not false "neither false nor not false."

非非。非不非。非亦非亦不非。非非非非不非。不非非。不非不非。不非亦非亦不非。不非非非非不非。亦非亦不非非。亦非亦不非不非。亦非亦不非　亦非亦不非。亦非亦不非　非非非不非。非非非不非非。非非非不非非非。非非非不非亦非亦不非。非非非不非非非非不非。[69]

The punctuation and numbers are modern additions to this passage. A look at the original text (especially if one mentally removes the punctuation) reveals an overwhelming amount of repetition of the character *fei* 非 ("false," "neither," "nor"), appearing up to five times in a row. Logically, this formula could continue to be compounded into infinity. For example, the cubed form of 16 would be: "to neither false nor not false 'neither falsing nor not falsing "neither false nor not false"'" 非非非不非非非非不非非非非不非. The resulting formulas may be difficult to grasp conceptually, but anyone can hear their haunting, incantatory rhythm. In his attempts to comprehensively account for metacognition, Guanding establishes an aesthetics of potentially endless repetition.

My purpose here is not to claim that poet-monks of the Late Tang memorized or even studied Guanding's commentary, although it is certainly the case that his and Zhiyi's teachings influenced many forms of Tang Buddhism, including those later designated "Chan." My purpose is to demonstrate that the very practice of reasoning by using the *catuṣkoṭi*, combined with the logographic Chinese script, opened up possibilities of repetitious language. The doubling of *shi* 是 ("true") and *fei* 非 ("false") had precedent in the Chinese classics. In the *Xunzi* 荀子, for example, we find the adage: "Regarding 'true' as true and 'false' as false—call it wisdom; regarding 'false' as true and 'true' as false—call it folly" 是是非非謂之知，非是是非謂之愚.[70] However, it was not until a Chinese commentator (who was likely familiar with *Xunzi*) elaborated on an originally Indian form of logic that we get the staggering heights of repetition found in Guanding.[71] It was such elite monks, drawing on the multiple traditions at their disposal, who created the aesthetic possibilities later fulfilled by poet-monks and Buddhist-adjacent poets at the end of the ninth century.

One such fulfillment can be found in another poem by Guanxiu. Here he opens with a reflection on the ontology and metacognition of true and false before pivoting to the more typical melancholic tone of exchange poetry.

Written Offhand, Having Thought of a Clergyman in the Mountains 偶作因懷山中道侶

> Guanxiu

Regarding the true as true and the false as false
    is not ultimately real.
Falling petals and flowing water
    bid verdant spring farewell.
The one named Liu and the one named Xiang—
    where are they now?[72]
They strove for fame, strove for fortune,
    grieving one to death.
In the end, there is always a stillness
    in losing to others;
In the same way, there is a painful stubbornness
    in victory.[73]

Clergyman of the deep clouds,
    do you think of me or not?
Come on back—*hey*—
    to the banks of the Xiang.

是是非非竟不真，
落花流水送青春。
姓劉姓項今何在，
爭利爭名愁殺人。
必竟輸他常寂默，
只應贏得苦沈淪。
深雲道者相思否，
歸去來兮湘水濱。[74]

Buddhist ontology is introduced here as a coping mechanism. The mundane world is not real: neither this separation nor these tears bear any ultimate significance. This contrasts with the verdant landscape (line 2), which teems with life. The focus on the landscape brings us to the sense of place that suffuses the poem. The allusion to Xiang Yu (232–202 BCE), the hero of Chu who famously battled future Han dynasty founder Liu Bang (256–195 BCE), grounds us in the Changsha region. Two allusions to the *Songs of Chu* (lines 6 and 8) reinforce this setting. Guanxiu lingers on the rich poetic history of the area, conjuring a tragic atmosphere with the phrase "the banks of the Xiang" 湘水濱, the place where the wrongly accused poet-minister Qu Yuan drowned himself. These cultural heroes, no matter their striving, are gone (lines 3–4)—a point emphasized with the "double drafting" technique, with "named" and "strove" repeated. Liu Bang and Xiang Yu show us that loss can be better than victory, in that it brings us stillness rather than suffering (lines 5–6). But all the lessons of antiquity and all the indeterminacies of Buddhist ontology are not enough. The speaker's emotions overwhelm him, his equanimity falters, and he ends up longing for his friend, begging him to return (lines 7–8). The tension between ideals and reality is set up by appealing to both metaphysical and historical justifications for detachment. The repetitious opening, with its echoes of *Xunzi* and the *catuṣkoṭi*, acts as a kind of thesis statement for the poem, only to find itself undermined by the conclusion. A correct attitude to truth and falsity cannot prevent sorrow.

The apophatic nature of much Chinese Buddhist doctrine lent itself to multiple layers of repetition. The *catuṣkoṭi* and Guanding's elaboration thereof established a negative discourse that later poets would draw on. A rare talent like Guanxiu could exploit these possibilities within the structure of regulated heptameter. More often, such repetitive discourse appears in song-style poems. Either way, the poems take a side effect of apophasis—its mesmerizing repetitions—and exploit its musical possibilities. The negations of Buddhist philosophy are one source of the poet-monks' tendency toward repetition.

Songs from the Dunhuang corpus also drew on this apophatic tradition, often in very conspicuous ways. Although we have no information about the author of the following verse (and therefore cannot definitively attribute it to a poet-monk), it is clearly Buddhist in theme and is written to a *yuefu* song title that had long been part of both the high literati and the Buddhist doctrinal traditions.[75] Given that the manuscript observes taboos related to the female Emperor Wu Zetian 武則天 (r. 690–705), it is one of the earlier surviving examples of retriplication. Characters of negation (*bu* 不, *fei* 非, and *wu* 無) appear twenty-seven times in twenty lines, creating an ontological maze. Although the reality of the concepts mentioned in the song would take some work to tease out, an oral performance would leave one overwhelmed by the repetitive quality of the soundscape.

[Traveling's Hard]
XVI

Do you not see
No-mind's great wisdom?
Bare and broad, bare and broad,
   it is without bounds or borders.
Without obstacle it interfuses,
   detached from being and non-.
Subtly it pervades,
   containing each and all.

Each and all it pervades,
   forgetting this and that.
As thus-thusness is equal,
   one can discuss denying affirming.
Denying affirming and affirming affirming,
   are labeled empty emptiness.
Empty emptiness is itself empty,
   and for all dharmas it is so.[76]

For all dharmas it is so: empty emptiness
   is without other or self.
The wisdom eye reflects brightly,
   forever not dualizing.
Not dualizing, it is without knowing
   and without not knowing.
Non-knowing not knowing—
   call this great knowledge.

Great knowledge is not brightness,
   and is not not bright.
Not bright is not brightness, is not bright,
   without bright brightness.
The reflecting of non-brightness
   does not reflect reflections.
The reflecting of not reflecting
   is without arising.

Traveling's hard,
Traveling's hard.

No-mind is truly pure and tranquil.
Showing no concern
   for nirvāna and samsāra,
It is vast vast as emptiness
   and without impediment.

[行路難]
第六˙十

君不見	-
無心之大慧	A
廓々落々無邊際	A
無礙虛融離有無	-
微妙疏通含一々	A
切々疏通忘彼此	B
如々平等論非是	B
非是是是号空空	-
空空亦空乃法尔	B

法爾空空無他自	C
慧眼明照恆不二	C
不二無知無不知	*C
無知不知稱大智	C
大智非明非不明	D
不明非明不明無明々	D
無明之照不照々	-
不照之照乃無生	D
行路々	E
難々	E
無心甚清泰	F
涅槃生死不關懷	*F
蕩々如空無罣碍	F[77]

Reduplication is abundant in the poem, and there are ten cases of anadiplosis in a total of twenty-two lines, in many instances of which the second line picks up the phrase from the first line only to subvert or negate it. Double negation is matter of course here. All of this rapid-fire repetition seems to have led to a breakdown of the poem's rhyme scheme: instead of one rhyme being carried from lines 2–17—as in the other poems in this cycle of "Traveling's Hard" found in the same manuscript—we have four (two of which are slant rhymes, which accord in ending but not tone). This breakdown reflects on a phonic level the breakdown of binaries when one has reached no-mind, and the mundane rhyme scheme, like the mundane world, falls to the wayside.

This Dunhuang song is an extreme example of what happens when the Buddhistic tendency toward repetition is combined with the euphonic yearnings of verse. I am not arguing that such songs influenced elite poet-monks like Guanxiu. We have scant evidence for such a claim.[78] What I do hope to show is that the propensity for repetition in the works of Guanxiu, Qiji, Shenyu, and other poet-monks comes out of the same discursive environment as the Dunhuang song. Buddhist apophasis encouraged a profusion of negative particles, and poets could draw on this resource to create unusual, sonorous rhythms.[79] It was a rhetorical strategy strongly associated with Buddhism in Tang China—one that pervaded the poet-monks' daily lives—that spurred the development of this poetic technique.

In this chapter, we have pulled on one thread of the poet-monks' poetics and seen how it is tangled up with a host of literary and religious practices. Retriplication is not only a real phenomenon that had previously gone all but unnoticed in literary history, it is one of the most obtrusive poetic techniques employed by monks of the late medieval period. It can be used to intensify (simple retriplication), force a reader to pause and parse (complex), and create connections across line breaks (anadiplotic). Although related to the technique of reduplication, retriplication is by no means a simple extension of it. Being so rarely used, it would have been utterly defamiliarizing to Tang audiences. Being rather cumbersome within the strict meters of classical poetry, it was also related to the practice of caesura violation. In this way, retriplication is one of the most conspicuous aspects of the poet-monks' literary style.

Retriplication is the most extreme version of one kind of technique employed by the poet-monks—the repetition of individual characters in startling ways. This literary technique shares key features with the apophatic discursive tradition in Buddhism, best exemplified by fourfold negation (the *catuṣkoṭi*). The tendency to define key concepts through negation, the negation of negation, the negation of negation of negation, and so on, leads to a peculiar use of language that sounded especially strange in the classical Chinese context. The elite poet-monk tradition (represented by Guanxiu) drew on the unusual rhythms of apophasis in order to establish new uses of language in poetry. This sonority was also, in the strictest sense of the term, incantatory. And incantation, we will see, formed another core element in the poet-monks' conception of Buddhist poetry.

CHAPTER 5

Incantation

Sonority and Foreignness

Spells were a common feature of the religious landscape of late medieval China. They were part of the shared common religion of the pre-imperial period, and they were widely used by Daoists and Buddhists in their ritual practices.[1] In Buddhism, they were not only a core feature of Tantrism and proto-Tantrism but also appeared next to texts associated with Chan lineages and in some cases were part of the necessary preparation for effective meditation.[2] They were part of a general, pan-Asian Mahāyāna culture from which most East Asian Buddhist traditions drew.[3] People at all levels of society, from commoners to conquerors, trusted that chanting and writing spells would bring them benefits. Spells were a kind of spiritual technology, and Buddhist monks were some of the chief technicians who wielded them. They were inscribed on *dhāraṇī* pillars all across the late medieval Sinosphere, often with supplementary text by eminent poets.[4]

In the same way, Buddhist scriptures were understood to be incredibly powerful as spiritual objects. They were not just literary texts that one could mine for allusions, like the *Book of Odes* or *Wenxuan*. The *Lotus Sūtra*, to take just one example, promises happiness, virtues of the senses, the protection of the Buddha, and ultimate enlightenment to those who copy, recite, expound, and uphold it.[5] Tales of its miraculous power were widespread in China from at least the fifth century and would appear all over East Asia in monks' hagiographies and other tales.[6] Two collections of miracle tales dedicated specifically to the *Lotus* survive from the Tang dynasty.[7] It was understood to be present not just in its written form but also on the tongues of those who recited it and in the minds of those who memorized it.[8] To those who upheld it, the *Lotus Sūtra* became an integral part of their very being.[9] Simply reciting or copying the *Lotus* or other scriptures could have enormous supernatural effects, and monks were in charge of these scriptures.

The recitation of both spells and scriptures are types of incantation. Incantation, broadly defined, refers to the use of sonorous, extraordinary language that, when properly activated, accesses spiritual powers to bring benefit or injury to oneself or others.[10] Incantatory language has two main characteristics: it is sonorous, and it is extraordinary, usually foreign. That is, the recitation of spells and scriptures depends on the proper articulation of their sounds and on their purported origins in a different realm. For Buddhists, this was usually India, which many understood to have a more authentic connection with the supramundane powers of the Buddha. Through such sonorous, extraordinary language, incantation connects one to other realms and the beings that dwell in them.

This chapter describes how poet-monks of the ninth and tenth centuries drew on incantatory patterns to lend power to their literary works. It begins by examining a set of rare manuscripts from Dunhuang to demonstrate how at least one community of early readers understood the compatibility of poetry and incantation. From there, I explore Guanxiu's and Qiji's fascination with the power of sonority and of the foreign. Both of these principles figure prominently throughout their extant collections and come together most effectively in their poems on recitations of the *Lotus Sūtra*, with which I conclude the chapter. In such poems, they articulate a new vision of the possibilities of Chinese Buddhist poetry, a poetry that would blend classically Confucian and Buddhist practices.

This is not to say that only poet-monks paid attention to sonority or foreignness in poetry. Scholars who have attempted to hear Tang poetry through reconstructions of Middle Chinese often find that it is richer in melopoeia than normally understood.[11] As Christopher Nugent has noted, Tang poetry was "intensely oral," and sound was one of the main media through which it was composed and circulated.[12] Likewise, the question of what constituted foreignness and how it should relate to

Tang culture (*wen*) was a central concern to many literati, with Han Yu being only the most prominent example.[13] Both of these concerns—sonority and foreignness—are also prominent in poems on music, albeit with very different connotations. What I am arguing in this chapter is that monks' relationship to performative speech was different from that of the literati. As specialists in the recitation of spells, scriptures, and ritual texts, they understood that, through certain locutionary acts, they could connect to and manipulate spiritual powers.[14] We can find evidence of these incantatory practices in poet-monks' works, traces that, in the aggregate, can help us understand some of their more striking aspects.

Spells and Scriptures

Though Guanxiu left behind nearly eight hundred poems in his extant collection, only three survive in manuscript form from the late medieval period.[15] The most accomplished of these describes an exemplary recitation of the *Lotus Sūtra*. The *Lotus* is perhaps the most influential Buddhist text in East Asia, and it is one that Guanxiu himself was personally invested in. He had spent his youth memorizing it a thousand characters at a time, and he later preached on it before crowds at Yuzhang 豫章, "clearly and diligently explaining its subtle, profound meaning" 精奧義講訓且勤, as one source puts it.[16] He alludes to the *Lotus Sūtra* in his poems and in notes he wrote to his poems, one of which describes other monks' appreciations of his own recitations.[17]

Guanxiu's poem on a *Lotus Sūtra* recitation demonstrates the depth of his faith in its power. The poem, with its overload of terms related to the body and to sound, stresses the efficacy of intoning spiritually potent texts. The chanting monk embodies the incantatory power of the *Lotus* through his recitation.

In Praise of the *Lotus Sūtra*-Reciting Monk 讚念法華經僧
Guanxiu

Beneath the gate of the King of Emptiness,
    there is a true son[18]
Who's willing to serve
    the King of Emptiness.[19]
He always upholds the lotus blossom,
    the pure *Lotus Sūtra*.[20]

Count it out on your fingers: none
    come close to his likeness.
    Beneath the tall pines,
    Within the deep windows:
Clear, clear are his pure tones,
    his resonant *gong*- and *zhi*-notes.
Short *gāthā*s and long lines:
    host and guest are distinct,[21]
Not letting idle sounds
    hang from his teeth.
    Outsiders hear,
    Heed their two ears:
A fragrant breeze enters their noses,
    and the hairs on their skin stand up.
They see only heavenly blossoms
    falling before his seat.[22]
Undoubtedly, there are spirits and ghosts
    in the sky.

My master must strive forth,
Having accumulated merit
    over many years.
Mulberry fields turn to seas,
    bones become dust,
But his roots are red like a lotus.

空王門下有真子，	A
堪以空王爲了使。	A
常持菡萏白蓮經，	-
屈指無人得相似。	A
長松下，	-
深窻裏，	A
歷々清音韻宮徵。	A
矩偈長行主客分，	B
不使閑聲掛牙齒。	A
外人聞，	B
聳雙耳，	A
香風襲鼻寒毛起。	A
只見天花落座前，	-
空中必定有神鬼。	A

吾師須努力,	C
年深已是成功積。	C
桑田變海骨爲塵,	-
根似紅蓮色。	C²³

Guanxiu underscores the monk's embodiment of the *Lotus Sūtra*'s numinous power by focusing on his physicality. The reciter's body becomes a site of passage, with incense entering, musical notes leaving, and no "idle sounds" hanging from his teeth (line 8). It is the very place where the sūtra abides for the duration of the recitation and is therefore a place worthy of attention and veneration.

The detail with which the poem describes the sound of the sūtra reciter stresses its spiritual efficacy. The reciting monk's voice is clear and precise (line 6), differentiating between the verse sections and the prose in his enunciation ("short *gāthās*" vs. "long lines"). His chanting affects the noses, skin hair, and visions of non-Buddhists (lines 9–11). The closing, exhortative stanza follows logically from this: the speaker encourages him to continue his recitations and add to his considerable merit (line 14). Even as his body and the whole world wear away, his "roots"—sensory organs, likely the tongue specifically here—remain miraculously vibrant (lines 15–16). The monk's oral recitation activates the sūtra's power. It unleashes a force of nature, the likes of which is normally seen only in miracle tales.

We can perceive further play on the sonic level. The poem declares its song-like sonority by remaining close to, but deviating just enough from, the norms of regulated heptameter 七言律詩. Most obviously, the poem's rhythm shifts for the closing quatrain, from the standard seven-beat pace to 5-7-7-5.²⁴ This final quatrain, in which the mood shifts from descriptive to exhortative, is also set off by a change in rhyme, from —*i* to —*ik*. Both rhymes belong to the deflected tonal class (*zesheng* 仄聲), so they would not be permitted under standard regulation. Nevertheless, they function as a euphonous half rhyme because the vowel remains the same even as the tone changes. Furthermore, the poem's tonal patterning tends toward standard regulation, but it does not conform completely. The two places where it deviates from normal meter can themselves be seen to comprise a pattern: both appear at the end of meaningful quatrains, both belong to opposite tonal classes, one invokes the poem's A rhyme, and the other internally rhymes with the poem's main subject.²⁵

Guanxiu's poem is incantatory because it demonstrates faith in sound as a means of accessing a supramundane force. The manuscript context in which it appears reinforces this. Immediately following Guanxiu's poem in both P.2104 and S.4037 is a long series of spells and mantras (see figure 5.1). Like the poem itself, these ritual texts emphasize sonority as a way to achieve religious efficacy. Guanxiu's poem and the spells are part of a sequence of ritual texts that appears in three separate manuscripts (S.4037, P.2104, and P.2105).[26] This sequence includes:

1. "Digest of the Essentials of Meditation" (Chanmen biyao jue 禪門秘要決), a long, tetrametric verse that serves as a primer on the basics of Buddhist practice; it is nearly identical with the received "Song of the Realization of the Way" (Zhengdao ge 證道歌) attributed to Yongjia Xuanjue 永嘉玄覺 (665–713).[27]
2. Several untitled didactic *gāthā*s that in other sources are attributed to the monks Benjing 本淨 and Judun 居遁.
3. A "Text for the Transfer of Merit after the Transfer of Scriptures" (Zhuanjing hou huixiangwen 轉經後迴向文).[28]
*4. Guanxiu's "In Praise of the *Lotus Sūtra*-Reciting Monk" (Zan nian Fahuajing seng 讚念法華經僧).
5. A spell to be recited "in order to get rid of all fear" (*chu yiqie weibu* 除一切怖畏).
6. "Inscription on Seated Meditation" (Zuochan ming 坐禪銘), a brief, trimetric verse on how to meditate.
7. A long sequence of other spells. These include "Spell for Release from Purgatory" (Diyu cuisui zhou 地獄摧碎呪), "Spell for Contemplating the Three Paths" (Ruo nian sandao zhou 若念三道呪), "Spell for Distributing Food" (Sanshi zhou 散食呪), spells to accompany offerings to bodhisattvas in each of the four seasons, and many others.[29]

All of these texts have practical purposes. The "Digest" and "Inscription" provide instructions on fundamental practices and doctrines associated with medieval Buddhism, the *gāthā*s illustrate some of these basic principles with brief analogies, the transfer of merit text instructs a monk on how a scribe may donate to a benefactor the good merit accumulated by copying a scripture, and the spells give one protection against malevolent forces or accompany various offerings to deities. As a whole, the manuscript functions as a ritual toolbox.[30] It contains a set of texts that a monk may wish to apply in various, commonly encountered circumstances: instructing a novice, encouraging a junior, copying a scripture, encountering fear, distributing meals, paying homage to bodhisattvas, and so on. One version (P.2104) is marked up in red to indicate section

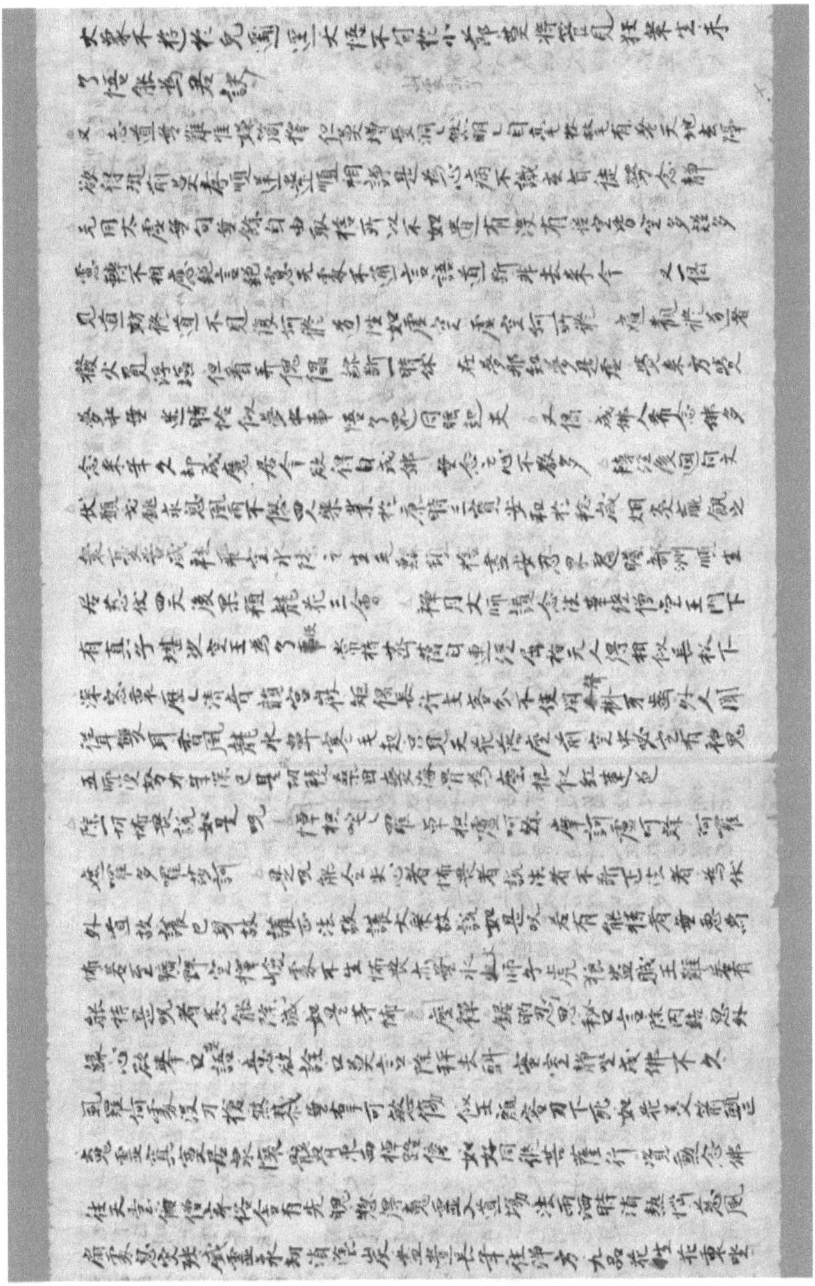

FIGURE 5.1. Detail from P. 2104, verso. Guanxiu's poem begins in the center of this section. The spell to get rid of all fear immediately follows it, just to the left of the vertical line where two sheets of paper have been glued together. The inclusion of Guanxiu's poem in such a ritual toolbox suggests lines of continuity between incantation, sūtra recitation, and poetry.

breaks and facilitate easier access to its various parts.³¹ This implies that these texts were copied to be used, not just venerated. These texts are tools that help a monk accomplish his professional duties.

The appearance of Guanxiu's poem in this sequence is no accident. Of the three versions of the ritual toolbox, two manuscripts include his poem (S. 4037 and P. 2104), while one does not (P.2105). We do not know whether the version lacking Guanxiu's poem is earlier or later than the other manuscripts, so we cannot say exactly what kind of editing happened in the process of copying this sequence. Whether Guanxiu's poem was added or deleted, it is clear that a historical actor intervened in the process of transmitting this sequence in order to adjust it. This implies that the ritual toolbox was a meaningful sequence of text, albeit one that could be tailored to different needs.

One reason Guanxiu's poem would have been included in such a ritual collection is because his poem illustrates the efficacy of incantation. It shows how the recitation of spiritually potent texts (such as scriptures and spells) can summon natural and supernatural forces. The poem itself is carefully crafted to sound pleasant to Late Tang ears, nearing but not slavishly following the norms of regulated verse. Its content too reinforces the importance of sound: the monk reciting the *Lotus Sūtra* in Guanxiu's poem gives the reader an ideal to strive for. He attends closely to his pronunciation and vocal modulation, and, as a result, the audience experiences a fragrant breeze, a vision of flowers falling from the sky, and the presence of gods and ghosts. The sound of the *Lotus Sūtra* creates miracles.

We can see the same incantatory logic at work in the spells in the ritual toolbox. The spell immediately following Guanxiu's poem, originally found in the *Mahāparinirvāṇa Sūtra*, illustrates this. It contains four elements: an introduction (A), the spell itself in transliterated pseudo-Sanskrit (B), a description of its powers (C), and a concluding phrase (D). It explicitly states the way that its recitation may quell fear by accessing paranormal forces.³²

[A]
In order to get rid of all fear, say this spell:
除一切怖畏說如是呪。
[B]
*Taki, tatarataki, rokarei, makarokarei, ara, shara, tara, shaka.*³³
悼枳，咃咃羅卓枳，嚧呵餘，摩訶嚧呵餘，阿囉，遮囉，多囉，莎訶。

[C]
This spell can put at ease one with a scattered mind, one who is terrified, one who is explaining the Dharma, and one who shall never be cut off from the true Dharma. For the purpose of overcoming heterodox ways, for the purpose of protecting oneself, for the purpose of protecting the true Dharma, and for the purpose of protecting the great assembly, say such a spell.

If there are any who can uphold it, they will be free of the fear of a mad elephant. If they reach an expanse of wilderness, an empty marsh, or a precipitous place, fear will not arise. Moreover, they will be free of the hardships of water, fire, lions, tigers, wolves, thieves, and hardship imposed by rulers.

是呪能合失心者，怖畏者，説法者，不斷正法者，為伏外道故，護己身故，護正法故，護大衆故，説如是呪。若有能持者，無惡象怖，若至曠野，空澤嶮?，不生怖畏，亦無水火、師子、虎狼、盜賊、王難。

[D]
If there are any who can uphold this spell, they will be able to rid themselves of all these things and such fears.

若有能持是呪者，悉能除滅，如是等怖。

The spell calms the mind in the face of many kinds of difficulties. It may be applied to specifically religious problems, such as trouble in explaining the Dharma, and it may also be applied to more mundane problems, such as wild beasts and corrupt officials. But this spell is effective only if it is said aloud (*shuo* 説) in transliterated Sanskrit, a string of syllables that is meaningless as Chinese but purports to represent the sounds of an Indic original. The spell's efficacy is so closely connected to its aural qualities that it cannot be translated into legible Chinese. Such faith in extraordinary, sonorous language as a means of activating spiritual power is the bedrock of incantation.

Sonority

Sonority is the root principle of incantation. Chants, spells, charms, prayers, and scripture recitations tend to be rhythmic, repetitive, and melodic. They often make use of poetic devices such as alliteration, assonance, and rhyme.[34] Northrop Frye summarized the views of many literary theorists when he described the deep formal similarities between lyric poetry and incantation: "The radical of *melos* is *charm*: the hypnotic incantation that, through its pulsing dance rhythm, appeals to involuntary physical response, and is hence not far from the sense of magic, or physically compelling power."[35] Tang documents as well often mention the aesthetic pleasures of hearing Buddhist monks recite or preach the scriptures.[36] The musical element of poetry, taken to its logical conclusion and given a more explicitly instrumental aim, is precisely incantation. Poetry, like incantation, declares faith in the power of the sound of abnormal, aestheticized language to move sentient beings. Guanxiu's poem on the *Lotus Sūtra* recitation stresses its aural power for this reason.

Spells, also known as *dhāraṇī* (Ch. *tuoluoni* 陀羅尼, *zhou* 呪, *zongchi* 總持, etc.) or *mantra* (Ch. *zhenyan* 真言), also rely on incantatory sonority for their power.[37] Even though spells and scriptures could be activated by ingesting, copying, or wearing them, sound was the primary medium through which one realized them.[38] Manuscript evidence, including that examined above, attests to the fact that spells are generally activated by speaking.

Given that spells were a common feature of the religious landscape of late medieval China, it should come as no surprise to find evidence of familiarity with these practices in the lives and works of late medieval poet-monks.[39] Though the poet-monks are most closely associated with meditative lineages and communities, they were also familiar with the esoteric ritual technologies that gained currency in the capital in the eighth century.[40] We can find some evidence for this in the poet-monks' activities outside of poetry. Wuke and his cousin Jia Dao, while the latter was still a monk, lived together at Qinglong Monastery 青龍寺 in Chang'an during the first decade of the ninth century at the same time that the esoteric master Huiguo 惠果 (746–805) resided there, training Kūkai and other monks.[41] Wuke was famous for his calligraphy of the *Uṣṇīṣavijayā-dhāraṇī Sūtra* 佛頂尊勝陀羅尼經 that was featured on a *dhāraṇī* pillar, and he also served as the editor of the court monk Ruichuan's 叡川 rendition of this same scripture.[42] Zhixuan 知玄 (809–881), a southwestern monk who had traveled to the capital, once recited a spell in hopes of correcting his accent. According to his hagiography, while living in the capital, "Zhixuan always despised his regional accent and was thus unwilling to engage in discussion or study. Then he recited the 'Spell of Great Compassion' at Mount Xiang'er [in his home region] and dreamed that a divine monk switched tongues with him. The next day his incorrect sounds turned into proper Chinese" 玄每恨鄉音不堪講貫，乃於象耳山誦「大悲呪」，夢神僧截舌換之，

明日俄變秦語矣。⁴³ He would later move back to the capital, where he used his newly honed voice to compose poetry; connect with literati such as Li Shangyin, Liu Deren, and Wen Tingyun 溫庭筠 (801?–867?); debate Daoists at court; and earn honors from multiple emperors. All of his later success, the hagiography implies, would not have been possible without the "Spell of Great Compassion." This powerful *dhāraṇī*, recited faithfully at a spiritually potent location, summoned a monk from the heavens to switch tongues with him. The sound of a spell cured the sound of his voice.

The monastic poet active in the latter half of the Tang who may have most clearly posed a connection between esoteric spells and literary writing is Kūkai. Regarded as the founder of Japanese Esoteric Buddhism (Shingon 真言), Kūkai traveled from 804 to 806 throughout Tang China, where he was formally consecrated as the dharma heir of the esoteric master Huiguo at Qinglong Monastery in Chang'an. Kūkai was a prolific writer in classical Chinese, composing original works and compiling others' on mantras and poetry alike. Though most of these were written after he had returned to Japan, many represent ideas he had picked up from Chinese teachers. A full accounting of Kūkai's views of the relationship between language, literature, and Buddhism would double the size of this book, but it is worth noting that he regarded them as deeply interconnected.⁴⁴ For example, in the preface to *Bunkyō hifuron* 文鏡秘府論, his collection and synthesis of Tang texts on poetics, he justifies his study of poetry by referring to the power of literary language:

> When the Great Transcendent brought benefit to the people, he used the teaching of names as his foundation.⁴⁵ When gentlemen came to the aid of their times, they took literature as their basis. . . . Thus the One was the beginning of names, and "patterns" (*wen*) was the well-spring of teaching.⁴⁶ When you consider the teaching of names as its ancestor, then literature is the key element of principles of order. Of those in the world or out of it, who can ignore this?⁴⁷ Therefore, the scriptures explain that an *avinivartanīya* bodhisattva must first understand literature.⁴⁸

> 夫大仙利物，名教爲基；君子濟時，文章是本也......然則一爲名始，文則教源，以名教爲宗，則文章爲紀綱之要也。世間出世，誰能遺此乎？故經說阿毗跋致菩薩，必須先解文章。

The key term in this passage is "the teaching of names" 名教, which has special significance to Kūkai. In other contexts, it may refer to the

Confucian project of rectifying names (*zhengming* 正名) and its resulting moral transformation, but here it refers to language instruction.[49] The idea that language functions as a kind of ancestor is one that Kūkai pulls from the treatise "On Literary Meaning" 論文意, likely written by Wang Changling and included in the "South" 南 section of *Bunkyō hifuron*.[50] Kūkai, however, puts a Buddhist spin on this statement, explaining how it is essential to a bodhisattva's training.

With this in mind, we should note how language instruction carries esoteric significance in one of his other works, "On the Meanings of Sound, Script, and Reality" 聲字實相義:

> The basis for taking refuge cannot be established without the teaching of names. The flourishing of the teaching of names cannot be established without clarifying sound and script. When sound and script are clear, reality will be revealed. What are called sound, script, and reality are the three esotericae of the universal dharma body, which is the basic *maṇḍa* of all sentient beings.
>
> 歸趣之本，非名教不立，名教之興，非聲字不立，聲字分明，而實相顯，所謂聲字實相者，即是法佛平等之三密，衆生本有之曼荼也。[51]

For Kūkai, language instruction is important because it highlights the need to understand sound, script, and reality. These form the three basic components of the dharma body of the glorified Buddha, which is equivalent to the essence of ultimate reality and sentient beings' basis in that essence. Connecting this insight with the preface from *Bunkyō hifuron*, it becomes clear that literature is of crucial importance for two reasons: first, it can help create and sustain societal order (*jigang* 紀綱); second, it has a privileged relationship to true language and thus the essence of ultimate reality.[52] While it is doubtful that every Chinese poet-monk shared Kūkai's esoteric view of language, it is important to understand it as one theoretical explanation that would connect literary and religious practices that these monks were familiar with.

We find evidence for poet-monks' familiarity with spells in their poetic works too. The monk Huaipu 懷浦 (dates unknown) describes another monk's daily devotion by referring to the ways the landscape intersects with his meditation and spell recitation: "The mountain snow, when encountered in meditation, is dark; / The sound of the pines, when entering spells, is cold" 嶽雪當禪暝，松聲入咒寒.[53] Spells, like the wind as it whistles through a pine forest, are sonic forces that produce tangible effects in the physical world. Huaipu presumes that spells are a fundamental part of a Buddhist monk's practice, on par with meditation, an assumption shared by Qiji: "Wielding spells requires a strength bestowed by fate, / And saving others necessitates a heart that resembles emptiness" 持咒力須資運祚，度人心要似虛空.[54] Both of these poems are written to monks with the title "Tripiṭaka" (Sanzang 三藏). This term refers to the "three baskets" into which the Buddhist scriptures are divided (*sūtra, śāstra,* and *vinaya*). As a title, it was used for Buddhist monks who had mastered all three of these baskets. The most famous monk with this title was Xuanzang 玄奘 (602-664), the pilgrim-translator, who became known popularly as "Tripiṭaka of the Tang dynasty" (Tang Sanzang 唐三藏). But the title was also given to many other monks, especially those who had greater familiarity with esoteric ritual technologies, such as Śubhakarasiṃha (Shanwuwei 善無畏, 637-735), Divākara (Rizhao 日照 or Dipokeluo 地婆訶羅, late seventh cent.), Cimin 慈愍 (also known as Huiri 慧日, 680-748), and Amoghavajra (Bukong 不空, 705-774).[55] There are nine Tang poems addressed to monks who hold the title Tripiṭaka, the earliest of which dates to the late eighth or early ninth century.[56] Most are addressed to monks who have access to esoteric spells and influence at court. Even in poetic discourse, spell recitation was understood to be one of the most powerful and most advanced practices that a Buddhist monk could master.

A poem written by Qiji for a monk named Tripiṭaka Zhiman 智滿三藏 is an especially clear example of this. It prominently features the specialized vocabulary of spells, bending the rules of Tang verse to include transliterated Sanskrit terms.

Given to Tripiṭaka Zhiman 贈智滿三藏
        Qiji

When you were anointed with a single, permeating drop
    of clear, cool water,
Mahāvairocana
    pervaded all of space.[57]
You want to soar like a champak
    blossom without limit,
But you must wait for your *dhāra-*
    ṇī to be efficacious.
Your adamantine-mallet power smashes
    the darkness of the demon realm,[58]

Your crystal light penetrates
    the red of night lanterns.[59]
Having been worthy of making offerings in the east
    to the bright Son of Heaven,
On you were bestowed a robe and a new response,
    in the service of the state's airs.[60]

灌頂清涼一滴通,
大毗盧藏遍虛空。
欲飛薝蔔花無盡,
須待陀羅尼有功。
金杵力摧魔界黑,
水精光透夜燈紅。
可堪東獻明天子,
命服新酬贊國風。[61]

Qiji's poem, first and foremost, is a flattering description of a ritual specialist summoned by one of the regional kings of the tenth century. As Zhiman heads east, Qiji wishes him well, using technical terminology to describe his spiritual prowess. Zhiman has been ritually purified and initiated into a tantric lineage (line 1), he sees Mahāvairocana, the Buddha's cosmic manifestation (line 2), and he wields an adamantine mallet (line 5) and emanates crystal light (line 6).

What makes this poem especially striking is Qiji's violation of poetic norms in lines 3–4. While the poem's rhymes and tonal pattern perfectly comply with the expectations of a regulated, heptametric octave, Qiji's enthusiasm for Buddhist vocabulary overrides the expected placement of the caesura after the fourth character. There is instead a pause after the fifth character, creating an unusual 2-3-2 rhythm: "You want to soar like | a champak blossom | without limit, / But you must wait for | your dhāraṇī | to be efficacious" 欲飛.薝蔔花.無盡, 須待.陀羅尼.有功. A significant deviation from the norms of Tang poetry, this very effectively grabs the reader's attention.[62] It is like seeing enjambment in a line by Alexander Pope. By violating normal caesura usage, Qiji stresses Zhiman's facility with the power of spells and his own facility with the vocabulary associated with it. We find similar deviations to emphasize transliterated Sanskrit words in poems by other monks, such as line 7 of Guanxiu's poem on the installation of a relic of the Buddha at Famen monastery in Chang'an in April 873, "Hearing that the True Body has been Received" 聞迎真

身: "The blossoms | of the utpala tree | are to be held dear" 可憐.優鉢羅.花樹.⁶³ In these poems, especially Qiji's, linguistic sound is used in an unconventional way to arrest the reader. In this way, we might liken it to a spell: it bends language to make it more sonorous and thereby create an effect in the world.⁶⁴

Guanxiu, like Qiji, was familiar with the ritual technologies of esoteric Buddhism. Both the *Lotus* and the *Śūraṃgama Sūtra*s, which we know Guanxiu studied intensely, contain long sections of *dhāraṇī* to which are attributed great spiritual powers. He also had some knowledge of the *Dhāraṇī Sūtra of the Jeweled Pavilion* (*Baolouge jing* 寶樓閣經) and the *Dhāraṇī Sūtra of the Great Protectress* (*Dasuiqiu tuoluoni jing* 大隨求陀羅尼經), as he mentions in a poem written for another monk who held the title Tripiṭaka.⁶⁵ In both cases, Guanxiu marvels at the power of the sound of these spells.

Written on the Temple of Tripiṭaka Hongyi 題弘顗三藏院⁶⁶

Guanxiu

Pure in demeanor, placid in bearing,
    with carved garnet rings;
You roll up your curtain, unruffled,
    without a speck of dust.
Your marchmount tea is frothy,
    the courtyard blossoms bloom,
And your faithful disciples
    come from time to time.

Gods fill up the adornments
    of your lustration platform,
And suffering is restrained
    by your thirty years' merit.
An Indic monk imparted subtle words
    to you in a dream;
On the snowy peaks, the white ox's
    strength is firmly attained.

A rope of crystal,
    a burner of incense—
From his red-lotus tongue
    comes ghee.

When I first listen to his throaty sounds
    of the Dhāraṇī of the Jeweled Pavilion,
It's like hearing of King Māra's
    palace being pulled down,
        its gold tiles falling.

Then I hear those marvelous sounds
    of the Dhāraṇī of the Great Protectress,
And further realize
That all events in the human realm
    are far, far away.
The four sounds combine to make
    the pure or the supple,
And the murky waves of the River of Desire
    flow backward.

They flow backward—*hey*—
    with nowhere to go:
Original nature's ocean contains emptiness,
    the glow of early dawn.

儀清態淡雕瓊環	-
捲簾瀟灑無塵埃	A
嶽茶如乳庭花開	A
信心弟子時時來	A
灌頂壇嚴神齟塞	*A
三十年功苦拘束	B
梵僧夢裏授微言	-
雪嶺白牛力深得	B
水精一索香一爐	C
紅蓮花舌生醍醐	C
初聽喉音寶樓閣	D
如聞魔王宮殿拉	*D
金瓦落	D
次聽妙音大隨求	E
更覺	
人間萬事深悠悠	E

四音俱作清且柔	E
愛河濁浪卻倒流	E
卻倒流兮無處去	F
性海含空日初曙	F

This poem unfolds in three stages. The first stage (lines 1–4) describes Hongyi's purity. His demeanor is perfect, bearing no trace of dust. He sips well-made mountain tea, surrounded by a retinue of faithful disciples. He represents the ideal state of detachment to be held by an eminent monk. Stage two (lines 5–10) is the natural result of stage one. Because of his purity, Hongyi has access to the supramundane. He is revealed to be a monk who has been consecrated into esoteric rituals. The merit he has accumulated over many years makes him practically invincible against the pain of life. Instead, he is shrouded in incense and jewels, surrounded by divine beings, and receives a spell from a foreign monk in a dream. For this reason, his tongue is likened to a red lotus, and his voice is said to be as pure as clarified butter. The third stage (lines 11–19) describes the effects of the *dhāraṇī* that Hongyi recites. They quell demons, transport listeners out of the mundane world, stem the tide of suffering, and ultimately lead one to realize the fundamental emptiness of all things. In short, they are capable of achieving both the immediate and the ultimate goals of a Buddhist monk.

The most noteworthy aspect of Guanxiu's poem is its attention to sound at the levels of both form and content. Guanxiu focuses on two *dhāraṇī* sūtras' sonic power, showing a causal connection between hearing the spells and feeling their effects. He also attends to the details of the spells' sounds—the *Jeweled Pavilion* is throaty, whereas the *Great Protectress* is more transcendent. Hongyi is adept at incantation because of the way he combines the four types of sounds—possibly the tones of Middle Chinese, possibly the initials—to create different effects. The power of his spells is directly related to their sonority. Guanxiu then echoes this in the very structure of his poem. Of the nineteen lines in the poem, fifteen are full rhymes and another two are partial rhymes. That is, 79–89 percent of the line endings resonate with one another, far more than 50 percent that is typical of Tang poetry. He also varies the rhythm of the poem by using the particle *xi* 兮 (line 18), adding a hypermetrical phrase (line 15), and including an extra three-syllable hemistich (line 13). While these flourishes are not remarkable in themselves for old-style verse, they break up the monotony of the standard seven-beat meter used throughout.

The tones are also patterned in meaningful ways: in the opening quatrain, the final three characters of each line are all level, extendable tones. This technique of repeating tones of a certain class, either in quick succession or in crucial positions, is what a contemporaneous poetry manual calls "cross-regulation" (*hulü* 互律).[67] Here Guanxiu uses it as a way to emphasize the incanting monk's spiritual purity, letting sounds of each length resonate. Similarly, in lines 12–13, which function as a single unit, line 12 opens with four level tones in a row, then come two three-character phrases with the tonal pattern of level-oblique-oblique, the hard stop of the entering tone at the end of the line aurally illustrating the crashing of Māra's abode. In its sound and sense, the poem takes a cue from its subject, emphasizing the power of the sonorous.

The sonic similarity between poetry and incantation is not just hidden in the formal features of Guanxiu's works. He explicitly states it in the opening lines of another poem. Written for a Buddhist monk and shown to a literati patron, this poem grounds itself in the compatibility of esoteric Buddhism and the fountainhead of the poetic tradition.

Inscribed on the Temple of Reverend Hongshi and Shown to Commissioned Lord Du 題弘式和尚院兼呈杜使君

Guanxiu

The two Elegantiae and the two Esotericae—[68]
In their sonority, we but delight in them ourselves.[69]
Your monastic years are so great that your cloud sandals are worn thin;[70]
Your visage is so ancient it could have been drafted by a painter.[71]
Digging ants rim your tin-ringed staff,
Hearth smoke stains your snowy brows.
When I hear that you've written new things,
I send off a letter to Qiu Chi at once.[72]

二雅兼二密，
愔愔祇自怡。
臘高雲履朽，
貌古畫師疑。
墊蟻緣金錫，
爐煙惹雪眉。
仍聞有新作，
祇是寄丘遲。[73]

In the poem's middle, descriptive couplets, Guanxiu focuses on his recipient's physical decay with age. Hongshi is old and revered, with a body worn down by years of intense religious practice. His eyebrows are white like snow (line 6), and he appears as tattered as a pair of old shoes (line 3). When we read about his face looking like it was "drafted by a painter" in line 4, we should keep in mind Guanxiu's own fame as a painter, celebrated especially for his depictions of arhats (*luohan* 羅漢, early disciples of the Buddha) as gnarled old men who take on the craggy features of the mountainous landscapes they resided in. Similarly, Guanxiu describes Hongshi as blending in with the landscape, as ants climb on his staff and gray smoke blends with his snowy brows (lines 5-6).

In the opening and closing couplets Guanxiu reflects on the nature of literature. In the last two lines he establishes a community of like-minded poets who can understand one another's works. Hongshi, Prefect Du (indirectly mentioned by reference to Qiu Chi), and Guanxiu must share any new works with each other, as those who truly get it are few. Literature, the speaker says, is elite by nature, grasped only by a handful of people in any generation. For this reason, the opening couplet's parallel references to the poetic tradition and Buddhist esotericae is justified. A small group of initiates keep the true flame alive even as it seems to fall apart in the hands of the masses. For poetry, this is the Elegantiae, the early layer of the *Book of Odes* that records the myths and rituals of the Zhou dynasty. For Buddhism, it is the two Esotericae, the Buddha's secret deeds and doctrines that only the most capable of his followers knew about. Many Mahāyāna innovations—such a new sūtras, rituals, and spells—claim such esoteric origins.

The term "two Esotericae" is given great weight here, being a cornerstone of Guanxiu's approach to poetry. "Doctrinal esoterica" (*limi* 理密) refers to the perfect interfusion (*yuanrong*) of the mundane and the ultimate, while "practical esotericae" (*shimi* 事密) refers to the actions, words, and thoughts of the three Buddhas of past, present, and future (Amitābha, Śākyamuni, and Maitreya). These two may appear to be in conflict to the uninitiated, but they are in fact in perfect accord, as described by Ennin.[74] Mundane and ultimate are interfused in doctrine, and doctrine and practice are interfused in the two Esotericae. At a third, higher level, the two Esotericae are themselves interfused with the "two Elegantiae" of poetry: both are "sonorous" (*yinyin* 愔愔) in the same way as the "Prayer Summons" ode referenced in the ancient *Zuozhuan*. Both are pleasant to hear, and both offer access to deeply resonant spiritual traditions. Guanxiu emphasizes this point with sound, using the "cross-regulation" technique in the first line to deviate from the prescribed meter in order to refer to the "two Esotericae." The fourth character of the line, *er* 二 (MC: *nyìj*), should be a level tone but instead is a deflected one.[75] This creates a staccato effect in the line, as four of its five characters are deflected and thus less prolongable.[76] Guanxiu's choice must have been deliberate, since the rest of the poem perfectly follows the tonal meter of regulated verse. Sound is used to emphasize sense.

Spells provided the poet-monks with a model for sonorous language with incredible spiritual effects. The major poet-monks Guanxiu, Qiji, and Wuke were familiar with spell recitation, esoteric scriptures, and the monks who specialized in them. It is likely that they themselves recited spells as part of their professional lives. When they wrote poems addressed to tantric monks, they matched their language to the topic, re-creating the sonority of recited spells in their verses. But they did not stop there. The poet-monks pushed further, claiming that literary and esoteric religious practices were fully consonant with each other, perfectly interfused just like the words and deeds of the Buddha in his cosmic manifestation. The poem, no less than the spell, is language at its utmost.

Foreignness

Aside from sonority, the other fundamental feature of incantatory language is its origins in another realm. For Chinese Buddhists, this usually meant India. By the time of our poet-monks in the ninth century, Sino-Indian relations had a long history founded on long-distance trade and the transmission of Buddhism, buttressed in the Tang by shared concerns over the expansion of the Tibetan empire.[77] However, despite this long history, direct contact between the two civilizations was limited. Prior to the modern period, much communication was conducted indirectly through travel accounts, translated Buddhist scriptures, and precious objects.[78] In the Tang, most people, including Buddhist monks, encountered South Asians rarely. To them, India remained a fully alien land, though one that was strongly associated with the spiritual power attributed to Buddhism.

Guanxiu's work in particular reveals a lifelong fascination with all things Indic, a fascination tied to the sounds of Sanskrit. Like several other poet-monks, he had the opportunity to meet and write about foreign monks from the west.[79] A series of five poems, likely written in 891 when he was nearly sixty years old, is addressed to an Indian monk traveling to Mount Wutai.[80] Mount Wutai had become widely known as the abode of the bodhisattva Mañjuśrī 文疏 since at least the sixth century and had been a site of pilgrimage for Indian Buddhists since at least the seventh. Indian pilgrimage continued to increase in the eighth and ninth centuries, and, by the eleventh century, one source purports that some five hundred Indian monks were present at a single temple on Mount Wutai.[81] Tang Buddhists were fascinated with these Indian pilgrims. The deities, people, languages, and writing systems of India were to them a source of spiritual power.

Guanxiu's poetic series on meeting an Indian pilgrim is filled with Buddhist allusions, including a reference to Śākyamuni Buddha as "*our early ancestor*" 吾上祖. Despite his recognition of a shared devotion to the Buddha, the speaker is obsessed with the Indian monk's foreignness. He has "blue lotus eyes" 青蓮目, carries "pressed Brāhmī writings" 梵夾 and "icons drawn up on piles of white cotton" 白疊還圖像, and he "travels through several realms, / transforming the minds of many kings and emperors" 經幾國，多化帝王心 by converting them to Buddhism.[82] Back in India, he imagines, the foreign monk had "sat atop the Snowy Peaks / And descended to the universe to look around" 雪嶺頂危坐，乾坤四顧低.[83] The fourth poem, in particular, contrasts the inscrutable powers held by this foreigner with the physical pain he has experienced on their journey.

Running into an Indian Monk Going to Mount Wutai: 4 of 5 遇五天僧入五臺五首（其四）

Guanxiu

Your foot-rub oil is nearly used up,[84]
And your *gandhāra* banner half-destroyed.[85]
You are a *Pratyeka-buddha* in your appearance,[86]
The son of a *Kṣatriya* family.[87]
The mudras you perform make demons weep,
Your mind roams to places unknown by sages.
I sigh deeply, hair turned white,
Unable to follow you afar.

塗足油應盡，
乾陁帔半隳。

辟支迦狀貌，
刹利帝家兒。
結印魔應哭，
遊心聖不知。
深嗟頭已白，
不得遠相隨。[88]

The poem is at pains to stress the monk's Indianness. Three lines open with transliterated Sanskrit terms (lines 2–4) and one more (line 1) with an object whose textual source is Faxian's western travelogue of the early fifth century, *Record of Buddhist States*. The monk is said to belong to the ruling Kṣatriya class and look like early ascetics (lines 3–4). The speaker's attitude toward him shifts between pity and awe. His banner has been beaten to tatters by the weather (line 2), his foot salve emptied (line 1), still not at his destination. At the same time, he can access incredible spiritual power through esoteric mudras (line 5) and can visualize unknown worlds in meditation (line 6). It is not clear if Guanxiu was able to communicate with this monk—he did not know any foreign languages as far as we know.[89] It may be that this monk was a Tantric master who claimed to wield such powers. Or Guanxiu may have just projected onto him an idea of Indian authenticity. Whatever may be the case, Guanxiu's five poems create a strong association between the concepts of Indianness, exoticism, and spiritual power.

The inscrutable yet potent nature of all things Indian in poet-monks' works is apparent in their interest in the Brāhmī script. Elite Buddhists had engaged with Indic writing for centuries. Examples include the *Lalitavistara Sūtra*'s 普曜經 (translated in 308) list of sixty-four scripts, Xie Lingyun's study of Siddham, Amoghavajra's championing of esoteric rituals at the Tang court, and the monk Zhiguang's 智廣 (d. 806) Siddham textbook written in 800, the *Xitanziji* 悉曇字記.[90] There also exists a fascinating suite of didactic songs attesting to monastic interest, "Siddhaṃ Stanzas for the Meditation Gate of the *Laṅkāvatāra Sūtra* Spoken by the Buddha" 佛説楞伽經禪門悉曇章, attributed to a monk called Dinghui 定惠, whom some scholars have identified as Huanzhong 寰中 (780–862), a student of Hongzhou-style Chan who lived in the southeast in his later years.[91] If this is correct, then this suite is the work of a monk whose presence in the southeast during his later years would have overlapped with Guanxiu's youth there.

Whatever the case may be, these songs were authored by a monk living in the Tang heartland during the early or middle phases of the poet-monks' development and, as evidenced by their multiple copies and variations at Dunhuang, remained popular through the tenth century.[92] Like the Guanxiu poem on the *Lotus Sūtra*–reciting monk at the beginning of this chapter, these are song-style verses written mostly in a seven-beat meter, with distinct descriptive and exhortative sections. These are different in that they are interspersed with lines of transliterated Sanskrit and pseudo-Sanskrit and in that they are linked to the *Laṅkāvatāra Sūtra*, a well-known Mahāyāna scripture expounding doctrines commonly held by many Tang Buddhists. Modern scholars have associated this scripture with the Northern School of Chan because a document of the early eighth century called the *Treatise on the Men and Dharma of Laṅkāvatāra* 楞伽人法志 outlines the Northern School lineage.[93] However, there is evidence that monks and literati with various doctrinal views were familiar with this scripture even past its eighth-century heyday, including Guanxiu, who twice refers to fellow monastics as "Masters of *Laṅkāvatāra*" (*lengqie zi* 楞伽子).[94]

In these songs about the written Siddhaṃ script, we see a close association between sonority and foreignness that is incantatory in nature.[95] As the preface to the "Siddhaṃ Stanzas" notes, the monk who compiled this text had both a didactic and auditory-aesthetic goal in mind: "He rendered [the *Laṅkāvatāra*] into Siddhaṃ stanzas to broadly open the gate of meditation and not impede the study of wisdom—to not write down words but merge them together with Chinese sounds" 翻出悉談章，廣開禪門不妨慧學，不著文字並合秦音. The eighth and final section of the "Siddhaṃ Stanzas" illustrates this careful attention to sound especially clearly.

From "Siddhaṃ Stanzas for the Meditation Gate of the *Laṅkāvatāra Sūtra* Spoken by the Buddha"

Bjuwk-ljak-yak
Bjuwk-ljak-yak
Eight:
The meditation gate removes overthinking:
Not high and not low,
    there are no towers and pavilions.
Not leaving and not entering,
    there are no inner and outer walls.[96]
This mental image actualized in sound
    is the beginning of learning.

Produce thought and stir the mind,
    but don't attach to them.
With lengthy sitting and hard work,
    do not-doing,
Non-joy can be enjoyed:
    this is eternal joy.[97]
The lamp of wisdom fully illuminates
    the outer limits of the trichiliocosm.[98]
Stilled water eternally purifies you of
    the eighty thousand kleśas.[99]
With the buddhas of the ten directions
    you will awaken together,
Awaken—*tèj-lì*—broaden![100]
r r̂ l l
Bjuwk-ljak-yak
Buddha-sons, abide in yourselves
    and do not make constraints:
The four directions and up and down
    cannot be crossed,[101]
So dwell in tranquil nirvāṇa,
    together at the gate's edge.
With utterly peaceful joy
There are no attachments,
Svāhā, may all awaken.

復畧藥	A
々々々	A
第八	A
禪门絕針酌	A
不高不下无樓阁	A
不出不入无城廓	A
是想現聲即初學	A
生心動念勿令著	A
久坐用功作非作	A
无樂可樂是常樂	A
慧燈一照三千廓	A
定水常清八万鑠	A
十方諸佛同開覺	A
々底裏博	A
魯留盧樓	-

復畧藥	A
諸佛子自在作莫制約	A
四維上下不可度	A
住寂涅槃同門廓	A
甚安樂	A
無著	A
娑訶耶等覺	A[102]

The most conspicuous aspect of this stanza, as of all the "Siddhaṃ Stanzas," is the presence of three-character hemistiches which carry no semantic significance but set the rhyme for the piece: the *"bjuwk-ljak-yak"* that appears twice in line 1 and once in line 13.[103] At its third appearance, it is preceded by four characters that represent the four vowels placed at the beginning of a Siddhaṃ primer mentioned in the preface and attributed to Kumārajīva.[104] These four liquid vowels of Sanskrit were typically placed at the end of Siddhaṃ primers because they are rarely used and difficult to pronounce, almost considered to be non-sounds, what Zhiguang calls "borderline letters" (*jiepanzi* 界畔字).[105] Thus, in the non-semantic line 13 of this song, there is a combination of pure aurality and its near absence.

The other striking aspect of this song is its rhymes. First, it employs an abruptly halting entering tone rhyme (*–ak*), which was generally forbidden in regulated verse but often used in old-style poetry, including by Guanxiu in the conclusion of his poem found on P. 2104. Second, the rhymes are strikingly abundant: all eighteen lines rhyme, plus some hemistiches. If we include all entering-tone characters as half rhymes, the number of characters that resonate with the main rhyme increases to 44 of 123 total (36 percent).[106] This does not include other internal rhymes (such as the *"tèj-lì"* of line 12) or instances of alliteration or assonance (such as the alliterative binom *zhenzhuo* 針酌, MC: *tsyim-tsyak*, in line 2).

This excessive sonority reinforces the song's message, a program for new Buddhist adepts. One begins by visualizing the absence of physical positions, objects, and movements and then attempts to actualize these in sound (line 5). If one works hard and spends much time meditating (line 7), one may achieve wisdom and stillness (lines 9–10, 14–16), which leads to nonattachment and enlightenment (lines 11, 17–18). Sound is primary, as the attempt to vocalize images is what initiates this whole process. Beyond this individual verse, if we think of the presence of purely sonic syllables and the whole suite's goal of merging the sounds of Sanskrit and Chinese, then this song is indeed a manifestation of incantatory logic.

Guanxiu, like the reciters and listeners of the "Stanzas," had a deep interest in Siddhaṃ. Two of his poems use the metaphor of the graph of the vowel *i* in Brāhmī to represent the truth.[107] This vowel looks like three dots in a triangle (∴), and it was used metaphorically to describe the nonhierarchical relationship between the Dharma, Buddha, and Prajñā (wisdom), since one cannot create the graph by arranging the dots along a single vertical or horizontal axis. As the Buddha explains in the *Mahāparinirvāṇa Sūtra*:

> What kind of name can be given to the hidden storehouse of my teachings? It is like the three dots of the *i*-graph: horizontally, they don't form *i*, and neither do they vertically. They are like the three eyes on the head of Maheśvara. The three dots form the *i*-graph together; when considered separately, they do not form it. It is like this with me too. The dharma of liberation is not nirvāṇa, the person of the Tathāgatha is not nirvāṇa, and *mahāprajñā* [great wisdom] is not nirvāṇa. These three dharmas are each unique and not nirvāṇa. I now firmly reside in these three dharmas, but for the sake of all sentient beings I declare my entrance into nirvāṇa, like the world's *i*-graph.
>
> 何等名爲祕密之藏？猶如伊字三點：若並則不成伊，縱亦不成。如摩醯首羅面上三目：乃得成伊三點，若別亦不得成。我亦如是。解脫之法亦非涅槃，如來之身亦非涅槃，摩訶般若亦非涅槃。三法各異亦非涅槃。我今安住如是三法，爲眾生故名入涅槃，如世伊字。[108]

The metaphor of the *i*-graph is just one manifestation of Chinese Buddhists' broad interest in South Asian writing.[109] Indic scripts, such as Brāhmī and Siddham, were associated with written and spoken spells that gave the practitioner access to esoteric powers.[110] One of Guanxiu's poems alludes to the *i*-graph to acknowledge the ultimate emptiness of this sign that points to ultimate reality.

Presented to the Reverend of Donglin Monastery 上東林和尚

Guanxiu

Declining purples, you returned to walls of green,[111]
Whence your great name is heard within the four seas.
Even so, you have no concern for such matters:

How could they compel my lord?
The Way is only conveyed with the graph *i*;
Poetry mostly laughs at clouds in the blue.[112]
So have pity on this traveler beneath your gate
Whose remaining energy will be put toward literature.[113]

讓紫歸青壁，
高名四海聞。
雖然無一事，
得不是要君。
道秪傳伊字，
詩多笑碧雲。
應憐門下客，
餘力亦為文。[114]

Likely written in 861 when Guanxiu first traveled to Mount Lu, this poem functions as a cover letter to a senior monk at Donglin monastery, meant to demonstrate his own skills and purpose while simultaneously flattering its recipient.[115] This reverend is not only famous but also wise, for he is indifferent to worldly matters. Guanxiu encapsulates this wisdom in a pithy contrast between Buddhism and poetry in lines 5-6. Whereas the Way is transmitted by empty signs that point toward ultimate reality, poetry gives one access to a detached perspective of the phenomenal world. That is, religion gestures toward higher truths, while literature encourages nonattachment to the lower, mundane world.[116] One is an imperfect approach to perfect things, the other a perfect approach to imperfect things.[117] The final lines see the speaker resolving to dedicate himself to literary activity. Both literature and religion are complementary approaches to understanding ultimate reality, and Guanxiu declares that he can contribute literature. This is politely referred to as an activity of "remaining strength" that seems to put the reverend (and religious practice) in the superior position. While the norms of exchange poetry demand such a polite gesture, the powerful parallelism of line 5-6 suggest that literary practice may be just as important as religious practice.

Guanxiu not only tells the reverend this, he also demonstrates it. Every couplet in this poem follows a hyper-regulated pattern, in which the tones of every character in a couplet are in parallel with each other.[118] The technical mastery is also on display in the poem's interlocking rhyme scheme. A schematic representation the poem's tonal structure and rhyme pattern, with filled-in circles representing oblique tones and empty circles representing level tones, looks like this:

讓紫歸青壁	●●○○●	A
高名四海聞	○○●●○	B
雖然無一事	○○○●●	C
得不是要君	●●●○○	B
道秖傳伊字	●●○○●	C
詩多笑碧雲	○○●●○	B
應憐門下客	●○○●●	A
餘力亦為文	○●●○○	B

All of this formal craft is in service of the poem's main point. The *i*-graph is a symbol of the ultimate truth of Buddhism, but it is still only a symbol. It is more fitting to "laugh at clouds in the blue" than to get bogged down in the fine points of doctrine. Poetry, Guanxiu suggests, may be Buddhism in practice.

The most well-known examples of Guanxiu's fascination with India are his sixteen arhat paintings.[119] These survive in several sets that have been copied from Guanxiu's originals.[120] It is clear from early descriptions of Guanxiu's paintings that people were struck by the strange power that seemed to exude from the arhats' exotic, gnarled appearances. The *Record of Famous Painters of Yizhou* 益州名畫錄 (preface dated 1006), the earliest prose description of them, describes their foreign features in detail.

> The sixteen arhat paintings he drew had enormous brows and large eyes, long necks and aquiline noses, and were leaning against pines and rocks and sitting among mountains and rivers. Their barbarian visages and Indic features are brought out everywhere. When someone asked about them, he said, "I saw them in a dream, and then I painted ten disciples of the Buddha accordingly."[121] Everyone marveled at them, and they were treasured by his disciples.[122]
>
> 畫羅漢十六幀，龐眉大目者，朵頤隆鼻者，倚松石者，坐山水者，蕃貌梵相，曲盡其態。或問之，云「休自夢中所覩，爾又畫釋迦十弟子亦如此類。」人皆異之，頗為門弟子所寶。

Guanxiu's arhat paintings were some of the most influential in the history of Chinese painting, inspiring poems and being offered as tribute

FIGURE 5.2. Depiction of the arhat Piṇḍola in the style of Guanxiu (11th–12th cent.). Held in the Museum of the Imperial Collections (Sannomaru Shōzōkan 三の丸尚蔵館), Tokyo. Source: The Imperial Household Agency website (https://shozokan.kunaicho.go.jp/en/collection/), modified from color to black and white. Arhats in the Guanxiu style were known for their exaggerated, foreign features.

to the Song emperor.[123] Their appeal is the result of their grotesque, foreign appearance. Critics dwell on their large noses, thick eyebrows, and other typically Indian features, visible in the painting of Piṇḍola Bhāradvāja 賓頭盧 attributed to Guanxiu that is found in the Museum of the Imperial Collection in Tokyo (see figure 5.2).[124] Ouyang Jiong 歐陽炯 (896–971), who wrote the earliest surviving appreciation of these paintings in verse, similarly observes that the arhats' "forms are like emaciated cranes, their essential spirits robust; / Their crowns are like crouching rhinoceroses, their skull bones massive" 形如瘦鶴精神健，頂似伏犀頭骨麤.[125] The arhats' unfamiliar images as emaciated foreigners startled Guanxiu's contemporaries, and it was precisely their strangeness that gave them power.[126] This shocked admiration continued into the twentieth century, as one critic compared them to the works of the surrealists.[127]

It is also important to note that Guanxiu painted these arhat images from dreams.[128] This implies that they were divinely inspired and attests to their significance as objects of religious devotion.[129] We must remember that Guanxiu's arhat paintings are not merely artistic portraits of a Buddhist subject but also religious icons. They were real manifestations of the arhats and thus worthy of worship by pious Buddhists.[130] The *Song Biographies of Eminent Monks* makes this clear, as it describes how Guanxiu's dreams only came about because of his own prayer requests.

> Guanxiu was skilled with the small brush and proficient in the six laws of painting, being especially adept at water and ink.[131] His ability to depict likenesses was remarkable. At the request of the Qiang family medical shop at Zhong'an Bridge, he produced a hall of arhats, saying that for each arhat he painted, he had to pray, then in a dream he would get to see his appearance in response, and then he made it accordingly. They are different from the ordinary style.[132]

> 休善小筆得六法，長於水墨，形似之狀可觀。受衆安橋強氏藥肆請，出羅漢一堂，云，每畫一尊必祈夢得應眞貌，方成之。與常體不同。

Guanxiu's arhat paintings were objects made for religious practice: they were created to be hung in a devotional hall associated with a medical shop, where the ill likely would have made offerings for healing.[133] But even more, these paintings are the products of religious practice. Guanxiu had to pray to see their faces in dreams before he could paint them. We do not know whether or not Guanxiu would have met any real Central or South Asians by 880, but it is clear that the dream is not only a source of visual cues for the arhat paintings. It is a sign of their spiritual efficacy as icons. Gods, dreams, and foreigners alike come from other worlds, bearing extraordinary powers.

Chanting the Lotus Sūtra

Guanxiu's incredible literary skills were honed through his religious practices as much as his literary ones. His fascination with India, and other realms more generally, worked its way into his aesthetic sensibility and manifested itself in both his painting and poetry.[134] Perhaps the most palpable representations of Indianness in the Tang empire were the *dhāraṇī* in transliterated Sanskrit and pseudo-Sanskrit.[135] In elite Buddhist circles of the late medieval period, these texts were not seen as mere nonsense. Rather, they were understood "not only to be coherent and semantically rich utterances but also to be complexly layered texts combining performative narrative, philosophical and ritual detail, and consecratory sound."[136] That is, the practices associated with *dhāraṇī* provided immersive sensory experiences in their recitation (sound), inscription (sight), infusion (smell), and ingestion (taste).[137]

For our purposes, the most salient experience is sound. Most *dhāraṇī* are highly repetitive, with the same series of transliterated words produced over and over again. In the twenty-sixth chapter of the *Lotus Sūtra* 法華經, there is a *dhāraṇī*, spoken by ten *rākṣasī* and their mother, which is said to protect those who uphold the *Lotus Sūtra*. It reads:

itime itini itime atime itime
nime nime nime nime nime
ruhe ruhe ruhe ruhe
stahe stahe stahe
stuhe nohe[138]

伊提履 伊提泯 伊提履 阿提履 伊提履
泥履 泥履 泥履 泥履 泥履
樓醯 樓醯 樓醯 樓醯
多醯 多醯 多醯
兜醯 㝹醯

Whether or not one understands the semantic meanings of these words, their very repetition creates an intense sonic experience, as a limited number of phonemes are combined in a variety of ways. Ten individual characters are used in forty-three positions, with *lü* 履 and *xi* 醯 (MC: *lij* and *xej*) each accounting for nine of them (21 percent of the total; combined 42 percent). The result is an extremely dense aural pattern. The combination of these various syllables, even when it is not simply a single word like *nime* or *ruhe* or *stahe* repeated three or more times in a row, create resonance. For a medieval Chinese listener, the experience would have been sonically overwhelming.

There is also the possibility that the repetitions embedded in these *dhāraṇī* had a more profound significance to the late medieval Buddhists who heard them. The mid-eighth-century monk Fachong 法崇, for example, explains that the doubling of the word *maotuoye* 冒馱野

(glossed as "able to awaken") in a different *dhāraṇī* represents the "two truths" of principle (*li* 理) and phenomena (*wu* 物).[139] As seen in chapter 3, the fundamental identity of principle and phenomena was an important doctrinal point in many varieties of Late Tang Buddhism, including the *Awakening of Mahāyāna Faith* that Guanxiu spent three years studying and the Hongzhou and Wei-Yang lineages familiar to many poet-monks. Verbal repetition, especially in a *dhāraṇī*, could provide a very clear illustration of the philosophical principle that there is identity in difference and difference in identity.

Elsewhere in the *Lotus Sūtra*, upholders of the text are promised incredible powers over sound. Chapter 19 of the *Lotus Sūtra*, "The Merits of the Dharma Preacher" 法師功德, describes the perfected sensory organs it promises to its holders, which include heightened audition and speech. A perfect ear can hear forty-two different kinds of sounds, ranging from the mundane (animals, humans, musical instruments) to the supramundane (gods, dragons, buddhas).[140] When describing the enhanced powers of the tongue attained by those who uphold the *Sūtra*, the main benefit is euphonic speech that compels joy in whoever hears it and commands the attention of buddhas.[141] Elsewhere, the *Lotus* describes the sound of bodhisattvas' voices as being especially euphonic.[142] Many other passages describe the benefits of hearing the *Lotus Sūtra*, that the merit accrued by listening to even a phrase of it is greater than many lifetimes of good deeds.[143] Notably, these passages always describe encounters with the *Lotus* through acts of hearing, not reading. It is sonority that moves.

The various aspects of incantation—foreignness, sonority, and a propensity to repetition—come together in several song-style poems about hearing recitations of the *Lotus Sūtra* by Guanxiu and Qiji.[144] To get a sense of the boldness of these later monks' poems, let us first examine a song on the same theme from the late-eighth century, written by the literatus Zhu Wan 朱灣 (fl. ca. 773–783) in conjunction with the early poet-monk Qingjiang 清江 (d. 811?). There is here a remarkable focus on the physical intensity and sonic beauty of the recitation. While it established the basic conventions of song-style verse on *Lotus Sūtra* recitations, we will see that it is relatively restrained compared to the later monks' writings.

A Song on Listening to the Venerable Jian and Zheng Recite the *Lotus Sūtra* in Huaizhou, with Master Qingjiang on a Moonlit Night 同清江師月夜聽堅正二上人為懷州轉《法華經》歌

Zhu Wan

A monk from Yunmen monastery
    by the bank of Ruoye Creek,[145]
Sits in peace at night
    and hears about the True Vehicle:

The *Lotus*'s esoteric *gāthās*
    and Parable of the Medicinal Herbs:[146]
The two masters' bodies rest,
    but their mouths do not.
If you drill a well to find water,
    you will surely reach the source;[147]
If you close doors to avoid fire,
    you will end up losing the path.[148]

Past mind and future mind
    are both this present mind.
The marvelous sounds of Indic sounds
    are delicate sounds.[149]
The clear, frosty stone chimes
    move sometimes;
A still, silent, empty hall
    befits the depths of night.

Why is it that
    we've never been able to sleep?
By finally producing the one thought,
    our hundred worries cease.[150]
The wind turns scattering leaves:
    there's a sound in the woods;
The snow reflects the quiet courtyard:
    there's no color in the moon.

It is hard to conceive of the hidden tracks
    at the Gates of the Arcane:
The sober awaken—*hey*—
    and the drunken doubt.
Who is the one who becomes aware of
    the jewel in his robe?[151]
The Governor of Linchuan
    got it.[152]

若耶溪畔雲門僧	A
夜閑燕坐聽真乘	A
蓮花秘偈藥草喻	B
二師身住口不住	B
鑿井求泉會到源	-
閉門避火終迷路	B
前心後心皆此心	C
梵音妙音柔軟音	C
清泠霜磬有時動	-
寂曆空堂宜夜深	C
向來不寐何所事	-
一念才生百慮息	D
風翻亂葉林有聲	-
雪映閒庭月無色	D
玄關密跡難可思	E
醒人悟兮醉人疑	E
衣中系寶覺者誰	E
臨川內史字得之	E[153]

This poem on two monks' recitation of the *Lotus Sūtra*, written while traveling with a third monk, combines a physical description of the monks' recitation with at least six references to the text of the *Lotus* (lines 3, 5, 6, 8, 12, 17). The setting is a quiet monastery next to a hillside creek, against which the monks' chants and bells resound all the more. The *Lotus* is so powerful that it leads the literati speaker, here figured as Xie Lingyun in line 18, to believe he may have realized his fundamental buddha-nature. Though metrically regular, Zhu Wan re-creates some of the recitation's sonority in his poem: there is slightly more rhyme than one might expect (lines 15–18 all rhyme), and he uses an expanded version of the "double drafting" technique discussed in chapter 4, as the same character is used three nonconsecutive times in a single line twice (lines 7–8). Zhu Wan cleverly depicts the "delicate sounds" of the recitation while managing to convey his own understanding of its import.

Guanxiu and Qiji develop Zhu Wan's approach to verse depictions of *Lotus Sūtra* recitations into something much more sonorous and foreign. We have already seen one example from Guanxiu at the beginning of this chapter, of a song that found its way into a manuscript of mostly practical ritual texts. Another example, found in Guanxiu's received collection, has similar ties to ritual texts. It not only describes the sound of a *Sūtra* recitation but also directly re-creates it with onomatopoeia in the poem's opening.

The *Sūtra*-Upholding Monk 長持經僧
Guanxiu

Lau-lau, long have you sat through the nights,
Lau-lau, long have you risen early.[154]
Shirt so dark, dark,
You can't see him,[155]
But his sounds run on and on
    like rushing water.
He strikes metal, beats jade:[156]
Exhales *gong*-notes, inhales *zhi*,[157]
Head drooping to plants and trees,
Hands clasping gods and ghosts.
He could consume three gold catties' worth daily,
    getting serenity through effort,[158]
But, being a dead tree with rotten branches,
    he eats just once.
I sigh with pain
    over the people of this floating world,
Who've never had
    such a good thing enter their ears.

嘮嘮長夜坐	-
嘮嘮長早起	A
衫森森	B
不見人	B
人聲續續如流水	A
摐金挣玉	C
吐宮咽徵	A
頭低草木	C
手合神鬼	A
日消三兩黃金爭得止	A
而槁木朽枝一食而已	A
傷嗟浮世之人	B
善事不曾入耳	A[159]

The opening brings the reader directly into the sonic world of the recitation. The setting is dark, so deep in the night or in the woods that the reciting monk's black robes cannot be distinguished against the background (line 3). But this only intensifies the auditory experience, loud and clear as a rushing stream (line 4). The reciter, as in Guanxiu's other poem, masterfully changes his pitch and breathing (line 6), and Guanxiu mirrors these verbal changes with his own frequent changes in meter. The rhymes on several odd-numbered lines reinforce the importance of sound. The reciting monk produces a soundscape so rapturous that the speaker pities those secular people who will never behold it (line 14). The sonic power of his recitation is based in his religious purity.

The line about "consuming three gold catties' worth" of provisions per day, which may at first strike us as a simple description, is in fact a crucial allusion. Guanxiu (or an early editor) highlights its importance with an "original note" saying, "The Buddha says that those who constantly uphold the scriptures can eat three gold catties' worth a day." Using daily consumption of gold to describe offerings to monks was common in this period. A line in the popular "Song of the Realization of the Way" (also in the "Digest of the Essentials of Meditation" in the ritual toolbox examined above) says that one who has the marvelous power of liberation may "consume ten thousand gold catties' worth" 萬兩黃金亦銷得.[160] The *Record of Linji* (*Linji lu* 臨濟錄) similarly states that those who understand that there is no real dharma "are true renouncers of home, and may consume ten thousand gold catties' worth a day" 是真出家，日消萬兩黃金.[161]

However, the precise number in Guanxiu's poem, three catties of gold, corresponds most closely to a veneration practice described in the *Ritual Instructions for Altar Records* (*Tanfa yize* 壇法儀則).[162] This text, a collection of esoteric rites attributed to Amoghavajra discovered in several Dunhuang manuscripts dating to the early tenth century, integrates practices that are now thought of separately as "Chan" and "Esoteric."[163] While there is some debate about whether the text as we now have it ever circulated outside of Dunhuang, it is very likely based on more widely practiced *maṇḍala* rites, and thus it is possible that Guanxiu knew of this rite or similar ones.[164] The section relevant to Guanxiu's poem is found at the end of the first part of the manuscript, the culmination of a seven-day ritual sequence.

> When you initiate this *maṇḍala*, employ thirty-seven monks to practice and thirty-six people to scatter flowers. When they perform the consecration, employ four serving lads holding a bottle each,

light seven sticks of precious incense, and scatter seven precious flowers. You should make offerings to the dharma masters using clothing and bedding of seven jewels and one hundred braids. Feed them three gold catties' worth a day, eating and drinking one hundred flavors. You must completely fulfill this, not slacking in the least. If you make your offering with a correct mind and do not permit anger, the results will be achieved.[165]

開此壇時，用行道僧三十七人，用散花十六人。授灌頂時，用四童子，各執一瓶，燒七寶香，散七寶花，應用七寶百總衣服臥具供養法師。日食三兩黃金，百味飲食，盡令充足，不令闕少。真心供養，不令嗔怒，果滿成就。

Donations of three gold catties' worth of flavor-rich food per day is extravagant. It is the most expensive amount given in *Ritual Instructions for Altar Records*, which most often instructs one to provide the "three white foods" 三白食—milk, yogurt, and rice—to the ritual participants. In Guanxiu's poem, then, the speaker is stating that the monk reciting the *Lotus Sūtra* is worthy of the utmost ritual veneration, the same given to monks performing a consecration ceremony at the culmination of an esoteric ritual program.

Even more striking than Guanxiu's poem is Qiji's longer treatment of a sūtra-reciting monk. This poem gives us a glimpse of one virtuoso performance of the *Lotus*, drawing on the power of incantation to propose a new vision of poetry.

Given to the *Lotus Sūtra*-Minding Monk 贈念法華經僧
Qiji

Minding, minding, minding—*hey*—
    it is easy to enter into evil;
Minding, minding, minding—*hey*—
    it is hard to enter into goodness.
By minding the *Sūtra* and minding the Buddha
    one is capable of everything.
Where the river of desire is dried up,
    a billowing wave comes forth.[166]

It is said that in your youth,
    you were a vessel of the true dharma,[167]
Never going out at day,
    never sleeping at night.

Your every thought connected to the *Sūtra*,
    your mouth connected to its words.
Your cell is empty, empty,
    a lantern lighting the ground.
Aloewood, sandalwood, and scrolls
    fill precious cases;[168]
The sweet smell of champak,
    and recollection of crystal.[169]

He rests in an old monastery
    on an empty mountain of fallen trees,
Frost and sleet dry up
    where a crane sleeps in pine branches.
At the root of his teeth and the root of his tongue,
    waterdrops chill—
Coral beaten by
    red gemstone jade.

I anticipate only
The seven lotuses
    will be snapped open in an instant:[170]
Each one is as pure as
    his inmost heart.

And I anticipate that a heavenly wind
    will blow heavenly blossoms[171]
Profuse as the rain,
    swirling about his *kāṣāya*.[172]
I have also heard that this *Sūtra*
    is so subtle and mysterious,
The true, esoteric essence
    of a hundred thousand buddhas.
After being proclaimed on Vulture Peak,
    it began to be transmitted:[173]
Those who hear it are many,
    but those who uphold it are few.

You can also chant it into
    dhāraṇī:
When Tang sounds and Brāhmic sounds
    are mixed together,

Shun's strings harmonize,
> sweet airs blow,
And the strings of King Wen and King Wu
> are all the more plaintive.

Thus
Ceaselessly striving in the azure heavens
> come dragons to heed,
> come ghosts to heed,
Making those in the human realm
> who hear them bow,
> who see them bow,
And spontaneously
> their hearts are emptied,
> their natures purified.

The true form of this *Sūtra*
> is Vairocana.
The white oxcart on the Snowy Peaks:
> do you not recognize it?[174]

念念念兮入惡易   -
念念念兮入善難   A
念經念佛能一般   A
愛河竭處生波瀾   A

言公少年真法器   B
白晝不出夜不睡   B
心心緣經口緣字   B
一室寥寥燈照地   B
沈檀卷軸寶函盛   -
薝蔔香熏水精記   B

空山木落古寺閑   C
松枝鶴眠霜霰幹   C
牙根舌根水滴寒   C
珊瑚搥打紅琅玕   C

但恐
蓮花七朵一時折   D
朵朵似君心地白   D

又恐天風吹天花	E
繽紛如雨飄袈裟	E
況聞此經甚微妙	F
百千諸佛真秘要	F
靈山說後始傳來	-
聞者雖多持者少	F
更堪誦入陀羅尼	G
唐音梵音相雜時	G
舜弦和雅薰風吹	G
文王武王弦更悲	G
如此	
爭不遣碧空中	-
有龍來聽	H
有鬼來聽	H
亦使人間	-
聞者敬	H
見者敬	H
自然	
心虛空	-
性清淨	H
此經真體即毗盧	I
雪嶺白牛君識無	I[175]

Qiji's poem is both a representation of the monk's recitation in song and a literary performance of song as a kind of recitation. As in Guanxiu's poem, the opening simple retriplications of "minding" (*nian* 念) mark off the world of the poem as a kind of sacred space, imitating the sound of the monks' chants. This incantatory quality continues throughout the poem with its dense rhymes: 30 out of 34 lines end with a rhyme word. The opening sounds give way to the message of the *Lotus Sūtra*: it is hard to maintain goodness, but the *Lotus Sūtra*, which gives one access to incredible powers (line 3) and is equated with the Buddha as his textual embodiment (line 33), can help.

The speaker then describes the intense training of the reciting monk: he spent every day and every night in his youth practicing (lines 5-6). Though his personal possessions are few, the *Lotus Sūtra* is properly venerated with incense and stored in a precious case (lines 9-10). Having memorized the text, the *Lotus* lives with him, is instantiated by him (line 7), making him a "vessel of the true dharma" (line 5). That is, he is a physical embodiment of the *Lotus Sūtra*, which is itself a textual embodiment of the Buddha and his dharma. The monk is deified. This brings the poem to the site of the *Sūtra*'s recitation, the body of a monk located in a humble mountain monastery in winter (lines 11-12). The speaker zeroes in on the monk's mouth, whence the sacred text issues forth into the world. He describes the mouth first in literal, visceral terms (drops of liquid on his teeth and tongue, line 13) and then in metaphoric, glorified terms (his teeth as coral, his tongue as red jade, line 14). As the site of the *Lotus Sūtra*'s re-creation, the monk's mouth is afforded the same veneration that the *Sūtra* itself received in lines 9-10.[176]

Next, the speaker anticipates internal and external signs confirming the efficacy of the *Sūtra* recitation. The internal sign of the *Sūtra*'s efficacy is the fact that the content of each fascicle, once opened, is revealed to be pure, just like the very ground of the reciting monk's mind (lines 15-16). Externally, flowers rain from the sky upon his recitation, as they did when the great monks of the sixth century chanted the text (lines 17-18). Like Guanxiu's arhat dreams, these visions are important markers of the spiritual power of the monk's recitation. Nevertheless, not everyone can grasp the *Sūtra* (line 22), for its power is "subtle," "mysterious," and "esoteric" (lines 19-20).

Also like Guanxiu's arhats, the *Sūtra*'s power is tied to its non-Chinese origins—in India (line 21) and, prior to that, in the heavenly realms of a hundred thousand buddhas (line 20). But the *Sūtra* does not remain irrevocably foreign, nor does it overpower the classical songs of China it comes into contact with. It brings out those songs in a new way, as a harmony to melody (line 25). Or, to switch metaphors, the *Lotus Sūtra* acts like salt, strengthening the inherent flavors that were already present in the original ingredients (see line 26). Qiji envisions a hybrid song in the form of a *dhāraṇī*: neither fully Chinese nor fully Indian, it has elements of the sounds of both (lines 23-24). Fitting into neither category, it would draw on the numinous powers of both traditions, attracting listeners in all human realms, and above and below (lines 27-28), transforming in an instant those who would hear or read it (lines 29-32). The spiritual power of Buddhism and the aesthetic power of classical Chinese music would meld into a new song for a new, post-Tang era. It would be, Qiji implies, something like the work of a poet-monk like himself. It would be Buddhist poetry.

Qiji's poem is both an homage to and exemplar of a tradition of Buddhist chanting, one that emerges from a fascination with the esoteric power of Indian languages and attempts to combine this power with the classical songs of the poetic tradition. It is incantatory: part of an oral performance that accesses esoteric power and wields it in order to aid others, especially in their spiritual transformation. Such incantations are not jumbles of meaningless syllables but rather sensory experiences whose meaning is performative. Unlike Zhu Wan's poem that described and alluded, Qiji's poem performs the recitation's power. Its very articulation enacts its purpose. It is not a mere sign pointing to a higher truth like the *i*-graph in the Brāhmī script. Rather, like Guanxiu's arhat paintings, the recitation of the *Lotus Sūtra* is both a product of and an object for religious devotion. Qiji's song simultaneously venerates and enacts such a recitation.

The oral recitation of sacred texts, including the incantation of *dhāraṇī*, stems from a larger fascination with the Indian origins of Buddhism and the sense of authenticity afforded to monks, scripts, images, and sounds associated with India. Though most closely associated with esoteric ritual technologies, incantation was also part of the shared culture of medieval Buddhism across Asia. *Dhāraṇī* could be extremely repetitive and semantically meaningless. However, the power of these texts came not from their semantic meaning or even their foreignness but rather their performance. That is, in the act of uttering spells or reciting sūtras, the practitioner became the very site of that sacred text's production and, as such, wielded its power. A poem like Qiji's song of the *Lotus Sūtra*-reciting monk both described and embodied this kind of recitation.

The repetitions found throughout the works of Guanxiu, Qiji, and other poet-monks are performative. Like incantations, their power is nonrepresentational. Their patterns of sound act on the audience *as sound*, not just as language. Thus, the aural quality of these works is what makes them, in one sense, religious. Such poems use the same mechanism as spells. They function according to the same logic. They are the same in practice. They could become Buddhist poetry.

But incantation was not the only Buddhist practice the poet-monks found to be fundamentally in accord with classical poetry. In the late medieval period, another spiritual technology that provided insight into the deeper levels of reality was gaining in popularity, and the poet-monks brought this into their literary works too. They were the first, we will see, to identify the fundamental unity of poetry and meditation.

CHAPTER 6

Meditation

Effort and Absorption

Poetry is meditation, meditation poetry. This claim, of the homology between poetry and meditation, has deep roots in traditional Chinese criticism. From at least the thirteenth century onward, there is a strong habit to use the terms of Chan Buddhism as metaphors for the experience of reading and writing poetry.[1] The metaphors were repeated so often that they became a cliché and soon seemed inevitable.[2] Poetry and meditation could help explain each other, since both were based in acts of self-cultivation that reflected privileged insight into the world. Poetry and meditation would be analogous ways of seeing.

But, despite what modern, popular writers on Zen poetry may say, this equation of poetry and meditation was neither inevitable nor unchanging.[3] It emerged in the second half of the Tang dynasty and transformed soon thereafter as the result of specific developments in the history of literary and Buddhist practice. As Qian Zhongshu 錢鍾書 (1910-1998) once noted, Tang and Song poets held profoundly different attitudes toward the relationship between poetry and meditation. Whereas Song poets take the relationship to be metaphorical, the Tang poets who mention the relationship "all combine into one the mind of poetry and the mind of Buddhism" 皆以詩心佛心，打成一片.[4] That is, during the Tang dynasty, the relationship between poetic and Buddhist practices was not metaphorical; it was equal. It is the purpose of the present chapter to explain exactly how several poet-monks of the Late Tang came to assert the fundamental unity of meditation and poetry.

While there have been many surveys of the relationship between Buddhism and poetry and many attempts to understand the "Buddhist thought" of lay Tang poets, few have traced the internal logic of the equation between poetry and meditation.[5] Those who have examined in detail the relationship between poetry and Buddhist practice have usually done so from the perspective of the Song Dynasty, after Chan had developed into a full-fledged institution and many assumptions about poetry had changed.[6] Those who have focused on the Tang period tend to see it as building toward this Song culmination.[7] This chapter, by contrast, takes seriously the claims of poet-monks who lived through the collapse of the Tang and its aftermath. It traces how, in the late ninth century, several strands in literary and Buddhist discourses converged to create a new understanding of poetry.

The most important of these strands was the *kuyin* aesthetic that was briefly introduced in chapter 3. Intense devotion to poetry, to the point of physical and mental suffering, was upheld as an ideal in this approach to writing. The legacy of Jia Dao was crucial to establishing and popularizing this particular sense of *kuyin*. At the same time, an older layer of the literary theoretical tradition, which saw poets as those who sent their spirit to roam the cosmos, was also given new life in the Late Tang as it mixed with the *kuyin* aesthetic and Buddhist meditation. This connection between *kuyin* devotion and religious asceticism helped create the very idea of "poet" as an identity in itself, as Stephen Owen has suggested.[8] But the poet-monks took this one step further. Buddhist monasticism did not just provide a model for the poet as literary ascetic. They asserted that the practices of poetry and meditation are not just analogous (as asserted in the Song) but fundamentally the same, being two gates to the same goal. Qiji articulated this view most clearly, but it has its roots in remarks made by earlier poet-monks like Jiaoran and Guanxiu. By asserting this fundamental unity, Qiji and others could turn the writing of poetry into a means of understanding the fundamental nature of all reality, on par with Buddhist enlightenment.

The Painstaking Couplet

In the first half of the ninth century, just as the term "poet-monk" began to spread throughout the Tang empire, a new trend in poetry emerged. This was the valorization of *kuyin*, particularly in one sense of that term, which crystallized around the ex-monk Jia Dao. Abundant evidence for this trend can be found not only in poetry written in the Late Tang but also in poetry manuals written at this time. As we have seen, these manuals are composed mainly of exemplary couplets classified by various poetic techniques and principles, which may or may not be accompanied by prose explanations. Many were written by poet-monks or their associates, and they obsess over Jia Dao.[9] In the poet-monk Xuzhong's *Handmirror of Streams and Categories* (*Liulei shoujian* 流類手鑑), Jia Dao is the most frequently quoted of any poet.[10] Qiji, in his *Exemplary Models of Poetry*, cites Jia Dao more often than anyone besides himself.[11] In Xu Yin's *Confidential Matters of the Way of Elegantiae*, Jia Dao is third-most cited (with eight citations), after two other self-described *kuyin* practitioners, Qiji (fourteen) and Zhou He (eleven).[12] Li Dong 李洞 compiled an entire manual from only Jia Dao's couplets.[13] Another manual, titled *Secret Exemplars of the Two "Souths"* (*Ernan mizhi* 二南密旨), was attributed to Jia Dao. Although probably not written by the master himself, it was likely compiled by one of his many admirers at the start of the tenth century and attests to how highly regarded his name was at the time.[14]

The central concern of the poetry manuals is the fine art of the individual couplet and its achievement via *kuyin*. The term *kuyin* first gained its technical sense in the work of Meng Jiao.[15] To Meng, *kuyin* was the vocal recitation of one's own verses during the process of composition and revision, done for the sake of achieving personal success in the imperial bureaucracy, often via the civil examination system. His concept of *kuyin* as the painstaking preparation for the exams, which function as a test of one's ability to contribute to the greater good, dominated as long as there was general faith in the examination system.

Stirred at Night, Dispelling My Sorrow 夜感自遣

Meng Jiao

Studying at night, still haven't stopped by dawn,
As I *kuyin*, the gods and ghosts worry.
How is it I can't rest?
My mind and body are enemies.
Disgrace in death is pain for a short while;
Disgrace in life is humiliation for many years.
The pure osmanthus has no straight branches,
By the sapphire river, I think of my old travels.

夜學曉未休，
苦吟神鬼愁。
如何不自閑，
心與身為讎。
死辱片時痛，
生辱長年羞。
清桂無直枝，
碧江思舊遊。[16]

The central preoccupation of this poem is success in the examinations: breaking off an osmanthus branch is a symbol of passing, and the fact that none of these branches are "straight" or "upright" causes the speaker much consternation (line 7). How is it, the speaker wonders, that the unworthy passed, while an upright poet like himself lingers in obscurity? Poetic composition was tested on the exams and valued by high officials. Consequently, circulating a brief scroll of one's verse (*xingjuan* 行卷) with the capital elites was a crucial first step in establishing one's reputation at the outset of a bureaucratic career.[17] It was therefore necessary to have a perfectly polished collection to succeed in Mid-Tang political and literary life. This led to an inflated rhetoric of intensity. To prove his worth, Meng Jiao describes how he never rests (line 3) and even comes to consider his tiring body the enemy of his mind (line 4). The logic is a strange reversal of the high-mindedness often found in medieval literature, in which one's historical legacy is more important than success in this life. Instead, Meng Jiao states that success in this life matters more than one's reputation after death, since the pain of deathbed regret is over quickly, while the suffering of lifelong humiliation lasts decades (lines 5–6). Examination poetry, as the hallmark of success, is more important than life itself.

Such stakes meant that it was necessary to constantly revise one's poems until each line was phrased perfectly. Liu Deren, also working through the night, describes the process: "Fixing lines of a poem until morning, / My neighbors dislike my *kuyin*" 到曉改詩句，四鄰嫌苦吟.[18] Liu Deren sat for the examinations multiple times over a twenty-year period but extant evidence suggests that he never passed. Despite his repeated failures, he felt the compulsion to keep working at it, to keep going over his writings, reading them aloud until they sounded just right. In one poem, he describes how he "cuts to the bone in search of new lines" 刻骨搜新句.[19] Elsewhere, he is ashamed for not having achieved anything despite how weary those same bones have grown.

Presented to Vice Director Cui on Taking the Examinations: 2 of 4 省試日上崔侍郎四首（其二）

Liu Deren

I've been like one sick or stupid
    for twenty autumns—
It's hard to succeed in seeking a name,
    but it's even harder to rest.
I should surely be ashamed
    when looking back at my flesh and bones:
Though I'm cloaked in coarse-hemp robes
    my head is white.

如病如癡二十秋，
求名難得又難休。
回看骨肉須堪恥，
一著麻衣便白頭。[20]

When one's sense of success is based on obtaining an official career after passing the examinations (politely referred to as "achieving a name" 得名, line 2), failure is devastating. Shame and poverty follow (lines 3–4). To Liu Deren and many others in the early and mid-ninth century, official success was a measure of self-worth. At best, failure meant remaining on the margins of elite culture; at worst, it meant an utter negation of one's very purpose in life.

This strain of *kuyin*—associated with Meng Jiao and success in officialdom—continued into the tenth century, but it did not become the dominant one. Rather, it was Meng's associate Jia Dao who became most fully identified with the *kuyin* aesthetic. The *New Tang History*'s assessment of Jia Dao, for example, refers explicitly to *kuyin* as part of his legacy.[21] His very person is defined by this term, as attested by many of the poems memorializing him.[22] In his own verse, Jia Dao too identified his very self with *kuyin*, referring to himself as "a *kuyin* person" 苦吟身 in one poem.[23] It is not just a stage in his life, the discomforting time between preparing for an official career and achieving it. It is his entire life. Although Jia Dao did take the examinations (and failed) soon after laicizing in 812, he rarely used the rhetoric of *kuyin* to talk about a path to officialdom. Rather, he effectively separated it from the narrative of a successful career. Like earlier *kuyin* poets, Jia Dao frequently complained of his poverty, but the cause is different.[24] It is his commitment to poetry as an end in itself, not as a means to an end, that causes this suffering.

Jia Dao fundamentally changed the meaning of *kuyin* by dissociating it from official success and tying it to the writing of poetry itself. The poverty, suffering, and failure in Jia Dao's life are presented not as an ironic contrast to his obsession with poetry but rather as precisely *the result of* his commitment to poetry.[25] This comes through in the way Jia Dao lets his readers know that he has put an enormous amount of effort into his lines. One poem, for example, contains the following, seemingly unremarkable couplet: "Alone I walk my shadows at the bottom of a pool, / And repeatedly rest my body beside the trees" 獨行潭底影, 數息樹邊身.[26] To these lines is appended an annotation in verse supposedly written by Jia Dao himself (*zizhu* 自注):

> These two lines were attained after three years:
> As soon as I intoned them, a pair of tears fell from my eyes.
> If the one who knows my tone does not appreciate them
> I will go back to lie down in my old hills.

> 二句三年得,
> 一吟雙淚流。
> 知音如不賞,
> 歸臥故山丘。

The claim to intensity (measured by time rather than physical breakdown) is used to prove the sincerity of the poet's pursuit of aesthetic truth, with a recognition of his worthiness.[27] One thinks of the stories of bodhisattvas pursuing enlightenment over countless eons of rebirth. The poet is the ascetic, willing to put aside material comforts in order to attain a long-term benefit.[28] By reorienting the *kuyin* rhetoric of passion toward poetry itself, and away from official success, Jia Dao wrote new ideals for the late ninth- and tenth-century poets to strive after.

Kuyin covered a range of phenomena and approaches to poetry, and these referents shifted over the course of the Late Tang and afterward. The Jia Dao strain, which separated *kuyin* from a bureaucratic career, became especially widespread in the late ninth and tenth centuries, in part due to the literati's waning faith in political stability and, hence, in officialdom and the examination system.[29] If getting a *jinshi* degree is not a sure path to success, if talented poets routinely failed, and if the unworthy were promoted due to corruption and factionalism, why bother with officialdom at all? Thus, by the very end of the ninth century, the idea of poetry as an end in itself—rather than as a means to a successful career—became much more popular than it had been.[30]

At the center of the term *kuyin* are two interrelated concepts: the intensity of one's devotion to poetry, especially its details, and the resulting toll on the body of the poet. The physical pain of *kuyin* came from the intensity with which poets worked on their craft. Multiple poets claimed that the process of composing poems ruined their hair.[31] Such an intense passion for poetry meant an attention to detail. The tenth-century poet Liu Shaoyu 劉昭禹 reportedly likened careless composition to murder, saying: "A pentametric poem is like forty worthy men. If you misplace one character, you're a butcher" 五言如四十箇賢人，亂著一字，屠沽輩也.[32]

Many poets, like Jia Dao, identified themselves with *kuyin*. Some even went so far as to proclaim that the writing of poetry was the very purpose of life. Du Xunhe 杜荀鶴 (846–904), another member of the elite who failed the exams many times, portrays himself this way repeatedly. In the opening of one poem he announces: "My Way is in pentameter" 吾道在五字.[33] That is, his Dao—the path that he sees himself as following, the principle that structures his life—is poetry. He elaborates on this theme in a poem on *kuyin*.

Kuyin 苦吟

Du Xunhe

Within this world, what is the finest?
Nothing is finer than poetry.
When I attain a line on my own,
Everyone already knows it the four realms over.
In life, we should have no days of rest,
For death is when we shall no longer intone.
Just as I prepare to go back to the mountains,
The path by the woody spring is right here.

世間何事好，
最好莫過詩。
一句我自得，
四方人已知。
生應無輟日，
死是不吟時。
始擬歸山去，
林泉道在茲。[34]

In this poem, *ku* clearly means "intense devotion" rather than "suffering" or "bitter." The first couplet states explicitly that the speaker regards poetry as the "finest" (*hao* 好) thing in the world. Therefore, to get the most out of life, one must spend every possible moment writing (line 5). Like his contemporary Cui Tu 崔塗 (*j.s.* 888), Du Xunhe seeks to "intone in the morning and intone at dusk" 朝吟復暮吟.[35] Poetic practice has changed from a means to an end in itself, at least in Du's self-presentation. Death is to be loathed not because it is an evil but because it provides no more opportunities for creating and reciting poetry (line 6). The closing couplet underlines this point by stating the speaker's desire to go enter reclusion (the "woody spring" of line 8) before he "returns to the mountains" for good (i.e., dies). Poetry is his very raison d'être. It is the meaning of his life.

The Poet-Monks' Effort

The poet-monks of the Late Tang and Five Dynasties were just as enthralled with the *kuyin* aesthetic as anyone else.[36] Given how well connected they were with the literati, it is no surprise to find them drawing on the Meng Jiao strand of *kuyin* when writing poems of encouragement to examination candidates.[37] But the Jia Dao strand was more attractive, for it proffered ideals similar to Buddhist monasticism: living in poverty and austerity, toiling away at self-cultivation, and sacrificing one's body out of intense devotion to a text.[38] The *Awakening of Mahāyāna Faith*, which Guanxiu knew intimately, also advocates a practice of zeal similar in kind to that expected in *kuyin* discourse—a person's resolution and effort are crucial to Buddhist soteriology, just as they are to one's literary reputation.[39] So did the *Treatise on the Essentials of Guarding the Mind* 守心要論, a set of practical instructions on meditation attributed to Hongren 弘忍, in which the patriarch says:

> Make effort! Make effort! Although it may seem futile now, it shall be the cause for your future enlightenment. Do not let time pass in vain while only wasting energy. The sūtra says: "Some will reside forever in hell as if pleasantly relaxing in a garden. There are no modes of existence worse than their present state." We sentient beings fit this description. Having no idea how horribly terrifying this world really is, we never have the intention of leaving! How awful!

> 努力努力。今雖無用，共作當來之因。莫使三世虛度，枉喪功夫。《經》云：「常處地獄，如遊園觀。在餘無惡道，如己舍宅。」我等眾生今現如此，不覺不知，驚怖殺人，了無出心。奇哉。[40]

The exertion of effort, fighting against deluded complacency, becomes here the basis of salvation. It is through striving that one achieves enlightenment. Passion is required, just as in *kuyin*. Similarly, the attention to detail espoused in the *kuyin* aesthetic—as in its precursor Jiaoran—is reminiscent of Mazu Daoyi's notion of insight through attention to detail.[41] Aspects of *kuyin* can be mapped onto discourses associated with both Northern and Southern Chan lineages. But, more important than their doctrinal associations, poet-monks like Guanxiu and Qiji portray themselves as having a passion for the art itself.

Guanxiu's writings on *kuyin* share many themes with his contemporaries'. He often describes poetic composition as *ku*: hard, bitter, painstaking. As one poem has it, "Endless is the hard work (*ku*) of seeking lines" 無端求句苦.[42] Elsewhere, he writes, "In literature, you should exhaust your energy" 文章應力竭.[43] Discussing the experience of his poetic practice, he says, "My mind labors bitterly (*ku*), but the taste isn't bitter" 心苦味不苦, that is, his mind works hard, but he becomes so absorbed in the process of composition that it does not feel laborious to him.[44] Poetry, rather, is his life's work. As he directly states in the opening of another poem, "What really is my purpose? / *Lau-lau*—I love only intoning" 我竟胡為者，嘮嘮但愛吟.[45] When he discusses the physical and spiritual toll of poetic composition on the poet, as well as the importance of individual lines, he sounds like any other *kuyin* poet.[46] At times, Guanxiu explicitly posits his *kuyin* ideal as a continuation of earlier masters. In this case, he sees himself as laboring for the sake of Jia Dao and Liu Deren.[47]

Reading the Poetry Collections of Liu Deren and Jia Dao: 2 of 2 讀劉得仁賈島集二首其二

Guanxiu

Laboring in thought, you once bumped into the governor.[48]
And you often spoke of preventing nearness to the state.[49]
How can one put a price to an osmanthus branch?
From lowly alleys, you never rose above poverty.
With a sick horse, it's hard to melt snow with boiling water.[50]
When gates have been deserted, few are the people there.
Mine own chanting, too, is bitter:
I knit my brows for you.

役思曾衝尹，
多言阻國親。
桂枝何所直，

陋巷不勝貧。
馬病難湯雪,
門荒劣有人。
伊余吟亦苦,
為爾一眉嚬。⁵¹

As with most poems about two people, this one begins by alternating between its two topics, with line 1 about Jia Dao and line 2 about Liu Deren. These are allusions to anecdotes about the two. In each case, the stories tell us how complete absorption in craft paradoxically leads to political power: Jia Dao once bumped into Han Yu while contemplating the best word for a line of poetry, leading to Han's patronage of Jia, and Liu's reclusion made him seem so authentically committed to purity that a prince once devoted enormous state resources to finding him. The middle couplets contrast this with the poverty, failure, and loneliness characteristic of the *kuyin* poet. The final couplet shifts its linguistic approach, using first- and second-person pronouns instead of implying them. In doing so, the speaker states his connection to the poets as directly as possible. Guanxiu can best honor their legacies by getting down to work and writing with the same dedication to craft.

Against the increasingly common *kuyin* ideal at the turn of the tenth century, the younger monk Qiji wrote his own response poem on "Cherishing Intoning" (*aiyin* 愛吟). While Qiji himself was as committed as anyone to the *kuyin* aesthetic, one can imagine him writing this poem in order to rethink the dying metaphor or perhaps to put a little nondualism into practice.

Cherishing Intoning 愛吟

Qiji

Just as I'm about to fix my thoughts
    and shut the gate to meditation,
This monk is once again
    vexed by the poetry demon.⁵²
Leaning for a moment against the shutters,
    I follow the falling light;
Unable to sleep, gusts of snow
    continue until the last watch.
Jiaoran need not have been
    misled by his karmic traces;⁵³
Zhi Dun would've been better off had he not

been aware of his future lives.
Their transmitted writings have met
    their purest mirror[54]
Who ought to understand this
    singing of idle feelings.

正堪凝思掩禪扃,
又被詩魔惱竺卿。
偶憑窗扉從落照,
不眠風雪到殘更。
皎然未必迷前習,
支遁寧非悟後生。
傳寫會逢精鑒者,
也應知是詠閒情。[55]

Poetry here is seen not as an investment, a craft that requires ultimate devotion, but rather as a distraction. It is an outside force, made manifest as the "poetry demon" (*shimo* 詩魔)—a metaphor comparing the desire to write poetry to the demon Māra, who attempted to break Śākyamuni's concentration under the Bodhi tree, a metaphor that first gained currency in the Mid-Tang.[56] The use of "poetry demon" is precise here. Qiji's desire to write poetry interrupts his attempts at meditation; thus, Māra succeeds here where he failed with the Buddha. The poet's gaze traces the last lights of dusk as they reach out from the horizon. His mind is filled with thoughts of past poet-monks, keeping him from sleep. He cannot focus. The poem is not his life's purpose but rather the distraction from the tasks of his everyday life—meditating, sleeping. This everyday life is described as "idle" (*xian* 閒)—that is, not engaged in the business of serving the state (which Qiji did, serving as Saṃgha Rectifier in Jingnan). In doing so, Qiji adopts the terms of mainstream political discourse, not the terms of the poetic outsider. He is just a lazy writer after all.

But the consequence of this rhetorical move is that Qiji thereby justifies his own idleness. He is unproductive in his normal affairs not because he is simply lazy but because he has been attacked by an outside force. His desire to write poetry is not self-motivated love of fame; it is the result of a haunting. He cannot control it. This portrayal of poetry reflects the fine art of the couplet found in *kuyin* discourse, wherein lines are things that are "sought" (*qiu* 求) and "attained" (*de* 得): poetry is external, and the poet, whether "affectionate" (*ai*) or "painstaking" (*ku*) in his pursuit of it, is at the mercy of larger forces.

Nevertheless, when Qiji writes about the composition of poetry, he normally adopts the common terms of post-Huang Chao poetics and stresses the kind of craftsmanship and intensity associated with *kuyin*. In the final, evaluative section of his poetry manual, Qiji divides poems into three types (*san ge* 三格), a "superior type, which uses ideas" 上格用意, a "middle type, which uses vital breath" 中格用氣, and an "inferior type, which uses allusions" 下格用事. Aversion to allusions was a hallmark of *kuyin* poetry, as it stressed an aesthetic of "purity" (*qing* 清) which emphasized more direct presentations of serene mind- and landscapes.[57] In keeping with this practice, Qiji's direct uses of allusion are few, especially in his regulated verses. Instead, Qiji's and others' *kuyin* poetry stressed formal craft that can be appreciated on the surface. In a eulogistic poem written upon Guanxiu's death, he praises the older monk for precisely this craft: "My master is a craftsman of poetry, / And he truly drifted off like a cloud in the blue" 吾師詩匠者，真個碧雲流.[58] The term used here for craftsman, *jiang* 匠, literally means "carpenter" and implies that the poet brings to language the same kind of attention to shaping linguistic details as a carpenter does to wood. Writing is a specific kind of labor, the kind of painstaking crafting and polishing performed by an artisan. Elsewhere Qiji stresses the intense devotion and physical breakdown of the *kuyin* ideal.

Sending Thoughts of Sengda, the Old Meditator of Jiangxi 寄懷江西僧達禪翁

Qiji

Often I recall those days on our old mountain
When we made sand stūpas together.[59]
Not yet able to focus on *patra*-leaves,[60]
You learned to sing of willow down.
You toiled (*ku*) until your mind and bones ached
For purity that chatters teeth.
What's stopping you from perpetuating your residual habits?[61]
You were of the poets in a previous era.

長憶舊山日，
與君同聚沙。
未能精貝葉，
便學詠楊花。
苦甚傷心骨，
清還切齒牙。

何妨繼餘習，
前世是詩家。[62]

Poetry composition is not just a physically and mentally exhausting activity (line 5) but also a commitment over multiple lifetimes. As the final couplet implies, Sengda has made a habit of it in his previous incarnations and shows no sign of stopping now. This is a playful allusion to Jiaoran's justification for his poetic practice, as discussed in chapter 2. But Qiji reverses Jiaoran's apologetic tone: Sengda's poetry is not a sign of weakness; it is the fruit of multiple lifetimes', even kalpas', labor. His verse is then so pure that it "chatters teeth" (line 6)—a reversal of the usual tropes of *kuyin*'s physical consequences. Instead of the poem affecting the poet's body, it brings about a reaction in the reader's body. Though the reference to previous lifetimes is certainly playful, the very possibility of its deployment reveals that poetry required the same level of effort and commitment as the monastic life.

Guanxiu and Qiji frequently drew on *kuyin* discourse, finding in it a match for many aspects of monastic ideals. The glorification of poverty and physical suffering was just the most conspicuous of these. As we have also seen, *kuyin* implies a direct correlation between energy invested and quality of poem produced. This kind of correlation is similar to the law of cause and effect (karma) so prominent in Buddhism, in which deeds of compassion and devotion lead to merit, while wicked deeds lead to rebirth in evil realms. By this logic, the mental and physical energy invested in poetry can be understood as a meritorious act in a different discursive system. One venerates *kuyin* masters like Jia Dao instead of Buddhas. One intones poems instead of scriptures or spells. The structure of the actions are the same; only the content is different. Both systems require complete devotion to their practice.

The Still Poet

The attention to detail and intense devotion to poetry that coalesced in *kuyin* is also related to an ideal of absorption: a person devoted to a singular goal by blocking out extraneous thoughts or sensory input. This involves a kind of mental strength beyond the abilities of most humans. Poets must have an extraordinary capacity for concentration and visualization if they are to take part in the process of fashioning (*zaohua* 造化), of shaping and re-creating the patterns of the cosmos in their literary works. Though this idea of a poet's concentration had deep roots in the classical literary tradition, its fullest flowering came when it cross-pollinated with the practices of Buddhist meditation.

The classical precedent for the poetic ideal of absorption was Lu Ji's "Rhapsody on Literature" ("Wen fu" 文賦). This text, anthologized in the influential *Wenxuan*, would have been well known to any Tang poet.[63] Lu Ji describes how the poet takes a visionary journey in preparation for the act of composition.

> In the beginning, the poet both
> Withdraws sight, suspends hearing,
> And deeply contemplates, seeks broadly,
> Letting his spirit race to the eight limits,
> Letting his mind roam ten thousand spans.
> Then, at the end,
> His feelings, first glimmering, become ever brighter,
> And things, clear and resplendent, reveal one another.[64]

> 其始也，
> 皆收視反聽，
> 耽思傍訊，
> 精騖八極，
> 心遊萬仞。
> 其致也，
> 情曈曨而彌鮮，
> 物昭晰而互進。

The "Rhapsody on Literature," one of the great achievements of literary criticism in the mainstream tradition, here echoes parts of the *Songs of Chu*, in which the speaker describes a spiritual journey to parts of the known world and beyond. He turns off his mundane senses to let his mind roam, revealing internal (*qing* 情) and external (*wu* 物) realities in ever brighter relief, at which point he can channel them into the linguistic medium of a poem.

Lu Ji's "Rhapsody on Literature" had a deep impact on literary theory and practice for centuries.[65] A poetry manual attributed to Wang Changling and collected in Kūkai's *Bunkyō hifuron* describes the process of composition in terms of a similar spirit journey, though giving the poet's mind a more active role:

> When mentally preparing to compose a poem, you must fix your mind, and your eyes will touch their objects. When you use your mind to touch them, you will deeply pierce their world. It is like

climbing the summit of a high mountain: when you look down on the ten thousand things, it is like they are in the palm of your hand. When you see images in this way, you will see them clearly in your mind, and thus can they be put to use.⁶⁶

夫置意作詩，即須凝心，目擊其物，便以心擊之，深穿其境。如登高山絕頂，下臨萬象，如在掌中。以此見象，心中了見，當此即用。

Before anything can happen, the mind must reach the same state of concentration as described in Lu Ji's rhapsody. Once it is settled and focused, it can be used to pierce objects in a way that sight alone cannot. That is, the mind does not just see phenomena, it sees through them to get to their cosmic significance as images. The poet can then recall these images and arrange them into the world of a poem. But this only comes through mental absorption of the kind that "tires (*ku*) your mind and exhausts your intelligence, wherein you must forget your person" 苦心竭智，必須忘身, as the author writes in the passage just preceding this one.⁶⁷ The mind, through the kind of toil in which one lets go of one's very self, can be trained to take hold of the images of the cosmos and re-create them in a poem.

As early as the late eighth century, Tang poets began to make explicit analogies between the kind of concentration espoused in poetic theory and the increasingly popular Buddhist practices of meditation. Yang Juyuan 楊巨源 (b. 755), for example, could write: "'Knocking on stillness' comes out of distant contemplation, / Finding the marvelous originates in comprehending meditative wisdom" 扣寂由來在淵思，搜奇本自通禪智.⁶⁸ The first line of Yang's couplet synthesizes two sections of the "Rhapsody on Literature." The sort of spirit journey we examined earlier is said to be the basis of another one of the poet's activities described in Lu Ji's rhapsody, in which the poet "tests the void and nonexistence to demand of it existence, / Knocks upon stillness and silence, seeking a tone" 課虛無以責有，叩寂寞而求音.⁶⁹ That is, the act of poetic creation, which seems to emerge out of nothing, is in fact the product of a spirit journey. The second line of Yang's couplet draws on the jargon of Buddhism to come at the same point from a slightly different angle. Intense mental concentration, divorced from sensory input, is what leads to new insight.

Later writers made this same point, that poetry requires the same kind of concentration as Buddhist meditation, using the language of *kuyin*. In a poem to Jia Dao, Yao He writes, "When madness erupts, you chant (*yin*) as if weeping, / When sorrow comes, you sit as in meditation" 狂發

吟如哭，愁來坐似禪。[70] And Pei Yue, in a fragmentary couplet, similarly writes: "*Kuyin*: a monk entering concentration, / Attaining a couplet: a general achieving success" 苦吟僧入定，得句將成功。[71] Pei Yue's lines are the more explicit of the two, making a direct analogy between meditation and *kuyin* across the caesura, but Yao He's are the more interesting. Not only do Yao's lines come from a poem addressed to the *kuyin* paragon Jia Dao himself, they also reconcile what seem to be two opposing qualities. Madness, an intense mania associated with wild calligraphers who give free reign to their imaginations, makes way for the stillness of meditation (*chan*). First, the intense emotion of madness overwhelms the poet, which he must let out in weeping or poetry or some combination of the two. This experience, subjective and isolating, then brings the poet to a state of sorrow, a calm in which he can enter meditation (presumably to send his thoughts forth to gather more prompts for artistic creation). Poetry can prepare one for meditation, just as meditation can prepare one for poetry.

Liu Yuxi, the exiled literatus who wrote the first history of poet-monks in the early ninth century, was perhaps the first to explicitly theorize the connection between meditation and poetic concentration. On the whole, he seems to have held ambivalent attitudes toward Buddhists' attempts at writing high literature. As noted in chapter 2, his preface to Lingche's collection praised its subject precisely for transcending the category of "poet-monk." However, in the preface to a parting poem given to the monk Hongju 鴻舉 in the fall of 814, Liu suggests the possibility that a Buddhist monk with literary inclinations may be capable of writing superior verse.

> When one is able to be free of desire, the ground of his heart is empty; when it's empty, the ten thousand images can enter; once they've entered, they must come out, and so they take shape in phrases. To be marvelous and deep, these phrases must follow tonal meter. Thus, from the recent past on down, Buddhists who are known throughout the world for their poetry have come one after another. When they attain a poem-world in concentration, it is natural and pure. When they send it off in language with wisdom, their works are refined and striking.

> 能離欲，則方寸地虛，虛而萬象入，入必有所泄，乃形乎詞，詞妙而深者，必依於聲律，故自近古而降，釋子以詩聞於世者相踵焉。因定而得境，故翛然以清；由慧而遣辭，故粹然以麗。[72]

Liu Yuxi blends the classical expressive theory of the "Great Preface" ("Da xu" 大序) to the *Book of Odes* with the idea of the poet as Fashioner and with Buddhist concepts of quietude and emptiness. The classical discourse maintains that things stirred inside a person must come out one way or another, whether through sigh, song, or dance.[73] But instead of saying those things inside are emotions (*qing*) stirred by events in the world, Liu Yuxi asserts that they are the very images (*xiang*) of the ten thousand things that make up reality, and that they will only enter into a mind that is completely still and empty. That is, poets are not passive recipients of events who respond spontaneously with accurate, authentic reactions to the world. Instead, poets are those who must first cultivate their minds in order to prepare them for the arrival of the images. Not everyone is capable of being a poet. It is the province of those with a superior control of their mind. For this reason, Buddhists have a potentially privileged relationship to poetry. They are experts in the mind, having honed it over many years of practice, cleansing it of desire's interference. In this way, the world of their poems and the perception that mediates (*jing* 境 refers to both) are also pure. Sun Guangxian, as noted in chapter 3, once praised Guanxiu for precisely this quality: "His poem-worlds and ideas (*jingyi*) were outstanding and unique, impossible to match" 境意卓異，殆難儔敵.[74] Monks' ability to concentrate (*ding* 定), to settle their minds, can be applied directly to poetry. There is no noise distorting the images as they enter the monks' minds, nor as they come out in words. Therefore, the monks' works are "refined and striking." In modern parlance, we might say that Buddhist monks have a transferrable skill set. A calm mind, imbued with the images of the cosmos, is precisely what is required of poets. They are, after all, fashioners of the world.

The Two Gates

The homology of poetic concentration and Buddhist meditation, suggested by Liu Yuxi and others, came to its fullest expression in the work of Qiji.[75] Qiji was familiar with monks associated with the Wei-Yang lineage, being a native of the Chu region and having exchanged poems with Wei-Yang monks.[76] The Wei-Yang lineage was particularly noted for its emphasis on the complementary nature of religious practice, ordinary life, and sudden enlightenment, and especially how the forms of the physical world can shed light on the mind (*ji se ming xin* 即色明心).[77] The Buddhist communities at Hongzhou, where Qiji, Guanxiu, and other poet-monks lived for many years, similarly stressed "non-cultivation," the possibility of turning any everyday action into meditation.[78] Texts associated with the Hongzhou communities often framed this in terms of meditating in any of the "four postures" 四威儀 in which all monastic activity is performed.[79] As one sermon attributed to Hongzhou patriarch Mazu Daoyi put it:

> All dharmas are Buddha-dharma, and all dharmas are liberation. Liberation is Thusness, and all dharmas never leave Thusness. Walking, standing, sitting, and lying—all these are inconceivable functions, which do not wait for a timely season.
>
> 一切法皆是佛法，諸法即解脫。解脫者即眞如，諸法不出於如。行住坐臥，悉是不思議用，不待時節。[80]

Given the fact that the ultimate and the mundane are perfectly interfused, completely dependent on one another, one need not sit in silence to meditate. Activity in any posture can give one access to the "inconceivable," that is, enlightenment which is beyond thought. The doctrine of the inseparability of principle and phenomena gave rise to the practice of non-meditation as meditation, something that came to be seen as a hallmark of Hongzhou and related Buddhist communities. Such doctrines left much room for an advanced practitioner to engage with the arts and would have been convenient justification for a poet-monk.

Often Qiji discusses poetry and meditation as the two distinct but complementary activities on which he spends most of his time. He opens several poems with lines like "Outside of meditation, I seek poetry's wonders" 禪外求詩妙 and "Outside of monasticism, the pleasure of idle chanting is purest" 僧外閑吟樂最清.[81] In these lines, his Buddhist practice is portrayed as primary, his poetic practice as secondary. Other times he reverses the terms. Another poem opens, "When I've no taste for chanting poems, I take up sūtras" 無味吟詩即把經.[82] In exchanges with other poet-monks, he describes their activities in a similar manner: "In addition to the work of sūtras and śāstras, you also take on the task of poetry" 經論功餘更業詩, he writes of a monk named Huixian 惠暹.[83] In a quatrain to a certain Venerable Guang, he echoes the *kuyin* language of Pei Yue.

Replying to the Venerable Guang 酬光上人

Qiji

After the difficulties of meditation discourse
    you come to poetic discourse.

Sitting on stones, your mind is the same
> as the soul of the moon out.
Recall how last autumn,
> when we met to intone,
We were still out at the fifth watch,
> by the roots of the old pines.

禪言難後到詩言，
坐石心同立月魂。
應記前秋會吟處，
五更猶在老松根。[84]

Qiji posits a sequential relationship between religious and literary activities and makes poetry the second stage—perhaps implying temporal sequence, perhaps implying that it is the more advanced of the two (line 1). In the second line, the Venerable Guang sits on stones, his mind pure and clear like the moon that shines overhead. This image of his physical and mental stillness could describe either seated meditation or poetry composition. The point is moot, because the two look the same. The very ambiguity of the line, as it provides a bridge to a description of poetic composition through the night, underscores a connection between these practices. Though still distinct, poetry and meditation require their practitioners' bodies to adopt similar poses. They share a physical repertoire.

When explaining his own approach to the composition of poetry, Qiji ties together many of the strands already mentioned. The complementary nature of poetry and meditation, the obsession with formal perfection, and the physical toll of *kuyin*-style devotion to the craft of verse are all mentioned and exemplified in one of his more self-conscious poems.

Explaining Intoning 喻吟
> Qiji

What do I focus on day to day?
When tired from intoning I sit in meditation.
Though this life is enjoyable,
Nothing else is related to it.
My head has whitened in pursuit of "no wrong";[85]
My spirit is purified before the real images.
Riverside flowers and fragrant grasses
Don't pollute the field of my inner self.[86]

日用是何專，
吟疲即坐禪。
此生還可喜，
餘事不相便。
頭白無邪裏，
魂清有象先。
江花與芳草，
莫染我情田。[87]

Qiji portrays poetry as his primary vocation and meditation as a welcome respite from it (line 2). These two activities constitute the majority of his daily life (line 1), taking pleasure in them and little else (lines 3–4). Poetry is labor, and his hard work pays off. He achieves two of the ideals described earlier: poetic perfection on par with the *Odes* (line 5) and an emphasis on the real images of the cosmos (line 6). The latter, moreover, is only possible because his spirit has attained purity and thus become capable of going on the kind of spiritual journey described by Lu Ji's "Rhapsody on Literature." The poem concludes by explicitly relating his poetic and religious practices. Contrary to what one may assume, the sensuous "riverside flowers" and "fragrant grasses" often depicted in poetry do not harm his unattached mind (lines 7–8). Qiji may be subtly depicting himself as having achieved an advanced level of detachment, in which the practitioner is permitted to enjoy sensory experience.[88] That is to say, poetic and religious practice are not oppositional. In fact, it is precisely because of Qiji's advanced meditative practice that he may be so bold in his literary works.

In poems written to Zheng Gu, Qiji further develops this relationship between poetry and meditation. One quatrain puts the two practices in parallel with each other, implying their fundamental unity.

Sent to Director Zheng Gu 寄鄭谷郎中

Qiji

I have recently come across a craftsman of poetry
    in the human realm,
And I once met a mind-stamped master
    beyond the birds.[89]
There is nothing so singularly marvelous
    besides these two gates—
Beneath a riverside pine,
    I trace my thoughts alone.

人間近遇風騷匠，
鳥外曾逢心印師。
除此二門無別妙，
水邊松下獨尋思。[90]

Poetry and Buddhism are "two gates" (line 3)—that is, two approaches to the same goal. In Buddhist writings, this phrase is often used to describe two seemingly contradictory approaches that are fundamentally interrelated and conditioned on each other, such as the Lesser and Greater Vehicles, or saṃsāra and true thusness (*zhenru*).[91] Qiji, in his own poetry manual, describes poetry's forty gates, which are various moods, attitudes, and realms—such as "satisfaction" (*deyi* 得意, no. 7), "turning one's back on the times" (*beishi* 背時, no. 8), "divinity" (*shenxian* 神仙, no. 30), and "purity" (*qingjie* 清潔, no. 40)—through which the poet must enter in order to attain his couplets.[92] They are all distinct approaches that lead to the same goal—a well-wrought poem. The gate metaphor, to Qiji, is pluralist. It stresses that there can be multiple ways to enter into something. In the quatrain to Zheng Gu, poetic composition and Buddhist meditation are two such gates. In the first couplet, they are embodied by the two guides mentioned in the first couplet, Zheng Gu (line 1) and an unspecified "mind-stamped master" who is part of an orthodox lineage (line 2). Qiji positions himself as one who, having gone through both gates, finds himself at the same realm on the other side, where he sits in absorption, no longer with any teacher, following his thoughts as they go by (line 4). That is, poetry and meditation are two ways in to the same thing—stillness. Both gates lead to heightened mental concentration.[93]

Qiji expands on this idea of mental concentration in another poem to Zheng Gu. Here he draws on the *kuyin* aesthetic to invert the normal way it conceives of absorption. Instead of being a means to achieve two different ends (religious insight and poetic creation), absorption becomes an end in itself, something attainable through either literary or religious training. Monasticism is not just a model for poetic pursuits—both meditation and poetry composition are forms of ascetic devotion that may lead one into an absorptive trance.

Sent to Director Zheng Gu 寄鄭谷郎中
Qiji

How could your poetry mind be passed on?
What you have realized is naturally the same as meditation.[94]

Seeking a couplet is like searching for a tiger;
Finding understanding is like reaching a transcendent.
Your spirit is pure, antiquity resides therein;
Your words lovely, filled with the Elegantiae and Airs.
You were once praised as a purified starry gentleman,[95]
But were embarrassed that this was too ostentatious.

詩心何以傳，
所證自同禪。
覓句如探虎，
逢知似得仙。
神清太古在，
字好雅風全。
曾沐星郎許，
終慚是斐然。[96]

The language of Buddhist practice pervades these lines, even as it draws on classical discourse. Zheng Gu's poetry is imbued with "antiquity" (*taigu* 太古) and the moral purity of the *Book of Odes* (lines 5–6). But Zheng Gu also has a "poetry mind" (*shixin* 詩心) that can be "passed on" (*chuan* 傳) to his followers, just like the mind of a Chan patriarch (line 1). This implies not only a sense of lineage but also a sense that poetry is itself a practice implying a certain view of reality, like meditation, that leads to higher insights. One can cultivate one's inherent poetry mind, just as one can cultivate one's Buddha mind (*foxin* 佛心). It is on this basis that Qiji gives Zheng Gu the highest possible compliment he can think of: he has proven the deep homology between poetry and meditation (line 2). Their fundamental root is not only theoretical but also something that Qiji has witnessed in the work of Zheng Gu. He has proven that one with a deeply cultivated poetry-mind can reach the same insights as one who has cultivated the Buddha-mind. The verb Qiji uses here, *zheng* 證 ("realized"), is used throughout texts on the nascent Chan lineages to describe both the attainment of enlightenment and the proof of it that one gives to others.[97] As in the quatrain written to Zheng Gu, Qiji again asserts that poetry and meditation are two gates to the same goal.

The second couplet then follows logically from the first. It explains how it is possible that poetry and meditation ascertain the same thing. The enormous effort a poet like Zheng Gu must make to achieve a perfectly wrought couplet is precisely the same effort needed to reach insight through religious practice. Qiji clearly thought it a good couplet, as he included it in his own poetics treatise to illustrate "Hardship" (*jiannan* 艱難), one of poetry's "Twenty Models" (*ershi shi* 二十式).[98] The third line, moreover, draws on one of the theoretical precursors to *kuyin*, a passage from Jiaoran's *Poetic Paradigms*:

> It is also said: "Hard (*ku*) thought is not necessary. When one thinks hard, he loses the substance of spontaneity." This too is wrong. If one won't enter a tiger's lair, how can one catch a tiger cub? When obtaining a poem-world, striking couplets only begin to reveal themselves after reaching difficulty and danger. Once you have composed a piece, observe its appearance: if it seems easy, attained without thought, this is the work of a superior hand.
>
> 又云：不要苦思，苦思則喪自然之質。此亦不然。夫不入虎穴，焉得虎子？取境之時，須至難、至險，始見奇句。成篇之後，觀其氣貌，有似等閒，不思而得，此高手也。[99]

Lines that appear effortless or spontaneous are never what they seem. That is the illusion of a master poet. As Borges once said, "Perfect things in poetry do not seem strange; they seem inevitable."[100] Underlying this breezy surface is the solid foundation of hard work. Poetry, like meditation, requires one to brave the rocky terrain of the human mind. Only through years of training, of concentration, of labor, can one attain the sort of perceptual awareness that is the fruit of both poetic and religious practice.

Qiji elaborated this equation between poetry and meditation not only in poems written to Zheng Gu. If that were the case, one may think that he is simply adopting the terms of his interlocutor for the sake of instruction, a form of *upāya*. Instead, even in poems describing his own meditation practice, he makes the same claim:

Sitting in Stillness 靜坐
    Qiji
Sitting, lying, walking, and standing
I enter meditation, still intoning out.
Over long days and months, this will
Wear down my body and mind.
Few things resemble silent communication;[101]
Huangmei's address was profound.[102]
On the path of old pines before my gate,
Sometimes I get up to walk in the cool shade.

坐臥與行住，
入禪還出吟。
也應長日月，
消得個身心。
默論相如少，
黃梅付囑深。
門前古松徑，
時起步清陰。[103]

The boldest claim here is the opening: poetry and meditation may be performed simultaneously. That is, the "non-cultivation" advocated in several late medieval Buddhist communities is limited not only to the four postures of sitting, lying, walking, and standing; it extends even to the composition of poetry itself. Qiji proceeds using the same logic as the previous poem, drawing on the rhetoric of *kuyin*. The activity he is describing—whether that is taken to be meditation, poetry composition, or a hybrid of the two—takes a physical toll on his body.

The third couplet then draws on the technical language of late medieval Buddhism to emphasize the complementarity of language and silence. In line 5, the rare teachings of a master are transferred to a disciple without using words—thus using silence to convey something normally understood through language. In line 6, the patriarch Hongren (here called Huangmei) wrote treatises on quiet meditation—thus using language to convey something normally understood through silence. The poem concludes with the speaker rising from his meditation to stroll through a path of old pines and, presumably, write a poem about them. That is, taking his own equation of meditation and poetry writing seriously, the speaker goes out to put it into practice.

Elsewhere Qiji uses the dialectical tension of parallelism to assert a fundamental identity between poetic and meditative practice, drawing again on the language of hardship.

Meeting a Poet-Monk 逢詩僧
Qiji

Meditation's mysteries—they cannot be equaled,[104]
Poetry's marvels—how can they be critiqued?
You suffer in five or seven characters
And are purified after hundreds or thousands of years.
Though hard to find, you arrive at principle,
When you "do not wither," you'll make a name.[105]

We cherish and value seeing each other often,
Forgetting plans and talking of these things.[106]

禪玄無可並,
詩妙有何評。
五七字中苦,
百千年後清。
難求方至理,
不朽始為名。
珍重重相見,
忘機話此情。[107]

In each of the first three couplets, Qiji focuses on meditation in the first line and poetry in the second. The opening presents us with a paradox: things that cannot be "equaled" or "critiqued" are beyond human comprehension, yet they are precisely the poet-monk's area of expertise. The word used at the end of line 1 for "equaled" (*bing* 並) more literally means "place side by side, in parallel with," so Qiji is saying that nothing can be put in parallel with the fruits of meditation. Yet he spends the rest of the poem doing just that: he matches poetry and meditation in parallel couplets. Thus the paradox at the heart of the poem: Qiji does what he claims cannot be done.[108]

The middle couplets present the path that the poet-monk must tread in similar terms. The goals, given in lines 5–6, are different: in poetry, one seeks to establish a reputation; in meditation, one strives for ultimate truth. Yet both promise a kind of transcendence beyond normal human life. A poet's words live on after death, and insight into Buddhist reality leads to the attainment of nirvāṇa. Both require long journeys of intense striving (lines 3–4), be it in the crafting of pentametric and heptametric lines or the countless rebirths on the bodhisattva path. Qiji stresses their similarity through a playful switch of words. "Suffering" (*ku* 苦, line 3) can be understood as a technical Buddhist term (*duḥkha*) for the misery of life in saṃsāra, the First Noble Truth, but here it is used to describe *poetic* practice, drawing on the rhetoric of *kuyin*. "Purified" (*qing* 清, line 4), on the other hand, is frequently used to describe austere, dignified descriptions of landscapes in poetry, but here it is used to describe the fruits of Buddhist—not poetic—practice. In this way, Qiji writes an underlying unity of literary and meditative practices into his poem, even as he denies its possibility in the first two lines. This is what poet-monks do, according to Qiji: live in the tension between the two truths of mundane and ultimate reality, use words to point to practice, practice to broach transcendent principle. The poet-monk he meets understands this as well, and the two become so absorbed in the conversation that they lose track of their plans (line 8).

This idea of the poet-monk as the one who understands and performs the underlying unity between poetry and meditation reaches its apex in a poem about Qiji. The audacious opening unfolds into an embodiment of its claim.

Reading the Venerable Qiji's Collection 讀齊己上人集

Qichan

[Your] poems are meditation for Confucians,
Their form is truly transcendent.
Ancient and elegant like the Hymns of Zhou,
Pure and harmonious as the strains of Shun.
Ice forms: your couplet on hearing the cascade.
A fragrance wafts: your piece on early plums.[109]
Contemplating them, I intone them until night,
And your literary star lights up the heavens of Chu.

詩為儒者禪，
此格的惟仙。
古雅如周頌，
清和甚舜弦。
冰生聽瀑句，
香發早梅篇。
想得吟成夜，
文星照楚天。[110]

The opening line states that poetry and meditation are fully identical at their roots: the only difference is that one is primarily the task of a Confucian scholar, the other the task of a Buddhist monk. And a poet-monk is someone who translates one into the other. The practices of meditation and of writing poetry are basically the same, even if their outward manifestations are different. Both poetry and meditation involve a heightened sense of perception, a knack for ordering thoughts and objects, countless hours of hard striving toward a suddenly realized goal, and a final achievement of supramundane insight. This sense of identity is reinforced by lines 3–4, which praise Qiji's work as being modern epigones of the most ancient, most orthodox (*guya* 古雅) poetry. The Hymns of Zhou are the oldest layer of the *Book of Odes*, and the strains of

Shun are the perfect songs of the most righteous sage-king in history. Qiji's work is poetry personified.

Furthermore, the very structure of the poem demonstrates the perceptual awareness that one cultivates in meditation, the powers of observation for which Sun Guangxian praised Guanxiu in the preface to Qiji's works. It proceeds through the six sense fields (Ch. *liujing* 六境, Skt. *ṣaḍ viṣayāḥ*) systematically. After line 1 states the process of meditation, line 2 begins with *shape* or *form* 色 (the field of sight), focusing on the poems' "structure" or "grid" 格. Lines 3–4 attend to *hearing* 聲, comparing Qiji's works to exemplary classics of music. Line 5 proceeds to *touch* 觸, as some of Qiji's best lines are said to have the coldness of ice, while still linking back to the sound emphasized in the previous couplet. Line 6 stresses *smell* 香 and *taste* 味, alluding to a poem that seems to exude the sweet smell and taste of the plums it describes: we must remember that "fragrant" 香 was applied as often to delicious food as it was to pleasing fragrances. Line 7 concludes with *thought* 法, the sensory field that integrates the other five, corresponding to the mind. Line 8 circles back to sight, as the speaker imagines Qiji lighting up the skies. Together, these six senses make up the totality of human experience. In this way, it mirrors some of the practices described in earlier meditation manuals translated from Indic languages, those forming the basis for later practices.[111] The *Śūraṃgama Sūtra* (which Guanxiu referred to as the "marrow of meditation" 禪髓) proceeds through the six sense faculties in the same way.[112] As Qichan methodically proceeds through all six senses in the course of meditation in his own poem, he enacts the claim of line 1 that "poetry is meditation for Confucians."

In these works, Qiji and Qichan bring to its fullest expression the assertion of a deep homology between religious and poetic practice. If one takes for granted the interfusion of ultimate and mundane reality, if one believes that enlightenment is the realization of this interfusion, and if one assumes that one may therefore practice meditation in the midst of any other activity, then their assertions make perfect sense. It is a small step to go from saying "Wearing clothes, eating food, talking and responding, making use of the six senses—all these activities are dharma-nature" 著衣喫飯，言談祗對，六根運用，一切施為，盡是法性 to saying that poetry may serve a soteriological purpose.[113] Qiji is merely bringing well-established practices into his own favored realm of activity, the writing of poetry. But this is not just a casual act of mindfulness; it is an act of asceticism. Both poetry and meditation require intense concentration that may lead to physical suffering, but the fruit of both is a profound, salvific insight into the very nature of reality. From this perspective, the term "religious poetry" is redundant, for religion and poetry are different paths to the same goal.

The homology between meditation and poetry came to its fullest expression in the work of the tenth-century poet-monk Qiji after it had been hinted at for much of the ninth century. The insight that these two practices are the same was made possible by the waxing of multiple aesthetic paradigms. On the one hand, the classical tradition, from Lu Ji's "Rhapsody on Literature" on down, stressed the importance of the poet's concentration and mental focus in the process of composition. On the other hand, the *kuyin* aesthetic, especially as it came to represent an ideal of pure poetry with Jia Dao, emphasized the importance of effort and intense devotion to the detail of couplet craftsmanship. When these two paradigms came together in the late ninth century, and poet-monks who had spent much of their lives devoted to meditation practices encountered them, the match was obvious. Poetry and meditation became two gates leading to a greater perceptual awareness. And precisely this, the awareness of phenomena and their deeper significance as images, is the trigger that may lead one to a sudden insight into the emptiness of all things, otherwise known as enlightenment.

This is an understanding of poetry that builds on, but is ultimately different from, what is usually put forth by scholars (and poets) of Tang China. To Qiji and other poet-monks, poetry is a verbal art, certainly, as well as a linguistic exercise, a social practice, an expression of one's mind, and all the other functions normally attributed to poetry. But it is not only that. It is also a religiously significant practice. Moreover, Qiji avoids putting poetry and religion in a hierarchical relationship, in which one is subordinate to the other. While religious goals are seen as primary, both meditation and writing are seen as legitimate paths to that goal. They are two gates to the same thing. One may even suppose that, since poets cultivate their practice without knowledge of their religious goals, they may be considered better Buddhists. A poet cannot be attached to the idea of enlightenment if one is unaware that one is pursuing it. Poetry is meditation, and meditation poetry.

Qiji's articulation of the identity of poetry and meditation is the beginning of a tradition. In his works we find the first clear statements that the writing of poetry and the practice of Buddhism lead to the same thing. For this reason, Qiji should be recognized as a pioneer in the history of Chinese poetics. But, just as importantly, Qiji's view was also the culmination of something. Building on other poet-monks such as Guanxiu and Jiaoran, he wove together several threads from the discourses of poetry and Buddhism—Lu Ji's spirit journey, Jia Dao's *kuyin*, and Hongzhou monks' non-meditation as meditation—to create a new idea of Buddhist poetry. The equation of poetry with meditation did not appear out of nowhere but rather emerged out of the poet-monk tradition traced throughout this book. Literary, religious, social, and political developments aligned to create the right conditions for their emergence in the late eighth century, ascendancy in the ninth, and heyday in the early tenth. Under these peculiar circumstances, Qiji claimed that poetry could serve as meditation not only for Confucians but even for Buddhist monks.

Though Chan metaphors for poetry (inspired, in part, by Guanxiu and Qiji's works) soon became popular, the poet-monks' particular idea of poetry and meditation's fundamental unity would not last. The reasons for this dissolution are closely connected to the declining popularity of Tang poet-monks, especially the Guanxiu-Qiji generation, as well as waning aesthetic paradigms and changing monastic regulations. Within about two generations, the poet-monks fell out of favor, and their bold vision of Buddhist poetry died with them. Some aspects of this vision were condemned for their unorthodoxy, while other aspects, such as the poetry-meditation equation, were repeated until they became meaningless clichés. Nonetheless, for a while, these poet-monks seemed like they were on the verge of restructuring the relationship between literary and religious practices. They had invented Buddhist poetry.

Conclusion

> When you get a line, you offer it first to the Buddha—
> No one understands this mindset.
> 得句先呈佛
> 無人知此心
>
> —Guanxiu 貫休, "Thinking of Qiyi of Wuchang: 2 of 2" 懷武昌棲一二首（其二）(Hu Dajun 9.453-55; *QTS* 830.9351-52)

The major poet-monks of the late medieval period placed themselves at the intersection of two distinct traditions—poetry and Buddhism—and attempted to harmonize these two traditions into a new synthesis. This synthesis is most conspicuous in the way they infused their poetry with three Buddhist practices: apophatic repetition, incantation, and meditation. In so doing, they invented Buddhist poetry for their time. They drew on multiple resources in the religious and poetic traditions to create a concept of Buddhist poetry that was ultimately different from anything that came before. It did more than allude to Buddhist texts in their poems. It did more than entice new converts through literature. It did more than describe Buddhist concepts in verse. To them, poetry could enact the Buddhist practices that they performed professionally, and these same practices could make for superior poetry. This was literature as a way of doing religion, and religion as a way of doing literature.

Experimentation may lead to innovation. Or it may lead nowhere. The deciding factor is its reception, the sympathy and knowledge of the audiences who encounter it. The poet-monks' unusual hybrid of religious and literary practices, on the whole, was not met by generous readers. Though we find admirers scattered across the centuries, most Buddhist readers found them too literary, and most literary readers found them too Buddhist. For this reason, their vision for a new kind of Chinese Buddhist poetry largely went unfulfilled in the poetic mainstream, and they came to be known as minor poets to later critics. Future poet-monks were plentiful, but few departed from norms like Jiaoran, Guanxiu, Qiji, and their contemporaries. These poet-monks succeeded in establishing the idea of the Buddhist poet but not of Buddhist poetry. Nevertheless, their vision has much to teach even modern scholars about the possibilities of religion and literature.

Buddhist Readers

The poet-monks' ability to combine Buddhist and classical literary practices should have made them very attractive to other elite monks. They had proved that it was possible to do both at the same time, to find in classical Chinese culture a way of serving the Buddha. They had been able to justify Buddhist teachings and rituals to the non-Buddhist literati using the literati's own terms. If their vision were fulfilled, Buddhism could be seen as a transformative force on Chinese culture, a purifying agent that somehow made the classical tradition more fully itself.

In one way, the late medieval poet-monks were successful. They became the archetypes of those who took seriously a literary approach to Buddhist practice. Occasionally, this was portrayed positively. Guanxiu's "Mountain-Dwelling Poems" 山居詩, for example, sparked centuries of imitations among literary monks. Just a few of the people who wrote their own versions include Yongming Yanshou 永明延壽 (904–975), Shiwu Qinggong 石屋清珙 (1272–1352), Hanshan Deqing 憨山德清 (1546–1623), Hanyue Fazang 漢月法藏 (1573–1635), and, in Japan, Zekkai Chūshin 絕海中津 (1336–1405).[1] Later monks also recognized the religious value of poems by poet-monks. The Dunhuang manuscript mentioned in chapter 5, which included Guanxiu's poem on sūtra recitation among a series of ritual texts, is just one example. Many poems by Jiaoran, Guanxiu, and Qiji were quoted in later sermons by such eminent monks as Yuanwu Keqin 圓悟克勤 (1063–1135), Chushi Fanqi 楚石梵琦 (1296–1370), and Shizhuo 實拙 (b. 1682). It is clear that later monastics read the later poet-monks' works, sometimes with admiration.

Sometimes with admiration, but sometimes with trepidation. As exemplars of a literary approach to Buddhist practice, the poet-monks represented a real danger to practitioners of the newly emerging Chan of the Northern Song dynasty. Many monastics worried that the poet-monks stood atop a slippery slope and would encourage the faithful to slide into complacent classicism. This is precisely the danger that Shenqing pointed out in his *North Mountain Record* from the early ninth century: poet-monks risk becoming "madmen" (*kuangjuan zhi fu* 狂狷之夫) who become attached to sensual pleasure. *North Mountain Record* gained renewed attention in the early eleventh century, just as Southern Chan was gaining institutional dominance and certain monks sought to harmonize Buddhism, Daoism, and Confucianism. It was debated by many leading monks at this time, including poet-monks Qisong 契嵩 (1007–10072) and Huihong, and attracted two commentaries that date to this period.[2] One of these commentaries, by a monk named Huibao 慧寶, updates Shenqing's criticism of poet-monks by referring to Kepeng 可朋, a younger contemporary of Guanxiu in Shu known as the "drunken shavepate" (*zuikun* 醉髡) for paying off his alcohol debts with the thousands of poems he wrote.[3] Huibao understood Shenqing's criticism of excessive monastic literary activity to have continued relevance to poet-monks of the late medieval period.

As Chan developed its formal institutions, new codes were written to regulate monastic activity. One of these, the *Rules of Purity for Gardens of Chan* 禪苑清規 of 1103, describes how poetry could seduce one away from monasticism. The section on scribes calls Guanxiu and Qiji "poet-monks" with a note of disdain and implies that they lost a true mind of renunciation.

> [A scribe] should read widely—ancient and modern correspondence, poetry, and prose—to improve his knowledge. If the language used by the scribe is refined and elegant and his style fits the forms, then a letter sent a thousand miles away can be regarded as glorious by erudite men. He must not use pen and ink to spite or intimidate his colleagues with no consideration for the Dharma. Guanxiu and Qiji were called nothing more than poet-monks. Jia Dao and Huixiu drifted away to become secular officials. But is this the real meaning of renunciation?
>
> 古今書啟疏詞文字，應須遍覽以益多聞。若語言典重式度如法，千里眉目一眾光彩。然不得一向事持筆硯輕侮同袍，不將佛法為事。禪月、齊已止號詩僧。賈島、慧休流離俗宦，豈出家之本意也。[4]

Literary ability, when deployed in written correspondence, can help promulgate the Dharma. It proves one's learning and situates one as having agency in the world of literate Chinese discourse. However, poetry is dangerous because it risks becoming a distraction from religious pursuits. It is at best supplemental, but sometimes antithetical, to the purposes of renunciation. This passage reflects a deep monastic anxiety over poetry that became widespread in the Song period, likely due to the institutionalization of Chan that took place in the later tenth and eleventh centuries (reflected in monastic codes like the *Rules of Purity*).[5] From this perspective, Guanxiu and Qiji are negative examples. They teetered on the brink of laicization, only one step away from being ex-monks like Jia Dao and Huixiu. The Chan practitioner would do well not to follow their lead.[6]

This same attitude appears in anecdotes about the poet-monks as well. In the 1238 collection *The Essential Stories of the Old Masters, Continued* 續古尊宿語要 we find a tale about Guanxiu, Qiji, and another poet-monk named Xuantai 玄泰 living at Mount Shishuang 石霜山 in the late 880s.[7] It describes how the lay person Zhang Zhuo 張拙 (834–898) came to Mount Shishuang to call on its head monk Shishuang Qingzhu 石霜慶諸 (807–888) and was unimpressed with what he saw.[8]

> Guanxiu—Meditation Master Chanyue—was serving as head cook at Mount Shishuang. One day Zhang Zhuo came to the mountain inquiring after Shishuang Qingzhu. When he saw that Shishuang's appearance was withered and his speech plain, he was unhappy and left with a flick of his sleeve. When he arrived at the guests' quarters, he saw Guanxiu, Qiji, and Xuantai debating in a sterling manner. Zhang asked them, "Why shouldn't one of the three of you be recommended to become abbot?" Guanxiu, understanding that Zhang meant to belittle Shishuang, said, "Five hundred people gather at this temple: 250 lowly seeming monks, and 250 superior monks. The head of our temple is a bodhisattva in the flesh." When Zhang heard this he fixed his attitude.

> 舉禪月休禪師，在石霜充典座。一日張拙入山，訪石霜，見其形貌枯悴，語言平淡，遂不喜之，拂袖而下。到知客寮，見禪月、齊巳、太布衲、議論琅琅。張乃問曰：「三人中，何不推一人作長老？」禪月知張之意，輕於石霜，乃曰：「堂中五百眾，似卑僧者，二百五十，勝卑僧者，二百五十。堂頭和尚，乃肉身菩薩。」張聞此語，再整威儀。[9]

Because of their gifted use of language, outsiders would suppose the poet-monks to be superior to the sickly, plainspoken Shishuang.

However, this would be incorrect. It is only Shishuang who is "a bodhisattva in the flesh" and worthy of being abbot. There is no relation between linguistic and religious achievement. Another version of this anecdote stresses that the main difference between the poet-monks and Shishuang is poetry, and Zhang Zhuo suggests that one of them become head abbot because "Shishuang was not skilled in poetry" 石霜不善詩筆.[10] Both versions of this story hinge on recognizing the late medieval poet-monks as the epitome of literary refinement. Such high worldly status puts Shishuang's simplicity in sharper relief. However, that literary refinement is precisely what keeps them from becoming worthy leaders. A poem by Foyin Liaoyuan 佛印了元 (1032–1098), quoted in the second version of the anecdote, states this clearly:

> When beginning your Buddhist studies, you're weak
>   and need to hold fast:
> Be fond of Chan
>   and don't study Confucianism.
> I have only seen enlightened minds
>   perfect the Buddha's way;
> I've never heard that itinerants
>   should read the *Odes* and *Documents*.
> If you teach that Confucius
>   transcended life and death,
> How can you proclaim that Gautama
>   is a great man?
> Though Qiji and Guanxiu's
>   reputations shook the land,
> Who would place them
>   in a chart of patriarchs?

> 教門衰弱要人扶，
> 好慕禪宗莫學儒。
> 祇見悟心成佛道，
> 未聞行脚讀詩書。
> 若教孔子超生死，
> 爭表瞿曇是丈夫。
> 齊己貫休聲動地，
> 誰將排上祖師圖。

Foyin understood there to be a sharp division between Buddhist and secular, Confucian learning. Guanxiu and Qiji fell under the latter's sway. Their fame as poets is nothing more than vanity, for they never became fully liberated, able to receive the orthodox transmission of the Dharma. They should not be admired. They were the ones who walked up to the edge of monasticism and leaned out over the abyss. They were not patriarchs, but poet-monks.

Foyin's attitude was common among Song dynasty monastics. While later, romanticized depictions might lead us to believe that Chan monks promoted an artistic, even antinomian lifestyle, contemporary evidence suggests that they harbored deep suspicions about classical literature. General literacy was necessary for scribes and senior monks, and familiarity with the classical tradition could be useful for garnering respect from non-monastics. But poetry was dangerous. It could distract. It could lead to arrogance or self-importance. It could plunge one into the boozy, sensual social circles of the literati. For this reason, it was strongly discouraged in monastic communities, especially among novices. Rules, of course, are created out of necessity. They curb behavior that is already underway. It should come as no surprise that some individuals admired and emulated the late medieval poet-monks. But on the whole, these admirers seem to be in the minority. The poet-monks were too literary for the Buddhists.

Literati Readers

The other main audience for the poet-monks was the literati. The poet-monks wrote in an elite style that implied a highly educated readership, and they sought precisely to synthesize the classical literary tradition and Buddhism. As noted in previous chapters, the late medieval poet-monks aligned themselves on the one hand with the song-style verse of Li Bai and Li He, and on the other hand with the *kuyin* aesthetic of Jia Dao. Neither association served them well among literati audiences in the coming centuries. In particular, the *guwen* 古文 ("ancient prose" or "ancient culture") movement that began to emerge as a major force in the late tenth and eleventh centuries rejected both of these ideals. The major *guwen* spokesperson Ouyang Xiu 歐陽修 (1007–1072) was particularly hostile to Jia Dao and the eleventh-century "Late Tang style" 晚唐體 that sought to imitate him.[11] He and other advocates of *guwen* objected to what they deemed the frivolity of verses in this style. This could take two forms, either smallness of subject matter (poems on mere objects instead of on grand ideas of governance) or obsession with craft at the expense of subject. Poets embracing a *kuyin* aesthetic could be accused of both. Similar objections could be brought to those who continued the tradition of Li He's fantastical, song-style verse, to those who filled their works with erudite allusions, and to those, like Guanxiu, who did both. Such writing styles implied a hierarchy of language over content, and they would not be promoted by *guwen* advocates. Add to this most *guwen* adherents' antipathy toward Buddhism, and it is no wonder that the Late Tang poet-monks were not highly regarded at this time.[12]

To later generations, the poet-monks of the Tang were mainly known through the works of Jiaoran, Guanxiu, and Qiji. In 1238 Li Gong 李龏 (b. 1194) compiled the first anthology of poetry by Tang monks, called *Collection of Tang Monks' Extensive Flowers* 唐僧弘秀集. Though it features five hundred poems by fifty-two monks, the distribution is skewed toward the three most famous poet-monks. With seventy poems by Jiaoran, sixty-one by Guanxiu, and sixty by Qiji, together they comprise 38 percent of the collection. In the mid-seventeenth century, Mao Jin 毛晉 (1599–1659) codified this canon when he put together a collection titled *The Collected Poetry of Three Eminent Monks of the Tang* 唐三高僧詩集, consisting of the collected works of Jiaoran, Guanxiu, and Qiji. Of the three, Jiaoran's reputation has fared the best in later centuries. Yan Yu, in his famous *Canglang shihua* (early or mid-thirteenth cent.), ranked Jiaoran's poetry "the best among monks in the Tang" 在唐諸僧之上.[13] In the late Ming anthology *Tang Poetry, Sorted* 唐詩歸, Zhong Xing 鍾惺 (1574–1624) distinguishes Jiaoran from other monks by saying that his works do not carry the flavor of monasticism: "Monkish poems have the air and habits of monkish poems. If you are a monk, you must not write monkish poetry, and then your works will not have the air and habits of monkish poetry. Jiaoran is pure and far-reaching: he must have attained this in poetry, not in monasticism" 僧詩有僧詩氣習，僧而必不作僧詩，便有不作僧詩氣習。皎然清淳淹遠，當於詩中求之，不當於僧中求之.[14] Zhong Xing praises Jiaoran at the expense of other poet-monks. He is exceptional precisely because he transcends his monastic identity and becomes a poet first and foremost. This is the same claim that Liu Yuxi made about Jiaoran in his notes on Lingche's works. He is a poet in spite of being a monk, not because of it.

Those poet-monks who lived through the collapse of the dynasty were not as fortunate as Jiaoran. Traditional criticism posits a necessary connection between the spirit of an age and the writings produced therein. The poems from a time of prosperity, such as the post–An Lushan restoration of the late eighth century, are necessarily superior to the poems from a time of collapse and disunity, such as the late ninth and tenth centuries. By this logic, then, Jiaoran must be superior to later poet-monks.

Qiji's reputation survived as a fragment of its former self. By the Song dynasty, he was known chiefly for his mastery of tonal prosody, despite the wide variety of styles that he wrote in.[15] Qiji, though generally regarded now as a minor poet, had some very devoted admirers throughout the centuries. Ji Yun 紀昀 (1724–1805), for one, ranked him above Guanxiu and Jiaoran, calling him "the foremost among poet-monks of the Tang" 唐詩僧以齊己為第一.[16] Zhong Xing, in his anthology of Tang poetry, remarked, "Qiji's poetry has a kind of air of lofty sincerity and divine marvel" 齊己詩有一種高渾靈妙之氣.[17] A Qing dynasty collection of regulated verse, the *Autumn Light of Recent-Style Poetry* (*Jinti qiuyang* 近體秋陽), said, "So many of [Qiji's] works are excellent that we cannot include them all" 篇多佳，收不可盡.[18] The continuity of regulated verse, which continued to be a favored form of poetic expression by educated Chinese all the way into the twentieth century, ensured that Qiji would find at least a small readership for centuries to come.

Indeed, when the editors of the annotated catalog for the *Siku quanshu* 四庫全書 evaluated Qiji's work in the late eighteenth century, they offered qualified praise precisely along these lines. Though Qiji's writings in looser meters are deemed unworthy of consideration, the editors maintain a fondness for some of his regulated heptametric poems.

> Many were the monks who were skilled in poetry during the Tang dynasty. But of those whose collections are currently extant, there are only Jiaoran, Guanxiu, and Qiji. Jiaoran is pure but weak. Guanxiu is bold but uncouth. Qiji's regulated heptametric poems do not break free of his contemporaries' exercises. His old-style heptametric poems take the styles of Lu Tong (775?–835) and Ma Yi (*j.s.* 784) and shorten them into briefer stanzas.[19] Being full of harsh and dissonant words, they are not worthy of consideration. Regulated heptametric poems, however, comprise 60 percent of his collection. Though they tend to follow the Wugong school [of Yao He], they are uniquely robust in style. For example, his poems "Swordsman," "Listening to a Zither," and "Zhurong Peak" contain remnants of the ideas of the Dali era [766–780] poets.[20] Among his quatrains, "Facing the Moon on the Fifteenth Night of the *Gengwu* Year [March 4, 910]" reads:[21]

> The sea clear, the sky blue,
>   the truly round moon.
> I intone and visualize Xuanzong
>   cold tonight.

The jade rabbit has feelings that
   ought to be recorded.[22]
From the western frontier, I cannot see
   old Chang'an.

Such earnest feelings about the former rulers is something that other Buddhists never reach. It is fitting that he was close with Sikong Tu.

唐代緇流能詩者眾。其有集傳於今者，惟皎然、貫休及齊己。皎然清而弱。貫休豪而粗。齊己七言律詩不出當時之習。及七言古詩以盧仝、馬異之體縮為短章，詰屈聱牙，尤不足取。惟五言律詩居全集十分之六。雖頗沿武功一派，而風格獨遒。如《劍客》、《聽琴》、《祝融峰》諸篇，猶有大曆以還遺意。其絕句中《庚午年十五夜對月》詩曰：「海澄空碧正團圞，吟想玄宗此夜寒。玉兔有情應記得，西邊不見舊長安。」惓惓故君，尤非他釋子所及。宜其與司空圖相契矣。[23]

Following long-running precedent in literary criticism, each poet-monk has a positive quality mixed with a negative one.[24] Qiji is no exception: the editors find his work in most forms derivative and harsh, but his regulated pentameter has moments of glory. The editors single out a quatrain mourning the collapse of the Tang dynasty for its pathos and patriotism. Out of all the ideas and images in Qiji's corpus, it is the feeling of sorrow over the empire's fall that the editors find praiseworthy. Such sentiments fit well a neo-classicist, "Confucian" idea of what poetry should be. Though the editors praise some of Qiji's work, they silently omit all Buddhist elements from it. The poet-monk is nothing more than a minor poet.

The reputation of the more stylistically audacious Guanxiu did not fare as well as Qiji over the years. Guanxiu's penchant for deploying a mix of colloquialisms and archaisms seems to have particularly annoyed literati of later dynasties. Hu Zi 胡仔 (1083–1143) reports that Su Shi 蘇軾 (1037–1101) complained of Guanxiu's poetry having "an uncouth air" 村俗之氣 and found it "very strange" that others "called him a man of discernment" 號有識者故深可怪.[25] He Chang 賀裳 (fl. 1681) described Guanxiu's verses as one of the more odious examples of the decadence rampant at the end of the Tang:

Poetry fell apart during the Late Tang.... Most extreme are the vulgar and deficient, such as Du Xunhe and the monk Guanxiu. I especially can't stand the coarse places in Guanxiu's work. For example, his "Song on Looking at Huaisu's Cursive Calligraphy" contains:

Swift as the Duke of Ezhou yelling at
    Shan Xiongxin,[26]
As the Prince of Qin bore on his shoulders
    lances of jujube.[27]

How is this any different than the prosimetric chanting of a country churl? Another example is the last couplet of the eighth of the "Mountain-Dwelling Poems":

Let other men chatter,
    let them laugh;
Earth upended and heaven overturned
    would be all right, too.[28]

How can you not detest this?

詩至晚唐而敗壞……甚則粗鄙陋劣，如杜荀鶴、僧貫休者。貫休村野處殊不可耐。如《懷素草書歌》中云「忽如鄂公喝住單雄信，秦王肩上搭著棗木槊」，此何異傖父所唱鼓兒詞。又如《山居》第八篇末句云「從他人說從他笑，地覆天翻也只寧」，豈不可醜。[29]

The focus of He Chang's criticism is Guanxiu's blasé attitude toward the norms of classical poetry. In the first example, Guanxiu flaunts the limitations of heptameter to indulge in enneameter (nine-beat lines), which He Chang likens to the chanted prose interludes of popular prosimetric entertainment in his day. No matter that many other great poets of the Tang used enneameter in their song-style verses as well.[30] To He Chang, classical verse must display a tightly crafted, crystalline structure. The second example fits into a proper meter, but it is inefficient. It uses informal language, repeats characters, and wastes space on grammatical particles such as *ye* 也 and *zhi* 只 in the second line. These departures from the norms of classical poetry are, to a late Ming reader, grating. They smack of amateurism more than experimentalism.

    Guanxiu's reputation also suffered due to the fact that he was seen as representing an outmoded approach to literature. Like many other poets of the late ninth and early tenth centuries, his embrace of *kuyin* made him a target of later writers' mockery. Ouyang Xiu undermined Guanxiu's reputation through satire. The following excerpt from his

Talks on Poetry (*Liuyi shihua* 六一詩話) uses Guanxiu as an example of a poet whose intention is profound but use of language inept.

> Mei Shengyu (1002–1060) often said: "Though the meaning of a line of poetry may be penetrating, it may be laughable if its wording is shallow and vulgar: this is a fault. . . . There is a 'Poem on Poetry' that reads:
>
> All day I search without finding it;
> Then it comes to me on its own.[31]
>
> These lines refer to the fact that a good couplet is hard to come by, but some explanations say: 'This is a poem about someone losing a kitten,' which everyone laughs at."
>
> 聖俞嘗云：「詩句義理雖通，語涉淺俗而可笑者，亦其病也。[……] 有《詠詩》者云：『盡日覓不得，有時還自來。』本謂詩之好句難得耳，而說者云：『此是人家失卻貓兒詩。』人皆以為笑也。」[32]

Although this poem is ostensibly about someone's misreading, it places the blame on the poet. The poet's meaning is easily misconstrued, and therefore it should not be considered good poetry. Moreover, the fact that this is a humorous story reveals that Guanxiu had a reputation for being especially serious about poetry.[33] The further the couplet strays from its original meaning and the no-nonsense mind behind it, the funnier it becomes. Thus, while Ouyang Xiu's remarks helped to erode Guanxiu's reputation, we can see its mirror image in this passage as well. Making Guanxiu the butt of such a joke only proves that he was known as a serious poet. Nonetheless, the damage was done, and it may have been hard for later readers to regard Guanxiu quite as seriously as they had before.

Although the poet-monks of the late medieval period never entirely faded from memory, their reputations gradually declined over the centuries. Every audience, it seems, could find fault with them. On the one hand, Buddhists worried that these monks were not taking their religious commitments seriously enough. On the other hand, literati faulted them for using unrefined language in elite verse and for their embrace of an old-fashioned style. A prose epistle by the poet Chen Shidao 陳師道 (1053–1102), written on the occasion of parting with the eleventh-century poet-monk Daoqian 道潛, sums up these contradictions nicely:

From "Essay on the Occasion of Seeing off Canliao" 送參寥序
Chen Shidao

We talked together in the evening until we reached the topic of Tang poet-monks. Master Canliao said: "Our era has low regard for the words of Guanxiu and Qiji. They had a capacious, unique spirit and world-transcending will. Even though they were praised throughout the whole land and honored by kings, nobles, generals, and ministers, they remained servants of Master Shishuang, never leaving him until the end of his life. Why do people focus on their poetry? It is not right to fault them for their skill or clumsiness in literature." From this I understood that what I value is what Canliao tosses aside as superfluous, and that I am a man you would call shallow!

夜相語，及唐詩僧，參寥子曰：「貫休、齊己，世薄其語，然以曠蕩逸群之氣，高世之志，天下之譽，王侯將相之奉，而爲石霜老師之役，終其身不去：此豈用意于詩者？工拙不足病也。」由是而知余之所貴，乃其棄餘，所謂淺爲丈夫者乎！[34]

It is clear that by the late eleventh century, late medieval poet-monks like Guanxiu and Qiji were not highly regarded. Presumably this is because their language appeared rough to literati who had absorbed the plain aesthetic of ancient prose (*guwen*). The monk Daoqian, for his part, changes the terms of the debate. First, he departs from other Buddhist sources, like the Chan rulebook we saw earlier, and praises Guanxiu and Qiji for their religious achievements. In particular, he singles out their devotion to the Chan master Shishuang—focusing on an incident likely drawn from an anecdote similar to the one examined earlier in this chapter. He then argues that their literary skill is a trivial matter by comparison. The poet-monks' most important quality is their religious loyalty. Daoqian does not deny his contemporaries' low regard for these poet-monks as poets; he only says that they have their priorities wrong. Chen Shidao, the secular literatus and friend of Su Shi who comments at the end, disagrees with Daoqian's hierarchy of Buddhism over literature but does not dispute his characterization of Guanxiu and Qiji's works. He silently agrees that they are not great poets. As Daoqian and Chen debate the merits of the late medieval poet-monks, they both seem to be in opposition to the monks' audacious vision of Buddhist poetry and instead focus on the general question of which is superior, poetry or religion. By this point, it seems, the poet-monks' reputations have significantly eroded in both literati and elite Buddhist circles.

In doing so, the Song poets reinstated the binary opposition between poetry and religion. This is the same dualism that emerged in the first sustained writings on poet-monks, examined in chapter 2. It was precisely this dualism that Guanxiu, Qiji, and others repeatedly equated with the illusory dualism of Buddhism's "two truths," the mundane and the ultimate—a dualism that they attempted to overcome by proposing ways of integrating the two into a harmonious whole. Poetic and religious practices, to the Tang poet-monks, should not be viewed as hierarchical. Nor should they be viewed as antithetical. Nor should they be viewed as entirely separate. Instead, they should be seen as harmonious—two gates leading to the same place. But instead, the Song reinscribed this dualism—the tension between religious and literary practices, in which the two are seen as fundamentally separate. It is this same dualism that plagues us to this day in the theorization of religious poetry.

Beyond Religion and Literature

In the introduction, I noted some limitations of previous scholarship on religion and literature. Largely shaped by modern Protestant assumptions about what religion is, they tend to privilege beliefs, worldviews, and sacred texts over practices. One problem with these approaches is that the attitudes of any person (especially historical persons) can never be fully known. They are easily misinterpreted. As Guanxiu wrote in the lines that serve as this chapter's epigraph, "No one understands this mindset" 無人知此意. A focus on worldviews leads either to some form of theological criticism (this person sincerely held a certain belief, which influenced his writing) or to a quest for paradoxes and tensions (this person is complex, because he worked in oppositional or contradictory fields). These approaches have sometimes been productive, but they lead to predetermined ends. In both cases, they assume two separate entities ("literature" and "religion"). These entities may influence or oppose one another, but in both cases they remain distinct. In these pages, I have argued that it is better to focus on religious practices—what people actually did with their bodies that were seen as meaningful within certain fields. This allows one to break free of historical mind-reading and, just as importantly, allow for the possibility of overlap or even unity between literature and religion.

CONCLUSION 227

Buddhist monks were not the only people who engaged in religious practices in medieval China. Lay Buddhists had their own sets of practices, some of which required an ascetic commitment to self-sacrifice. Daoists too engaged in methods of incantation, drew on the powers of deities, and enacted rituals that patterned their lives. Though perhaps not as numerically dominant as Buddhism, Daoism was the official religion of the Tang ruling house and enjoyed widespread participation throughout the empire.[35] "Popular" religious rituals also helped shape the lives of people at all levels of society. A careful consideration of these various religious practices would likely bring to light other important elements of medieval Chinese poetry. Perhaps other poets sought to synthesize their literary and religious practices in ways completely different from those of the poet-monks. There is much potential for future research to recover other marginalized figures and uncover new dimensions of beloved classics.

Guanxiu, Qiji, and others sought to break down the opposition between literary and Buddhist practices in their own works. Following their lead, I have sought to break down the opposition between literary and Buddhist studies in my own. Paradoxically, in the process, I have had to reassert this opposition—between "Confucian" and "Buddhist" traditions as they were understood in the Tang, echoing my sources—in order to attempt to overcome it. The poet-monks cannot be understood only as literary actors, separated from the religious practices of meditation, incantation, and apophatic repetition. Likewise, they cannot be understood only as religious actors, separated from their centrality in literary networks, their adaptations of literary forms, their use of *kuyin* discourse, and their presence in poetry manuals. If, as scholars, we do not break down the normal barriers between literary and religious studies, between the Tang and the Five Dynasties, between principle and phenomena, between poet and monk, we will continue to overlook such figures as the late medieval poet-monks, and we will keep reifying our old categories of understanding Chinese cultural history. But those categories cannot hold. To regard the true as true and the false as false is not ultimately real. Poetry is meditation for Confucians. Tang sounds and Brahmic sounds do mix together. Those who would uphold creation, in its religious and literary guises, must drive all its subtleties into their forge.

Notes

Introduction

1. Wang Xiulin 7.405; Pan Dingwu 7.402; *QTS* 844.9550.
2. The above dramatization of Qiji's composition of this poem is fictional.
3. Chapter 6: "Once you understand Heaven and Earth to be a great forge and the fashioned world to be a great foundry, where can you go that will not be acceptable?" 今一以天地為大鑪，以造化為大冶，惡乎往而不可哉 (Guo, *Zhuangzi jishi*, 6.262). This whole poem makes liberal use of Zhuangzian terminology. For example, "single breath" (*yiqi* 一氣) comes from chapter 6 of *Zhuangzi*, in which exemplary people are described as "roaming in the single breath of heaven and earth" 遊乎天地之一氣 (Guo, *Zhuangzi jishi*, 6.268), and "unspeaking" (*buyan* 不言) is used in chapter 22 to describe the magnificence of the cosmos, which only the ultimate man perceives: "Heaven and earth have great beauty but do not speak. The four seasons have a clear rule but do not discuss. The myriad things have a perfect inherent pattern but do not explain. The sage finds the origin of heaven and earth's beauty and perceives the myriad things' inherent pattern. For this reason, the ultimate man does not act and the great sage does not create. That is, they observe heaven and earth" 天地有大美而不言，四時有明法而不議，萬物有成理而不說。聖人者，原天地之美而達萬物之理，是故至人无爲，大聖不作，觀於天地之謂也 (Guo, *Zhuangzi jishi*, 22.735).
4. Lines 3 and 4 of the above poem are also quoted in two poetry manuals from the tenth century, *Exemplary Models of Poetry* (*Fengsao zhige* 風騷旨格), by Qiji himself, and *Essential Forms of Poetry* (*Fengsao yaoshi* 風騷要式), by Xu Yan 徐衍 (dates unknown). In both manuals the poem is given as an example of "Great Elegantiae" (*Daya* 大雅). Qiji offers no further explanation, but other parts of his manual suggest that it refers to the cosmic grandeur of the imagery. Xu Yan takes this a step further, stating that "Great Elegantiae" are called such because their grand imagery can be allegorically interpreted to describe matters of empire and its rulership.
5. In this book I use "Confucian" or "classicist" as translations for "Ru" because of their familiarity to the Anglophone reader, despite the increasing popularity of the transliterated term "Ruist." "Ru" refers to the shared classical heritage of the elites, which was not necessarily centered on Confucius himself. See Nylan, *The Five "Confucian" Classics*, 364–65, on why "Confucian" is an imperfect translation of "Ru."
6. *QTS* 848.9609–10. This poem and its central claim will be examined in detail in chapter 6.

7. From "Matching 'Lying at Ease,' Shown to Me by Minister Wei" 和韋相公見示閑臥 (Hu Dajun 2:12.606–11; *QTS* 831.9372–73). This poem was likely written in 910, as its recipient Wei Zhuang was on his deathbed. We could also translate this line as "Yao-deva is Brahma-deva."

8. For example, Qiji's poetry manual *Fengsao zhige* describes poetry's forty "gates" (*men* 門), a term with Buddhist overtones. On this, see Zhang, *Chan yu shixue*, 30–34; Wang, *Wan-Tang Wudai shiseng*, 363–64; and Li, *Wan-Tang Wudai shige*, 204–05.

9. For an example of the former, see Hinton, *Awakened Cosmos*; for an example of the latter, see Hu, *Baihua wenxue shi*, 132–52.

10. Wang Fuzhi, *Jiangzhou shihua jianzhu*, 2.144, and Chen Qiyuan, *Yongxianzhai biji*, 12.290, respectively.

11. On the history of this criticism, see Protass, "The Flavors of Monks' Poetry."

12. In Chinese, *Three Hundred Tang Poems* 唐詩三百首 (1763) includes just one poem by a monk (Jiaoran); *Poems of the Masters* 千家詩 (13th cent.) has only three poems by monks; and Wang Li's four-volume *Gudai Hanyu* 古代漢語 (1962) has no Buddhist writing of any sort. None of the 160 poems in Matsuura Tomohisa's *Kōchū Tōshi kaishaku jiten* are by monks. Burton Watson's *Columbia Book of Chinese Poetry* has one poem by a monk (Jiaoran). Most English anthologies and textbooks exclude Buddhist monks entirely: for example, Wai-lim Yip's *Chinese Poetry* (1976), Victor Mair's *Columbia Anthology of Traditional Chinese Literature* (1994), Zong-qi Cai's *How to Read Chinese Poetry* (2008), and Michael Fuller's *Introduction to Chinese Poetry* (2017).

13. For example, there is little attention given to Buddhism and almost no mention of poet-monks in Su, *Tangshi gailun*; Xu Zong, *Tang shi shi*; Zhang Peiheng and Luo, *Zhongguo wenxue shi*; Nie, *Tangdai wenxue shi*; and Li Congjun, *Tangdai wenxue yanbian shi*. In Kojo, *Shina bungaku shi*, only one poet-monk is given in a list of famous Tang poets (358–60).

14. Sizes of corpora have been counted by number of characters: Guanxiu's is 40,196, Qiji's is 38,563, and Jiaoran's is 28,165; *QTS* as a whole is 2,571,526. I have excluded linked verses (*lianju* 聯句) from my *QTS* corpus, and anonymous poems from my rankings of corpora. My corpora of *QTS* authors can be found in "QTS_authors_clean" in the Digital Appendix; rankings can be found in "0-1 QTS Corpora Sizes." Ranking corpus size by number of poems produces similar results: Qiji is ranked 5, Guanxiu 9, and Jiaoran 14 (Liu Chao-lin, Mazanec, and Tharsen, "Exploring Chinese Poetry with Digital Assistance," 288).

15. See, for example, the minor roles given to poet-monks in Liu Ning, *Tang-Song zhi ji shige* (especially 125–26 and 247–57); Zhang Xingwu and Wang, *Tang-Song shiwen yishu*; and Li Dingguang, *Tangmo Wudai luanshi*. In English, Stephen Owen has stated that Buddhism matters in Tang poetry in three ways: as a "turn of mind" for literati poets like Wang Wei, as the subject of didactic verse by Wang Fanzhi and Hanshan, and as a model of "discipline" for poets of the ninth and tenth centuries ("How Did Buddhism Matter," 405). I engage and extend this third claim, which he also makes in *The Late Tang* (91), in the third and sixth chapters of this book.

16. In this, Chinese Buddhist poetry resembles other "traditions" that claim invariant connections to the past even as they must be actively invented, reinvented, and perpetuated by their practitioners. See Hobsbawm, "Introduction"; and Prickett, *Modernity and the Reinvention of Tradition*, 15 ("*all traditions . . . are the product of some degree of self-conscious creation*"; emphasis in the original).

17. For a general survey of scholarship on intersections between the Chinese poetic tradition and Buddhism, see Mazanec and Protass, "Buddhist Poetry of China."

18. Zürcher, *Buddhist Conquest*, 26–27, states that the first sign of the existence of a Buddhist community appeared in 65 CE at the court of Liu Ying 劉英, King of Chu. It is unclear, however, to what extent there was a recognizably Buddhist community at the time, versus the Buddha simply being incorporated into a pantheon of local gods. See Wu Hung, "Buddhist Elements in Early Chinese Art," 264–72, and Sharf, *Coming to Terms*, 21–23.

19. Dating the earliest *shi*-poems presents enormous challenges, thanks to both intertextual and bibliographic factors. However, most scholars agree that the process began in the first century BCE and came to full maturity at the turn of the third century CE with the literary circle around the royal Cao 曹 family. See Holzman, "Les Premiers vers pentasyllabiques," 113; Lu Qinli, "Hanshi bielu," 69; and Muzhai, *Gushi shijiushou*, 2.

20. On this early period and its relationship to the Tang, see Li Xiaorong, *Jin-Tang Fojiao wenxue shi*, 123–232. On the Buddhist influence on one crucial development in poetry during this early period, see Xiaofei Tian, "Seeing with the Mind's Eye."

21. Huixiu: secular surname Tang 湯, whose "Sorrows of Parting" was commemorated in the *Wenxuan* 文選 through an imitation by Jiang Yan 江淹 (444–505), 31.1480. More on his life can be found in the biography of Xu Zhanzhi 徐湛之 in Shen, *Songshu*, 71.1847. On Jiang Yan's poem, see Williams, *Imitations of the Self*, 208. Baoyue: monk who had one of his poems, a version of "Traveling's Hard" 行路難, collected in the famed anthology *New Songs from a Jade Terrace* 玉臺新詠. It describes a moon emerging from clouds to shine on a soldier's lonely wife (Lu Qinli, 1480; *Yuefu shiji* 70.1001; *Yutai xinyong jianzhu* 9.415–16).

22. On this period, see Protass, *Poetry Demon*.

23. On poetry associated with arcane studies, see Williams, "The Metaphysical Lyric." For a general introduction to arcane studies, see Chai, *Dao Companion to Xuanxue*.

24. On the scope of *qingtan*, see Jack Chen, *Anecdote, Network, Gossip, Performance*, 14–17. We should note that the actual term *qingtan* is a later coinage, but similar terms can be found in the *Shishuo xinyu* 世說新語 and other texts of the medieval period (Tang, *Wei Jin qingtan*, 1–29).

25. The latter likely was not meant to be taken seriously as the name of an approach to poetry but rather as a self-deprecating reference to Huihong's own verse (Protass, *Poetry Demon*, 130–42).

26. Wu Ke, *Canghai shihua*, 1.8a; and Lu You, *Jiannan shigao*, 79.6a.

27. Su, *Tangshi gailun*, 173–74. See also Xu Zong, *Tang shi shi*, 2:424–25; Zhang Xingwu and Wang, *Tang-Song shiwen yishu*, 251; Zhang Xingwu, *Wudai zuojia de renge yu shige*, 181–215; and Peng Wanlong, "Wudai shige kaolun," 443.

28. For example, the last *shi*-poet included in Fuller, *An Introduction to Chinese Poetry*, is Yu Xuanji 魚玄機, who died around 868 (347–50). Cai, *How to Read Chinese Poetry*, includes no *shi*-poetry from this period. Mair, *Columbia Anthology of Traditional Chinese Literature*, includes just two poems from this period, by Pi Rixiu 皮日休 and Sikong Tu 司空圖 (240–41).

29. Kroll, "Poetry of the T'ang Dynasty," 312–13. Kroll's chapter in *The Columbia History of Chinese Literature* ends with the fall of the Tang in 907; the *Columbia History*'s next chapter on *shi*-poetry, Michael Fuller's "Sung Dynasty Shih Poetry," begins with the founding of the Song in 960.

30. Owen, *The Late Tang*, 7–8. Owen has articulated similar ideas more briefly in "The Cultural Tang," 1:359 and "Periodization and Major Inflection Points," 13–14.

31. Owen, *The Late Tang*, 567.

32. In the conclusion to this book I explain how changes in literary and monastic cultures of the Northern Song led to the late medieval poet-monks' low status in literary history.

33. For more on the history of denigrations of Late Tang poetry, see Tian Gengyu, *Tangyin yuyun*, 73–81; and Li Dingguang, *Tangmo Wudai luanshi*, 1–8. The view is prevalent in Japanese criticism too. See, for example, Ogawa, *Tōshi gaisetsu*, 76, and Yoshikawa, *Chūgoku bungakushi*, 186.

34. Li Dingguang, *Tangmo Wudai luanshi*, 153–72, for example, has shown how the art of regulated verse forms (*lüshi* 律詩 and *jueju* 絕句) developed in significant ways during this period. Liu Ning, *Tang-Song zhi ji shige*, also traces the influence of Bai Juyi and Yuan Zhen through this period without an abundance of negative comments. The more narrowly focused study of Duan, *Tangmo Wudai Jiangnan*, is similarly illuminating without using much negative language.

35. Agosti, "Greek Poetry"; McGill, "Latin Poetry"; Formisano, "Towards an Aesthetic Paradigm of Late Antiquity"; and Shanzer, "Literature, History, Periodization." The same criticisms of decadence are often attributed to the Qi and Liang 齊梁 periods (479–557), on which see Goh, *Sound and Sight*, 2–4; Xiaofei Tian, *Beacon Fire*, 2–3; and Fusheng Wu, *Poetics of Decadence*.

36. Li Jiangfeng, *Wan-Tang Wudai shige yanjiu*, is an important step forward in this approach. Bender, *Du Fu Transforms*, explains how and why the biographical mode became the privileged way of reading poetry following Du Fu's canonization in the Song.

37. Relatedly, this period has also long been seen as a low point in the history of Chinese Buddhism. For an account of the origins of this view, see Brose, "Credulous Kings and Immoral Monks."

38. I combine here Claudio Guillén's idea of "system" as the conjuncture of textual forms, genres, expectations, and relations, and Pierre Bourdieu's idea of the "field" of production as a set of structural relations in which actors take positions. On these concepts, see Guillén, *Literature as System*, 468–69; and Bourdieu, "The Field of Cultural Production."

39. For a study that explicitly aims to make a methodological point, see Long, *The Value in Numbers*.

40. On some new aspects of the late medieval literary world that can be revealed through the network analysis of over ten thousand poems, see my "Networks of Exchange Poetry," part of which has been incorporated into chapter 1 of this book.

41. On the development of *ci* in this period, see Wagner, *Lotus Boat*; and Shields, *Crafting a Collection*. On *gāthā*s, see my "Medieval Chinese *Gāthā*"; and Protass, *Poetry Demon*, 33–75.

42. My characterization of monks derives from Kieschnick, "Buddhist Monasticism." On Sikong Tu, see Wah, *Ssu-K'ung Tu*. On Hanshan's verse, see Rouzer, *On Cold Mountain*.

43. These statistics come from Wang Xiulin, *Wan-Tang Wudai shiseng*, 4. Zha gives slightly different numbers: 114 poet-monks in *QTS*, to whom are attributed 3,127 poems, plus an additional 800 monastic poems from Dunhuang manuscripts and 960 from *QTSBB* (*Zhuanxingzhong de Tang Wudai shiseng*, 26). Peng Yaling's count of 420 Tang monks to whom are attributed 6,269 extant poems and 251 fragmentary couplets is problematic for numerous reasons, not least of which is its inclusion of non- and ex-monastics like Jia Dao, Hanshan, and the putative author of military *ci* Yi Jing 易靜 ("Tangdai shiseng de chuangzuolun," 190).

44. On Zhenguan's collection, see his biography in fascicle 30 of *Xu gaoseng zhuan* 續高僧傳, in *T* no. 2060, 5:703c; on Tanyu's and Guangbai's, see Toqto'a, *Songshi*, 161.5387.

45. Buddhist monasteries used Confucian texts, such as the *Mengqiu* 蒙求, to teach literacy in Chinese even beyond the frontiers of the Tang, on which see Galambos, "Confucian Education in a Buddhist Environment."

46. For a more comprehensive study of themes in one poet-monk's entire oeuvre, see Kao, "Guanxiu ji qi *Chanyue ji*," 107–93.

47. See, for example, Guanxiu's two "Songs of Abundance" 富貴曲, which give extravagant descriptions of wealth in the process of criticizing it (Hu Dajun 1.49–52; *QTS* 826.9306).

48. Chau, *Religion in China*, 189–90.

49. On the "documentary" versus "literary" dichotomy, see, for example, Pollock, "The Cosmopolitan Vernacular," 8. Michael Fuller's definition of literature as "aesthetically organized language" is also helpful but risks asserting this dichotomy by invoking the "aesthetic," for which he refers to Kant's definition of beauty as "purposiveness without a purpose" (*Drifting among Rivers and Lakes*, 10).

50. Guanxiu wrote an especially interesting inscription (*ming*), which I have translated and studied in "Of Admonition and Address."

51. Some of the assumptions include the centrality of worldviews, beliefs, the supernatural, and sacred texts to a definition of "religion." On the early history of the religion and literature field, see Hesla, "Religion and Literature." More recent representative titles in this field include Jasper, *Study of Literature and Religion*; Knight, *Introduction to Religion and Literature*; and Knight, *Routledge Companion to Literature and Religion*, which continue to privilege modern Christianity.

For example, the *Routledge Companion*, published in 2016, contains thirty-eight contributions, only three of which (7.9 percent) directly address non-Abrahamic traditions (all in modern, Western literature). Anthony Yu, *Comparative Journeys*, demonstrates the potential of comparative work to shake open the field, and Ni, *Pagan Writes Back*, offers a promising alternative through a post-secular "pagan criticism" that foregrounds deconstruction.

52. Bourdieu, *Logic of Practice*, 69–70.

53. Campany, "On the Very Idea of Religions," 305. Campany states elsewhere in his article that there is not a clear religion/non-religion boundary in medieval China but, in a qualifying footnote, admits that there were debates about how pursuit of the Dao related to the state, often in terms of separate realms (314–15). T. H. Barrett, in an essay responding to and qualifying some of Campany's statements, has shown how many Buddhists and Daoists were invested in a distinction between themselves and "the world" (*shijian* 世間) in the medieval period ("The Advent of the Buddhist Concept of Religion in China"). Our poet-monks also saw Daoist clergy as fellow "men of the Dao" (*daoren* 道人) distinct from the literati. For example, throughout his works, Guanxiu uses "men of the Dao" to refer both to Buddhist monks ("On Hearing of Wuxiang, Man of the Dao, Passing Away: 5 Poems" 聞無相道人順世五首, in Hu Dajun 9.445, *QTS* 830.9350; "Written on the Hovel of Wuxiang, Man of the Dao" 書無相道人庵, in Hu Dajun 12.482, *QTS* 831.9369) and to Daoist priests ("Sent to Li You, Man of the Dao" 贈李佑道人, in Hu Dajun 10.499, *QTS* 830.9357; "Sent to Zheng of Xin'an, Man of the Dao" 贈信安鄭道人, in Hu Dajun 12.591, *QTS* 831.9370; "Staying at the Mountain Abbey of Red Pine, Written on the Man of the Dao's Waterside Pavilion and Sent to the Prefect" 宿赤松山觀題道人水閣兼寄郡守, in Hu Dajun 25.1045, *QTS* 837.9433).

54. Yang Jingqing's *Chan Interpretations of Wang Wei's Poetry*, for example, has carefully documented the errors of reading Wang Wei as a Chan Buddhist poet, given that Wang's connections to actual Chan lineages and practices were tenuous at best. Building on Yang, Nicholas Morrow Williams offers a more compelling account of Wang Wei's Buddhist poetics in "Quasi-Phantasmal Flowers." For a historically grounded analysis of monks' verse from the Song period, see Protass, *Poetry Demon*. For a study of pilgrimage verses related to a specific place in the medieval period, see Cartelli, *Five-Colored Clouds*.

55. Smith, "Religion, Religions, Religious," 269–70.

56. Many of these studies have been summarized in Johnson, *Embodied Mind*; Fincher-Kiefer, *How the Body Shapes Knowledge*; and Soliman et al., "It's Not 'All in Your Head.'"

57. See, for example, Stainton, *Poetry as Prayer*; Ogunnaike, *Poetry in Praise of Prophetic Perfection*; and Haeri, *Say What Your Longing Heart Desires*.

Chapter One. Introducing Poet-Monks: History, Geography, and Sociality

1. Burton Watson, for example, admits that the term came into being at a specific time but sees no problem using it "retroactively to refer to Buddhist writers of the early T'ang" ("Buddhist Poet-Priests of the T'ang," 31). Zha, *Zhuanxingzhong de Tang Wudai shiseng*, 1, says essentially the same thing. More

nuanced views can be found in Wang Xiulin, *Wan-Tang Wudai shiseng*, 1–5; and Sun Changwu, *Chansi yu shiqing*, 316.

2. "Men of Chu": Qu Yuan 屈原 (399–? BCE), Song Yu 宋玉 (ca. 319–298 BCE), and others associated with the *Songs of Chu* (*Chuci* 楚辭).

3. "Floating cloud": well-established metaphor for impermanence in the Buddhist canon. This line closely echoes the phrasing in chapter 2 of the *Vimalakīrti Sūtra*: "This body is like a floating cloud, changing and disappearing in an instant" 是身如浮雲，須臾變滅 (*Weimojie suoshuo jing* 維摩詰所說經, trans. Kumārajīva 鳩摩羅什; *T* no. 475, 14:539b; cf. McRae, *Vimalakīrti Sutra*, 83).

4. *QTS* 818.9217. On the dating of this poem, see Jia, *Jiaoran nianpu*, 82–83. On it being the earliest appearance of the term "poet-monk," see Ichihara, "Chū-Tō shoki ni okeru," 219.

5. Poems addressed to Shaowei by Huangfu Zeng 皇甫曾 (d. 785), Qian Qi 錢起 (710?–782?), Yan Wei 嚴維 (*j.s.* 757), Gu Kuang 顧況 (727?–816?), Dai Shulun 戴叔倫 (732–789), Lu Lun 盧綸 (d. 799?), Li Duan 李端 (d. 785?), Ouyang Zhan 歐陽詹 (757?–802?), and Xiong Rudeng 熊孺登 (fl. c. 815) survive. These can be found in *QTS* 210.2183, 237.2634, 263.2923, 267.2969, 273.3082, 280.3180, 285.3244, 349.3905, and 476.5421. None of these poems addressed use the term "poet-monk," nor does a surviving essay of departure for Shaowei written by Dugu Ji 獨孤及 (725–777). The indirect evidence for the twenty-seven other officials comes from a parting essay that Dugu Ji wrote for Shaowei, for which see Liu Peng and Li, *Piling ji jiaozhu*, 16.359, *QTW* 388.3949.

6. Source for clergy: Gernet, *Buddhism in Chinese Society*, 6. Source for number of registered households at the time (4,955,151): Wang Pu, *Tang huiyao*, 84.1552. The number of clergy may have been even higher. In 830, when the government instituted examinations for the ordinary of Buddhist clergy, 700,000 registered for the exam (chapter 42 of *Fozu tongji* 佛祖統紀, comp. Zhipan 志磐 in 1269, in *T* no. 2035, 49:385a), against 4,357,575 registered households at the time (Wang Pu, *Tang huiyao*, 84.1552), giving us a ratio of 160 clergy per 1,000 households. The variation in the former period is due to the different numbers of registered households for the years 726 (7,069,565) or 742 (8,525,763). See Twitchett, "Hsüan-tsung (reign 712–56)," 419, and references therein.

7. Source for number of clergy: US Bureau of Labor Statistics, "Employment and Earnings Online," 393. Source for number of households (116,716,292): US Census Bureau, "Households and Families: 2010," 2.

8. See, for example, Xiao, *Fofa yu shijing*, 11–76; and Li Xiaorong, *Jin-Tang fojiao wenxue shi*, 125–42.

9. I put "Chan" 禪 in scare quotes because I follow Foulk, Sharf, and other scholars in understanding that, although the Chan lineages and their surrounding communities developed in the Mid and Late Tang, the more fully codified and formal monastic institution emerged only in the tenth century and developed further in the Song. See Foulk and Sharf, "On the Ritual Use of Ch'an Portraiture in Medieval China"; Foulk, "The Ch'an *Tsung*"; Foulk, "Chan Literature"; and Sharf, "The Idolization of Enlightenment." On the transformation and institutionalization of Chan in the tenth and eleventh centuries, see Brose,

Patrons and Patriarchs; Schlütter, *How Zen Became Zen*; Buckelew, "Becoming Chinese Buddhas"; and Sun Changwu, *Chansi yu shiqing*, 350–81.

10. See, for example, Jia, "The Hongzhou School of Chan Buddhism and Tang Literati," 180–88; Williams, "The Taste of the Ocean"; Owen, "How Did Buddhism Matter"; Zhao, *Zhao Changping zixuanji*, 170–77; and Zhou Yukai, *Zhongguo Chanzong yu shige*, 89.

11. On this point, see Kawachi, "'Tetsu shōnin bunshū jo' kanki"; and Jiang Yin, *Dali shiren yanjiu*, 326.

12. See, for example, fascicle 6 of the *Mūlasarvāstivāda-vinaya-kṣudraka-vastu* (Ch. *Genben shuo yiqie youbu pinaiye zashi* 根本說一切有部毘奈耶雜事, trans. Yijing 義淨 in 710, *T* no. 1451, 24:232b); fascicle 4 of Zhanran's 湛然 eighth-century commentary to Zhiyi's 智顗 *Mohe zhiguan* 摩訶止觀 known as *Zhiguan fuxing zhuan hongjue* 止觀輔行傳弘決 (*T* no. 1912, 46:266a); and fascicle 5 of the *Bodhisattva-bhūmi-sūtra* (Ch. *Pusa dichi jing* 菩薩地持經, trans. Dharmakṣema 曇無讖 in the early fifth century, *T* no. 1581, 30:915b–c). For more on *waixue* and its relationship to monastic poetry, see Protass, *Poetry Demon*, 158–93.

13. Shenqing, "Other Learning" 異學, in *Beishan lu jiaozhu*, 9.705–57; and *T* no. 2113, 52:626b–30c. On Shenqing, see Wong, "Mid-Tang Scholar-Monk"; and Adamek, *The Mystique of Transmission*, 276–83.

14. Ornate speech is listed as one of the ten wicked actions (*shi'e* 十惡) in canonical Indic sources such as the Sarvāstivādin *Ten Recitations Vinaya* (Ch. *Shisong lü* 十誦律, Skt. *Daśabhāṇavāra-vinaya*, *T* no. 1435, 23:452a). Shenqing discusses their avoidance as the ten good actions (*shishan* 十善) in his essays (*Beishan lu jiaozhu* 2.78, 10.798). Ornate speech is also frequently listed as one of several types of bad speech. In the *Great Wisdom Śāstra* (Ch. *Da zhidu lun* 大智度論, Skt.: *Mahāprajñāpāramitā-śāstra*), for example, it is one of five types of "harmful speech" 苦切語 (*T* no. 1509, 25:252a).

15. Statistics on how destructive the An Lushan Rebellion was are hard to confirm. The disparity of thirty-six million between the censuses of 755 and 764, which some cite as the number of fatalities, is unlikely to be entirely due to deaths resulting from the rebellion. It is probably also due to decreased reliability of the census caused by the destruction of infrastructure.

16. On the southeast as an alternative cultural center, see Jing, *Jiangnan wenhua*, 301–35, which counts at least forty-eight important literati who moved from the capital region to Jiangnan after the rebellion. On the importance of the military governor system to the literary history of the latter half of the Tang, see Dai, *Tangdai shifu*.

17. Zürcher, *Buddhist Conquest*, 97, 114.

18. On Huiyuan's life and teachings, see Knechtges and Chang, *Ancient and Early Medieval Chinese Literature*, 1:410–13; and Zürcher, *Buddhist Conquest*, 204–39. A testament to the Daoist presence there is Jianji Abbey 簡寂觀 built in 461 for the eminent codifier of Lingbao Daoism, Lu Xiujing 陸修靜 (406–477), on whom see Verellen, *Imperiled Destinies*, 123–215.

19. Duan, *Tangmo Wudai Jiangnan*, 12, drawing on Li Yinghui, *Tangdao fojiao dili yanjiu*. Duan, following Li, includes monks who are listed in *SGSZ*, compiled by Zanning 贊寧 (920–1001) in the late tenth century. It is possible that Zanning, himself from Jiangnan, had a geographical bias that favored monks from

his home region. For more on Zanning, his life, and his motivations for composing *SGSZ*, see Yang Zhifei, *Song gaoseng zhuan yanjiu*, 38-94.

20. See Ye, *Lushan Taiping xingguo gong*, 1.3b-4a; Reiter, "Investigation Commissioner."

21. De Meyer, *Wu Yun's Way*, 51-94, and, on his anti-Buddhist writings, 128-46.

22. Bol, *"This Culture of Ours,"* 109-11.

23. DeBlasi, *Reform in the Balance*, 19-44.

24. McMullen, *State and Scholars*, 237-41.

25. DeBlasi, *Reform in the Balance*, is especially clear on how alienated the *guwen* reformers were from the Tang mainstream.

26. For example, we can understand the imperial commissioning of Jiaoran's collected works in 792 as part of the increased patronage of literary activity.

27. See Zürcher, "Buddhism and Education," 32-33.

28. Weinstein, *Buddhism under the T'ang*, 77.

29. Poceski, *Ordinary Mind as the Way*, 148-49.

30. On this mainstream "poetic orthodoxy," see Owen, *The Great Age of Chinese Poetry*, 253-57. On the influence of Buddhism on Wang Wei's poetics, see Williams, "Quasi-Phantasmal Flowers."

31. On the shifting center of the Tang literary world, see Wang Zhaopeng and Qiao, "Geographic Distribution." On developments in the spatial imaginary, see Ao Wang, *Spatial Imaginaries*.

32. For a summary of evidence for this local turn, see, for example, Hartwell, "Demographic, Political, and Social Transformations of China." On the way that recently recovered tomb epitaphs suggest the Huang Chao Rebellion as a more decisive factor, see Tackett, *Destruction of the Medieval Chinese Aristocracy*.

33. Fu, *Tang wudai wenxue biannian shi*.

34. The definition of "poet-monk," for the purposes of these visualizations, is broad. Simply put, I have included those monks for whom *some* poetic writings and biographical information have survived (forty-eight in total). I have excluded only those monks without extant poems or whose only surviving verses are didactic reformulations of Buddhist doctrine in verse. For the full list of poet-monks and events, see "1-1 Poet Monk Events" in the Digital Appendix.

35. Compare Zha, *Zhuanxingzhong de Tang Wudai shiseng*, 32-36, which provides three tables of poet-monks' geographical and temporal distribution compared with literati poets, *jinshi* candidates, eminent monks, and Daoist poet-priests. Zha's conclusions, despite using differently structured data, are consistent with my own: 1) poet-monks tend to be from the south; 2) poet-monks are often in places not considered Buddhist centers; 3) poet-monk activities tend to take place in the cultural, political, and economic centers of Chang'an, Luoyang, and Jiangnan; 4) the places that produce poet-monks tend to be less developed; 5) there is a distinct increase in the number of extant monastic poems after the An Lushan Rebellion; and 6) a region's literary development does not correspond to its development in terms of monastic poetry.

36. See Zhao, *Yinhua lu*, in *Tang guoshi bu, Yinhua lu*, 4.94. On the pronunciation of the place-name Guiji 會稽 (sometimes called "Kuaiji"), see Hargett, "會稽: Guaiji? Guiji? Huiji? Kuaiji?"

37. See Yu Di 于頔 (d. 818), "Preface to *Zhushan Collection* by Jiaoran" 釋皎然杼山集序 (*QTW* 544.5519–20); and "Imperial Letter to the Surveillance Commissioner of Zhexi, Commissioning the Collection of Meditation Master Jiaoran of Huzhou" 敕浙西觀察使牒湖州當州皎然禪師集, in Jiaoran, *Zhushan ji*, 1.

38. *Tang guoshi bu*, 3.9a.

39. On Guangxuan, see Hirano, "Kōsen Hōnen hō"; Wang Zaojuan, *Tangdai Chang'an fojiao wenxue*, 287–306; and Yang Fenxia, *Zhong Tang shiseng*, 193–201.

40. On Zhixuan, see his biography in *SGSZ*, fascicle 6 (*T* no. 2061, 50:743b–44c).

41. On poet-monks at court, see Zha, *Zhuanxingzhong de Tang Wudai shiseng*, 37–51.

42. On the growth of the Buddhist community in Hongzhou, see Jia, *The Hongzhou School*, 17–19.

43. For a vivid summary of the Huang Chao Rebellion and its devastating effect on the elites of the capital, see Tackett, *Destruction of the Medieval Chinese Aristocracy*, 187–234. For more on the capital's collapse during this time, see Schafer, "The Last Years of Ch'ang-an."

44. On the southern shift following Huang Chao's destruction, see Brose, *Patrons and Patriarchs*, 34. Buddhist monasteries located in the mountains often served as refuges in times of trouble, which helped establish a common trope of literati poems written on the occasion of visiting Buddhist monasteries (Li Xiaorong, *Jin-Tang Fojiao wenxue shi*, 221–22).

45. On communities of poets at Mount Lu, see Jia, *Tangdai jihui zongji*, 237–56. On the shifting fortunes of monastic networks in this region, which followed the rise and fall of prominent patrons, see Brose, *Patrons and Patriarchs*, 43–46.

46. Although the south witnessed great destruction as well, it was relatively brief and limited in scale compared to the north, and the strength of the de facto local rulers (first military governors, then kings) allowed for a speedier recovery from the general chaos of the 880s. On this point, see Gu, *Zouxiang nanfang*, 32–43.

47. Wang Ming, *Wunengzi jiaozhu*, 78. For more on *Wunengzi*, see Steavu, "Cosmogony."

48. *QTS* 720.8269.

49. "Shangyuan County" 上元縣. See Nie Anfu, *Wei Zhuang ji jianzhu*, 4.148; *QTS* 697.8017. On the surface, this poem is about the Three Kingdoms period (220–280), but the topic is clearly used as a figure to describe current events.

50. Zu and Tao, *Sikong Biaosheng shiwen ji jianjiao*, 3.79; *QTS* 633.7264.

51. For more such examples, see Li, *Tangmo Wudai luanshi*, 59–67.

52. It is difficult to state the exact number of poets in *QTS* with precision, since there are numerous anonymous poems, mistaken attributions, and generic designations. My own corpus gives 2,618 poets in *QTS*. One may object that the statistics given here represent only an increase in the number of *records*

for poet-monks and not an increase in their actual numbers. However, this only leads us back to the same conclusion: people with a higher status in literary society are more likely to have had their records preserved, and therefore if we see a great number of records for poet-monks, they most likely have moved up a notch in society.

53. See Song Chen, "Review of *The Destruction of the Medieval Chinese Aristocracy*," 236.

54. On the political and economic power of the southern kingdoms during the tenth century, see, for example, Schottenhammer, "Local Politico-Economic Particulars"; Clark, "Quanzhou (Fujian)"; and Worthy, "Diplomacy for Survival."

55. For more on the former Shu regime, see Hongjie Wang, *Power and Politics*. An overview of Wei Zhuang's life can be found in Yates, *Washing Silk*, 1–35. On Du Guangting, see Verellen, *Du Guangting*.

56. See, for example, Sun Guangxian's 孫光憲 narration of this episode in his preface to Qiji's works, "Preface to the *White Lotus Collection*" 白蓮集序 (*QTW* 900.9390–91; Pan Dingwu, 598–99; Wang Xiulin, 619).

57. On the *Collection among the Flowers* and its relation to Shu literary culture in the tenth century, see Shields, *Crafting a Collection*, 106–18.

58. That many of these rulers began their careers as leaders of bands of outlaws, often from humble origins, was beside the point. Military success and strategic patronage could overcome such biases. On the small-time origins of several founders of the southern kingdoms, see Clark, "Scoundrels, Rogues, and Refugees."

59. Brose, *Patrons and Patriarchs*, especially 30–47. Poet-monks' cultural capital, being tied to their literary abilities, was similar but not entirely identical to that possessed by other prominent monks. It is also important to remember that the "regions" under discussion were not stable entities but had to be actively reconstituted and reimagined as such, especially as central power faded away in the late ninth century and led to new divisions and unifications in the tenth century. For one example of such spatial reconceptualization, see Liu Xinguang, "Tang-Song Jiangnan diyu kongjian."

60. Robson, *Power of Place*, 258.

61. This section is adapted from my article "Networks of Exchange Poetry."

62. The monk Shangyan, for example, could still bring glory to the Xue 薛 clan by being a poet-monk (*QTW* 829.8730–31); see discussion in chapter 3. Jiaoran too in multiple places speaks with pride of being a descendant of the poet Xie Lingyun (e.g., *QTS* 815.9173).

63. Byrne, "Poetics of Silence," 155, lists 140 of Hongzhi's 175 exchange poems as being addressed to monks.

64. On the social function of poetry and its relationship to money and Buddhist merit, see Mazanec, "Literary Debts in Tang China."

65. See Protass, *Poetry Demon*, 205–37.

66. The only Tang poets who have no exchanges with monks are those who have too few surviving poems to be statistically significant, or those with a skewed surviving corpus (such as Zhou Tan 周曇, whose only surviving works are poems on famous rulers and ministers from history).

67. For a full discussion of the methodology used to create these networks, along with several other conclusions that can be drawn from them, see my "Networks of Exchange Poetry."

68. For an introduction to betweenness, see Easley and Kleinberg, *Networks, Crowds, and Markets*, 66–74; and Newman, *Networks*, section 7.7. On some of the advantages and shortcomings of betweenness as a measure of power, see Easley and Kleinberg, *Networks, Crowds, and Markets*, 303–8.

69. Ryan and Ahnert, "The Measure of the Archive."

70. The algorithm used for these calculations is described in Brandes, "A Faster Algorithm."

71. In my data set of 487 named, contemporaneous poets, of whom 51 are monks, we would expect to see 1.7 monks in the top 16 and 3.7 in the top 35. The precise numbers here differ slightly from "Networks of Exchange Poetry" due to randomness in Brandes's betweenness algorithm, but general trends are the same.

72. Qu, *Liu Yuxi ji jianzheng*, 19.519–24; *Wenyuan yinghua*, 713.3684; and *QTW* 605.6113–14.

73. Jianfu monastery, established in the Jinglong 景龍 period (707–710), was located in Futu cloister 浮圖院 in Chang'an's Anren ward 安仁坊. It was dedicated to and patronized by the court ladies. See Xiong, *Sui-Tang Chang'an*, 317.

74. Wuzhen's mission to Chang'an and its documentation have received much attention in Dunhuang studies. For an introduction, see Galambos, "Composite Manuscripts"; and Hu Kexian and Yu, "You 'Wuzhen shoudie.'" On the establishment and early history of the Return to Allegiance Army more generally, see Yang Jidong, "Zhang Yichao."

75. Falan: Zhu Falan 竺法蘭, Indian monk said to have brought Buddhism to Luoyang in the first century CE and later worked as a translator at White Horse monastery 白馬寺.

76. Bowang: Zhang Qian 張騫 (d. 113 BCE), Marquis of Bowang 博望侯, was a Han dynasty diplomat, the first known to establish contact with many of the peoples of Central Asia. There is no record of him having created a diagram or map, but his firsthand knowledge of Xiongnu 匈奴 terrain is said to have been an enormous help to Han military forces.

77. The Pass: border between the Central Plains (Guanzhong 關中) and the western regions. "Long" roughly corresponds to modern Gansu province in the west.

78. The Yellow River 黃河; "Huang": the Huangshui River 湟水, a large tributary of the Yellow that flows through Qinghai and Gansu provinces.

79. P. 3886 and S.4654. A typeset edition can be found in Zhang Xihou, *Quan Dunhuang shi*, 7:58.2914–16.

80. He Guangyuan, *Jianjie lu*, 5.11b. For a discussion of the sources for this episode, see Hu Dajun, 1127–29.

81. A common critique of monks' poetry in later periods in imperial China was that their poetry was bland because the monks lacked experience in the real world. The classic example of this criticism is Ouyang Xiu's 歐陽修 (1007–1072) remark that, at a gathering held by Xu Dong 許洞 (976–1015), monks failed to produce poetry when they were forbidden from using language about natural

landscapes (Ouyang, *Liuyi shihua*, 1.4b; English translation and discussion in Protass, "The Flavors of Monks' Poetry," 131-32).

82. Owen has also noted that "in their social relations and in their poetic practice, the poet monks [of Jiaoran's circle] were an integral part of the later eighth century" (*The Great Age of Chinese Poetry*, 282), but I depart from him in that I do not understand this to be because the monks were practically indistinct from their secular contemporaries, for which see chapters 2 and 3.

Chapter Two. Inventing Poet-Monks: The First Generation and Their Reception, 760–810

1. On "mainstream" Mid-Tang literary culture, see DeBlasi, *Reform in the Balance*, 3-7. On Buddhist monks as a "secondary elite," see Zürcher, "Buddhism and Education," 23-26.

2. See, for example, Liu Yuxi 劉禹錫 (772-842), "Notes on Venerable Lingche's Literary Collection" 澈上人文集紀 (discussed below); and Sun Guangxian 孫光憲 (d. 968), "Preface to the *White Lotus Collection*" 白蓮集序 (discussed in chapter 3).

3. Liu Peng and Li, *Piling ji jiaozhu*, 9.203-04; *QTW* 390.3962b-3964a. This inscription serves as the basis of Zanning's biography of Lingyi in *SGSZ*, for which see *T* no. 2061, 50:799a-b.

4. *Tangren xuan Tangshi*, 516. For more on this collection, see Kroll, "Anthologies in the Tang," 309-10.

5. For Dugu Ji, "reviving antiquity" meant that literature should be rooted in the classics, written with authenticity, and delivered in a relatively plain style, which would lead to society's moral transformation (Bol, *"This Culture of Ours,"* 116-18).

6. McMullen, "Historical and Literary Theory," 312. Dugu Ji was not alone in this: a whole group of fellow literati in the southwest took an interest in eclectic forms of religious contemplation during this period. This group included Dugu Ji's student Liang Su 梁肅 (753-793) as well as Quan Deyu 權德輿 (759-818), on which see McMullen, *State and Scholars*, 106-07.

7. On this phenomenon, see Sokolova, "Master Shanghong."

8. See his biography in *SGSZ*, *T* no. 2061, 50:796b-c.

9. "Buoy" (literally, "floating sack") is a metaphor for monastic regulations, which keep a monk afloat on the "sea of suffering" (*kuhai* 苦海).

10. Guo Qingfan, *Zhuangzi jishi*, 3.267-68; translation adapted from Ziporyn, *Zhuangzi*, 46.

11. There is an interesting question of agency here: is Dugu Ji responsible for applying this discourse to Lingyi, or is whoever commissioned Dugu Ji to write "Inscription" (who may have been a monk)? If the latter, we should assign some of the responsibility for the poet-monks' discursive box to Buddhist monastic community itself.

12. Berkowitz, *Patterns of Disengagement*, 20-35.

13. On Tao Qian as recluse, see Berkowitz, *Patterns of Disengagement*, 215-26, and Holzman, "A Dialogue with the Ancients." On Tao's ambivalent reputation in the Tang, see Swartz, *Reading Tao Yuanming*, 48-73.

14. Berkowitz, *Patterns of Disengagement*, 47, 56–58. To be more precise, the description of Lingyi here falls under the "Untroubled Idler" subcategory of Perfect Man.

15. *Tangren xuan Tangshi*, 516.

16. Owen, *The Great Age of Chinese Poetry*, 253–57.

17. "Stone chamber": in Daoist mythology, the dwelling place of gods and immortals. Here this refers to Numinous Grotto Abbey.

18. "Transcendent": in Daoist mythology, one who has achieved long life and extraordinary powers through bodily and spiritual cultivation. Here the word refers to a Daoist priest.

19. "Subdue dragons" refers to a story in which a man named Uruvilvā Kāśyapa offered the Buddha a room to stay in for the night that was filled with flames and a *nāga* (naturalized as *long*, "dragon," in Chinese). The Buddha remained calm in the face of this danger and subdued the nāga using his alms bowl. This story can be found in the "Lofty Pillar" chapter 高幢品 of the *Incremental Āgama Sūtra* (Ch. *Zengyi ahan jing* 增一阿含經, Skt. *Ekōttarāgama-sūtra*, trans. Zhu Fonian 竺佛念, *T* no. 125, 2:615a-624b), and in the "Three Kāśyapa Brothers" chapter 迦葉三兄弟品 in the *Sūtra of the Collected Deeds of the Buddha* (Ch. *Fo benxingji jing* 佛本行集經, Skt. *Buddhacarita-saṃgrāha*, trans. Jñanagupta 闍那崛多, *T* no. 190, 3:837c-851a). The story is alluded to in other elite and religious verse of the time, such as Dai Shulun's 戴叔倫 (732–789) "Given to an Itinerant Monk" 贈行腳僧 (*QTS* 273.3077) and the "Song of the Realization of the Way" 證道歌 (*T* no. 2014, 48:396a). The ability to subdue dragons in alms bowls, perhaps inspired by this story, was also attributed to the Chinese monks Shegong 涉公 of the fourth century (*Song gaoseng zhuan* 高僧傳, *T* no. 2059, 50:389b-c) and Huineng 慧能 (638–713, see the "External Record of the Origins of the Sixth Patriarch" 六祖大師緣起外紀 attributed to his disciple Fahai 法海 and appended to the *Taishō* edition of *The Platform Sūtra of the Sixth Patriarch* 六祖大師法寶壇經, in *T* no. 2008, 48:363a).

20. *Tangren xuan Tangshi*, 517; *QTS* 809.9123-24.

21. "Seeing off Lu Qianfu to Maoshan to Look for a Friend Again" 又送陸潛夫茅山尋友, line 5 (*QTS* 250.2818).

22. Jia, *Jiaoran nianpu*, 15–19; Yang Fenxia, *Zhong Tang shiseng*, 109–16. On Madhyamaka, see Zhang Jing, "Jiaoran shilun yu Fojiao de Zhongdao guan." On his association with Oxhead (Niutou 牛頭) Chan, see Zhang Yong, *Beiye yu yanghua*, 133–37. Jiaoran also wrote encomia praising teachers and patriarchs of both Northern and Southern Chan (*QTW* 917.9555).

23. On the Hongzhou school's advocacy of "the ordinary mind is the way," see Poceski, *Ordinary Mind as the Way*, 182–86; and Jia, *The Hongzhou School of Chan Buddhism*, 67–82. On Jiaoran's relation to Hongzhou doctrine, see Jia, *Jiaoran nianpu*, 15–19; Jia, "The Hongzhou School of Chan Buddhism and the Tang Literati," 180–84; and Williams, "The Taste of the Ocean."

24. Jia, for example, understands Jiaoran's occasional use of the term "independent enlightenment" (*duwu* 獨悟) and gentle mockery of traditional Buddhist practices (like sūtra chanting) to be evidence of his adherence to Hongzhou doctrine. However, such claims are related to doctrines shared by

many varieties of Mahāyāna Buddhism, including the "dharma gate of nonduality" (*bu'er famen* 不二法門), which can be found in earlier Mahāyāna texts like the *Vimalakīrti Sūtra* 維摩詰經 and the *Brāhma's Net Sūtra* 梵網經.

25. Zhang Jing, "Jiaoran shilun yu Fojiao de Zhongdao guan," 109–12, for example, mentions that much of Jiaoran's poetic theory in the *Poetic Paradigms* 詩式 is undergirded by the concept of the "lack of discrimination" (*wu fenbie* 無分別) between subject and object that was characteristic of Madhyāmaka.

26. On religions as repertoires, see Campany, "On the Very Idea of Religions," 317–19.

27. From "Stele Inscription for Miaoxi Monastery on Zhushan in Wucheng County, Huzhou" 湖州烏程縣杼山妙喜寺碑銘 (Huang Benji, *Yan Zhenqing ji*, 130; *QTW* 339.3436). There is a textual variant in the last clause, where, instead of *wei* 味 ("tasted of"), *Yan Lugong wenji* 顏魯公文集 in *SBCK* gives *mei* 昧 / *mo* 昧 ("ignorant of"), while *Yan Lugong ji* 顏魯公集 in *SKQS* gives *zhao* 昭 ("perceptive in"). These variants have not been noted in *Yan Zhengqing ji* or any edition of this work. *Mei* / *mo* is easily explained as a transcription error for *wei* 味, reinforced by the commonality of the expression *mei yu* ("to be ignorant of") in the Tang. *Zhao* would make for a more positive comment here but would still imply a distinction between Buddhist and literary activities.

28. Huida is mentioned in the title of one of Jiaoran's poems presented to Yan Zhenqing and other literati, "At [Hui]da's Meditation Studio in Miaoxi Monastery, Sent to Rectifier Li Gongsun, Capital Minister Fang Deyu, Retainer [Pei] Fangzhou, and Yan Shi'e of Wukang: Forty-two Rhymes" 妙喜寺達公禪齋寄李司直公孫、房都曹德裕、從事方舟、顏武康士騁, 四十二韻 (*QTS* 815.9173–74).

29. Li Zhuangying, *Shishi jiaozhu*, 1; Zhang Bowei, *Quan Tang-Wudai shige huikao*, 222; *QTW* 817.9553; cf. Williams, "The Taste of the Ocean," 12.

30. The term "subcreation" was first coined by J. R. R. Tolkien in a 1939 lecture that was later published as "On Fairy-Stories," 67. For more on subcreation, see Wolf, *Building Imaginary Worlds*.

31. See *Liji* 禮記, in *Chongkan Songben Shisan jing zhushu*, 19.669; translation adapted from Legge, *Li Chi*, 2:100.

32. See, for example, the *Record of Music* 樂記: "Ritual, music, punishment, and governance are one in the end: they are means by which the people's minds are unified, producing the Way of order" 禮樂刑政, 其極一也, 所以同民心而出治道也 (in *Liji* 19.663). For a discussion of this passage and other early texts on music and governance, see Owen, *Readings in Chinese Literary Thought*, 49–56.

33. On the trope of the poet as a creator in Han Yu, see Shang, "Prisoner and Creator," 31–40.

34. See Yu Di, "Preface to *Zhushan Collection* by Jiaoran" 釋皎然〈杼山集〉序 (*QTW* 544.5519–20); and "Imperial Letter to the Surveillance Commissioner of Zhexi, Commissioning the Collection of Meditation Master Jiaoran of Huzhou" 敕浙西觀察使牒湖州當州皎然禪師集, in *Zhushan ji* 杼山集 (*SBCK* ed.), 1. Yu Di, the scion of a prominent military family, had supported popular irrigation development as prefect of Huzhou (Jiaoran's place of residence) and Suzhou after helping to secure the Tibetan border in the 780s. By the year

800, he had gained considerable political clout as well as a "reputation for arbitrary rule, for cruelty and violence, for avarice, for extravagant expenditure, for rapacious exploitation of the people under his administration by his ruthless subordinates, and for harshness toward his own staff" (Twitchett, "Seamy Side," 41–42).

35. "This western mountain": Zhushan 杼山, located in the west of Huzhou.

36. Lines 23–28 from "Respectfully Replying to the Poem Vice Director Yu Sent Me, 'Laid up with Illness at My Prefectural Studio'" 奉酬于中丞使君郡齋臥病見示一首 (QTS 815.9170).

37. Zizhen (first century BCE), also known as Zheng Pu 鄭樸, was a self-cultivator from Gukou 谷口 who refused to serve when summoned by the Han government. His biography can be found in Ban, Hanshu, 27.3056–57. Cf. Williams, "Taste of the Ocean," 10, which takes zi 子 to be a second-person pronoun ("you") and zhen 真 to be an adverb ("truly"). Zong Bing (375–443) was a famed painter, calligrapher, and writer who associated with leading Buddhist teachers of his day.

38. "Pitched Chu" is the name of an ancient melody. "Singing in Ying" refers to a traveler who sang several well-regarded songs in Ying, the capital of Chu, from Song Yu's "Questions for the King of Chu" 對楚王問 (Wenxuan, 45.1999).

39. Following Jiang Yin and Peng Yaling, I take liao 聊 to be a full verb in this line ("depend on"), rather than an adverb ("for a while") as Williams does. In his extant oeuvre, Jiaoran uses liao in both ways.

40. QTS 815.9173. See also the discussions in Jiang Yin, Dali shiren yanjiu, 362–63; Peng Yaling, Tangdai shiseng de chuangzuolun, 138–42; and Williams, "The Taste of the Ocean," 10–11.

41. On the trope of the "mountain mind" in Jiaoran and its religious significance, see Xiao, Fofa yu shijing, 151–53.

42. "Sent to the Venerable Jiaoran" 寄皎然上人, in Sun Wang, Wei Yingwu shiji xinian jiaozhu, 4.441; QTS 188.1925. In Buddhist discourse, "religious mind" (daoxin 道心) referred more narrowly to the mind set on enlightenment (bodhicitta).

43. "Gem in your hand" refers to Wei Yingwu's poem addressed to Jiaoran. The rose-gem (qiong 瓊) could refer metaphorically to anything of great inherent beauty.

44. Simurgh tunes: the yuezhuo 鷟鸞, a type of simurgh, is notable because it called out from the Qi Mountains 岐山 (in modern Shaanxi province) when the Zhou dynasty was at its peak (Xu Yuangao, Guoyu jijie, "Zhou yu" 周語, #12, 1.29). Yunhe is the name of a mountain in modern Zhejiang province, the trees of which were used to make particularly fine string instruments. By metonymy, "Yunhe" may refer to any exquisite music. One might also read this couplet as continuous, with the negative wu 無 modifying the next line's verb "add to" (ji 繼), to read "I can make no Simurgh tunes / To add to your Yunhe piping." However, this reading seems unlikely both on internal grounds (the parallelism of "Simurgh tunes" and "Yunhe pipings" encourages us to read the lines contrastively) and on external grounds (this very poem, in fact, adds to Wei's).

45. Lines 15–30, in Sun Wang, *Wei Yingwu shiji xinian jiaozhu*, 4.442; *QTS* 815.9172–73.

46. This same range can be found in another of Jiaoran's poems from roughly the same period, "Replying to Zheng Fanghui" 答鄭方回 (*QTS* 815.9173), written in 785 (Jia, *Jiaoran nianpu*, 124–27). This poem claims that poetry may be a refreshing distraction from meditation (line 4), that religious pursuits may help literary ones (line 16), and that explaining poetry may lead one into delusion (line 37).

47. "Replying to Retainer Quan Deyu's Letter" 答權從事德輿書, in *QTW* 917.9551–52 and Jiang Yin, *Quan Deyu shiwen ji biannian jiaozhu*, 799; "Letter to Vice Director Secretary Li" 贈李舍人使君書, in *QTW* 917.9552. On the dating of these letters, see Jia, *Jiaoran nianpu*, 102–3, 138–39.

48. Yu Di repeats this trope in his preface to Jiaoran's collected works but, perhaps jokingly, misunderstands Jiaoran's karmic traces to be an inherited family trait passed down from his ancestor Xie Lingyun. See Yu Di, "Preface to the *Zhushan Collection* by the Monk Jiaoran" 釋皎然杼山集序 (*QTW* 544.5519–20).

49. We can also read in these lines Jiaoran's growing interest in the teachings of the Hongzhou school (Xiao, *Fofa yu shijing*, 138–39; Zhao Changping, *Zhao Changping zixuanji*, 174–75).

50. Li Zhuangying, *Shishi jiaozhu*, 1.42; trans. adapted from Bender, "Against the Monist Model," 656–57.

51. The preface to *Baolin zhuan* is attributed to a monk named Lingche, with the second character being the near-homophonous *che* 徹 (MC: *trhjet*) for *che* 澈 (MC: *drjet*). This is likely an alternate transcription of the same name for the same person, for which see Tosaki, "*Horinden* no josha Reitetsu to shisō Reitetsu." On the dating and authorship of *Baolin zhuan*, see Jorgensen, *Inventing Hui-neng*, 644–51; Yanagida, *Shoki zenshū shisho no kenkyū*, 6:351–65; and Jia, "*Baolin zhuan* zhuzhe."

52. On the dating of Lingche's visit to Jiaoran, see Jia, *Jiaoran nianpu*, 104–7. For Jiaoran's poems written to Lingche, see *QTS* 815.9171, 9183, 9184; 818.9225; 820.9245; and 821.9265. In addition to the recommendation letter examined below, Jiaoran also recommended Lingche to Quan Deyu in a letter from 790, which is quoted in part above.

53. For the entirety of this letter, see *QTW* 917.9552–53.

54. This alludes to the well-known story of Cui Junmiao 崔君苗 (late third cent.), who so admired Lu Ji 陸機 (261–303) that reading works by Lu made him want to destroy his own writing utensils. See *Quan Jin wen* 全晉文, 102.4089, in Yan Kejun, *Quan shanggu sandai*; and Lu Ji's biography in Fang Xuanling, *Jinshu*, 24.1480.

55. Dao'an (312–385): prodigious writer, translator, and Buddhist master. He was the teacher of Huiyuan, among hundreds of others, and well-connected to literary and courtly circles. For more, see Zürcher, *Buddhist Conquest*, 184–204.

56. Some sources in the Song and Yuan list this work with the alternative title *Origins of the Practices of the Vinaya School* (*Lüzong xingyuan* 律宗行源). See, for example, Zuxiu 祖琇, *Longxing biannian tonglun* 隆興編年通論, comp. 1164

(Z no. 1512, 75:204a); Benjue 本覺, *Shishi tongjian* 釋氏通鑑, preface written in 1270 (Z no. 1516, 76:105a); and Jue'an 覺岸, *Shishi jigu lüe* 釋氏稽古略, comp. 1354 (T no. 2037, 49:830b).

57. Guo Guangwei, *Quan Deyu shiwen ji*, 123–24; *QTW* 493.5027.

58. *Tang guoshi bu*, 3.9a; see also the early-twelfth-century anecdote collection of Wang Dang, *Tang yulin*, 2.46b.

59. These pieces were likely composed on multiple occasions, which scholars have recently dated to 801, 803, and 806. See the editors' discussion in Yin Zhanhua and Han, *Liu Zongyuan ji jiaozhu*, 25.1669–70.

60. "Essay on Parting with Buddhist Master Wenchang" 送浮屠文暢師序, in Liu Zhenlun and Yue, *Han Yu wenji huijiao jianzhu*, 10.1073; trans. adapted from Hartman, *Han Yü and the T'ang Search for Unity*, 148. Shao-yun Yang believes that Han Yu's Confucian chauvinism here is a veiled critique of Liu Zongyuan and others' support of Buddhism (*The Way of the Barbarians*, 45).

61. Lines 5–8, 17–18 from "Seeing Master Wenchang Off on a Northern Journey" 送文暢師北游 (Fang Shiju, *Han Changli shiji bianian jianzhu*, 4.238; *QTS* 337.3779; cf. Zach, *Han Yu's Poetische Werke*, 50–51). Han Yu here likens Wenchang's tonsure to the mutilating punishments of antiquity, alluding to chapter 6 of *Zhuangzi*, in which the recluse Xu You 許由 tells Master Yi'er 意而子, "Yao [the sage-king] has branded your face with humaneness and duty, and cut off your nose with right and wrong" 夫堯既已黥汝以仁義，而劓汝以是非矣. To this Yi'er replies hopefully: "How do you know that the Fashioner of Things may not erase my branded face and restore my cut-off nose, enabling me to avail myself of wholeness so that I may become your disciple?" 庸詎知夫造物者之不息我黥而補我劓，使我乘成以隨先生邪 (Guo Qingfan, *Zhuangzi jishi*, 6.280; trans. Mair, *Wandering on the Way*, 62–63, modified).

62. *QTS* 371.4167. For a translation and discussion of the full poem, see Rouzer, "Early Buddhist *Kanshi*," 435.

63. See Liu Yuxi's essay on parting with the monk Hongju 鴻舉, translated and discussed in chapter 6. On the tension between monks' ideal nonattachment and parting poetry genre expectations in the Song, see Protass, *Poetry Demon*, 205–37.

64. The locus classicus for this slogan is Lu Ji's "Rhapsody on Literature" 文賦, in *Wenxuan*, 17.766. The phrase "stems from the emotions" (*yuan qing* 緣情) appears 115 times in *QTW*, mainly in writings on poetry, such as Yu Di's preface to Jiaoran's collection.

65. On Liu Zongyuan's Buddhist sympathies, see Jo-shui Chen, *Liu Tsung-yüan*, 172–80.

66. "Essay on Seeing Off Venerable Wenchang to Ascend Mount Wutai and Traveling to Heshuo" 送文暢上人登五臺遂遊河朔序, in Yin Zhanhua and Han, *Liu Zongyuan ji jiaozhu*, 25.1667; and *QTW* 579.5841.

67. Yin and Han, *Liu Zongyuan ji jiaozhu*, 25.1664–66; *QTW* 579.5850–51.

68. Liu Yuxi 劉禹錫 reports that Fangji spent some ten years at Mount Lu 廬山, where many of the first community of poet-monks also lived, and Liu personally met both Lingche and Fangji. See his "Seeing Off the Monk Fangji to Call upon Supernumerary Liu Zongyuan, with Preface" 送僧方及南謁柳員外并引 (Qu, *Liu Yuxi ji jianzheng*, 2:29.960–62; *QTS* 354.3970–71).

69. Wong, "Mid-Tang Scholar-Monk," 61–69.

70. "Sheep monks," also written as "dumb sheep monks" (*yayang seng* 啞羊僧), are a type of monk described in *Great Wisdom Śāstra* thus (fascicle 3, in *T* no. 1509, 25:80a):

> Though they don't break the precepts, they are dull and lacking in wisdom, do not distinguish between good and bad, do not understand light and weighty, and do not understand sinful and sinless. If there's something the matter in the saṃgha and two people quarrel, they will not be able to resolve it but will remain silent, saying nothing. They are just like white sheep that, on the way to slaughter, are unable to make a sound.

> 雖不破戒，鈍根無慧，不別好醜，不知輕重，不知有罪無罪；若有僧事，二人共諍，不能斷決，默然無言。譬如白羊，乃至人殺，不能作聲。

71. Shenqing, *Beishan lu jiaozhu*, 9.739–40; *T* no. 2113, 52:629a.

72. Other examples include Liu Yuxi referring to Lingche as Huixiu in his poem "Seeing Off the Monk Zhongzhi on Eastward Travels and Sent to Be Shown to Venerable Lingche" 送僧仲剬東游兼寄呈靈澈上人 (Qu, *Liu Yuxi ji jianzheng*, 29.947–49; *QTS* 356.4005), and comparing the two in his "Notes," discussed below. Zanning's biography of Jiaoran reports that in 789 the official Li Hong 李洪, a lay Buddhist himself, praised Jiaoran's poetry for exceeding Huixiu's (fascicle 9 of *SGSZ*, in *T* no. 2061, 50:892a; trans. Nielson, *Chiao-jan*, 59).

73. Daobao: scion of the influential Langya Wang 琅琊王 clan and younger brother of minister Wang Dao 王導 (276–339), who became a Buddhist monk. Brief biographical notes on him can be found in the fourth fascicle of the *Biographies of Eminent Monks* 高僧傳, in *T* no. 2059, 50:350c. "Cup-floating trickle": a flow of water barely strong enough to convey a light cup.

74. "Rice-patty robes": monastic robes short enough to not touch the water in a rice patty (Dajue 大覺 [early eighth cent.], *Sifenlü xingshi chaopi* 四分律行事鈔批, in *Z* no. 736, 42:976c). Shenqing's point is that Buddhist monks should prioritize doing basic Buddhist things, such as wearing monastic robes and using clay begging bowls, before engaging in other pursuits.

75. Shenqing, *Beishan lu jiaozhu*, 9.742; *T* no. 2113, 52:629b–c.

76. "Preface to 'Ten Rhymes Inscribed for the Venerable Daozong'" 題道宗上人十韻序, in Zhu Jincheng, *Bai Juyi ji jianjiao*, 21.1445–49; *QTS* 444.4978. This work was probably written sometime in 827–828.

77. "Doctrine-discussions": a technical Buddhist term, Chinese translation of the Sanskrit *upadeśa*, referring to expositions of doctrine in catechistic format.

78. "The Buddha's work": work that enables the salvation of sentient beings and the propagation of the dharma. See, for example, chapter 10 of Kumārajīva's 鳩摩羅什 rendition of the *Vimalakīrti Sūtra* 維摩詰所說經, in which the Buddha describes how Vimalakīrti's powers are "extremely great." "He sends transformations to all the ten directions, where they carry out the Buddha's work and benefit sentient beings" 甚大，一切十方皆遣化往，施作佛事饒益眾生 (*T* no. 475, 14:552b; trans. McRae, *Vimalakīrti Sutra*, 151).

79. "One Sound": the single, unified truth of the Buddha-Dharma.

80. The second couplet of Jiang Yan's Imitation of Huixiu's "Sorrows of Parting" reads: "The sunset merges with clouds in the blue, / The fine one, faraway, has yet to come" 日暮碧雲合，佳人殊未來 (*Wenxuan* 31.1480).

81. On this, see Mazanec, "Medieval Chinese *Gāthā*."

82. Qu, *Liu Yuxi ji jianzheng*, 19.519-24; *Wenyuan yinghua*, 713.3684; and *QTW* 605.6113-14. For a Japanese translation of this entire essay, see Kawachi, "'Tetsu shōnin bunshū jo' kanki," 83-85.

83. Huiyue 慧約 (c. 452-535), secular surname Lou 婁, was a monk known for his learning and intelligence. Though the poem mentioned here (presumably on the powerful patron Fan Tai 範泰 [335-428]) is no longer extant, he was an associate of many prominent poets, including Shen Yue 沈約 (441-513). His biography can be found in *Xu gaoseng zhuan* (T no. 2060, 50:468b-70a).

84. That is, his conversation was multifaceted, since he could speak on both literary and Buddhist matters.

85. Liu Yuxi's other writings confirm his curious but condescending attitude toward poet-monks. In the preface to his poem "Parting with Master Haochu at Haiyang Lake" 海陽湖別浩初師, for example, he marvels at Haochu's "grasp of external teachings" 得執外教 and the "purity" of his poetry 為詩頗清, which, along with his ability to play chess, "brought him favor from the literati" 以取幸於士大夫 (Qu, *Liu Yuxi ji jianzheng*, 29.965; *QTS* 362.4086). In the preface to another exchange poem, Liu worries that when his fellow literati see him reading Buddhist writings, they will blame him "for being dragged into Buddhism after becoming sleepy, saying that there are two Ways" 誚予困而後援佛，謂道有二焉 (Qu, *Liu Yuxi ji jianzheng* 29.942; *QTS* 357.4014). This implies that the literati around Liu regarded Buddhism as a separate path, even a trap into which one could fall.

86. "White Horse monastery": located in Luoyang, where Buddhism reputedly first came to China in 64 CE; "Redcrow": literal translation of the name of the Chiwu era (238-251).

87. "Yellow ears": dogs.

Chapter Three. Becoming Poet-Monks: The Formation of a Tradition, 810–960

1. On the importance of the capital corridor, see Tackett, *Destruction of the Medieval Chinese Aristocracy*, 82-88. For a brief overview of Chang'an as the center of Late Tang literary culture, see Linda Feng, *City of Marvel*, 6-9. On Chang'an generally, see Xiong, *Sui-Tang Chang'an*.

2. For overviews of Jia Dao's life and works in English, see Owen, *The Late Tang*, 123-31; and Witzling, "The Poetry of Chia Tao." For a chronology of Jia Dao's life, see Qi Wenbang, *Jia Dao ji jiaozhu*, 739-82.

3. Owen, "The Cultural Tang," 349.

4. For more on the importance of *kuyin* to the idea of the poet-monk, see chapter 6 of this book, as well as Wang Xiulin, *Wan-Tang Wudai shiseng*, 269-76.

5. This strand begins with the comment of Ouyang Xiu 歐陽修 (1007–1072): "Jia Dao was once a monk, therefore he had this flavor of austerity

and stillness that also manifested itself in his poetry in such a way" 島嘗為衲子，故有此枯寂氣味，形之於詩句也如此 (quoted in the thirteenth-century Wei, *Shiren yuxie*, 15.22). Later critics who follow this line include Wang Fuzhi 王夫之 (1619-1692), Lu Shiyong 陸時雍 (mid-17th cent.), Wen Yiduo 聞一多 (1899-1946), Li Dingguang 李定廣 (b. 1966), and Zhang Zhenying 張震英 (b. 1972). See, respectively, Wang Fuzhi, *Jiangzhai shihua jianzhu*, 2.144; Lu Shiyong, "Shijing zonglun," 1.29; Wen, *Tangshi zalun*, 37; Li Dingguang, *Tangmo Wudai luanshi*, 52; and Zhang Zhenying, *Hanshi de diyin*, 60-66.

6. The earliest evidence I have found of Jia Dao being labeled a "poet-monk" comes from Yan Yu's thirteenth-century *Canglang shihua*, 1.15a. The term is never applied to him in any contemporaneous records, and he never uses the term himself. One apparent usage, in the *QTS* edition of line 3 of "Seeing off Adjutant Wang of Shan Prefecture" 送陝府王司馬, is in fact an error for *chiseng* 持僧, a monk who upholds and venerates the scriptures, as attested in earlier editions (Qi Wenbang, *Jia Dao ji jiaozhu*, 9.515; Lee Chien-k'un, *Jia Dao shiji jiaozhu*, 9.354-55; *Wenyuan yinghua*, 278.1441; and *QTS* 574.6678).

7. *QTS* 813.9154.

8. Wu Heqing, *Yao He shiji jiaozhu*, 4.176-78; *QTS* 497.5644-45.

9. There is no way to know in which year this poem was composed, but it likely dates to the period of 823-843 when Wuke lived in the capital region and exchanged many poems with Yao He. For more on Wuke, including a tentative chronology of his activities during this period, see Yang Fenxia, *Zhong Tang shiseng*, 203-33.

10. Luo, *Dingmao ji jianzheng*, 1.12-13; *QTS* 528.6037-6038. Little is known of "Venerable Zhongyi" other than a brief mention in Yuanhao's 元浩 biography in *SGSZ* (*T* no. 2061, 50:740b) and one other poem addressed to him by Zhang Hu 張祜 (782?-853?). Tianxiang Monastery was located in Runzhou 潤州, near modern Suzhou. "Recluse Sun" refers to Sun Lu 孫路, also addressed in a poem by Xiang Si 項斯. Fuchun, famous for having been the former dwelling place of eminent recluse-fisherman Yan Ziling 嚴子陵 (first cent. CE), is the name of a mountain located in the western part of modern Tonglu county 桐廬縣 in Zhejiang province.

11. Goosegate (Yanmen) is the name of a commandery located in modern northwest Shanxi.

12. The similarity may have been reinforced by the half-rhyme of "monk" 僧 (MC: *song*) with "man" 翁 (MC: *'uwng*).

13. See Sima Qian, *Shiji*, 32.1477-79. Fishermen could also be stereotyped as "wise rustics"—uneducated people who prove to be smarter than their famous or noble interlocutors. For more on this type, see Berkowitz, *Patterns of Disengagement*, 27-29.

14. For example, Lai Peng's 來鵬 (fl. 840s-880s) "Rising from an Illness" 病起 describes both teetotaling poet-monks and drunken lay poets as part of the landscape, coming together to exchange verses and celebrate the mountains (*QTS* 642.7357).

15. See, for example, Kenneth Ch'en, *Buddhism in China*, 389-90.

16. Weinstein, *Buddhism under the T'ang*, 119, explains that the "undesirable" monks who were forced into laity in 842 "were defined as those who

mutilated themselves with fire, practiced magic, or bore tattoos or lash marks on their bodies, i.e. were ex-convicts. Also to be laicized were monks who were deserters or ex-artisans as well as those monks who failed to keep their vow of chastity."

17. For an overview of these reasons, see Gernet, *Buddhism in Chinese Society*, 29-62.

18. Ennin 圓仁 (794-864), *Nittō guhō junrei kōki* 入唐求法巡禮行記, qtd. in Weinstein, *Buddhism under the T'ang*, 119.

19. Weinstein, *Buddhism under the T'ang*, 138.

20. Contra Wang Xiulin, *Wan-Tang Wudai shiseng*, 18. For more on the swift recovery of Buddhism after the Huichang suppression and the continuity of Buddhist traditions from the mid-ninth to mid-tenth centuries, see Brose, *Patrons and Patriarchs*, 33-41, and Shi, "Buddhism and the State in Medieval China," 197-207. Brose argues that it was the Huang Chao Rebellion's widespread massacre of elite patrons that led to more substantive changes in Buddhist history that we normally associate with the Huichang persecutions (such as the rise of institutional Chan).

21. Liu Ning, *Tang-Song zhi ji shige*, 245, makes a hard distinction between poet-monks celebrated at court in the latter half of the ninth century (such as Yuanfu, Qibai, Zilan, and Kezhi) and those who maintained an attitude of reclusion (Shangyan, Xuzhong 虛中, Chumo, and Qiji). However, there do exist poems that connected the two groups: Qiji, for example, has one poem addressed to Qibai (*QTS* 843.9530), and Guanxiu (whom Liu Ning admits does not fall comfortably into either group) wrote numerous poems to Qibai, Qiji, Shangyan, Xuzhong, and Chumo. Moreover, the "reclusive" group was anything but: Shangyan (who we will see below) was close with his powerful cousin Xue Neng, and Qiji served as the highest overseer of Buddhist monks (Saṃgha Rectifier 僧正) in the Kingdom of Jingnan 荊南 for over seventeen years.

22. Fan Zhilin, *Li Yi shizhu*, 140; *QTS* 789.8890.

23. *Śrāmaṇera*: novice monk. Here the term refers more generally to any Buddhist monk.

24. "Current Highness ascended as a dragon": when Muzong assumed power in 821.

25. "Creek in the apricots": Li Yi lived in Apricot Creek Grove 杏溪園 in Lanling Ward 蘭陵坊 in Chang'an.

26. "Buddha ground": the state of Buddhahood; "mind's ground": common Buddhist locution for the mind, so named because of its productive capacity.

27. "Intoning": orally composing and reciting poetry; "upholding": practicing religious piety. Fan Zhilin interprets this couplet somewhat differently: "Having discussed seeking the mind's ground on these Buddha grounds [i.e., monastery], / I delight only that the one constantly intoning is the upholder who dwells here [i.e., the monk Guangxuan]." This reading seems unlikely to me because it disregards the grammatically parallel structure of these lines: adverbs as character 1 in each line, verbs as characters 2 and 5 in each line (oral verbs as character 2), and two-character nouns as characters 3-4 and 6-7 in each line (gerunds in line 8).

28. Fan Zhilin, *Li Yi shizhu*, 130; *QTS* 283.3230.

29. Despite having sat for the civil service examinations several times, Chen never passed. Afterward he lived as a recluse in Hongzhou, where he exchanged poems with Guanxiu, among others. Anecdotes about him and evaluations of him stress his purity and unwillingness to get mixed up in political life (Fu, *Tang caizi zhuan jiaojian*, 3:8.414–20). Confusingly, there were two men named Chen Tao who lived in Hongzhou during the late ninth and early tenth centuries: one lived roughly 803–879, the other roughly 894–968. This has been the source of much confusion since the Song dynasty, introducing many errors into the historical record, some of which have probably not been properly sorted out.

30. "Versifying": literally "stanzas and lines," the two main units of compositions in verse; "Indic eaves" metonymically refers to a Buddhist monastery.

31. Orchids hanging like pendants from the waist is unmistakably an image borrowed from the *Lisao* 離騷, in which Qu Yuan wears them as symbols of his virtues (according to traditional commentaries). For an English rendering, see Hawkes, *Songs of the South*, 67–95.

32. "Blue-cloud horse": a horse that travels into the horizon of clouds set against the blue sky, metonymically referring to parting.

33. "Hanlin whip": a writing brush. The couplet is describing his skill in the writing of parting poetry.

34. Lord Paulownia: the Yellow Emperor's healer. This obscure couplet likely refers to images mentioned in Yuanfu's now-lost literary collection.

35. Hongyan (502–564) was a monk of the Chen dynasty, famed for both Buddhistic and literary writings. See his biography in *Xu gaoseng zhuan* (*T* no. 2060, 50:476b–78c).

36. This refers to a story in the *Liezi* 列子 in which the Yellow Emperor dreams of the realm of Huaxu, where a kind of enlightened ambivalence pervades the land and none suffer. It is said that the Yellow Emperor spent twenty-eight years to get his own kingdom up to the same level, and then, when he had finally achieved his goal, he ascended to heaven. See Yang Bojun, *Liezi jishi*, 2.39–43; English translation in Graham, *The Book of Lieh-tzŭ*, 33–35.

37. The animals in this couplet refer figuratively to Yuanfu at the beginning and end of his career.

38. The *zouyu* 騶虞 comes from Ode 25 of the *Book of Odes*. According to the orthodox Mao commentary, it is a righteous animal that does not eat of any living creature (only those that have died natural deaths) and that appears when a sage-ruler is on the throne.

39. *QTS* 745.8470.

40. See *Xu gaoseng zhuan* (*T* no. 2060, 50:476c).

41. For an overview of Xue Neng's biographical sources, see Fu, *Tang caizi zhuan jiaojian*, 3:7.308–20 and 5:7.364–70. He is perhaps most famous for being the military governor of Zhongwu 忠武節度使 who was overthrown by his mutinous officer Zhou Ji 周岌 (d. 884) and killed along with his family as they attempted to flee to Xiangyang 襄陽 (see Sima Guang, *Zizhi tongjian*, 253.8233–34). Xue's reputation has not fared well after his death in 881, despite having been highly regarded in his own day. See Wang Dingbao, *Tang zhiyan jiaozhu*, 6.119; Fu, *Tang caizi zhuan jiaojian*, 4:6.408.

42. *QTW* 829.8730-31.

43. The fact that Shangyan could increase the glory of his birth family by becoming a monk may also seem counterintuitive. But the Buddhist monk's act of renunciation was never so absolute as we like to imagine it. Many writings, particularly those that do not belong to an explicitly Buddhist tradition, connect monks to their birth families. See, for example, Hao, *Tang houqi Wudai Songchu Dunhuang sengni*, 76-96; Shinohara, "Taking a Meal at a Lay Supporter's Residence," 18-42; and Jinhua Chen, *Monks and Monarchs*, 34-50.

44. The image here is that Shangyan is a superior glory, a shining light among practitioners of both Confucianism and Buddhism, not that his work sheds light on these traditions. While this phrase is found nowhere else in extant Tang literature, it is comparable to the common praise that one is "a light of our land" (*bangjia zhi guang* 邦家之光), which comes from the *Book of Odes* 詩經 (namely, Odes 172 and 290). It can later be found in, for example, the "Rhapsody on the Dawn Presentation at the Temple of Supreme Clarity" 朝獻太清宮賦 by Du Fu 杜甫 (Xiao, *Du Fu quanji*, 11:21.6134; Owen, *The Poetry of Du Fu*, 6:258-59).

45. Compare Lu Ji, "Rhapsody on Literature" 文賦: "The poet tests the void and nonexistence to demand of it existence, / Knocks upon stillness and silence, seeking a tone" 課虛無以責有，叩寂寞而求音, in *Wenxuan*, 17.765. For other translations into English, along with commentary, see Owen, *Readings in Chinese Literary Thought*, 118-19; and Knechtges, *Wen Xuan*, 3:217.

46. "Confucian works": works of the "six arts" 六藝 propounded by the Confucian classics: rites, music, archery, charioteering, calligraphy, and mathematics. This phrase calls to mind the description of Mencius and Xunzi in the *Shiji*: "Hunting down the remaining writings of Confucian ink, Xunzi illuminated the system of ritual duty; cut off from the desired end of King Hui, Mencius listed out the gains and losses of the past world" 獵儒墨之遺文，明禮義之統紀，絕惠王利端，列往世興衰 (Sima Qian, *Shiji*, 130.3314).

47. *QTW* 829.8731. *QTW*'s only note on Li Tong is that he lived during the Guanghua era (898-901).

48. Other writings about poet-monks from this period use similar, Confucian-inflected descriptions. See, for example, Li Xianyong 李咸用 (late ninth/early tenth cent.), "Looking over a Literary Monk's Scroll" 覽文僧卷 (*QTS* 645.7395), which compares the unnamed monk's music to the legendary Shao 韶 and his integrity to Xu You 許由.

49. See chapter 1.

50. For example, *SGSZ* mentions the poetry of thirty-four monks, seventeen of whom were active during the Late Tang or Five Dynasties (841-960), despite this only being about one-third of the total time period it covers (608-960).

51. The genealogy is among the oldest genres of writing in Chinese. Many bronze inscriptions from the tenth century BCE onward list out or narrate family lineages (Brashier, *Ancestral Memory in Early China*). The concern with ancestral lineages remained strong into the Tang and is most conspicuous in tomb epitaphs (*muzhiming*), which nearly always begin with an account of one's ancestors. On tomb epitaphs, see Davis, *Entombed Epigraphy*; and Tackett, *Destruction*

of the Medieval Chinese Aristocracy, 13–25. Buddhist, Daoist, and Confucian traditions all demonstrate an acute concern with mapping and evaluating the various lines of transmitted teachings. On Buddhism, see McRae, *Seeing through Zen*, 1–21; Morrison, *The Power of Patriarchs*, 13–90; and Cole, *Fathering Your Father*. On lineages in Daoism, see Skar, "Lineages"; and Charles H. Benn, "Transmission." On Confucian lineages, see McMullen, *State and Scholars*, 49. On the possible relationship between elite genealogies and Buddhist lineages, see Jorgensen, "The 'Imperial' Lineage of Ch'an Buddhism." For literary theory, see, for example, the "Revering the Classics" 宗經 chapter of *Wenxin diaolong*, which explains how each named genre grew out of one of the classics (Liu Xie, *Zengding Wenxin diaolong jiaozhu*, 3.26–27).

52. For an overview of biographical sources on Zheng Gu, see Fu, *Tang caizi zhuan jiaojian*, 4:152–72. For more on his life and poetry, see the introduction to Yan Shoucheng, Huang, and Zhao, *Zheng Gu shi jianzhu*, 1–20.

53. Qingsai (early ninth century) is better known to literary history by his secular name, Zhou He; little is known of Huaichu 懷楚 (late ninth century) aside from a few references in *Jingde chuandenglu* 景德傳燈錄 and a pair of poems by Guanxiu. See Fu, *Tang caizi zhuan jiaojian*, 5:3.117–18.

54. Yan Shoucheng, Huang, and Zhao, *Zheng Gu shi jianzhu*, 3.395–96; *QTS* 676.7754. Wenxiu, also known in some texts as Yuanxiu 元秀, was a southern poet-monk of the late ninth century.

55. For the original line, see *T* no. 2008, 48:349a. For an English translation, see Yampolsky, *Platform Sutra*, 133.

56. Wu Rong, "Preface to the *Collected Works of Master Chanyue*" 禪月集序 (Hu Dajun, 1292–94; *Wenyuan yinghua*, 714.3688–89; *QTW* 820.8643). On Wu Rong's life and reputation, see his biography in Ouyang and Song, *Xin Tangshu*, 203.5792; and Fu, *Tang caizi zhuan jiaojian*, 4:9.221–32. Wu Rong's preface is also analyzed in Kobayashi, *Zengetsu daishi*, 233–34, and Kao, "Guanxiu ji qi *Chanyue ji*," 257–58.

57. This likely refers to the poetry written by aristocrats such as Han Wo in the pre–Huang Chao Rebellion period. On this group, see Liu Ning, *Tang-Song zhi ji shige*, 106–14.

58. On this theme in the "Great Preface" 大序 to the *Book of Odes*, see Van Zoeren, *Poetry and Personality*, 99–115.

59. Though Li Bai is often thought of as a kind of carefree romantic, ninth- and tenth-century writers appreciated him just as much for his poetry's ability to instill classical values in its audience. For example, in a preface to a poetry collection written the summer of 892, Gu Yun 顧雲 (d. 894?) compared the work of Zhang Shu 張曙 (*j.s.* 891) to both Li Bai and Du Fu after claiming that Zhang's works "can make greedy officials honest, crooked ministers upright, fathers compassionate, sons filial, elder brothers good, younger brothers compliant, and human relations and the social order perfect" 能使貪吏廉，邪臣正，父慈子孝，兄良弟順，人倫綱紀備矣 ("Preface to *Airs of the Tang Collection*" 唐風集序, *QTW* 815.8585).

60. Halperin, "Heroes, Rogues, and Religion," 426–29. For more on Sun Guangxian and *Beimeng suoyan*, see Fang, *Sun Guangxian*.

61. "Vivid poetics": literally "melodies and variegated colors."
62. "Refined Way": the practice of the classical arts.
63. From "Preface to the *White Lotus Collection*" 白蓮集序, in Pan Dingwu 598–99; Wang Xiulin 619; *QTW* 900.9390–91.
64. See Jiaoran, "Obtaining the Poem-World" 取境, in Li Zhuangying, *Shishi jiaozhu*, 1.39–41. I translate and discuss this passage in chapter 6; it is also alluded to in Williams, "The Taste of the Ocean," 8.
65. On the various meanings of *yi* in poetry manuals of this period and their importance to Tang poetics, see Li Jiangfeng, *Wan-Tang Wudai shige*, 59–74.
66. "Shi you sanjing" 詩有三境, *Shige* 詩格, in Zhang Bowei, *Quan Tang-Wudai shige huikao*, 172–73. These refer to how one should approach landscape, expressive, and philosophical types of poems. See the discussion of Wang Changling's list in Li Jiangfeng, *Wan-Tang Wudai shige*, 63–65.
67. "Zhu tuo ru jingyi" 杼柝入境意, *Wenyuan shige* 文苑詩格, in Zhang Bowei, *Quan Tang Wudai shige huikao*, 365.
68. Canonical scriptures like the *Lotus Sūtra* and meditation manuals like the *Introduction to the Methods of Contemplation* 思惟略要法 alike make explicit claims about how Buddhist practice could lead to improved perception. See chapter 10 of the *Lotus Sūtra* (*T* no. 262, 9:30b–32b) and *Siwei lüeyaofa* 思惟略要法, trans. Kumārajīva 鳩摩羅什 (*T* no. 617, 15:300c; cf. Eugene Wang, *Shaping the Lotus Sutra*, 20).
69. Zhao Mu: Xiumu, with his secular surname used in lieu of the first character of his dharma name.
70. "*Sao*-poets" refers to "Lisao" (Encountering sorrow), the inaugural poem of the *Songs of Chu* attributed to Qu Yuan. "Lisao" was generally considered the fountainhead of mixed-metered, song-style poetry (see, e.g., the remarks by Zhi Yu 摯虞 [late third cent.] in his *Discussion of Literary Genres* 文章流別論, collected in *Quan Jin wen* 全晉文, 77.1905, in Yan Kejun, *Quan shanggu sandai Qin Han sanguo liuchao wen*).
71. The "bend-slack" 屈軼 flower, also known as the "flatterer-pointing" 佞指 flower, is a legendary plant said to grow up during the rule of sage-kings such as Yao 堯. Tian Qiuzi 田俅子, quoted in Li Shan's 李善 *Wenxuan* commentary, tells us: "In the time of the Yellow Emperor a plant grew on the steps to the Imperial Hall. When a flattering minister would enter the court, the flower would point to him. It was called the 'bend-slack' flower. In this way, no eloquent man dared approach it" 黃帝時，有草生於帝庭階，若佞臣入朝，則草指之，名曰屈軼，是以佞人不敢進也 (*Wenxuan*, 46.2063).
72. *QTS* 644.7386.
73. Guanxiu's *SGSZ* biography agrees with Li Xianyong's evaluation, declaring that "his style is not inferior to the two Lis, Bai and He" 體調不下二李、白、賀也 (*T* no. 2061, 50:897b).
74. The most well-known of these monks who practiced "mad cursive" (*kuangcao* 狂草) calligraphy is Huaisu 懷素 (b. 737), but others include Guanxiu, Bianguang 晉光 (late ninth cent.), Yaqi 亞栖 (late ninth cent.), and Gaoxian 高閑 (early ninth cent.). See Lu, "Wild Cursive Calligraphy"; Wang Yuanjun, *Tangren shufa yu wenhua*, 47–68; and Wang Yuanjun, *Tangdai shufa yu wenhua*, 16–26, 90–98.

75. Liu Ning and Xue Tianwei have both noticed how Guanxiu occupies a unique place in the development of *yuefu* and song-style poetry during this time, writing both political critiques in the Bai Juyi style and supernatural fantasies in the Li He style, but neither pursues this line of inquiry very far. See Liu, *Tang-Song zhi ji shige*, 205, and Xue, *Tangdai gexing lun*, 419–22, 429–30.

76. Earlier records include the biography of Faru 法如 in 689 and the *Lidai fabao ji* 歷代法寶記 composed around 774 (Yanagida Seizan, *Shoki zenshū shisho no kenkyū*, 6:335–46).

77. On *Baolin zhuan*, see Jorgensen, *Inventing Hui-neng*, 644–51; Yanagida, *Shoki zenshū shiso no kenkyū*, 6:351–65; and Jia, "*Baolin zhuan* zhuzhe." On *Zutang ji*, see Anderl, "Studies in the Language of *Zu-tang ji*," 20–43; and Welter, *Monks, Rulers, and Literati*, 59–114. On *Yunmen guanglu*, see App, "The Making of a Chan Record," 13–33. On *Jingde chuandenglu*, see Welter, *Monks, Rulers, and Literati*, 115–60.

78. See Foulk, "The Ch'an *Tsung*"; Foulk, "Myth, Ritual, and Monastic Practice"; Sharf, *Coming to Terms*, 7–10; and Welter, *Monks, Rulers, and Literati*.

79. Duke of Lu 魯公: Yan Zhenqing, famed calligrapher and friend of Jiaoran who held this title (not, as suggested by Hu Dajun, the legendary carpenter Gongshu Ban of Lu 魯公輸班). On Yan Zhenqing, see McNair, *The Upright Brush*.

80. Hu Dajun 2:16.775–76; *QTS* 833.9397.

81. Zhou He was described by contemporaries as "being pure and refined in poetic structure" 詩格清雅 and as "emphasizing the pure, marvelous, upright, and refined" 清奇雅正主. See Wang Dingbao, *Tang zhiyan jiaozhu* 10.207, and Zhang Wei, *Shiren zhuke tu*, 8.

82. See Yan Zhenqing's Miaoxi Monastery stele inscription, cited in chapter 2.

83. Elsewhere, Guanxiu compares his own friendship with a literatus to Jiaoran's friendship with Qin Xi 秦系 in "Given to Summoned Gentleman Xu" 贈許徵君 (Hu Dajun 15.722–23; *QTS* 832.9390), further demonstrating the fact that he saw Jiaoran as a model on which to base his own poet-monk persona.

84. Tanyu, "Preface to the *Collected Works of Master Chanyue*" 禪月集序 (Hu Dajun 1294–96; *QTW* 922.9604–05).

85. For English translations of this text, see Hakeda, *The Awakening of Faith*; and Jorgensen et al., *Treatise on Awakening Mahāyāna Faith*.

86. "Sent to Master Wenxiu" 寄文秀大師, in Wang Xiulin 1.56–57; Pan Dingwu 1.59; *QTS* 838.9454–55.

87. "Written on the Road to Xunyang" 尋陽道中作, in Wang Xiulin 3.163; Pan Dingwu 3.171; *QTS* 840.9482.

88. That is, he appears to have become the most prominent as judged by surviving records. Guanxiu's disciple Tanyu 曇域 is said to have left behind a ten-fascicle poetry collection (titled *Longhua ji* 龍華集) and a highly regarded commentary to the etymological dictionary *Shuowen jiezi* 說文解字, but very little of this survives. However, we do know that he and Qiji were in contact with each other in the years following Guanxiu's death, as evidenced from their exchange poetry.

89. *SGSZ*, in *T* no. 2061, 50:899a.

90. Wang Xiulin 4.200-01; Pan Dingwu 4.206; *QTS* 841.9493.

91. On Dushun, see Tao Jiang, "The Problematic of Whole-Part." On Fazang, see Jones, "The Metaphysics of Identity." On Dushun and Zhiyan more generally, see Gimello, "Chih-yen." On Chan affiliates, see Kimura, "Huayan and Chan"; Benicka, "(Huayan-like) Notions"; and Wei, *Zhongguo Huayanzong tongshi*, 202-11.

92. For the *Awakening of Mahāyāna Faith*, see *T* no. 1666, 32:576a-c; translations in Jorgensen et al., *Treatise on Awakening Mahāyāna Faith*, 68-71, and Hakeda, *The Awakening of Faith*, 38-43. For Lingyou, see *Jingde chuandenglu*, *T* no. 2076, 51:282b; and *Weishan jingce* 溈山警策, in *T* no. 2023, 48:1043a-b; translation in Poceski, *Ordinary Mind as the Way*, 138. For Weijin 惟勁, see his "Hymn on the Grounds of Realization" 覺地頌, in *Jingde chuandenglu*, *T* no. 2076, 51:453c).

93. *Mazu Daoyi chanshi guanglu* 馬祖道一禪師廣錄, in *Z* no. 1321, 69:3b; translation adapted from Poceski, *Ordinary Mind as the Way*, 184.

94. Youru Wang, "Philosophical Interpretations," 380.

Chapter Four. Repetition: Retriplication and Negation

1. Ruan Sizong: the reclusive poet Ruan Ji 阮籍 (210-263). It is said that he could become so absorbed in his reading that he would shut his door and block out the world, showing no concern for the public good (Fang Xuanling, *Jinshu*, 49.1359-62).

2. Zhu Yun and "balustrade-breaking": Zhu Yun lived during the time of Emperor Cheng of Han 漢成帝 (r. 33-7 BCE). He bravely criticized Zhang Yu 張禹, the Councilor in Chief 丞相 and Marquis of Anchang 安昌侯. Enraged, the emperor ordered Zhu Yun's execution, but he grabbed hold of a nearby balustrade with such strength that it broke when imperial guards attempted to pull him away. Thanks to the intervention of other ministers, he was banished from court rather than executed (Ban Gu, *Hanshu*, 67.2915).

3. Fang and Du: two celebrated Grand Councilors (*zaixiang* 宰相), Fang Xuanling 房玄齡 (578-648) and Du Ruhui 杜如晦 (585-630), who served under the Tang emperor Taizong 唐太宗 (r. 626-649).

4. Lord Wei: Wei Zheng 魏微 (580-643); Lord Yao: Yao Chong 姚崇 (650-721); Commander Song: Song Jing 宋璟 (663-737). All of these men were considered exemplary ministers.

5. "Graylife": the common people.

6. Hu Dajun 1:1.5-8; *QTS* 826.9302. According to the *Yuefu jieti* 樂府解題, the function of the "Song of Bright Spring" was to "lament the season" 傷時 (quoted in *Yuefu shiji*, 50.730). Its name is a variant of the famed "White Snow in Bright Spring" 陽春白雪 attributed to Song Yu, a song so noble that no matter how many people tried, no one could write a worthy matching poem.

7. Sima Guang, *Zizhi tongjian*, 253.8208, describes how Huang Chao's troops, unable to defeat the Tang forces Xuanzhou 宣州, attacked the lower Yangtze region (which included Wuzhou) and continued their destruction into the Fujian 福建 area.

8. On Guanxiu's otherworldly imagination, see Schafer, "Mineral Imagery."

9. Statistics on the number of poems from the pre-Song period come from Liu Chao-lin, Mazanec, and Tharsen, "Exploring Chinese Poetry," 279, to which is added the total number of poems from *QTSBB* (6,327). I have excluded five spurious instances of retriplication. Four of these spurious results come from the corpus of Lü Dongbin 呂洞賓 (798–?), a Daoist transcendent who was likely a legend conjured up by Song dynasty writers (see Fu, *Tang caizi zhuan jiaojian*, 4:10.392–404). The final spurious result is the first line of Luo Binwang's 駱賓王 (622–684?) juvenilia "On the Goose" 詠鵝 (*QTS* 79.864), which is of doubtful authenticity and for which the earliest editions give reduplication instead of retriplication in its first line (*Tangshi jishi jiaojian*, 7.176). For a full spreadsheet of instances of retriplication in pre-Song poetry, see "4-1 All Retriplication" in the digital appendix.

10. One instance comes from the Daoist Du Guangting, and seven are from poets whose religious affiliations are unknown.

11. Li Dingguang, *Tangmo Wudai luanshi*, 157, briefly notes the phenomenon of retriplication in the ninth and early tenth century but not its relationship to Buddhism. Yang Xiaoshan has also noted the presence of repeated characters (though not retriplication) in the Buddhist-themed poetry of Wang Anshi 王安石 (1021–1086), for which see Yang, *Wang Anshi*, 214–24.

12. Jingtao Sun, "Reduplication in Old Chinese," 171–72.

13. Kao, "Guanxiu ji qi *Chanyue ji*," 227–30, has also noticed Guanxiu's unusual proclivity for repeating characters or phrases and attributes this to inspiration from folk songs.

14. Zhang Bowei, *Quan Tang-Wudai shige huikao*, 135–36.

15. Zhang Bowei, *Quan Tang-Wudai shige huikao*, 59–61.

16. Zhang Bowei, *Quan Tang-Wudai shige huikao*, 412; Li Jiangfeng, *Wan Tang-Wudai shige*, 371.

17. On the prevalence of the "AXAY" pattern in the *Book of Odes*, see Kern, "*Shi jing* Songs as Performance Texts," 107–9. "Double drafting" was also listed as a "gate" in the *Confidential Matters of the Way of Elegantiae* (*Yadao jiyao* 雅道機要) by Xu Yin 徐寅, a manual that draws heavily on Qiji's (Zhang Bowei, *Quan Tang-Wudai shige huikao*, 424–25).

18. Duan, *Tangmo Wudai Jiangnan*, 187. Duan argues that the prominence of this technique in the works of the western Jiangnan poets Du Xunhe 杜荀鶴 and Zheng Gu (the latter of whom Qiji greatly admired) is evidence of Buddhist influence on their works. See Duan, *Tangmo Wudai Jiangnan*, 183–95.

19. For a spreadsheet of my full results, see "4-2 DD Ratio" and "4-3 DD Ratio over 500" in the digital appendix. For the code, see "4-4_QTS_double_draft." I have not counted the legendary figures Hanshan and Shide 拾得 as monks. If we include them, since their works draw heavily on Buddhist rhetoric, there would be fourteen of twenty-two monks whose ratio is above the average. If we look at the median ratio of double drafting instances among *QTS* authors with corpora of at least 500 characters (instead of the average of *QTS* as a whole), the number is lower—1.9 per 1,000—and we have even more monks above the median, fourteen of twenty (sixteen of twenty-two if we include Hanshan and Shide). This does not mean that the poet-monks are the most frequent users of this technique. Guanxiu, Lingche, and Qiji

rank 14, 17, and 82 out of 374 authors. The poet with the highest ratio is Lai Peng with 11.4 per 1,000 characters.

20. "Shige" 詩格, in Zhang Bowei, *Quan Tang-Wudai shige huikao*, 489. Not much is known about Shenyu. Zhang Bowei speculates that his manual was compiled sometime in the mid-tenth century (*Quan Tang-Wudai shige huikao*, 486–87). Shenyu's five ways of proceeding from topics are: 1) following the topic 就題, 2) conveying straightaway 直致, 3) leaving the topic 離題, 4) sticking to the topic 粘題, and 5) entering the arcane 入玄.

21. From "Thinking of Minister Xue [Xue Neng] and Shown to Commissioned Lord Wang of Dongyang [Wang Zao 王慥]" 懷薛尚書兼呈東陽王使君 (Hu Dajun 18.832; *QTS* 834.9406). The *QTS* version of the second line gives "loud" (*gao* 高) for "with pain" (*ku* 苦).

22. From "Given unto Magistrate Lu of Qiantang County" 貽錢塘縣路明府 (*QTS* 648.7444; He, *Jianjie lu*, 8.9). The *QTS* version does not include the repetition, reading instead: "Though I've not been successful in the task I've set upon (*zhi*), / I still intone with pain to (*dao*) this day" 志業不得力, 到今猶苦吟.

23. The source poem for this couplet is not extant.

24. "Nineteen Old Poems, #1," in Lu Qinli, *Xian-Qin Han Wei Jin Nanbeichao shi*, 329; *Wenxuan*, 29.1343.

25. The source poem for this couplet is not extant.

26. The importance of *kuyin* in poet-monks' poetry is explored in chapter 6.

27. *SBCK* and a few other editions give *ke* 客 ("guest, traveler") for *rong* 容 ("face, appearance"). I follow *SKQS*, *QTS*, and *Tang sanseng shiji* in giving *rong*, since it makes for stronger parallelism.

28. Wang Xiulin 10.543; Pan Dingwu 10.519; *QTS* 847.9583-84.

29. From "Autumn's End, Written at Changxing Monastery" 秋末長興寺作 (Hu Dajun 14.682–683; *QTS* 832.9384).

30. I translate this line as "mind upon mind the mind" to emphasize the repetition in the original. A more semantic-focused translation would read "Through each thought, the mind."

31. *Dingzhen* is short for *dingzhen xuma* 頂真續麻 ("thimble phrasing"), a poetic game played in the Song-Yuan period. See Williams, "A Conversation in Poems," 505. For one conspicuous example in the *Book of Odes*, see Ode 247, "We Are Drunk" (Jizui 既醉). On the English word "anadiplosis," see Lanham, *A Handlist of Rhetorical Terms*, 8.

32. "Goldbird": the sun. In this metaphor its "feet" are the rays of the sun.

33. That is, it blows to the eastern and western edges of the known world. "Withered mulberries": a play on Fusang 扶桑, the name of a mythical tree in the far east.

34. "Single Breath": the original energy of the cosmos; "formless": the only appearance of this term (*wutai* 無態) prior to Guanxiu can be found in the abridged translation of the *Pañcaviṃśati-sāhasrikā-prajñāpāramitā sūtra* known as the *Fangguang bore jing* 放光般若經 (trans. Mokṣala 無叉羅 on June 23, 291). In that text, it refers to a type of *samādhi* (concentration) in which the practitioner "does not attain the appearance of the dharmas" 不得諸法態 (T no. 221, 8:24a; also quoted in *Yiqiejing yinyi* 一切經音義, T no. 2128, 54:357a).

35. Hu Dajun 26.1065-66; *QTS* 20.235; *QTS* 826.9303. According to the *Yuefu shiji*, the "Ballad of the Bitter Cold" is one of six songs of the "clear tones" 清調 variety that were sung from the Jin 晉 to the Qi 齊 (265-502) dynasties but were no longer sung afterward (*Yuefu shiji* 33.495).

36. For a translation of this poem, see Watson, *The Columbia Book of Chinese Poetry*, 107-8.

37. See Roth, "Evidence for Stages." Roth's scope is a handful of texts from early times through the completion of the *Huainanzi* 淮南子 in 139 BCE, which he calls "early Daoism"—a term I hesitate to use because "early Daoism" is best applied to self-conscious religious organizations associated with the term in their formative period, from the revelations received by Zhang Daoling 張道陵 in 142 CE until their consolidation at the start of the Tang. On the problems (and necessity) of limiting the scope of "early Daoism" in this way, see Bokenkamp, *Early Daoist Scriptures*, 10-15, and Strickmann, "On the Alchemy of T'ao Hung-ching," 165-67.

38. On *xuanxue*'s relationship to early Chinese gentry Buddhism, see Zürcher, *Buddhist Conquest*, especially 87-92.

39. "You": spring; "Vast Furnace": Heaven and Earth.

40. Hu Dajun 21.915-16; *QTS* 836.9417.

41. Nattier, "The *Heart Sūtra*," 182-91, has raised serious doubts about the authenticity of earlier translations of the *Heart Sūtra* into Chinese, especially the version attributed to Kumārajīva. It is most likely that Xuanzang revised an existing version of the *Heart Sūtra* that he encountered while in Shu in the mid-seventh century.

42. On commentaries, see McRae, "Ch'an Commentaries on the *Heart Sūtra*." On *Heart Sūtra* lore across East Asia, see Mair, "*The Heart Sutra* and *The Journey to the West*"; Tanahashi, *The Heart Sutra*, 39-41; and Eubanks, *Miracles of Book and Body*, 161-62.

43. Bai Juyi, "Stele for a Scripture [Inscribed on] a Stone Wall of Dharma-Blossom Hall at Chongyuan Monastery in Suzhou" 蘇州重元寺法華院石壁經碑文 (Xie, *Bai Juyi wenji jiaozhu*, 32.1884; *QTS* 678.6926).

44. For Xuanzang's use of the *Heart Sūtra*, see Huili 慧立, "Biography of the Dharma Master Tripiṭaka of Daci'en Monastery of the Great Tang" 大唐大慈恩寺三藏法師傳, completed April 20, 688 (*T* no. 2053, 50:224b). For the Dunhuang colophons, see S. 3252, 4216, and 4441, respectively. For other Dunhuang colophons' claims of the *Heart Sūtra*'s efficacy, see Fukui, *Hannya shingyō no rekishiteki kenkyū*, 232-35.

45. See his poem "Autumn, Sent to Qiyi" 秋寄棲一 (Hu Dajun 2:13.614-615; *QTS* 831.9373). To the couplet "The scarring in your eye has healed not: / Do you uphold the *Prajñā gāthā* or no?" 眼中瘡校未，般若偈持無 is appended an original note: "At the time, he had scarring in his eye, so I encouraged him to recite the *Heart Sūtra*" 公時有眼瘡，因勸之念多心經.

46. *T* no. 251, 8:848c. Translation adapted from Nattier, "The *Heart Sūtra*," 160-61.

47. From the *Cūḷamālunkya Sutta*, translated from the *Majjhima-Nikāya*, in Nanamoli and Bodhi, *The Middle Length Discourses of the Buddha*, 533-36.

48. For this plain English rendition, see Priest, "The Logic of the *Catuskoti*," 25.

49. *Cūḷmālunkya Sutta*, in Nanamoli and Bodhi, *The Middle Length Discourses of the Buddha*, 533, translation modified. The Chinese translation comes from the *Arrow Parable Sūtra* 箭喻經 in the *Middle-Length Āgama Sūtras* 中阿含經 (trans. Gautama Saṃghadeva 瞿曇僧伽提婆 in 397–398), *T* no. 26, 1:805a–b.

50. In particular, he used the *catuṣkoṭi* when discussing six subjects: 1) causation, 2) the totality of factors in relative truth, 3) no-self, 4) the conditioned nature of reality (dependent origination), 5) the existence of the Buddha after death, and 6) nirvāṇa (Ruegg, "Uses of the Four Positions," 3–16).

51. See, for example, *Mahāyāna Nirvāṇa Sūtra* 大般涅槃經 (*T* no. 374, 12:526a, 572b for the northern edition; *T* no. 375, 12:770b, 819b for the southern) and *Great Wisdom Śāstra* (*T* no. 1509, 25:259c, 454c, 517b). We will look at an example from a commentary below.

52. "Chin couplet": the second of four couplets in a regulated verse.

53. Fragmentary couplet that early sources attribute to a monk of the Southern Tang 南唐 (937–976) named Qianming 謙明 (see the discussion in *QTSBB*, 475). Huang Che 黃徹 (1093–1168) mistakenly attributes it to Guanxiu in *Gongxi shihua*, 3.3a.

54. From the poem "Words on Behalf of an Autumn Fan" 代秋扇詞 by Zheng Gu, in Yan Shoucheng, Huang, and Zhao, *Zheng Gu shiji jianzhu*, 3.397–98; *QTS* 676.7748.

55. From the poem "Willow, in the Long Line" 柳長句 by Du Mu 杜牧 (803–852), in He Xiguang, *Fanchuan wenji jiaozhu*, 3.349; *QTS* 522.5972.

56. From a poem by Qiji, in Wang Xiulin 1.22, Pan Dingwu 1.23, and *QTS* 838.9445–46.

57. Zhang Bowei, *Quan Tang-Wudai shige huikao*, 490. This passage is also quoted and discussed at length in Li Jiangfeng, *Wan Tang Wudai shige*, 275–79.

58. For example, *Confidential Matters of the Way of Elegantiae* (*Yadao jiyao*), in Zhang Bowei, *Quan Tang Wudai shige huikao*, 438–39. This is also mentioned in Li Jiangfeng, *Wan-Tang Wudai shige*, 275.

59. Interestingly, Shenyu's precise phrasing here, about the two levels of meaning reaching their audience or not, can also be found in a number of early records of Chan masters. Li Jiangfeng has argued that both Shenyu and the Chan masters are drawing on colloquial sayings popular in tenth- and eleventh-century Chan communities (*Wan-Tang Wudai shige*, 277–79).

60. *T* no. 374, 12:487a (trans. Dharmakṣema 曇無讖 in 421).

61. A quick search of the *Taishō* canon lists 4,731 occurrences of this formula.

62. "Great Lu": Huineng, secular surname Lu, later considered to be the Sixth Patriarch of Chan Buddhism, whose legend is famously depicted in the *Platform Sūtra*. He was said to be an illiterate woodcutter from the south. On Huineng's biographies, see Jorgenson, *Inventing Hui-neng*.

63. That is, Huineng discovered universal Buddha nature (and thus awakening) in this world. "Morel pearl": an extremely hard-to-find treasure hidden beneath the chin of a black dragon. See *Zhuangzi* 莊子, chapter 32, "Lie Yukou" 列禦寇 (Guo Qingfan, *Zhuangzi jishi*, 32.1061–62). "Bellows": metaphor for the world, emphasizing its emptiness. The locus classicus is *Daodejing* 5: "The space between heaven and earth, is it not like a bellows? Emptied but not diminished, moving and further exceeding" 天地之間，其猶橐籥乎？虛而不屈，動而愈出.

64. Hu Dajun 19.872-73; *QTS* 835.9411.

65. See, for example, Zongmi 宗密 (780-841), in his commentary on the *Sūtra of Perfect Enlightenment*: "Situated in the currents of birth and death, the morel pearl shimmers in the watchet sea alone. Squatting on the banks of nirvāṇa, the cassia wheel glows in the cyan heavens by itself" 處生死流，驪珠獨耀於滄海。踞涅槃岸，桂輪孤朗於碧天 (*Yuanjue jing dashu* 圓覺經大疏, Z no. 243, 9: 323c). "Cassia wheel": the moon, which is round like a wheel and where a cassia tree is said to grow.

66. See Penkower, "In the Beginning," on Guangding's role in shaping the legacy of Zhiyi.

67. Penkower, "T'ien-t'ai during the T'ang dynasty," 317.

68. Guanding 灌頂, *Sub-Commentary to the Mahāparinirvāṇa sūtra* 大般涅槃經疏, T no. 1767, 38:83a.

69. *T* no. 1767, 38:83b-c. In my translation, "to false" means "to regard as false." The verb *fei* 非 is used putatively here: it imputes its properties onto its object. I use this awkward translation method to give the reader a sense of the repetition in the original.

70. In chapter 2, "Cultivating the Person" 修身, in Wang Xianqian, *Xunzi jijie*, 1.24.

71. Other monks, especially those like Dushun 杜順 (557-640) who taught Huayan doctrine, oscillated between negative and positive approaches (Gimello, "Apophatic and Kataphatic Discourse in Mahāyāna").

72. Liu and Xiang: Liu Bang 劉邦 and Xiang Yu 項羽, who famously battled each other in the "Chu-Han contention" during the Han dynasty's ascension in the late third century BCE.

73. This alludes to a few lines from the "Nine Laments" 九歎 of the *Songs of Chu*: "Sad that the men of this age are so unequal—*hey*- / Some so short-sighted and some so far-seeing: / Some so stubborn that they have no comprehension—*hey*- / Some of clear vision who cannot win a hearing" 惜今世其何殊兮，遠近思而不同。或沈淪其無所達兮，或清激其無所通 (*Chuci buzhu*, 16.305; trans. adapted from Hawkes, *Songs of the South*, 297).

74. Hu Dajun 21.924-25; *QTS* 836.9418. Likely written in 898 or 899, when Guanxiu lived briefly in the Changsha area.

75. On Buddhist uses of the *yuefu* "Traveling's Hard" 行路難, which began very early on, see Wang Xiaodun, "'Xinglunan' yu Wei-Jin Nanbeichao," 9-13; and Zheng, *Dunhuang Fojiao wenxian*, 305-36.

76. "Empty emptiness is itself empty": the *Great Wisdom Śāstra* defines this as "when all dharmas are empty, and this emptiness itself is empty" 一切法空，是空亦空 (*T* no. 1509, 25:393c16-17). In the *Mahāprajñāpāramitā Sūtra* 大般若波羅蜜多經 itself, "empty emptiness" is listed as the third of twenty varieties of emptiness (see *T* no. 220, 5:13b). A more doctrinally precise but less literary translation of this phrase would be something like "the emptiness of emptiness," meaning that the linguistic concept of emptiness is itself metaphysically empty.

77. The main source for this song is the manuscript labeled Ryūkoku 024.3-4-1 (labeled as such in a cross-reference in Soymié, *Catalogue*, 334-35). Photographic reproductions and a transcription can be found in Yoshimura, "Chōshin kōronan zankan kō," 189-91. Modern collections of songs and poems

found in Dunhuang manuscripts identify this song as being from the same cycle as the poems of two other manuscripts, Dx.665 and S.6042. See Ren, *Dunhuang geci zongbian*, 2:1146–1220; and Xiang, *Dunhuang geci zongbian huibu*, 204–13.

78. The elite Japanese monk Kūkai, however, did write a series of verses that share a title and themes with a series of Dunhuang songs, on "Contemplating Nine [Stages of Bodily Decay]" 九想. On these poems, see Zheng, *Dunhuang Fojiao wenxian*, 276–304.

79. It is possible that Daoists, who shared many concepts and terms with Buddhists at this time, also used some of these techniques in their works. The corpus of poetry attributed to Lü Dongbin, of dubious authenticity, also shows a propensity toward repetition.

Chapter Five. Incantation: Sonority and Foreignness

1. On early Chinese spells, see Harper, "A Chinese Demonography"; Poo, "Ritual and Ritual Texts in Early China"; and Poo, "Images and Ritual Treatment." On Daoist spells, see Capitanio, "Sanskrit and Pseudo-Sanskrit"; and Shu-wei Hsieh, *Dafan miluo*. On Daoist spells' relationship to poetry, see Kroll, "Daoist Verse," 972–75.

2. Lin Pei-ying, "A Comparative Approach."

3. See McBride, "Dhāraṇī and Spells"; Sørensen, "The Presence of Esoteric Buddhist Elements"; Strickmann, *Mantras et mandarins*, 70–71; Sharf, *Coming to Terms*, 264; Copp, *The Body Incantatory*, esp. 3; Kieschnick, *The Eminent Monk*, 82–96; Mollier, *Buddhism and Taoism Face to Face*, 20–22; Bentor and Shahar, *Chinese and Tibetan Esoteric Buddhism*, 2–3. For more on esoteric lineages and their influence on Buddhist culture in the Late Tang, see Orzech, "After Amoghavajra."

4. We know of at least forty-two excavated *dhāraṇī* pillars that date prior to the Song dynasty reunification in 974, located in every corner of the Tang and post-Tang world. See the table in Liu, *Miezui yu duwang*, 54–60. Even the Daoist Li Bai wrote one such text. See "Hymn, with Preface, for the *Exalted Buddha's Uṣṇīṣa Dhāraṇī* at Chongming Monastery" 崇明寺佛頂尊勝陀羅尼幢頌並序 (Qu and Zhu, *Li Bai ji jiaozhu*, 28.1608–16; *QTW* 348.2–5; English translation and study in Kroll, *Dharma Bell*, 39–75).

5. See Lowe, *Ritualized Writing*, 32–33.

6. There are many tales of the *Lotus Sūtra*'s power in the late fifth-century collection of miracle tales, *A Record of Signs from the Unseen Realm* (*Mingxiang ji* 冥祥記) by Wang Yan 王琰, many of which were reproduced in Huijiao's 慧皎 *Biographies of Eminent Monks* (*Gaoseng zhuan*), completed in 519 (*T* no. 2059). For a study and translation of the former text, see Campany, *Signs from the Unseen Realm*. On related texts, see Campany, "Miracle Tales as Scripture Reception." On Japanese miracle tales of the *Lotus Sūtra*, see Dykstra, *Miraculous Tales*.

7. These are Huixiang 慧祥, *Accounts of Propagation and Praise of the Lotus Sūtra* (*Hongzan fahua zhuan* 弘贊法華傳), completed around 706 (*T* no. 2067), and Sengxiang 僧詳, *Accounts on the Transmission of the Lotus Sūtra* (*Fahua jing zhuanji* 法華經傳記), completed around 754 (*T* no. 2068).

8. There are numerous tales of monks whose tongues remain intact after death because of their devotion to reciting the *Lotus* during their lifetimes. See, for example, the stories of the skull presented to Emperor Wucheng and of the monk Zhiye's unburied body (in *T* no. 2067, 51:31c and 34c; the latter is translated in Stevenson, "Tales of the Lotus Sūtra," 326-27).

9. Stevenson, "Buddhist Practice," 139.

10. Definition loosely adapted from Ludwig, "Incantation," 4406. For more on spells as a means of accessing and manipulating spiritual powers in the ancient west, see Graf, *Magic in the Ancient World*, 118-74. For medieval China, see Strickmann, *Chinese Magical Medicine*, 89-122; and Mollier, *Buddhism and Taoism*, 90-93.

11. The poetry of Li Bai is perhaps the most prominent example of this. See, for example, Eide, "On Li Po"; and Kroll, "Lexical Landscapes." The pioneer in anglophone sinology in this field is Stimson, "The Sound of a Tarng Poem." For a general study of the aural aspects of Tang poetry, see Zhu Zihui, *Tangshi yuyanxue piping yanjiu*, 111-94; and of Chinese poetry more broadly, Wang Li, *Hanyu shilüxue*.

12. Nugent, *Manifest in Words*, 127.

13. On Han Yu's idea of "ethnicized orthodoxy" and its debates among prominent intellectuals in the Mid and Late Tang, see Shao-yun Yang, *The Way of the Barbarians*, 24-73.

14. Literati were also ritual specialists of a sort, albeit in Confucian rituals. For a case study of medieval literati poetry's relationship to Confucian ritual, see my "Righting, Riting, and Rewriting."

15. On these, see Chi-yu Wu, "Trois poèmes inédits de Kouan-hieou."

16. Guanxiu's biography in *SGSZ*, *T* no. 2061, 50:897a. Guanxiu's memorization of the *Lotus Sūtra* and skill in preaching on it are also noted in Tanyu's preface to Guanxiu's works (Hu Dajun 1294-96; *QTW* 922.9604-05).

17. For an example of an allusion, see "Presented to Master Gu" 上顧大夫, which uses the metaphor of the dharma being the jewel hidden in the king's topknot from chapter 14 of the *Lotus* (Hu Dajun 5.257; *QTS* 828.9326-27). For an original note, see the note to line 10 of "Written on the Temple of Tripiṭaka Hongyi" 題弘顗三藏院, which explains that the term "white ox" is a metaphor for the Mahāyāna (Hu Dajun 3:122-26; *QTS* 827.9313-14). On the appreciative reaction, see the original note to the final line of "On Hearing that the Reverend Dayuan Passed Away: 3 of 3" 聞大願和尚順世三首（其三）(Hu Dajun 12.576-580; *QTS* 831.9368).

18. "King of Emptiness": an epithet of the Buddha in the *Lotus Sūtra*; "true son" (son of the Buddha): an ardent Buddhist, presumably one who has taken bodhisattva vows, like those in the *Brahma Net Sūtra* 梵網經, which are addressed to "sons of the Buddha" (*Fozi* 佛子) (*T* no. 1484, 24:1004b-1009a).

19. The original manuscript gives the final character as *shi* 事 (MC: *dzri*), which is corrected to *shi* 使 (MC: *sri*) in red on the manuscript. I follow the latter for the sake of a better rhyme; it is also the more difficult reading, since *liao shi* 了事 is a common phrase meaning "taking care of business."

20. The second character for "lotus blossom" (*handan* 菡萏) is written in P. 2014 as ⺿ over 阝+晶.

21. P.2104 mistakenly writes *ju* 矩 (carpenter's square, measure) for *duan* 短 (short). I follow S.4037 in emending it to *duan*. "Short *gāthās*": the verse sections of the *Lotus Sūtra*; "long lines": the prose sections.

22. In chapter 10 of the *Lotus Sūtra*, the teacher "who is able to explain the unsurpassable Dharma in this wicked world should be offered heavenly flowers and incense, as well as robes of heavenly jewels" 能於此惡世，廣説無上法，應以天華香，及天寶衣服 (*T* no. 262, 9:31a; cf. Hurvitz, *Scripture of the Lotus Blossom*, 161).

23. This text is based on P.2104, which I have checked against S.4037 and the modern, typeset editions found in Hu Dajun 1096-97; Chi-yu Wu, "Trois poèmes inédits de Kouan-hieou"; *QTSBB* 1538-39; Zhang Xihou, *Quan Dunhuang shi*, 7:55.2797-2800; and Xu Jun, *Dunhuang shiji canjuan jikao*, 18.

24. Lines 5 and 9, which appear as pairs of 3-beat lines in my presentation, are metrically equivalent each to one 7-beat line with a pause in the middle.

25. The tonal deviations are in character 6 of line 4 (level *sjang* 相 where we expect oblique) and character 2 of line 8 (oblique *srĭ* 使 where we expect level). *Srĭ* rhymes with the poem's A rhyme, while *sjang* rhymes with "the King of Emptiness" (*khung-hwjang* 空王) in lines 1 and 2.

26. These texts are difficult to date with precision. A colophon to the *Shidi yishu* 十地義疏 (Commentary to the Notes on the Ten Bodhisattva Grounds) on the opposite side of P. 2104 is dated to July 13, 980, and a circular written on the opposite side of S. 4037 is dated to February 23, 975. There is no indication of date on P. 2105. This, of course, does not tell us when these texts were written or first brought together, only that 975 is the sequence's terminus ante quem.

27. The received version can be found in *T* no. 2014, 48:395c-396c. On the "Digest" and its relation to the "Song," see Tanaka, *Tonkō Zenshū bunken no kenkyū*, 306-8.

28. For more on "transfer of merit" texts and the ritual programs they were embedded in, see Teiser, "Ornamenting the Departed"; and Teiser, "Literary Style."

29. For a description of the complete contents of P.2104, see Sørensen, "Dunhuang Buddhist Texts in Transition," 5-9.

30. I coined the term "ritual toolbox" to describe this manuscript in a presentation at the "Prospects for the Study of Dunhuang Manuscripts" conference in 2014. My thanks to Stephen F. Teiser, Wang San-ch'ing 王三慶, and others for their feedback on it. In a research note published in 2022, Henrik Sørensen similarly concluded that "P.2104 may be envisaged as a compilation of material to be used in various ritual performances" ("Dunhuang Buddhist Texts in Transition," 18), though he does not comment on the poem by Guanxiu.

31. For more on the use of similar markings in sūtra commentaries found in Dunhuang, see Hureau, "Les commentaires de *sūtra* bouddhiques."

32. P. 2104 remains my base text, checked against S.4037 and P.2105. This spell is adapted from the *Daban niepan jing* 大般涅槃經 (Skt.: *Mahāparinirvāṇa sūtra*), trans. Dharmakṣema 曇無讖 in 421, *T* no. 374, 12:370a.

33. Transliteration and punctuation of this spell follows Yamamoto, *The Mahayana Mahaparinirvana Sutra*, 10. Unfortunately, very little of the Sanskrit

version of the *Mahāyāna Mahāparinirvāṇa sūtra* survives, so it is impossible to render this into a meaningful Indic original.

34. I include "prayer" in this list because the line dividing prayer from incantation is blurry. Early Christian leaders explicitly described prayer as "sacred incantation" that could replace the spells of magicians, for which see Kahlos, "The Early Church," 170. On euphonic devices in Latin and Greek incantations, see Versnel, "The Poetics of the Magical Charm."

35. Frye, *Anatomy of Criticism*, 278 (emphasis in the original). See also Welsh, *Roots of Lyric*, 133–61.

36. Zhang Peifeng, *Fojiao yu chuantong yinchang*, 265–67.

37. On the definitions of *dhāraṇī*, see Copp, "Notes on the Term 'Dhāraṇī.'" On the interchangeability of *dhāraṇī* and *mantra* in medieval China, see Strickmann, *Chinese Magical Medicine*, 103.

38. On these practices, see Copp, *The Body Incantatory*. On the process of *dhāraṇī*'s movement from the Indic to the Sinitic Buddhist world, see Shinohara, *Spell, Images, and Maṇḍalas*.

39. While I have focused on spells in the Buddhist context below, it is important to note that spells were a central part of Late Tang Daoism, and many of these spells evolved along similar lines as their Buddhist equivalents. On these, see Verellen, *Imperiled Destinies*, 286–87.

40. Robert Sharf has argued that eighth-century Chan doctrine and ritual were indebted to the "Buddhist Veda" that we now associate with eight-century esoterism ("Buddhist Veda and the Rise of Chan"). Similarly, Henrik Sørensen has demonstrated that many teachers associated with Chan, especially Northern Chan, were familiar with esoteric practices, even if the doctrinal basis and significance of these practices could vary considerably ("Meeting and Conflation").

41. Qi, *Jia Dao ji jiaozhu*, 742–43, dates their residence at Qinglong Monastery to 801.

42. See, for example, the Ming critic Zhao Han's 趙崡 praise of Wuke's written rendition of this *dhāraṇī* (Zhao Han, *Shimojuan hua*, 4.16b); and Gu Yanwu's 顧炎武 (1613-1682) notes on seeing Ruichuan's preface at Hundred-Pagoda monastery 百塔寺 in Xi'an (*Jinshi wenzi ji*, 4.43a). Ruichuan served as abbot of Chongsheng monastery 崇聖寺 and received a purple robe of honor from Emperor Xuanzong 宣宗 (r. 846-849). On Ruichuan, see the brief remarks in the hagiography of Huiling 慧靈 in *SGSZ* (T no. 2061, 50:807c). The *Uṣṇīṣavijayā-dhāraṇī sūtra* was very popular in the Tang, for more on which see Lin Yun-jo, "Tangdai 'Foding zunsheng tuoluoni jing'"; and Liu Shufen, *Miezui yu duwang*.

43. T no. 2061, 50:743c. The "Spell of Great Compassion"—a list of epithets for Thousand-Armed Avalokiteśvara 千手觀音 written in transliterated Sanskrit—was particularly popular in the late medieval period, as attested by many narratives and poems from this time. See Yü, *Kuan-yin*, 271–75; and Kobayashi, "Tōdai no Daihi Kannon," 85–92.

44. The fullest accounts in English of Kūkai's views on language are Abé, *The Weaving of Mantra*; Hare, "Reading Writing and Cooking"; and Williams,

"Beyond Arbitrariness." For a study and translation of some of Kūkai's Buddhist song-style poetry, see Rouzer, "Early Buddhist *Kanshi*."

45. "Great Transcendent": the Buddha.

46. "The One": according to chapter 1 of the *Daodejing*, "The Way produced the One, the One produced two, two produced three, and three produced the ten thousand things" 道生一，一生二，二生三，三生萬物.

47. "Those in the world or out of it": non-monastics and monastics.

48. Lu Shengjiang, *Wenjing mifulun*, "Heaven" 天, 1; trans. adapted from Bodman, "Poetics and Prosody," 162. *Avinivartanīya*: non-regressing.

49. In this, I follow Lu Shengjiang's note in *Wenjing mifulun*, "South" 南, 1288, against Bodman, "Poetics and Prosody," 112, and Hakeda, *Kūkai*, 235.

50. Lu Shengjiang, *Wenjing mifulun*, "South," 1282.

51. *Teihon Kōbō daishi zenshū*, 3:33–49; trans. adapted from Hakeda, *Kūkai*, 235. "Three esotericae": the body, mind, and voice of the Buddha's universal body; *maṇḍa*: essence.

52. This interpretation of the importance of language in the *Bunkyō hifuron*'s preface largely follows Konishi Jin'ichi's 小西甚一 in *Bunkyō hifuron kō: kenkyū hen (jō)* 文鏡秘府論考：研究篇（上）, quoted in Lu Shengjiang, *Wenjing mifulun*, "Heaven," 9–11.

53. "Given to Tripiṭaka Zhizhou" 贈智舟三藏 (*QTS* 850.9623).

54. "Seeing Off Tripiṭaka Tan to the Capital" 送譚三藏入京 (Wang Xiulin 7.393–394; Pan Dingwu 7.392–93; *QTS* 844.9548).

55. On these monks, especially Amoghavajra, and the ascendancy of formal esoteric Buddhism in the mid-seventh century, see Goble, *Chinese Esoteric Buddhism*.

56. This is Wu Yuanheng 武元衡 (758–815), "Looking for the Venerable Tripiṭaka" 尋三藏上人 (*QTS* 317.3573).

57. "Mahāvairocana": the glorified form of Buddhahood, identified with the true, empty nature of the cosmos. See Sørensen, "Central Divinities," 90–92.

58. "Adamantine-mallet": *jinchu* is an abbreviation of *jin'gang chu* 金剛杵, that is, a weapon made of *vajra* (indestructible metal or thunderbolt). It symbolizes the power of wisdom to defeat ignorance and evil spirits.

59. Red lanterns, in China as in the West, were associated with the pleasure quarters. Zhiman's mystic light overcomes and purifies such worldly impurity.

60. Wang Xiulin emends *chou* 酬 ("response") in this line to *lei* 酹 ("libation") based on the *SBCK* edition of Qiji's works. I follow all other editions, including Pan Dingwu, in keeping it as *chou*, which also preserves standard tonal patterning (*lei* would be an unexpected oblique tone, MC: *lwòj*, while *chou* would be the expected level tone, MC: *dzyuw*). "State's airs" (*guofeng* 國風) alludes to the name of the first section of the *Book of Odes* and their power of moral suasion in the political and cultural realms.

61. Wang Xiulin 7.347–48; Pan Dingwu 7.357–58; *QTS* 844.9538.

62. Kūkai, for example, notes that the normal rhythm of a heptametric line was 4-3: "In heptameter, the first four characters form a phrase, and the latter three form a phrase" 上四字為一句，下三字為一句，七言 (Lu Shengjiang, *Wenjing mifulun huijiao huikao*, 173). Some linguists have found uses of a 2-5 rhythm, but, on closer inspection, these examples nearly always resolve into

2-(2-3) (see, e.g., Zhu Zihui, *Tangshi yuyannxue pipingyanjiu*, 134–36). We do occasionally find the 2-3-2 rhythm, as in Du Fu's lines "I do not see | the Prince of Ding's city's | old location, / I often think of | Tutor Jia's well | the same as before" 不見. 定王城，舊處，長懷. 賈傳井. 依然 (from "Qingming: 1 of 2" 清明二首其一, in *QTS* 233.2577). However, this is quite rare.

63. *QTS* 836.9417; Hu Dajun 21.916–17. Literati poems that use Sanskrit vocabulary appear to deviate less frequently from caesura norms. See, for example, the second couplet of Tang Qiu 唐求 (early tenth cent.), "Given to Lord Chu" 贈楚公: "*Prajñā*: you are always adding to your power from upholding the precepts. / *Lākṣā*: who can count your merit from reciting scriptures?" 般若恒添持戒力，落叉誰算念經功 (*QTS* 724.8310). Note how the two transliterated terms *prajñā* (wisdom) and *lākṣā* (one hundred thousand) are found before the light caesura in the first hemistich of each line.

64. Kao, "Guanxiu ji qi *Chanyue ji*," 202–4, also points out Guanxiu's penchant for breaking conventional rhythms but does not associate it with incantation.

65. The *Dhāraṇī Sūtra of the Jeweled Pavilion* exists in three Chinese translations: by an unknown Liang dynasty (502–557) monk (*T* no. 1007), by Bodhiruci 菩提流志 (572–727) (*T* no. 1006), and by Amoghavajra 不空 (705–774) (*T* no. 1005). The *Dhāraṇī Sūtra of the Great Protectress* exists in two Chinese translations: one by Amoghavajra (*T* no. 1153) and the other by Maṇicinta 寶思惟 (d. 721) (*T* no. 1154). The "Great Protectress" is the bodhisattva Mahāpratisarā (Dasuiqiu 大隨求). For more, see Huang, "Lüelun Tang-Song shidai"; and Li Ling, "Dasuiqiu tuoluoni zhoujing."

66. Hu Dajun 3.122–126; *QTS* 827.9313–9314. Further details of Hongyi are unknown.

67. Wang Rui 王睿 (ninth cent.), "Master Greasepot's Poetry Standards" 炙轂子詩格, in Zhang Bowei, *Quan Tang-Wudai shige huikao*, 388.

68. The "two Elegantiae" are two early sections of the *Book of Odes* (the "Greater Elegantiae" 大雅 and "Lesser Elegantiae" 小雅) devoted to Chinese civilization's founding rituals and rulers. "The two Esotericae" 二密 are the esoterica of meaning 理密 (secret doctrines taught by the Buddha) and the esoterica of actions 事密 (secret deeds performed by the Buddha). The Japanese monk Ennin, who codified many esoteric teachings he learned while visiting the Tang, associates the esoterica of meaning with the *Lotus* and *Nirvāṇa* sūtras, and the esoterica of actions with dhāraṇī texts. See Ennin's commentary to the *Susiddhi-kara-mahā-tantra-sādhanōpāyika-paṭala* (*Soshitsujikyara kyō sho* 蘇悉地羯羅經疏, in *T* no. 2227, 61:393b).

69. "Sonority" (*yinyin* 愔愔): the locus classicus for this term is the "Prayer Summons" 祈招 ode quoted in the *Zuozhuan*, which opens: "Sonorous is the Prayer Summons, / Showing forth the sound of virtue" 祈招之愔愔，式昭德音 (Duke Zhao; trans. Durrant, Li, and Schaberg, *Zuo Tradition*, 1484–85). In his commentary, Du Yu glosses *yinyin* as "tranquil and harmonious" 安和.

70. *Yunji* 雲屐 ("cloud sandals"): a variant of *yunlü* 雲履, which refers to a kind of footwear popular during the Tang.

71. Reading the final character as *ni* 疑 instead of *yi*.

72. Qiu Chi 丘遲 (464–508): famed literatus of the southern Qi and Liang dynasties, best known for his "Letter to Chen Bo" 與陳伯之書. For more, see

Knechtges and Chang, *Ancient and Early Medieval Chinese Literature*, 1:738–41. Here Qiu Chi stands for Prefect Du, to whom the poet-monk is sending a transcription of this poem. A manuscript variant found in *SBCK*, *QTS*, and the Jiguge version replaces "Qiu Chi" 丘遲 with "thinking of you" 相思. I follow Hu Dajun in giving "Qiu Chi."

73. Hu Dajun 14.675–676; *QTS* 832.9383. "Commissioned Lord Du": prefect of Quzhou 衢州 whom Guanxiu refers to as Du Mou 杜某. Guanxiu wrote some ten poems to him in the years 885–886.

74. Ennin, *Soshitsujikyara kyō sho*, in *T* no. 2227, 61:393b.

75. There is also the possibility that *er* 二 ("two") is a scribal error for *san* 三 ("three"). The latter character is level tone and would resolve the metrical irregularity. "Three Esotericae" (*sanmi* 三密) is also a more common term, referring to the body, mind, and mouth of the universal Buddha, which practitioners realize through mudras, visualizations, and spells. In the poem, this term would make essentially the same point as the "Two Esotericae," that different aspects of esoteric Buddhism are unified among themselves and with poetry. However, I find this emendation unlikely because it is unattested in any extant edition of Guanxiu's poems.

76. Qiji also used "cross-regulation" to emphasize an important term in the opening line of a poem. For example, the opening couplet to his regulated verse "Written at Seventy" 七十作 reads: "Seventy: only thirty springs / Away from one hundred" 七十去百歲, 都來三十春 (Wang Xiulin 3.177–178; Pan Dingwu 3.186–187; *QTS* 840.9486). Line 1 contains all deflected tones.

77. Sen, *Buddhism, Diplomacy, and Trade*, 1–54; and Xinru Liu, *Ancient India and Ancient China*.

78. Kieschnick and Shahar, introduction, 2–5.

79. For other poet-monks' encounters, see Kezhi, "Seeing Off a Brahmin Monk" 送婆羅門僧 (*QTS* 825.9292); and Zhou He, "Sent to a Foreign Monk" 贈胡僧 (*QTS* 503.5718–19).

80. "Running Into an Indian Monk Going to Mount Wutai: Five Poems" 遇五天僧入五臺五首 (Hu Dajun 14.655–61; *QTS* 832.9380).

81. Sen, *Buddhism, Diplomacy, and Trade*, 76–86.

82. "Blue lotus eyes": a description of the Buddha's eyes (see, e.g., the opening of *Lengyan jing* 楞嚴經, *T* no. 945, 19:107a, which mentions the "Tathāgatha's blue lotus eyes" 如來青蓮花眼), here applied to the Indian monks; "pressed Brāhmī writings": literal translation of the term for Chinese-style *pothi*, a kind of text-binding that imitated the Southeast Asian style of pressing palm leaves between two wooden blocks.

83. "Snowy Peaks": the Himālayas.

84. "Foot-rub oil": translation of Sanskrit *pāda-mrakṣaṇa*, protective oil used to wash one's feet. It is described in the *Record of Buddhist States* 佛國記 by Faxian 法顯 (320?–420?), also known as the *Biography of the Eminent Monk Faxian* 高僧法顯傳. See *T* no. 2085, 51:859b; English translation in Legge, *A Record of Buddhistic Kingdoms*, 44.

85. *Gandhāra*: type of tree named after the region in ancient northwestern India (modern-day southern Afghanistan and northern Pakistan) in which it grows. Its thick, brown bark was used to dye monks' robes. See Li Shizhen, *Bencao gangmu*, 37.31b. Here it refers to a brown banner dyed in the same manner.

86. *Pratyetka-buddha*: solitary realizer. The term was mainly used in a disparaging manner in Mahāyāna forms of Buddhism.

87. *Kṣatriya*: the class of the military and ruling elite in ancient India into which Śākyamuni Buddha was born.

88. Hu Dajun 14.658–60; *QTS* 832.9380.

89. Poet-monks from earlier generations certainly did not understand Indic languages. Jiaoran once wrote, "I hate foreign languages and will never study them" 虜語嫌不學 ("By Chance: 4 of 5" 偶然五首（其四）, *QTS* 820.9252), and Zhou He wrote that foreign monks' "chatter is like spells" 閒話似持咒 ("Sent to a Foreign Monk" 贈胡僧, *QTS* 503.5718–19).

90. *T* no. 2132, 54:1186a–90a. See Chaudhuri, "Siddham in China and Japan," 12–42; and Van Gulik, *Siddham*, 22–24.

91. Dating these songs is quite difficult, with scholars' estimates ranging from the mid-eighth to the mid-ninth century depending on how they triangulate bibliographic references, internal textual features, and doctrinal content. See the review in Anderl and Sørensen, "Northern Chán and the Siddhaṃ Songs," 105–9. I find the later dates proposed by Ren, *Dunhuang geci*, and Zhou, "Dunhuang Guangrong *Xitanzhang* geci," more convincing because Anderl and Sørensen's argument against it, based in part on Takise, "Jōkaku hasen," relies mainly on the presence of Northern Chan doctrines and phrases that they suppose a "Southern Chan" monk like Huanzhong would not have promoted. Ren and Zhou, by contrast, argue for the later date based on textual features, such as how the liquid vowels of Sanskrit are placed at the beginning of a Sanskrit primer referenced. Biographical information on Huanzhong can be found in fascicle 9 of *Jingde chuandenglu*, in *T* no. 2076, 51:226c–27a.

92. The songs, in whole or in part, appear on seven manuscripts: P.2204, P.2212, P.3082, P.3099, S.4583v, BD.00041-1, and Dx.492. P.2204 has a colophon that dates its copying to January 13, 942. These songs were also translated into Old Uighur sometime between the tenth and thirteenth centuries, for which see Zieme, "Old Uighur Translation."

93. Anderl and Sørensen, "Northern Chán and the Siddhaṃ Songs," 106–7, following McRae, *The Northern School*, 27–30, and McRae, *Seeing through Zen*, 61–62.

94. For example, Hongzhou patriarch Mazu Daoyi alludes to the *Laṅkāvatāra Sūtra* six times in his sermons (Poceski, *Ordinary Mind*, 144). Many literati of the post-An Lushan Rebellion period also mention in their poems reading, reciting, or listening to sermons on the *Laṅkāvatāra Sūtra*, including Li He 李賀 (*QTS* 392.4416–17), Yuan Zhen (*QTS* 401.4487), and Bai Juyi (*QTS* 432.4772–73, 437.4843, 439.4881, 459.5222). On Guanxiu, see his poems "Bidding Farewell to a Monk Returning to Mount Shan" 送僧歸剡山 (Hu Dajun 16.753; *QTS* 833.9393) and "Seeing Off Grandmaster Mingjue and Sent to Mountain Man Zheng" 送明覺大師兼寄鄭山人 (Hu Dajun 18.834; *QTS* 834.9406).

95. For fuller studies of this whole suite of songs, see Jao and Demiéville, *Airs de Touen-houang*, 86–87, 330–31; Kobayashi Enshō, "Tonkō shahon *Shittan shō*"; and Sørensen, "Meeting and Conflation" in addition to the studies cited earlier.

96. Reading *guo* 郭/塬 (outer wall) for *kuo* 廓 (broad) based on the other manuscripts.

97. P.2204 lacks "can be enjoyed" (*kele* 可樂), but I have added it based on P.2212, 3082, 3099, and S.4583.

98. "Trichiliocosm": in Buddhist cosmology, the universe is composed of a system of three thousand realms.

99. "Stilled water": common metaphor for a mind calmed through meditation; "eighty thousand *kleśas*": I follow Anderl and Sørensen, as well as the Old Uighur translation, in reading *shuo* 鑠 (MC: *syak*) as an abbreviation of a transliteration of *kleśa*. "Eighty thousand" is rounding of "eighty-four thousand" (*bawan siqian* 八萬四千), a generic term for a very large number in Indic texts.

100. I follow Anderl and Sørensen in rendering *dili* 底裏 (MC: *tèj-lì*) as purely phonetic.

101. The four directions (north, south, east, and west) plus up and down can be combined to form every possible direction to move in three-dimensional space. Anderl and Sørensen transcribe the second character of this line as *wei* 維 as I do but interpret it as *fu* 縛 (fetters).

102. My transcription is based on P.2204, available online at Gallica (Bibliothèque nationale de France), https://gallica.bnf.fr/ark:/12148/btv1b83040217, with reference to the other manuscripts as well as Ren, *Dunhuang geci*, 940. For slightly different transcriptions and translations, see Anderl and Sørensen, "Northern Chán and the Siddhaṃ Songs," 130–33.

103. Zhang Peifeng has likened the presence of these transliterated Siddhaṃ syllables to the "evocations" (*xing* 興) found in the *Odes* and other early poetry (*Fojiao yu chuantong yinchang*, 274–76).

104. See the discussion of this text in Anderl and Sørensen, "Northern Chán and the Siddhaṃ Songs," 112.

105. Zhiguang, *Xitanzi ji*, in *T* no. 2132, 54:1187c; Chaudhuri, "Siddham in China and Japan," 39.

106. Anderl and Sørensen have also pointed out the "'overuse' of rhymes" in these songs ("Northern Chán and the Siddhaṃ Songs," 103).

107. In addition to the poem analyzed below, Guanxiu uses the metaphor in "On Hearing that the Reverend Dayuan Passed Away: 3 of 3" 聞大願和尚順世三首（其三）(Hu Dajun 12.576–80; *QTS* 831.9368).

108. *T* no. 374, 12:376c.

109. See, for example, "Responding to Wang Wei" 酬王維 by Yuan Xian 苑咸 (mid eighth cent.), in which he also uses the *i*-graph metaphor and describes in the preface how Wang Wei "studied Indian writing" 學天竺書, and ascribes divine origins to the foreign script: "The lotus Brāhmī characters originally came from heaven" 蓮花梵字本從天 (*QTS* 129.1317).

110. Van Gulik, *Siddham*, 72, 78–79; and Shu-wei Hsieh, "Writing from Heaven," 205.

111. "Declining purples": refusing official recognition in the form of a "purple robe" 紫衣 bestowed on eminent monks by the emperor or others in high office; "walls of green": mountains covered in vegetation.

112. The phrase "clouds in the blue" (*biyun* 碧雲) is used here instead of *qingyun* 青雲 to fit prosodic requirements: *bi* (MC: *pjaek*) is oblique tone, while *qing* (MC: *tsheng*) is level. One may take it metonymically to refer to the act of

parting with a friend or relative, but it does not necessarily refer to Jiang Yan's imitation of Huixiu's "Sorrows of Parting" 別怨, mentioned in chapter 2. While *duo* 多 between the subject and predicate of a clause is often used as a postpositional adjective modifying the subject ("Most poems laugh..."), I take it here as an adverb modifying the main verb ("Poetry mostly laughs...") because of the parallelism with line 5 ("The Way is only conveyed..." 道祇傳). One could also read this couplet as a more specific statement about the reverend of Donglin's teaching and poetry writing.

113. See *Analects* 1.6: "The Master said: 'At home, a young man must respect his parents; abroad, he must respect his elders. He should talk a little, but with good faith; love all people, but associate with the virtuous. Having done this, if he still has any remaining energy, let him study literature'" 子曰：弟子入則孝，出則弟，謹而信，汎愛眾，而親仁。行有餘力，則以學文 (trans. adapted from Leys, *Analects of Confucius*, 4).

114. Hu Dajun 14.665–66; *QTS* 832.9381.

115. On the rhetorical strategies of Tang cover letters, see Ditter, "Civil Examinations and Cover Letters," 671.

116. This reading holds whether or not we take "clouds in the blue" to refer to parting—poetry helps one deal with the very human pain of separation in saṃsāra.

117. Qiji contrasts poetry and the Way in similar terms to Guanxiu in another poem, stressing poetry's immutable purity as opposed to how the Way is apprehended through imperfect symbols: "A pure breeze does not change—poetry still remains; / The bright moon is traceless—the Way can be conveyed" 清風不變詩應在，明月無蹤道可傳 ("Thoughts of Encouragement at Jingmen: Sent to My Friends at Daolin Monastery" 荊門勉懷寄道林寺諸友, in Wang Xiulin 7.359–360; Pan Dingwu 7.367; *QTS* 844.9540–41).

118. By a "hyper-regulated pattern," I mean that normally, within a given couplet in a regulated verse, only characters 2, 4, and 5 in a line need to alternate tonal class. In Guanxiu's poem, by contrast, these rules have been extended to characters 1 and 3 as well. This kind of patterning is not unique to Guanxiu, but it marks an extra effort beyond the minimal requirements of regulated verse.

119. "Arhat" (literally "worthy" or "praiseworthy"), in the Chinese Buddhist context, refers to an early disciple of the Buddha.

120. For a review in English of several sets of arhat paintings attributed or stylistically indebted to Guanxiu, see Loehr, *The Great Painters of China*, 54–60. One scholar has made the tenuous claim that a recently discovered hemp-cloth painting comes from Guanxiu's own hand (Yang Xin, *Wudai Guanxiu luohan tu*).

121. An early inscription on one set of paintings indicates that Guanxiu produced the first ten arhats at 880 while at He'an monastery 和安寺 and then another six some four years later at Jiangling 江陵. See Fong, "Five Hundred Lohans," 43–44, 54–55. However, it is very likely that he produced more after he moved to Shu.

122. Huang Xiufu, *Yizhou minghua lu*, 3.4; cf. Pearce, "Images of Guanxiu's Sixteen Luohan," 26–27.

123. For discussions, see Fong, "Five Hundred Lohans," 30–76; Kent, "Depictions of Guardians of the Law"; Hsu, *Monks in Glaze*, 102–31; Kobayashi Taichirō, *Zengetsu daishi*, 379–403; Miyazaki, "Sōdai butsugashi," 214; and Yang Xin, *Wudai Guanxiu luohan tu*.

124. On Piṇḍola, see Strong, "The Legend of the Lion-Roarer."

125. From "A Song of the Arhat Paintings Guanxiu Produced after a Dream" 貫休應夢羅漢畫歌 (*QTS* 761.8638–39). "Crouching rhinoceroses" refers to the rounded bulges in a person's frontal bone located about three centimeters above the brows, known in English as the frontal eminence or *tuber frontale*.

126. See too the notes on Guanxiu's arhats in the imperial catalog of paintings commissioned by Emperor Huizong 徽宗 (r. 1100–1126) (*Xuanhe huapu*, 3.12a; cf. Fong, "Five Hundred Lohans," 62).

127. Kobayashi Taichirō, *Zengetsu daishi*, 15.

128. On the importance of dreams to Guanxiu's work, see Kobayashi Taichirō, *Zengetsu daishi*, 341–46; and Schafer, "Mineral Imagery," 86–88.

129. See, for example, Robert Campany, summarizing the attitude toward dreams portrayed in the late fifth-century collection of Buddhist miracle tales *Mingxiang ji* 冥祥記: "Dreaming is a mode of real contact with other beings, not a mental event merely internal to the dreamer" (*Signs from the Unseen Realm*, 58).

130. Fong, "Five Hundred Lohans," 70–71. Koichi Shinohara has stated that, in medieval China, "paying respect to the Buddha appears to have been understood largely as a matter of paying respect to physical images" ("Stories of Miraculous Images," 184).

131. "Six laws of painting": those described by Xie He 謝赫 (late fifth cent.), for which see Hay, "Values and History."

132. *SGSZ*, in *T* no. 2061, 50:897a; cf. Fong, "Five Hundred Lohans," 36.

133. Guanxiu believed in the efficacy of such healing rituals. In a poem accompanying his giving someone a cure-all pill, he instructs the recipient: "To the Jade-Browed, the Tamer of People, lift up your praises, / To the Gold-Wheel King, Indra, and Brahma, offer your rites" 玉毫調御偏讚揚，金輪釋梵咸歸禮; and then "all the patients who take the medicine became clear-headed" 病者與藥皆惺憦. "Jade-Browed" and "Tamer of People" are epithets for Śākyamuni Buddha, and the "Gold-Wheel King" is the highest of the four Wheel-Turning Sage-Kings (*cakravartin*) who rule the earth with righteousness. For the poem, see "Giving a Pill for Myriad Ailments" 施萬病丸, in Hu Dajun 6.315–18; *QTS* 828.9332–33.

134. These likely played a part in Guanxiu's fame as a calligrapher too. Though none of his calligraphy survives, early descriptions note that he was famous for his cursive calligraphy (especially a style later known as "mad cursive" 狂草), similar in style to Huaisu 懷素 (b. 737). Huaisu was himself described as one who "swallows potions and chants spells" (*juetang songzhou* 嚼湯誦咒), as Wang Yong 王邕 (j.s. 751) wrote in a poem on his calligraphy ("A Song on the Venerable Huaisu's Cursive Calligraphy" 懷素上人草書歌, *QTS* 204.2133–34). Hui-Wen Lu has argued that "Tang Buddhist monks were typecast as practicing *shentong* [神通] spiritual powers or illusion magic when performing wild cursive calligraphy," and that, by the turn of the tenth century, wild calligraphy

had turned into a practiced skill with its own lineages of master-disciple transmission ("Wild Cursive Calligraphy," 373, 375–76). On the connection between wild calligraphy and the "sudden enlightenment" doctrine current in the Chan lineages that Guanxiu was familiar with, see Wang Yuanjun, *Tangren shufa yu wenhua*, 47–68.

135. As James Robson has noted, spells, talismans, and other kinds of magical writings in Chinese Buddhism were written in esoteric Chinese scripts as well as Indic scripts ("Signs of Power").

136. Copp, "Anointing Phrases and Narrative Power," 146.

137. See Copp, *The Body Incantatory*, for many examples of the power of inscribed, infused, and ingested spells. Ingestion involves more than the sensory experience of taste, including embodiment and corporeal merging with a spell.

138. *T* no. 262, 9:59b; cf. Hurvitz, *Scripture of the Lotus Blossom*, 322. I have broken up the spell into lines for the sake of clarity. This incantation is also collected as "a spell spoken by a rakṣasī" 羅刹女所説呪 in the fifth-century *Sūtra Spoken by the Buddha on the Great Golden Peahen Queen Spell* 佛説大金色孔雀王呪經, attributed to Śrīmitra 尸梨蜜 (*T* no. 987, 19.481c). On this text and its relatives, see Sørensen, "The Spell of the Great, Golden Peacock Queen."

139. *T* no. 1803, 39:1032b. This passage is translated and discussed in Copp, "Anointing Phrases and Narrative Power," 158–59.

140. *T* no. 262, 9:47c–48a; trans. Hurvitz, *Scripture of the Lotus Blossom*, 243.

141. *T* no. 262, 9:49b–c; trans. Hurvitz, *Scripture of the Lotus Blossom*, 250.

142. See, for example, chapter 17, "The Discrimination of Merits" (*T* no. 262, 9:44b; trans. Hurvitz, *Scripture of the Lotus Blossom*, 227); and chapter 25, "The Gateway of the Bodhisattva Sound Observer" (*T* no. 262, 9:58a; trans. Hurvitz, *Scripture of the Lotus Blossom*, 293).

143. See, for example, chapter 18, "The Merits of Appropriate Joy," which describes how giving away millions of valuables pales in comparison to hearing the *Lotus Sūtra* (*T* no. 262, 9:46c; trans. Hurvitz, *Scripture of the Lotus Blossom*, 238).

144. In addition to the poems analyzed in this chapter, see Qiji, "Given to the *Lotus Sūtra*-Upholding Monk" 贈持法華經僧 (Wang Xiulin 10.554–557; Pan Dingwu 10.535–36; *QTS* 847.9587); Qiji, "Given to the *Lotus Sūtra*-Reciting Monk" 贈念法華經僧 (Wang Xiulin 10.586–87; Pan Dingwu 10.567; *QTS* 847.9593); and Xiuya 修雅 (tenth cent.), "Song on Hearing a Recitation of the *Lotus Sūtra*" 聞誦法華經歌 (*QTS* 825.9298). Zhang Peifeng has also noted the aestheticization of scripture recitation from the Mid-Tang onward, which he attributes to the emerging Chan school's advocacy of freedom over rule and ritual. Elsewhere, however, he admits that this is a broad generalization and that scripture recitation remained guided by ritual (*Fojiao yu chuantong yinchang*, 257–60, 265).

145. Ruoye Creek is located in modern Shaoxing 紹興, Zhejiang province.

146. "Parable of the Medicinal Herbs": expounded in chapter 5 of the *Lotus Sūtra*, it offers a justification of the differences among the various forms of Buddhism. Just as the same rain falls on different forms of vegetation regardless of rank, and each receives it and grows according to its ability, so too the

same Dharma is received by different beings in different ways according to the ability of each.

147. In chapter 10 of the *Lotus Sūtra*, the Buddha illustrates the necessity of seeking the Dharma by comparing it to a man digging a well. If he digs on a high plain, he will find no water, but if he digs in moist earth, he will find it quickly. See *T* no. 262, 9:31c; Hurvitz, *Scripture of the Lotus Blossom*, 163–64.

148. In chapter 3 of the *Lotus Sūtra*, the Parable of the Burning House describes how a strong man lures distracted children out of a burning house with a narrow gate by means of promising them three vehicles on the other side.

149. In chapter 1 of the *Lotus Sūtra*, Maitreya describes the voices of buddhas preaching the scriptures: "Their voices are pure, emitting delicate sounds, with which they teach bodhisattvas in numberless millions of myriads. Their Brahmic sounds are subtle and profound, making men desire to hear them" 其聲清淨、出柔軟音、教諸菩薩、無數億萬、梵音深妙、令人樂聞. See *T* no. 262, 9:2c; trans. adapted from Hurvitz, *Scripture of the Lotus Blossom*, 7. "Marvelous Sound" is also the translated name of the bodhisattva Gadgadasvara (Miaoyin pusa 妙音菩薩), after whom chapter 24 of the *Lotus Sūtra* is named.

150. The *Lotus Sūtra* several times mentions the salvific power of just "one thought" of faith or delight in the *Sūtra*. See *T* no. 262, 9:30c (chapter 10), 44c, and 45a (chapter 17).

151. Refers to the Parable of the Jewel in the Robe, found in chapter 8 of the *Lotus Sūtra*. A rich man sews a valuable jewel into the robe of his sleeping friend, who, unaware of this treasure, soon falls into poverty. He later meets the rich friend, who tells him of the jewel, which the sleeper is able to use to get out of his dire straits. In the same way, all sentient beings already possess the buddha-nature that they may use to save themselves, even if they are unaware of it.

152. "Governor of Linchuan": Xie Lingyun.

153. *QTS* 306.3479. "Venerable Jian and Zhen": unknown; Huaizhou: located in modern Qinyang 沁陽, Henan province.

154. *QTS* lacks *chang* 長 in line 2, but most other early versions (*SBCK*, the Liu Qian 柳僉 manuscript of 1514, and the early seventeenth-century Jiguge 汲古閣 edition) retain it.

155. Following the edition of Hu Dajun, based on *SBCK*, Liu Qian, and Jiguge. *QTS* gives "Cypresses so thick, thick / You can't see far" 杉森森, 不見長.

156. "Strikes metal, beats jade": bells made of metal and chimes made of jade. Hu Dajun proposes emending *zheng* 揨 ("beat") to *cheng* 琤 (an onomatopoeia for the sound of jades tinkling). I have not followed this because it is not attested in any of the manuscripts.

157. *Gong* 宮 and *zhi* 徵 are the first two of the five notes 五音 of traditional Chinese music theory.

158. An "original note" 原注 reads: "The Buddha says that those who constantly uphold the scriptures can eat three gold catties' worth a day" 佛言常持經者可日食三兩黃金.

159. Hu Dajun 1:2.104–105; *QTS* 826.9311.
160. *T* no. 2014, 48:396c.
161. *Zhenzhou Linji Huizhao chanshi yulu* 鎮州臨濟慧照禪師語錄, *T* no. 1985, 47:498b; trans. adapted from Sasaki, *Record of Linji*, 13.
162. The most complete manuscript of this text is P.3913. To date, the most thorough study of this text in English is Goodman, "The *Ritual Instructions for Altar Methods*." Tanaka, "Relations between the Buddhist Sects," summarizes a foundational Japanese scholar's views on it, and Sørensen, "Meeting and Conflation," 348–55, outlines its ritual content in relation to Late Tang Chan and esoteric practices. For a critical edition based on several Dunhuang manuscripts, see Hou, *Jin'gangjun jing*.
163. Most prominently, *Ritual Instructions for Altar Methods* includes a lineage chart in part 2, integrating many figures normally associated with Chan. Tanaka Ryōshō presents these lineages as a kind of syncretism of two separate "Chan" and "Esoteric" schools (*Tonkō Zenshū bunken no kenkyū*, 135), while Robert Sharf and Amanda Goodman have argued that this text, among others, questions the very idea that there were such separate schools (Sharf, *Coming to Terms*, 268–69; Goodman, "Ritual Instructions," 51–55). Henrik Sørensen, by contrast, sees the text as mainly an Esoteric one "onto which a Chan Buddhist lineage has been grafted" ("Meeting and Conflation," 354).
164. This is not to say that Guanxiu is directly alluding to this text in his poem, only that he is referring to specific veneration practices that emerge out of the same ritual complex that produced the *Ritual Instructions*. Liying Kuo has suggested that the text is specific to the Dunhuang region ("Mandala et rituel de confession à Dunhuang," 227–28; "Sur les apocryphes bouddhiques chinois," 696–98). Amanda Goodman has argued that the *Ritual Instructions* offers an "upgrade" of existing esoteric ritual technologies that were reorganized into "a single, unified composition" ("The *Ritual Instructions for Altar Methods*," 81).
165. Hou, *Jin'gangjun jing*, 98a.
166. "River of desire": metaphor of the danger of the passions, which can drown a person. In the *Huayan jing* 華嚴經, the Buddha vows to dry it up (*T* no. 279, 10:352c).
167. "Vessel of the true dharma": the Buddha tells his disciples "You are vessels of the true dharma" 汝是眞法器 in the *Huayan jing* (*T* no. 279, 10:428a). In chapter 12 of the *Lotus Sūtra*, Śāriputra supposes that a female nāga cannot become a bodhisattva because "a woman's body is filthy, it is not a vessel of the dharma" 女身垢穢, 非是法器. The female nāga then offers a precious gem to the Buddha, turns into a man, and quickly attains bodhisattvahood. See *T* no. 262, 9:35c; trans. adapted from Hurvitz, *Scripture of the Lotus Blossom*, 184.
168. In chapter 17 of the *Lotus Sūtra*, one miraculous confirmation of the benefits gained by those who uphold the Dharma is a spontaneous rain of "finely powdered sandalwood and aloes" 細末栴檀沈水香 (*T* no. 262, 9:44b; Hurvitz, *Scripture of the Lotus Blossom*, 234).
169. Chapter 17 of the *Lotus Sūtra* instructs its readers: "Make offerings to the scriptural scroll, scattering flower perfume and powdered incense; or take

sumanā, champak, and *atimuktaka*, and, extracting their fragrant oil, ever burn it: he who makes offerings like these shall gain incalculable merit" 及供養經卷，散華香末香；以須曼舊蔔，阿提目多伽，薰油常燃之：如是供養者，得無量功德 (*T* no. 262, 9:46a; trans. adapted from Hurvitz, *Scripture of the Lotus Blossom*, 235).

170. "Seven lotuses": the *Lotus Sūtra*, which comprises twenty-eight chapters 品 in seven fascicles 卷.

171. Heavenly blossoms are said to have fallen when eminent monks like Fayun 法雲 (467-529) or Jizang 吉藏 (549-623) recited the *Lotus Sūtra* (*Xu gaoseng zhuan*, *T* no. 2060, 50:465a; *Fozu tongji*, *T* no. 2035, 49:187a). Many other similar stories abound in Buddhist hagiographies.

172. *Kāṣāya*: monastic robe.

173. Vulture Peak: Lingshan 靈山 (literally "sacred mountain") is an abbreviation of Lingjiushan 靈鷲山, "Sacred Vulture Peak" (Skt.: Gṛdhakūṭaparvata), where the *Lotus Sūtra* is said to have been preached by the Buddha.

174. Snowy Peaks: the Himālayas; "white oxcart," from the parable of the burning house from chapter 3 of the *Lotus Sūtra*, refers allegorically to the Mahāyāna. See *T* no. 292, 9:12c; Hurvitz, *Scripture of the Lotus Blossom*, 60.

175. Wang Xiulin 10.563-69; Pan Dingwu 5.545-47; *QTS* 847.9589. "Being mindful of the scriptures" (Skt. *sutrānusmṛti*) and "being mindful of the Buddha" (Skt. *buddhānusmṛti*) by extension indicate the practice of recitation.

176. See Stevenson, "Buddhist Practice," 138-43, on the rituals for consecrating, venerating, and reciting the *Lotus Sūtra*.

Chapter Six. Meditation: Effort and Absorption

1. This chapter is adapted from my article "How Poetry Became Meditation."

2. Yan Yu 嚴羽 (1180-1235), who helped establish this discourse, probably owed as much to Neo-Confucian habits of debate as he did to Chan philosophy. See Lynn, "Orthodoxy and Enlightenment." For more on the formation of the analogy between poetry and Chan in the Song dynasty, see Lynn, "The Sudden and the Gradual."

3. For the modern Zen writings, see, for example, Hamill and Seaton, *The Poetry of Zen*, 7; Blyth, *Zen in English Literature and the Oriental Classics*, 33; Wu Yansheng, *The Power of Enlightenment*, 9; and Suzuki, *Essays in Zen Buddhism*.

4. Qian Zhongshu, *Tanyi lu*, 260.

5. The concept of meditation examined here is one that gained ascendancy in the early eighth century with the rise of those teachers who would later be identified as some of the founders of the Chan school. In contrast to earlier meditation practices, which stressed the importance of confirmatory visions authorized by a meditation master, meditation from the eighth century onward increasingly stressed stillness as a final (rather than preliminary) goal. On this development, see Greene, *Chan before Chan*, 205-48.

6. See Lynn, "The Sudden and the Gradual"; Protass, *Poetry Demon*; Byrne, "Poetics of Silence"; Ding-Hwa Hsieh, "Poetry and Chan 'Gong'an'"; and Grant, *Mount Lu Revisited*. Protass, in *Poetry Demon*, 14-20, laudably contextualizes his

study as growing out of a specifically Northern Song monastic culture. Du Songbo takes a synchronic approach to the poetry-meditation question: drawing from nearly every corner of the classical tradition of poetry criticism, he nevertheless favors the Song and later periods because of the relative scarcity of materials in the Tang (*Chanxue yu Tang-Song shixue*, 611–728).

7. Jorgensen, "The Sensibility of the Insensible," for example, explores Tang poems and meditation texts as background for understanding debates between Song Buddhists and Neo-Confucians on theories of insentience and nature; there are also elements of this Song teleology in Hsiao, "Wenzi chan" shixue de fazhan guiji.

8. Owen, *The Late Tang*, 91; and Owen, "How Did Buddhism Matter," 405.

9. Zhou Yukai and Hsiao Li-hua have also noted the close relationship between poet-monks, poetry manuals, and late medieval currents in Buddhist thought (Zhou, *Wenzi chan yu Songdai shixue*, 147–54; and Hsiao, "Wenzi chan" shixue, 69–97). On Jia Dao's importance in these manuals, see Yugen Wang, "Shige," 85; Hartman, "The *Yinchuang zalu*," 215; and Zhou Yukai, "Jia Dao ge shige yu Chanzong," 429.

10. Zhang Bowei, *Quan Tang-Wudai shige huikao*, 417–23.

11. Zhang Bowei, *Quan Tang-Wudai shige huikao*, 397–416.

12. Zhang Bowei, *Quan Tang-Wudai shige huikao*, 424–49.

13. This manual is listed in the Song dynasty imperial catalogue but no longer survives. See Toqto'a, *Songshi*, 209.5410.

14. Zhang Bowei, *Quan Tang-Wudai shige huikao*, 370–83. This is listed as *Jia Dao's Secret Exemplars of Poetry Standards* 賈島詩格密旨 in the Song imperial catalog in *Songshi* 209.5409. Li Jiangfeng has argued that the work is genuine, but this claim does not appear to have been widely accepted (*Wan-Tang Wudai shige*, 293–309).

15. The following description of *kuyin* in the ninth and tenth centuries draws on Lee, *Zhong-Wan Tang kuyin shiren yanjiu*; Wu Zaiqing, "Lüelun Tangdai de kuyin shifeng"; and Li Dingguang, *Tangmo Wudai luanshi*, 77–109.

16. Han, *Meng Jiao ji jiaozhu*, 3.118; QTS 374.4203; cf. Owen, *The Poetry of Meng Chiao and Han Yü*, 57; Owen, "Spending Time on Poetry," 169; and Shang, "Prisoner and Creator," 20.

17. On this practice, see Mair, "Scroll Presentation"; Fu, *Tangdai keju yu wenxue*, 247–86; and Nugent, *Manifest in Words*, 214–35.

18. From "Events on a Summer Day" 夏日即事, in QTS 544.2685–86; cf. Owen, "Spending Time on Poetry," 171; Owen, *The Late Tang*, 93.

19. "Baring my Feelings, Presented to One Who Knows Me" 陳情上知己 (QTS 544.6291).

20. QTS 545.6303–04. "Vice Director Cui": Cui Yu 崔璵 (mid-ninth cent.), younger brother of Chancellor Cui Gong 崔珙 (d. 854?).

21. Ouyang and Song, *Xin Tangshu*, 176.5268.

22. See, for example, Zhang Pin 張蠙 (*j.s.* 895), "Grieving Jia Dao" 傷賈島 (QTS 702.8084); Kezhi 可止 (860–934), "Weeping over Jia Dao" 哭賈島 (QTS 825.9292); Xue Neng, "At Jialing Station, Seeing One of Jia Dao's Old Inscriptions" 嘉陵驛見賈島舊題 (QTS 560.6499); and Li Ying 李郢 (*j.s.* 856), "Grieving Jia Dao and Wuke" 傷賈島無可 (QTS 590.6853).

23. "The Last Day of the Third Month, Sent to Judge Liu" 三月晦日贈劉評事 (Qi, *Jia Dao ji jiaozhu*, 10.597; Lee, *Jia Dao shiji jiaozhu*, 10.415–17; *QTS* 574.6687).

24. See, for example, "Morning Hunger" 朝飢 (Qi, *Jia Dao ji jiaozhu*, 1.7; Lee, *Jia Dao shiji jiaozhu*, 1.5–7; *QTS* 571.6618); and "Singing My Feelings" 詠懷 (Qi, *Jia Dao ji jiaozhu*, 10.567; Lee, *Jia Dao shiji jiaozhu*, 10.395–96; *QTS* 574.6684).

25. On the connection between suffering (*ku* 苦) and purity (*qing* 清) in Jia Dao's aesthetic, see Xiao, *Fofa yu shijing*, 207–33.

26. From "Seeing Off the Venerable Wuke" 送無可上人, in Qi, *Jia Dao ji jiaozhu*, 3.140; Lee, *Jia Dao shiji jiaozhu*, 3.100–01; *QTS* 572.6633; cf. Owen, "Spending Time On Poetry," 162. In the second line, "repeatedly rest" (*shuxi* 數息) may also allude to *anapasati*, a meditative exercise that involves counting breaths. This practice is described at length in the *Great Sūtra on Minding Inhalation and Exhalation* 大安般守意經 (*T* no. 602) attributed to An Shigao 安世高 (fl. 148–170) and alluded to in many other canonical sūtras.

27. For more on *kuyin* poetry as a return on a temporal investment, see Owen, "Spending Time on Poetry."

28. An anecdote that is spurious, but nonetheless captures the deeper truth (as a myth often does), tells us how, "at the end of the year, Jia Dao would take out the poems he finished that year and make an offering of food and ale to them, saying: 'I have strained my spirit. With these I restore it'" 賈島常以歲除取一年所得詩，祭以酒食曰：「勞吾精神，以是補之」. The story is preserved in the *Yunxian zaji* 雲仙雜記, which is attributed to the Late Tang but likely dates to the mid-Song. See *Tangren yishi huibian*, 1:20.1114.

29. If extant records can be trusted, Jia Dao was by far the most popular poet of the ninth and tenth centuries. See my "Networks of Exchange Poetry." On waning faith in officialdom, see Moore, *Rituals of Recruitment*, 72, 91; and Xu Lejun, *Wan-Tang wenren shijin xintai yanjiu*, 252–58.

30. On this point, see Li Dingguang, *Tangmo Wudai luanshi*, 78–87, 100–01; and Tao, "Tangmo shige gainian," 215–16.

31. See, for example, Fang Gan, "Given to Yu Fu" 贈喻鳧 (*QTS* 648.7444); Lu Yanrang 盧延讓 (*j.s.* 900), "*Kuyin*" 苦吟 (*QTS* 715.8212); Li Pin, "Going Back after Passing the Exams" 及第後歸 (*QTS* 587.6819); and Pei Yue, "Sent to Cao Song" 寄曹松 (*QTS* 720.8261).

32. Ruan, *Shihua zonggui*, 10.6. Compare the similar passage Huang Che, *Gongxi shihua*, 7.6.

33. "Thinking of My Old Residence on Mount Jiuhua on an Autumn Day" 秋日懷九華舊居, in *QTS* 691.7941.

34. *QTS* 691.7944–45.

35. From another poem titled "*Kuyin*" 苦吟, in *QTS* 679.7771.

36. It is important to note that Guanxiu and Qiji were not the only poet-monks who promoted the *kuyin* aesthetic. Guiren 歸仁, a relatively unknown poet-monk of the late ninth and early tenth century, also writes in a poem "Every day I suffer for poetry" 日日爲詩苦 and "If I'm satisfied with a single couplet, / I forget all my ten thousand worries" 一聯如得意，萬事總忘憂 ("Diverting Myself" 自遣, in *QTS* 825.9293).

37. See, for example, Guanxiu's "Seeing Off a Friend to Lingwai" 送友人之嶺外 (Hu Dajun 13.627–28; *QTS* 831.9375) and "Seeing Off Liu Ti to His

Appointment at Min" 送劉迒赴閩辟 (Hu Dajun 12.588-89; *QTS* 831.9370); Shangyan's "Seeing Off 'Sure to Succeed' Liu" 送劉必先 (*QTS* 848.9600); Qiji's "Seeing Off Scholar Zhu to Min" 送朱秀才歸閩 (Wang Xiulin 王秀林 6.327; Pan Dingwu 6.338-39; *QTS* 843.9533); and Muyou's 慕幽 (mid-tenth cent.) "A Response Matching Something Sent by a Friend" 酬和友人見寄 (*QTS* 850.9624-25).

38. On Chinese Buddhist ascetic ideals, see Kieschnick, *The Eminent Monk*, 16-50. Stephen Owen has also noted similarities between the poet's and the monk's sense of self-denial in "How Did Buddhism Matter," 405.

39. See *The Awakening of Mahāyāna Faith*, in *T* no. 1666, 32:582a; English translations in Hakeda, *The Awakening of Faith*, 90; and Jorgensen et al., *Treatise on Awakening Mahāyāna Faith*, 127.

40. Chinese text is based on the critical edition compiled from seven Dunhuang manuscripts, as well as a few other sources, by McRae in *The Northern School*. This passage appears on the page labeled *ba* 八 (eight) in the back of the book. The translation is also McRae's, in *The Northern School*, 126-27.

41. On Jiaoran's attention to detail and its similarity to Mazu's "*samādhi* of the oceanic imprint" 海印三昧, see Williams, "The Taste of the Ocean," 25-26.

42. "Autumn Gazing, Sent to Commissioned Lord Wang" 秋望寄王使君 (Hu Dajun 15.710-11; *QTS* 832.9387-88). "Commissioned Lord Wang" refers to Wang Zao 王慥, one of Guanxiu's frequent addressees and magistrate of his hometown of Wuzhou 婺州 from 878 to 880.

43. "On Hearing that Supernumerary Li Pin Died" 聞李頻員外卒 (Hu Dajun 12.603-04; *QTS* 831.9372). Although Guanxiu is ostensibly describing Li Pin's practice, it is clear that they agree on this view of literature.

44. "On a Winter's Night, Sent to Executive Assistant Lu: 2 of 2" 夜寒寄盧給事二首（其二）(Hu Dajun 12.569-71; *QTS* 831.9367).

45. "Written Lakeside" 湖上作 (Hu Dajun 15.731; *QTS* 832.9391).

46. See his poem "*Kuyin*" 苦吟 (Hu Dajun 22.968-69; *QTS* 836.9423).

47. Beyond Jia Dao and Liu Deren, Guanxiu is quite taken by the idea that previous poets strained themselves with their hard (*ku*) thought. For example, he describes Miu Duyi 謬獨一, a contemporary mentioned several times by Guanxiu but not otherwise known, by saying, "His thinking is hard (*ku*) like mine" 思還如我苦 ("Thinking of Miu Duyi" 懷謬獨一, in Hu Dajun 14.668-69; *QTS* 832.9382).

48. "Bumped into the governor" refers to a well-known anecdote about Jia Dao, in which Jia is so absorbed in his choice of words for a couplet ("pushing" 推 or "knocking on" 敲 a door) that he wanders oblivious through the streets of the capital and runs into the metropolitan governor Han Yu, who finally tells him to pick "knock." For the original anecdote, see He Guangyuan, *Jianjie lu*, 8.6; for a translation and discussion, see Owen, *The Late Tang*, 97-98.

49. This line refers to an anecdote related to Liu Deren, in which Liu, despondent after failing the examinations for twenty years, decided to hide away in the mountains. When word got out, an imperial scion sent a thousand chariots to find him. None were successful in their search. See Fu, *Tang caizi zhuan jiaojian*, 3:6.184-85.

50. This line refers to Liu Deren's difficulty in finding a government job due to his lack of connections with the imperial court. "Melting snow with boiling water" had been a metaphor for something easy to achieve since the fourth century at the latest. See, for example, Fan, *Hou Han shu*, 711.2302-03: "Dissolving strongholds is easier than turning snow into boiling water" 消壘甚於湯雪.

51. Hu Dajun 7.368-71; *QTS* 829.9340.

52. "Monk": literally "officer in the Indian [religion]."

53. This refers to Jiaoran's justification for his obsession with poetry, as stated in his letters. See chapter 2.

54. Purest mirror: one with great discernment. In this case, Qiji is referring to himself as one who understands Jiaoran and Zhi Dun.

55. Wang Xiulin 7.385-86; Pan Dingwu 7.387-88; *QTS* 844.9546; cf. Jorgensen, "Sensibility of the Insensible," 217; Protass, *Poetry Demon*, 196-97. My reading departs from Protass in that I understand Qiji to be playfully responding to the common literary trope of *kuyin*, not describing a contradiction between his religious and literary practices.

56. The earliest uses of the term "poetry demon" are by Liu Yuxi and Bai Juyi. On the trope of the "poetry demon" more generally, see Protass, "Buddhist Monks and Chinese Poetry," 96-102.

57. Other poetry manuals, such as the *Poetic Paradigms* by Jiaoran and the *Secret Exemplars of the Two "Souths"* attributed to Jia Dao, also remark that allusions may only be used when they "connect implicitly" (*minghe* 冥合) to the author's ideas—that is, they should not be used as mere ornamentation. For Jiaoran, see Zhang Bowei, *Quan Tang-Wudai shige huikao*, 230, and Li Zhuangying, *Shishi jiaozhu*, 31-32; for pseudo-Jia Dao, see Zhang Bowei, *Quan Tang Wudai shige huikao*, 377, and Li Jiangfeng, *Wan Tang-Wudai shige*, 320.

58. "Hearing that Guanxiu Left this World" 聞貫休下世 (Wang Xiulin 2.94-96; Pan Dingwu 2.102-03; *QTS* 839.9464-65).

59. "Made sand stūpas": *jusha* 聚沙 (literally "gather sand") is short for *jusha chengta* 聚沙成塔, "gather sand to make stūpas." This refers to a children's game (similar to modern children's sandcastle building) that nevertheless produces merit for the children. The locus classicus is the second chapter of the *Lotus Sūtra* (T no. 262, 9:8c; trans. Hurvitz, *Scripture of the Lotus Blossom*, 38-39).

60. "*Patra*-leaves": the material on which South Asian texts were commonly written. Here it refers to Buddhist scriptures.

61. "Residual habits": lingering effects of past karma that can only be eliminated by a Buddha.

62. Wang Xiulin 2.113-14; Pan Dingwu 2.122-23; *QTS* 839.9469-70.

63. Qiji, for example, praised Guanxiu's work by comparing it to the *Wenxuan*: "He strove for equality with the Crown Prince of Liang, / To be esteemed like [those poets of] the *Wenxuan* tower" 爭得梁太子，重為文選樓 (Qiji, "Hearing that Guanxiu Parted from this World" 聞貫休下世, in Wang Xiulin 2.94-96; Pan Dingwu 2.102-03; *QTS* 839.9464-65). Crown Prince of Liang: Xiao Tong 蕭統 (501-531), compiler of the *Wenxuan*.

64. *Wenxuan*, 17.763; trans. adapted from Knechtges, *Wen Xuan*, 3:215.

65. Its impact can be felt perhaps most acutely in the "Daimonic imagination" (*shensi* 神思) chapter of *Wenxin diaolong*, which also points out the necessity of mental stillness, the spirit journey of the imagination, the arrangement of mental objects, and the difficulty in putting all of this into poetry. See Egan, "Poet, Mind, and World."

66. From "A Discussion of Ideas in Poetry" 論詩意, in *Shige* 詩格, attrib. Wang Changling. See Zhang Bowei, *Quan Tang-Wudai shige huikao*, 162; Lu Shengjiang, *Wenjing mifulun*, 3:1312; cf. Bodman, "Poetics and Prosody," 371.

67. Zhang Bowei, *Quan Tang-Wudai shige huikao*, 162; Lu Shengjiang, *Wenjing mifulun*, 3:1309; cf. Bodman, "Poetics and Prosody," 371.

68. "Given to My Cousin Maoqing" 贈從弟茂卿 (*QTS* 333.3717).

69. *Wenxuan* 17.765. For other translations, with commentary, see Owen, *Readings in Chinese Literary Thought*, 118–19; and Knechtges, *Wen Xuan*, 3:217.

70. *QTS* 497.5634.

71. *QTS* 720.8269. The earliest extant source for this couplet is the twelfth-century *Tangshi jishi* 唐詩紀事 (*Tangshi jishi jiaojian*, 65.1748).

72. Liu Yuxi, "Introduction to 'Stopping by the Temple Hall of Dharma Master Hongju on an Autumn Day and Seeing Him Off to Jiangling'" 秋日過鴻舉法師寺院便送歸江陵引 (Qu, *Liu Yuxi ji jianzheng*, 29.956–58; *QTS* 357.4015–16). Cf. Lynn, "The Sudden and the Gradual," 384.

73. See *Maoshi zhushu*, 1.13. Translation and discussion in Van Zoeren, *Poetry and Personality*, 95, 108–11; and Owen, *Readings in Chinese Literary Thought*, 41–43.

74. "Preface to the *White Lotus Collection*" 白蓮集序 (Wang Xiulin 619; Pan Dingwu 598–99; *QTW* 900.9390–91).

75. Others have recognized the close relationship between poetry and meditation in Qiji's poetry (e.g., Hsiao, "Wan-Tang shiseng Qiji de shichan shijie"; Jiang Yin, *Gudian shixue de xiandai quanshi*, 59; Owen, "How Did Buddhism Matter"; and Protass, *Poetry Demon*, 189–200). My readings of Qiji differ from Jiang and Owen in that I understand Qiji's claims to be more than metaphorical. I also differ from Protass, who reads Qiji's verse as being evidence of a fundamental difference between poetry and monastic ideals, and from Hsiao, who sees contradictions in Qiji's view of the relationship between poetry and meditation.

76. See, for example, "Leaving an Inscription at the Pagoda of the Master of Mount Yang" 留題仰山大師塔院 (Wang Xiulin 1.17–19; Pan Dingwu 1.20–21; *QTS* 838.9445), "Sent to Elder Guangwei of Mount Yang" 寄仰山光味長者 (Wang Xiulin 5.236–7; Pan Dingwu 5.244–5; *QTS* 845.9564), and "Sent to the Monk of Bright Moon Mountain" 寄明月山僧, which may refer to Mingyue Daochong 明月道崇, a disciple of Wei-Yang patriarch Huiji 慧寂 (814–890) (Wang Xiulin 2.108–9; Pan Dingwu 2.117; *QTS* 839.9468).

77. In the record of Huiji in *Jingde chuandenglu*, one monk describes how he and the master were "discussing the Way, how form (Skt. *rūpa*) can illuminate the mind and how connections to phenomena can reveal the truth" 商量道，即色明心，附物顯理 (*T* no. 2076, 51:284b–c). On these teachings of the Wei-Yang lineage, see Yin, "Hu-Xiang shiseng Qiji," 24–25; Liu Luming, "Wei-Yangzong Chanfa," 267–68; and Wu Xianlin, "Wei-Yangzong de Chanxue sixiang."

78. Jia, *The Hongzhou School*, 76–79.

79. A precedent for this idea can be found in the *Treatise on Perfect Illumination* (*Yuanming lun* 圓明論), which advocates an ideal of permanently residing in meditation and wisdom, "never quitting during walking, standing, sitting, or lying down" 行住坐臥，無有廢息 (McRae, *The Northern School*, *ershiba* 二十八 (twenty-eight); full translation on 212).

80. *Jingde chuandenglu*, in *T* no. 2076, 51:440a; translation adapted from Jia, *The Hongzhou School*, 77.

81. From "On Myself" 自題 (Wang Xiulin 6.318–319; Pan Dingwu 6.329; *QTS* 843.9530) and "Sent to My Brother Liao Kuangtu" 寄廖匡圖兄弟 (Wang Xiulin 10.599–600; Pan Dingwu 10.583–84; *QTS* 847.9596), respectively.

82. "Written by Chance at the Isles of Jing" 荊渚偶作 (Wang Xiulin 9.479; Pan Dingwu 9.460–61; *QTS* 846.9568).

83. "Given unto the Venerable Huixian" 貽惠暹上人 (Wang Xiulin 7.397; Pan Dingwu 7.395–96; *QTS* 844.9548).

84. Wang Xiulin 10.597; Pan Dingwu 10.579–80; *QTS* 847.9596.

85. "No wrong": poetry. In *Analects* 2.2, Confucius describes the *Book of Odes* as having "no wrong" (*wuxie* 無邪) in them.

86. Field of my inner self: reference to the *Book of Rites* (*Liji*, 9.439–40):

The sage kings cultivated the lever of righteousness and the sequences of ritual to put the inner selves of humans in order. Consequently the inner selves of humans were the field of the sage kings. They cultivated ritual to plough them. They laid out righteousness to plant them. They instituted learning to weed them. They rooted it in humaneness to collect them, and they employed music to give them peace.

聖王修義之柄、禮之序，以治人情。故人情者，聖王之田也。修禮以耕之，陳義以種之，講學以耨之，本仁以聚之，播樂以安之。

87. Wang Xiulin 6.300–01; Pan Dingwu 6.311–12; *QTS* 843.9525; cf. Owen, "How Did Buddhism Matter," 399–400.

88. If we take Qiji's connections to the Wei-Yang lineage seriously, we can see how this echoes the teachings of its founder Lingyou, who is said to have once preached: "At all moments, see and hear what is ordinary—it is without any twists and turns—and don't close your eyes or block your ears, but don't let your emotions become attached to phenomena" 一切時中視聽尋常更無委曲，亦不閉眼塞耳，但情不附物 (*Jingde chuandenglu*, in *T* no. 2076, 51:264c). Compare this too to the highest stage of practice of the Hongzhou patriarch Baizhang Huaihai 百丈懷海 (720–814), in which one may indulge in the senses without risk of defilement (Poceski, *Ordinary Mind as the Way*, 211).

89. "Mind-stamped master": Chan texts describe a person who has received the true transmission of the dharma as having been "stamped with the mind of the Buddha" (*Foxin yin* 佛心印); "beyond the birds": high up in the sky (it is possible that this refers to Huiji, who was very influential in the western Jiangnan region where Qiji grew up and whose life overlapped with Qiji's by about twenty years).

90. Wang Xiulin 10.582; Pan Dingwu 10.563; *QTS* 847.9592.

91. On the latter, see the *Awakening of Mahāyāna Faith*, in *T* no. 1666, 32:576a.

92. Zhang, *Quan Tang-Wudai shige huikao*, 407-14; Li Jiangfeng, *Wan-Tang Wudai shige*, 369-71.

93. For more on the Buddhist origins of the term "gate" in this sense and its influence on late medieval poetic theory, see Zhang Bowei, *Chan yu shixue*, 11-15; Wang Xiulin, *Wan-Tang Wudai shiseng*, 363-64; and Peng Yaling, "Tangdai shiseng de chuangzuolun," 98-102.

94. My reading of these lines parts with Owen's in significant ways. He understands line 1 to be a general statement about poetry ("How can one explain the poetic mind?"), whereas I understand it as invoking the notion of master-disciple transmission, a play on the notion of "passing on the Buddha mind" (*chuan foxin* 傳佛心) in Chan lineages. The conventions of social verse encourage this reading, in that it is directly addressed to Zheng Gu. Moreover, the three other instances of *heyi chuan* 何以傳 found in extant Tang sources all come from inscribed memorials, where they clearly indicate transmission. See, for example, Han Yu's conclusion to the verse inscription of an epitaph, "His events live on in others, / Daily further, daily forgotten. / How do we pass them on? / Carve them into this epitaph" 事在于人，日遠日忘，何以傳之，刻此銘章 ("Zhongsan dafu Henan Yin Du jun muzhiming" 中散大夫河南尹杜君墓誌銘, in Liu Zhenlun and Yue Zhen, *Han Yu wenji huijiao jianzhu*, 16.1747; *QTW* 566.5729). For the other examples, see Cui Youfu 崔祐甫 (712-780), "Gu Changzhou cishi Dugu gong shendao beiming" 故常州刺史獨孤公神道碑銘（並序）(*QTW* 409.4195); and anon., "Tang gu Suichao san dafu Tian jun (shi) ji furen Zhang shi (fei) muzhiming" 唐故隨朝散大夫田君（仕）及夫人張氏（妃）墓誌銘 (Wu, *Quan Tangwen buyi*, 261-62). Additionally, Owen interprets *zi* 自 in line 2 as the speaker's self-reference ("what I offer as proof is that it is the same as Chan"), whereas I interpret it as an adverb ("naturally"). A switch of subjects between lines 1 and 2, from "one" to "I," would be unusual in Tang social verse, and since the poem is clearly addressed to Zheng Gu throughout (apparent in the latter half of the poem, which Owen does not translate), it is best not to force the switch. Moreover, in most other collocations of *zi* and *tong* in extant Tang poetry, we must interpret *zi* as an adverb meaning "naturally" that modifies *tong*. See, for example, Du Fu, "Three Couplet Poems: 3 of 3" 三韻三篇（其三）: "The ardent gentleman hates many kinds of things, / the lesser naturally just go along" 烈士惡多門，小人自同調 (*QTS* 221.2333; trans. Owen, *The Poetry of Du Fu*, #14.47, 4:57). In the "Song of the Realization of the Way," which was popular in Buddhist circles of the ninth and tenth centuries, *zitong* is used to describe the inseparability of emptiness and the universal buddha-nature: "Never attach to the twenty gates of emptiness: / They are naturally the same in essence as the one-natured Tathāgata" 二十空門元不著，一性如來體自同 (*T* no. 2014, 48:396b). Finally, Owen understands the verb in line 2 (*zheng* 證) to be proof that Qiji is offering to Zheng Gu that he is practicing meditation without knowing it. However, *zheng* is a technical term in late medieval Buddhism, referring to the realization of enlightenment and its communication, on which see below. The verb *zheng* here refers to what Zheng Gu has already attained, not to proof that Qiji is directing to Zheng Gu.

95. "Starry gentleman": flattering nickname for those who held high office.

96. Wang Xiulin 3.151-53; Pan Dingwu 3.158; *QTS* 840.9478; cf. Owen, "How Did Buddhism Matter," 402; Jorgensen, "Sensibility of the Insensible," 215.

97. For example, Zongmi uses *zheng* in these senses over fifty times in his "Preface to the Collection of Chan Sources" 禪源諸詮集都序. For example: "How could there be a real practice called great wisdom? Just to attain [the state wherein] feelings have nothing to think about, ideation has nothing to do, mind has nothing that arises, and wisdom has no place to abide, is real faith, real understanding, real practice, real realization [*zheng*]" 豈有定行名摩訶般若。但得情無所念。意無所為。心無所生。慧無所住。即真信真解真修真證也 (*T* no. 2015, 48:400a; trans. Broughton, *Zongmi on Chan*, 107).

98. Zhang Bowei, *Quan Tang-Wudai shige huikao*, 405; Li Jiangfeng, *Wan-Tang Wudai shige*, 364-65.

99. Jiaoran, "Obtaining the Poem-World" 取境, in Li Zhuangying, *Shishi jiaozhu*, 1.39-41. This passage also made a deep impression on Guanxiu, who alluded to it when he praised a fellow poet-monk with the line, "You once ran into a tiger while seeking lines" 覓句曾衝虎 (Hu Dajun 13.615-17; *QTS* 831.9373).

100. Borges, *This Craft of Verse*, 4.

101. "Silent communication": also written as *moqi* 默契, the transmission of teachings from a master to a student without using language. In the Wei-Yang lineage, this was often associated with the drawing of a circle (*yuanxiang* 圓相) to indicate the fact that the Buddha nature encompasses and pervades all reality. A verse by a later monk, Shouzhi 守芝 (eleventh cent.), describes the Wei-Yang lineage's most distinctive emphases as "circles" and "silent communication" (preserved in Huihong [1071-1128], *Chanlin sengbao zhuan* 禪林僧寶傳, in *Z* no. 1560, 79:525c). See also Shanqing 善卿, *Zuting shiyuan* 祖庭事苑 (preface 1108), in *Z* no. 1261, 64:332a; as well as Liu Luming, "Wei-Yangzong Chanfa," 264-64; and Wu Xianlin, "Wei-Yangzong de Chanxue sixiang," 57-60.

102. Huangmei: alternate name for Hongren 弘忍 (601-674), based on one of his places of residence, Mount Huangmei 黃梅山. He is the putative Fifth Patriarch of Chan. His "address" refers to his teachings, most likely his advocacy of silent meditation as seen in the *Treatise on the Essentials of Cultivating the Mind* 修心要論 attributed to him (McRae, *The Northern School*, 127) and in his biography in the *Record of the Dharma Transmission of the True Lineage* 傳法正宗記, comp. Qisong 契嵩 (1007-1072), *T* no. 2078, 51:746c.

103. Wang Xiulin 3.143-144; Pan Dingwu 3.152; *QTS* 840.9477

104. Some editions give *shi* 示 ("shown") for *bing* 並 ("equaled"). I follow Wang Xiulin and Pan Dingwu in giving *bing*, since it is found in a majority of authoritative editions.

105. "Do not wither": a circumlocution for "establishing oneself through words" 立言. See *Zuozhuan* 左傳, Duke Xiang, year 24: "I have heard: 'The highest of all is to establish virtue; next to that is to establish achievements; next to that is to establish words.' Even with the passage of time these glories are not cast aside. This is called 'never perishing.'" 豹聞之：大上有立德，其次有立功，其次有立言，雖久不廢，此謂之不朽 (Durrant, Li, and Schaberg, *Zuo Tradition*, 1124-25).

106. "These things" is an idiomatic translation of *ciqing* 此情, which more literally means "the circumstances we are in and the inner mental and emotional responses to them." I take *ciqing* to refer to all subjective and objective experience shared by Qiji and his interlocutor, for which the first six lines of the poem are metonymy.

107. Wang Xiulin 5.242; Pan Dingwu 5.249-50; *QTS* 842.9506-07; cf. Owen, "How Did Buddhism Matter," 403; Jorgensen, "Sensibility of the Insensible," 215-16.

108. If we follow *Tangseng hongxiu ji* 唐僧弘秀集 (comp. 1258) in giving *shi* for *bing* in line 1, we come out with essentially the same paradox: poetry is used to "show" the same marvels as meditation, despite the first line's claim.

109. Lines 5 and 6 refer to Qiji's two most famous poems, "Listening to a Wellspring" 聽泉 and "Early Plums" 早梅. They have received much critical attention over the centuries and were called "preeminent poems on objects" 詠物之矯矯 (Zhou Ting 周珽, *Tangshi xuanmai huitong pinglin* 唐詩選脈會通評林, qtd. in Chen Bohai, *Tangshi huiping*, 3:3120).

110. *QTS* 848.9609-10.

111. The *Dharmatara-dhyāna sūtra* (Ch: *Damoduoluo chan jing* 達摩多羅禪經), for example, proceeds through the six senses, likening each to an animal that must be leashed (*T* no. 618, 15:322c, translated by Buddhabhadra 佛陀跋陀羅 at Mount Lu in the early fifth century). The *Candraprabha-samādhi sūtra* (Ch: *Yuedeng sanmei jing* 月燈三昧經) takes a different approach, systematically deconstructing the six organs 根, their corresponding senses 情, and consciousness 識 of them for 105 lines (*T* no. 641, 15:624c-25c, translated by Xiangong 先公 in the mid-fifth cent). Interestingly, the order of the senses given by this text (sight, sound, smell, taste, touch, and thought) is very close to that presented by Qichan in the poem (sight, sound, *touch*, smell, taste, and thought).

112. *T* no. 945, 19:114c-15c, trans. attrib. Pramiti 般剌蜜帝 in 705. Scholars believe that the *Śūraṃgama Sūtra* was at least significantly altered through a highly nativizing translation process in the early eighth-century, if not written completely anew (Jia, "Translation and Interaction," and Benn, "Another Look"). Although this text only became widely influential on literati culture in the Northern Song, it was in fact explicitly recommended to the literatus Wei Zhuang by Guanxiu, for which see "Matching 'Lying at Ease,' Shown to Me by Minister Wei" 和韋相公見示閑臥 (Hu Dajun, 2:12.606-11; *QTS* 831.9372-73).

113. These words are attributed to Mazu Daoyi in *Tiansheng guangdenglu* 天聖廣燈錄, comp. Li Zunxu 李遵勗 in 1036, *Z* no. 1553, 78:449a; trans. Jia, *The Hongzhou School*, 76.

Conclusion

1. For a translation of Guanxiu's poems, see my "Guanxiu's 'Mountain-Dwelling Poems.'" For a translation of Shiwu Qinggong's mountain-dwelling poems, see Red Pine, *The Mountain Poems of Stonehouse*. On Buddhist mountain-dwelling poems from the Tang to the Ming, see Qi, *Fojiao shanjushi yanjiu*. For a more detailed study of late Ming and early Qing mountain-dwelling poems

by Chan monks, see Liao, "Wan-Ming sengren 'Shanjushi' Lunxi." On Zekkai Chūshin, see Nishiguchi, "Kankyū 'Sankyoshi' shiyakuchō," 399–400.

2. Wong, "Mid-Tang Scholar-Monk," 69–74.

3. Shenqing, *Beishan lu jiaozhu*, 9.740. On Kepeng, see Wu Renchen, *Shiguo chunqiu*, 57.830.

4. Zongze 宗賾 (d. 1107?), *Chanyuan qinggui* 禪苑清規 (comp. 1103), in *Z* no. 1245, 63:532a; cf. Yifa, *The Origins of Buddhist Monastic Codes in China*, 159; and Protass, "Buddhist Monks and Chinese Poems," 83–84.

5. This phenomenon is described in Protass, *Poetry Demon*, first generally in 14–20, then with more specificity in 121–201.

6. Literati also noted that poetry composition was in tension with monastic regulations. Hu Zhenheng 胡震亨 (1569–1645), for example, speculates that poet-monks' anxiety over this is why they produced inferior poetry and ran afoul of authorities (*Tangyin tongqian*, 29.5b–6a).

7. Xuantai 玄泰: Southern poet-monk who had studied meditation with Deshan Xuanjian 德山宣鑑 (782–865) and Shishuang Qingzhu. None of his extant poems survive, but we have poems written to him by Li Xianyong (*QTS* 645.7395; 645.7397), Qiji (Wang Xiulin 7.341–42; Pan Dingwu 7.351–52; *QTS* 844.9537; and Wang Xiulin 9.528; Pan Dingwu 9.504; *QTS* 846.9580), Qichan (*QTS* 848.9609), and Xiumu (*QTS* 849.9618). See also his biography in *SGSZ* (*T* no. 2061, 50:818a).

8. Shishuang Qingzhu: famous meditation master, considered by some to be the fourth Dharma heir of Southern Chan. During the tenth century, he was also understood to have been the founder of his own lineage (Shishuang), which was considered one of the eight major Chan lineages at the time, along with Wei-Yang 潙仰, Cao-Dong 曹洞, Deshan 德山, Linji 臨濟, Xuefeng 雪峰, Yunmen 雲門, and Fayan 法眼. See Jia, *The Hongzhou School*, 115.

9. Huishi Shiming 晦室師明, *Xu guzunsu yuyao* 續古尊宿語要 (published 1238), in *Z* no. 1318, 68:397a.

10. See the commentary to the thirteenth case in Zhengjue Niangu 正覺拈古, comp., *Wansong laoren Pingchang Tiantong Jue heshang niangu qingyi lu* 萬松老人評唱天童覺和尚拈古請益錄, annot. Xingxiang Pingchang 行秀評唱, (published 1230, republished 1607), in *Z* no. 1307, 67:467c. In this version, Xuantai is the one who delivers the words that reveal Zhang's prejudice, since he is said to be the only one among them who was fully enlightened.

11. On Ouyang Xiu's attitudes toward poetry, see Egan, *The Literary Works of Ou-yang Hsiu*, 78–122. For detailed studies of Ouyang's literary style, see Feng Zhihong, *Bei-Song guwen yundong*, 164–82; and Zhu, *Tang–Song "guwen yundong" yu shidafu*, 154–73.

12. This is not to say that everyone who promoted *guwen* was averse to Buddhism. One early eleventh-century monk, Gushan Zhiyuan 孤山智圓 (976–1022), attempted to reconcile *guwen* and Buddhism. See Skonicki, "Viewing the Two Teachings."

13. Yan Yu, *Canglang shihua*, 1.15a

14. Zhong, *Tangshi gui*, j. 17.

15. For example, Wang Mao 王楙 (1151–1213) cited one of Qiji's poems to make a point about the proper pronunciation of *zhong* 中 in one of its less common uses (*Yeke congshu*, 24.4).

16. Quoted in Fang Hui, *Yingkui lüsui huiping*, 12.437.
17. Zhong, *Tangshi gui*, 36.844.
18. Quoted in Chen Bohai, *Tangshi huiping*, 3:3117.
19. This echoes a line of criticism written by Zhang Biaochen 張表臣 (early twelfth cent.): "The prose of Han Yu and the poetry of Li Bai were full of new meanings. But when we come to the imitations of knitted brows by Lu Tong, Guanxiu, and their like, or the borrowing of their footsteps by Zhang Ji, Huangfu Shi, and their like, they're strange and ugly, stiff and slavish" 韓文公之文、李太白之詩多出新意。至於盧仝、貫休輩效其顰，張籍、皇甫湜輩舉其步，則怪且醜，僵且仆矣 (Zhang Biaochen, *Shanhu gou shihua*, 1.1b).
20. For "Swordsman," see Wang Xiulin 1.48-49; Pan Dingwu 1.50; *QTS* 838.9452. "Listening to a Zither" refers to Qiji's much-admired "Listening to the Venerable Ye Play the Zither on an Autumn Evening" 秋夜聽業上人彈琴 (Wang Xiulin 4.209-10; Pan Dingwu 4.215-16; *QTS* 841.9495). "Zhurong Peak" refers to "Climbing Zhurong Peak" 登祝融峰 (Wang Xiulin 4.185; Pan Dingwu 4.192; *QTS* 841.9489). Zhurong: the god of fire.
21. Wang Xiulin 10.597-98; Pan Dingwu 10.581; *QTS* 847.9596.
22. "Jade rabbit": Chinese legend states that a jade rabbit lives on the moon. This figure was often used as a synecdoche for the moon in poetry.
23. *Siku quanshu zongmu tiyao*, 151.40b-41a.
24. This precedent goes back to Cao Pi's 曹丕 (187-226) evaluation of recent poets in *Dianlun lunwen* 典論論文. For an English translation and commentary, see Owen, *Readings in Chinese Literary Thought*, 61-64. On the historical context of Cao Pi's evaluations, see Xiaofei Tian, *Halberd at Red Cliff*, 11-30.
25. Hu Zi, *Tiaoxi yuyin conghua qianji*, 5.2b.
26. Duke of Ezhou: Yuchi Gong 尉遲恭 (585-658), a general famed for aiding in the establishment of the Tang dynasty, loyal to Li Shimin 李世民 (598-649), the eventual Emperor Taizong 唐太宗. According to Yuchi Gong's biography in the *Old History of the Tang* 舊唐書 (*Jiu Tangshu* 618.2496):

> While hunting among a crook of elms, Li Shimin happened on [enemy leader] Wang Shichong's leading infantry and cavalry, who were coming by the tens of thousands for battle. Shichong's valiant general, the head rider Shan Xiongxin, immediately rushed toward Taizong, whereupon Yuchi Gong yelled, horse leaping, and thrust his spear into the side of Xiongxin, knocking him from his horse.

> 因從獵於榆窠，遇王世充領步騎數萬來戰。世充驍將單雄信領騎直趨太宗，敬德躍馬大呼，橫刺雄信墜馬。

27. Prince of Qin: a position Li Shimin held before deposing his father and becoming Emperor Taizong.
28. He Chang is actually quoting the twelfth of Guanxiu's "Mountain-Dwelling Poems." See Hu Dajun 23.986; *QTS* 837.9426; Mazanec, "Guanxiu's 'Mountain-Dwelling Poems,'" 115.
29. He Chang, *Zaijiuyuan shihua* 載酒園詩話, quoted in Chen Bohai, *Tangshi huiping*, 3:3111.
30. Many canonical poets also wrote enneametric lines, including Li Bai 李白 in "The Way to Shu Is Hard" 蜀道難 (Qu and Zhu, *Li Bai ji jiaozhu*, 3.199;

QTS 162.1680); Bai Juyi 白居易 in "Song of Nothing Can Be Done" 無可奈何歌 (Zhu Jincheng, *Bai Juyi ji jianjiao*, 39.2638; *QTS* 461.5248), and Li Shangyin 李商隱 in "The Stele of Han Yu" 韓碑 (*QTS* 539.6154).

31. From "Poetry" 詩, in Hu Dajun 16.779; *QTS* 833.9397. In the received edition of Guanxiu's works, the first two characters of the first line read "In many places" 幾處 instead of "All day" 盡日.

32. Ouyang, *Liuyi shihua*, 1.7b.

33. On humor and its relationship to literary criticism in the eleventh century, see Rao, "Tales of Wit and Enlightenment."

34. Chen Shidao, *Houshan ji*, 11.11b–12a; cf. Protass, "Buddhist Monks and Chinese Poems," 42. Canliao: cognomen of Daoqian.

35. Xiong, *Sui-Tang Chang'an*, lists only 48 Daoist abbeys at the capital during the Sui-Tang period, compared to 193 Buddhist monasteries. This numeric difference may be exaggerated due to surviving sources and the fact that Buddhist monasteries seem to have been renamed more often than Daoist abbeys. On Daoism's importance during the Tang, see Barrett, *Taoism under the T'ang*, and Verellen, *Imperiled Destinies*, 217–323. An excellent study of one Daoist poet-priest's overlapping religious and literary practices is De Meyer, *Wu Yun's Way*.

Bibliography

Editions of Premodern Works
Abbreviations

QTS *Quan Tang shi* 全唐詩.
QTSBB *Quan Tang shi bubian* 全唐詩補編.
QTW *Quan Tang wen* 全唐文.
SBCK *Sibu congkan* 四部叢刊.
SGSZ *Song gaoseng zhuan* 宋高僧傳.
SKQS *Wenyuange Siku quanshu* 四庫全書.
T   *Taishō shinshū daizōkyō* 大正新脩大藏經.
Z   *Shinsan Dainihon Zokuzōkyō* 新纂大日本續藏經.

Ban Gu 班固. *Hanshu* 漢書. Annotated by Yan Shigu 顏師古. ZHSJ, 1962.
Chao Gongwu 晁公武. *Junzhai dushu zhi* 郡齋讀書志. SKQS ed.
Chen Bohai 陳伯海, ed. *Tangshi huiping* 唐詩匯評. Hangzhou: Zhejiang jiaoyu chubanshe, 1995.
Chen Qiyuan 陳其元. *Yongxianzhai biji* 庸閒齋筆記. ZHSJ, 1989.
Chen Shidao 陳師道. *Houshan ji* 後山集. SKQS ed.
Chuci buzhu 楚辭補注. Collated by Hong Xingzu 洪興祖. ZHSJ, 1983.
Ding Fubao 丁福保, ed. *Lidai shihua xubian* 歷代詩話續編. ZHSJ, 1983.
Fan Ye 范曄. *Hou Han shu* 後漢書. ZHSJ, 1965.
Fan Zhilin 范之麟, ed. and annot. *Li Yi shizhu* 李益詩註. SHGJ, 1984.
Fang Hui 方回. *Yingkui lüsui huiping* 瀛奎律髓彙評. Annotated by Li Qingjia 李慶甲. SHGJ, 1988.
Fang Shiju 方世舉, annot. *Han Changli shiji biannian jianzhu* 韓昌黎詩集編年箋注. Edited by Hao Runhua 郝潤華 and Ding Junli 丁俊麗. ZHSJ, 2012.
Fang Xuanling 房玄齡. *Jinshu* 晉書. ZHSJ, 1974.
Gu Yanwu 顧炎武. *Jinshi wenzi ji* 金石文字記. SKQS ed.
Guo Guangwei 郭廣偉, ed. *Quan Deyu shiwen ji* 權德輿詩文集. SHGJ, 2008.
Guo Qingfan 郭慶藩, ed. and annot. *Zhuangzi jishi* 莊子集釋. ZHSJ, 2012.
Han Quanxin 韓泉欣, ed. and annot. *Meng Jiao ji jiaozhu* 孟郊集校注. Hangzhou: Zhejiang guji chubanshe, 1995.
He Guangyuan 何光遠. *Jianjie lu* 鑒誡錄. SKQS ed.
He Xiguang 何錫光, ed. and annot. *Fanchuan wenji jiaozhu* 樊川文集校注. Chengdu: Ba-Shu shushe, 2007.
Hou Chong 侯沖, comp. *Jin'gangjun jing, jin'gangding jing yiqie rulai shenmiao bimi jin'gangjie dasanmaye xiuxing sishierzhong tanfa jing yong weiyi faze, Da*

Pilushe'nafo jin'gang xindi famen mifa jietanfa yize 金剛峻經金剛頂一切如來深妙秘密金剛界大三昧耶修行四十二種壇法經作用威儀法則 大毘盧遮那佛金剛心地法門密法戒壇法儀則. In *Zangwai Fojiao wenxian* 藏外佛教文獻, vol. 11, ed. Fang Guangchang 方廣錩, 17-144. Beijing: Zongjiao wenhua chubanshe, 2008. Online: https://cbetaonline.dila.edu.tw/zh/ZW11n0091.

Hu Dajun 胡大浚, ed. and annot. *Guanxiu geshi xinian jianzhu* 貫休歌詩繫年注. 3 vols. ZHSJ, 2011.

Hu Zhenheng 胡震亨. *Tangyin tongqian* 唐音統籤. SKQS ed.

Hu Zi 胡仔. *Tiaoxi yuyin conghua qianji* 苕溪漁隱叢話前集. SKQS ed.

Huang Benji 黃本驥, ed. *Yan Zhenqing ji* 顏真卿集. Annotated by Ling Jiamin 凌家民. Harbin: Heilongjiang renmin chubanshe, 1993.

Huang Che 黃徹. *Gongxi shihua* 䂬溪詩話. SKQS ed.

Huang Xiufu 黃休復. *Yizhou minghua lu* 益州名畫錄. SKQS ed.

Huang Zheng 黃徵 and Wu Wei 吳偉, eds. *Dunhuang yuanwen ji* 敦煌願文集. Changsha: Yuelu shushe, 1995.

Jiang Yin 蔣寅, ed. *Quan Deyu shiwen ji biannian jiaozhu* 權德輿詩文集編年校注. Shenyang: Liaohai chubanshe, 2013.

Jiaoran 皎然. *Zhushan ji* 杼山集. SKQS ed.

Jiu Tangshu 舊唐書. Compiled by Liu Xu 劉昫 and Yang Jialuo 楊家駱. Taipei: Dingwen shuju, 1981.

Lee Chien-k'un 李建崑, ed. and annot. *Jia Dao shiji jiaozhu* 賈島詩集校注. Taipei: Liren shuju, 2002.

Li Gong 李鞏. *Tangseng hongxiu ji* 唐僧弘秀集. SKQS ed.

Li Shizhen 李時珍. *Bencao gangmu* 本草綱目. SKQS ed.

Li Zhuangying 李壯鷹, ed. and annot. *Shishi jiaozhu* 詩式校注. Beijing: Renmin wenxue chubanshe, 2003.

Liji 禮記. In *Chongkan Songben Shisan jing zhushu fu jiaokan ji* 重刊宋本十三經注疏附校勘記. Taipei: Yiwen yinshuguan, 1965.

Liu Peng 劉鵬 and Li Tao 李桃, ed. and annot. *Piling ji jiaozhu* 毗陵集校注. Shenyang: Liaohai chubanshe, 2006.

Liu Xie 劉勰. *Zengding Wenxin diaolong jiaozhu* 增訂文心雕龍校注. Annotated by Huang Shulin 黃叔琳 et al. 3 vols. ZHSJ, 2012.

Liu Zhenlun 劉真倫 and Yue Zhen 岳珍, eds. *Han Yu wenji huijiao jianzhu* 韓愈文集彙校箋注. ZHSJ, 2010.

Lu Qinli 逯欽立, ed. *Xian-Qin Han Wei Jin Nanbeichao shi* 先秦漢魏晉南北朝詩. ZHSJ, 1983.

Lu Shengjiang 盧盛江, ed. and annot. *Wenjing mifulun [Bunkyō hifuron] huijiao huikao: fu Wenbi yanxin chao* 文鏡秘府論彙校彙考: 附文筆眼心抄. 4 vols. ZHSJ, 2006.

Lu Shiyong 陸時雍. "Shijing zonglun" 詩境總論. In *Gushijing* 古詩境. SKQS ed.

Lu You 陸游. *Jiannan shigao* 劍難詩稿. SKQS ed.

Luo Shijin 羅時進, ed. *Dingmao ji jianzheng* 丁卯集箋証. 2 vols. ZHSJ, 2012.

Maoshi zhushu 毛詩注疏. In *Chongkan Songben Shisan jing zhushu fu jiaokan ji* 重刊宋本十三經注疏附校勘記. Taipei: Yiwen yinshuguan, 1965.

Nie Anfu 聶安福, ed. and annot. *Wei Zhuang ji jianzhu* 韋莊集箋注. SHGJ, 2002.

Ouyang Xiu 歐陽修. *Liuyi shihua* 六一詩話. SKQS ed.

Ouyang Xiu and Song Qi 宋祈. *Xin Tangshu* 新唐書. ZHSJ, 1975.
Pan Dingwu 潘定武, Zhang Xiaoming 張小明, and Zhu Dayin 朱大銀, ed. and annot. *Qiji shi zhu* 齊己詩注. Hefei: Huangshan shushe, 2014.
Qi Wenbang 齊文榜, ed. and annot. *Jia Dao ji jiaozhu* 賈島集校注. ZHSJ, 2020.
Qu Tuiyuan 瞿蛻園, ed. *Liu Yuxi ji jianzheng* 劉禹錫集箋證. SHGJ, 1989.
Qu Tuiyuan and Zhu Jincheng 朱金城, ed. and annot. *Li Bai ji jiaozhu* 李白集校注. SHGJ, 1980.
Quan Tang shi 全唐詩. Compiled by Peng Dingqiu 彭定求 et al. ZHSJ, 1960.
Quan Tang shi bubian 全唐詩補編. Compiled by Chen Shangjun 陳尚君. ZHSJ, 1992.
Quan Tang wen 全唐文. Compiled by Dong Hao 董浩 et al. ZHSJ, 1983.
Ren Bantang 任半塘, ed. and annot. *Dunhuang geci zongbian* 敦煌歌辭總編. 3 vols. SHGJ, 1987.
Ruan Yue 阮閱. *Shihua zonggui* 詩話總龜. *SKQS* ed.
Shen Yue 沈約. *Songshu* 宋書. ZHSJ, 1974.
Shenqing 神清. *Beishan lu jiaozhu* 北山錄校注. Annotated by Huibao 慧寶 and Degui 德珪. Collated and annotated by Fu Shiping 富世平. ZHSJ, 2014.
Shinsan Dainihon Zokuzōkyō 新纂大日本續藏經. Edited by Nishi Giyū 西義雄 et al. Tokyo: Kokusho Kankōkai, 1975–1989.
Sibu congkan 四部叢刊. Edited by Zhang Yuanji 張元濟. Shanghai: Shangwu yinshuguan, 1919.
Siku quanshu zongmu tiyao 四庫全書總目提要. Shanghai: Shangwu yinshuguan, 1933.
Sima Guang 司馬光. *Zizhi tongjian* 資治通鑑. ZHSJ, 1956.
Sima Qian 司馬遷. *Shiji* 史記. Taipei: Dingwen shuju, 1981.
Song gaoseng zhuan 宋高僧傳. Compiled by Zanning 贊寧. *T* no. 2061, 50:709a–900.
Sun Wang 孫望, ed. and annot. *Wei Yingwu shiji xinian jiaozhu* 韋應物詩集繫年校箋. ZHSJ, 2002.
Taiping yulan 太平御覽. Compiled by Li Fang 李昉 et al. Taipei: Taiwan shangwu yinshuguan, 1975.
Taishō shinshū daizōkyō 大正新脩大藏經. Edited by Takakusu Junjirō 高楠順次郎 et al. Tokyo: Taishō Issaikyō Kankōkai, 1924–1935. Online editions at https://cbetaonline.dila.edu.tw/ and https://21dzk.l.u-tokyo.ac.jp/SAT/satdb2015.php.
Tang guoshi bu 唐國史補. Compiled by Li Zhao 李肇. *SKQS* ed.
Tang guoshi bu, Yinhua lu 唐國史補、因話錄. Compiled by Li Zhao 李肇 and Zhao Lin 趙璘. Shanghai: Gudian wenxue chubanshe, 1957.
Tangren xuan Tangshi xinbian: zengdingben 唐人選唐詩新編：增訂本. Edited by Fu Xuancong 傅璇琮, Chen Shangjun 陳尚君, and Xu Jun 徐俊. ZHSJ, 2014.
Tangren yishi huibian 唐人軼事彙編. Edited by Zhou Xunchu 周勛初. 4 vols. SHGJ, 2006.
Tangseng hongxiu ji 唐僧弘秀集. *SKQS* ed.
Teihon Kōbō daishi zenshū 定本弘法大師全集. Kōyasan, Wakayama-ken: Mikkyō bunka kenkyūjo, 1992–1997.
Toqto'a 脫脫 et al. *Songshi* 宋史. ZHSJ, 1977.
Wang Dang 王讜. *Tang yulin* 唐語林. *SKQS* ed.

Wang Dingbao 王定保. *Tang zhiyan jiaozhu* 唐摭言校注. Edited and annotated by Jiang Hanchun 姜漢椿. Shanghai: Shanghai shehui kexue xueyan chubanshe, 2003.
Wang Fuzhi 王夫之. *Jiangzhai shihua jianzhu* 薑齋詩話箋注. Edited and annotated by Dai Hongsen 戴鴻森. Beijing: Renmin wenxue chubanshe, 1981.
Wang Mao 王楙. *Yeke congshu* 野客叢書. SKQS ed.
Wang Ming 王明, ed. and annot. *Wunengzi jiaozhu* 無能子校注. ZHSJ, 1981.
Wang Pu 王溥. *Tang huiyao* 唐會要. ZHSJ, 1960.
Wang Xianqian 王先謙, annot. *Xunzi jijie* 荀子集解. ZHSJ, 1988.
Wang Xiulin 王秀林, ed. *Qiji shiji jiaozhu* 齊己詩集校注. Beijing: Zhongguo shehui kexue chubanshe, 2011.
Wei Qingzhi 魏慶之. *Shiren yuxie* 詩人玉屑. SKQS ed.
Wenxuan 文選. Compiled by Xiao Tong 蕭統. SHGJ, 1986.
Wenyuan yinghua 文苑英華. ZHSJ, 1966.
Wenyuange Siku quanshu 四庫全書. Edited by Yang Ne 楊訥 and Li Xiaoming 李曉明. Taipei: Shangwu yinshuguan, 1983–86.
Wu Gang 吳鋼, ed. *Quan Tangwen buyi* 全唐文補遺. Xi'an: San Qin chubanshe, 2005.
Wu Heqing 吳河清, ed. and annot. *Yao He shiji jiaozhu* 姚合詩集校注. SHGJ, 2012.
Wu Ke 吳可. *Canghai shihua* 藏海詩話. SKQS ed.
Wu Renchen 吳任臣. *Shiguo chunqiu* 十國春秋. Edited by Xu Minxia 徐敏霞 and Zhou Ying 周瑩 Beijing: Zhonghua shuju, 2010.
Xiang Chu 項楚. *Dunhuang geci zongbian kuangbu* 敦煌歌辭總編匡補. Taipei: Xinwenfeng chubanshe, 1995.
Xiao Difei 蕭滌非, ed., *Du Fu quanji jiaozhu* 杜甫全集校注. 12 vols. Beijing: Renmin wenxue chubanshe, 2012.
Xie Siwei 謝思煒, ed. and annot. *Bai Juyi wenji jiaozhu* 白居易文集校注. ZHSJ, 2010.
Xu Jun 徐俊. *Dunhuang shiji canjuan jikao* 敦煌詩集殘卷輯考. ZHSJ, 2000.
Xu Yuangao 徐元誥, annot. *Guoyu jijie* 國語集解. ZHSJ, 2002.
Xuanhe huapu 宣和畫譜. SKQS ed.
Yan Kejun 嚴可均, comp. *Quan shanggu sandai Qin Han sanguo liuchao wen* 全上古三代秦漢三國六朝文. ZHSJ, 1958.
Yan Shoucheng 嚴壽澂, Huang Ming 黃明, and Zhao Changping 趙昌平, ed. and annot. *Zheng Gu shi jianzhu* 鄭谷詩集箋注. SHGJ, 1991.
Yan Yu 嚴羽. *Canglang shihua* 滄浪詩話. SKQS ed.
Yang Bojun 楊伯峻, ed. and annot. *Liezi jishi* 列子集釋. ZHSJ, 1979.
Ye Yiwen 葉義問. *Lushan Taiping xingguo gong Caifang zhenjun shishi* 廬山太平興國宮採訪真君事實. In *Zhengtong daozang* 正統道藏. Shanghai: Shangwu yinshuguan, 1923–26. Online: https://www.kanripo.org/text/KR5g0095/.
Yin Zhanhua 尹占華 and Han Wenqi 韓文奇, ed. and annot. *Liu Zongyuan ji jiaozhu* 柳宗元集校注. ZHSJ, 2013.
Yuefu shiji 樂府詩集. Compiled by Guo Maoqian 郭茂倩 (1041–1099). 4 vols. ZHSJ, 1979.
Yutai xinyong jianzhu 玉臺新詠箋注. Edited by Xu Ling 徐陵 and annotated by Wu Zhaoyi 吳兆宜. ZHSJ, 1985.

Zhanguo ce 戰國策. SHGJ, 1978.
Zhang Biaochen 張表臣. *Shanhu gou shihua* 珊瑚鉤詩話. *SKQS* ed.
Zhang Bowei 張伯偉, ed. and annot. *Quan Tang-Wudai shige huikao* 全唐五代詩格彙考. Nanjing: Jiangsu guji chubanshe, 2002.
Zhang Wei 張為, *Shiren zhuke tu* 詩人主客圖. In *Lidai shihua xubian* 歷代詩話續編, coll. Ding Fubao 丁福保, vol. 1. Taipei: Yiwen yinshuguan, 1960.
Zhang Xihou 張錫厚, ed. *Quan Dunhuang shi* 全敦煌詩. 15 vols. Beijing: Zuojia chubanshe, 2006.
Zhao Han 趙崡. *Shimojuan hua* 石墨鐫華. *SKQS* ed.
Zhong Xing 鍾惺. *Tangshi gui* 唐詩歸. In *Xuxiu Siku quanshu* 續修四庫全書. SHGJ, 2002.
Zhu Jincheng 朱金城, ed. and annot. *Bai Juyi ji jianjiao* 白居易集箋校. SHGJ, 1988.
Zu Baoquan 祖保泉 and Tao Litian 陶禮天, eds. and annots. *Sikong Biaosheng shiwen ji jianjiao* 司空表聖詩文集箋校. Hefei: Anhui daxue chubanshe, 2002.
Zuozhuan 左傳. In *Chongkan Songben Shisan jing zhushu fu jiaokan ji* 重刊宋本十三經注疏附校勘記. Taipei: Yiwen yinshuguan, 1965.

Modern Works

Abé, Ryūichi. *The Weaving of Mantra: Kūkai and the Construction of Esoteric Buddhist Discourse.* New York: Columbia University Press, 1999.
Adamek, Wendi L. *The Mystique of Transmission: On an Early Chan History and Its Contexts.* New York: Columbia University Press, 2007.
Anderl, Christoph. "Studies in the Language of *Zu-tang ji*." 2 vols. PhD dissertation, University of Oslo, 2004.
Anderl, Christoph and Christian Wittern, eds. *Chán Buddhism in Dūnhuáng and Beyond: A Study of Manuscripts, Texts, and Contexts in Memory of John R. McRae.* Leiden: Brill, 2021.
Anderl, Christoph and Henrik H. Sørensen. "Northern Chán and the Siddhaṃ Songs." In Anderl and Wittern, *Chán Buddhism*, 99–40.
Agosti, Gianfranco. "Greek Poetry." In *The Oxford Handbook of Late Antiquity*, ed. Scott Fitzgerald Johnson, 361–404. Oxford: Oxford University Press, 2012.
App, Urs. "The Making of a Chan Record: Reflections on the History of the *Records of Yunmen* 雲門廣錄." *Zenbunka kenkyūjo kiyō* 禅文化研究紀要 17 (1991): 1–90.
Bao Deyi 包得義, Chen Xingyu 陳星宇, and Wang Shuping 王樹平. *Nanchao shiseng yanjiu* 南朝詩僧研究. Chengdu: Sichuan daxue chubanshe, 2012.
Barrett, Timothy H. "The Advent of the Buddhist Concept of Religion in China and Its Consequences for the Analysis of Daoism." *Sungkyung Journal of East Asian Studies* 9.2 (2009): 149–65.
—. *Taoism under the T'ang: Religion and Empire during the Golden Age of Chinese History.* London: Wellsweep, 1996.
Bender, Lucas Rambo. "Against the Monist Model of Tang Poetics." *T'oung Pao* 107 (2021): 633–87.

———. *Du Fu Transforms: Tradition and Ethics amid Societal Collapse*. Cambridge, Mass.: Harvard University Asia Center, 2021.
Benicka, Jana. "(Huayan-like) Notions of Inseparability (or Unity) of Essence and its Function (or Principle and Phenomena) in Some Commentaries on 'Five Positions' of Chan Master Dongshan Liangjie." In *Reflecting Mirrors: Perspectives on Huayan Buddhism*, ed. Imre Harar, 211-40. Wiesbaden: Harrassowitz Verlag, 2007.
Benn, Charles H. "Transmission." In *Encyclopedia of Taoism*, ed. Pregadio, 1:13-15.
Benn, James. "Another Look at the Pseudo-*Śūraṃgama sūtra*." *HJAS* 68.1 (2008): 57-89.
Bentor, Yael, and Meir Shahar, eds. *Chinese and Tibetan Esoteric Buddhism*. Leiden: Brill, 2017.
Berkowitz, Alan J. *Patterns of Disengagement: The Practice and Portrayal of Reclusion in Early Medieval China*. Stanford: Stanford University Press, 2000.
Blyth, R. H. *Zen in English Literature and the Oriental Classics*. Tokyo: Hokuseido Press, 1942.
Bodman, Richard Wainwright. "Poetics and Prosody in Early Mediaeval China: A Study and Translation of Kūkai's *Bunkyō hifuron*." PhD diss., Cornell University, 1978.
Bokenkamp, Stephen R. *Early Daoist Scriptures*. Berkeley: University of California Press, 1997.
Bol, Peter K. *"This Culture of Ours": Intellectual Transitions in T'ang and Sung China*. Stanford: Stanford University Press, 1992.
Borges, Jorge Luis. *This Craft of Verse*. Edited by Calin-Andrei Mihailescu. Cambridge, Mass.: Harvard University Press, 2000.
Bourdieu, Pierre. "The Field of Cultural Production, or: The Economic World Reversed." Translated by Richard Nice. In *The Field of Cultural Production: Essays on Art and Literature*, ed. Randal Johnson, 29-73. New York: Columbia University Press, 1993.
———. *The Logic of Practice*. Translated by Richard Nice. Stanford: Stanford University Press, 1990.
Brandes, Ulrik. "A Faster Algorithm for Betweenness Centrality." *Journal of Mathematical Sociology* 25.2 (2001): 163-77.
Brashier, K. E. *Ancestral Memory in Early China*. Cambridge, Mass.: Harvard University Asia Center, 2011.
Brose, Benjamin. "Credulous Kings and Immoral Monks: Critiques of Buddhists during the Five Dynasties and Ten Kingdoms." *Asia Major*, 3rd ser., 27.1/2 (2014): 73-98.
———. *Patrons and Patriarchs: Regional Rulers and Chan Monks During the Five Dynasties and Ten Kingdoms*. Honolulu: University of Hawaii Press, 2015.
Broughton, Jeffrey. *Zongmi on Chan*. New York: Columbia University Press, 2009.
Buckelew, Kevin. "Becoming Chinese Buddhas: Claims to Authority and the Making of Chan Buddhist Identity." *T'oung Pao* 105 (2019): 357-400.
Byrne, Christopher H. "Poetics of Silence: Hongzhi Zhengjue (1091-1157) and the Practice of Poetry in Song Dynasty Chan Yulu." PhD diss., McGill University, 2015.

BIBLIOGRAPHY

Cai, Zong-qi. *How to Read Chinese Poetry: A Guided Anthology*. New York: Columbia University Press, 2008.

Campany, Robert Ford. "Miracle Tales as Scripture Reception: A Case Study Involving the *Lotus Sutra* in China, 370–750 CE." *Early Medieval China* 24 (2018): 24–52.

———. "On the Very Idea of Religions (in the Modern West and Early Medieval China)." *History of Religions* 42.4 (2003): 287–319.

———. *Signs from the Unseen Realm: Buddhist Miracle Tales from Early Medieval China*. Honolulu: University of Hawaii Press, 2012.

Capitanio, Joshua. "Sanskrit and Pseudo-Sanskrit Incantations in Daoist Ritual Texts." *History of Religions* 57.4 (2018): 348–405.

Cartelli, Mary Anne. *The Five-Colored Clouds of Mount Wutai: Poems from Dunhuang*. Leiden: Brill, 2012.

Chai, David., ed. *Dao Companion to Xuanxue* 玄學 *(Neo-Daoism)*. Cham, Switzerland: Routledge, 2020.

Chang, Kang-i Sun. *The Evolution of Chinese Tz'u Poetry: From Late T'ang to Northern Sung*. Princeton: Princeton University Press, 1980.

Chau, Adam Yuet. *Religion in China: The Ties That Bind*. Cambridge, Mass.: Polity Press, 2019.

Chaudhuri, Saroj Kumar. "Siddham in China and Japan." *Sino-Platonic Papers* 88 (1998): 1–124.

Chen, Jack W. *Anecdote, Network, Gossip, Performance: Essays on the* Shishuo xinyu. Cambridge, Mass.: Harvard University Asia Center, 2021.

Chen, Jinhua. *Monks and Monarchs, Kinship and Kingship: Tanqian in Sui Buddhism and Politics*. Kyoto: Scuola Italiana di Studi sull'Asia Orientale, 2002.

Chen, Jo-shui. *Liu Tsung-yüan and Intellectual Change in T'ang China*. Cambridge: Cambridge University Press, 1992.

Ch'en, Kenneth K. S. *Buddhism in China: A Historical Survey*. Princeton: Princeton University Press, 1964.

Chen, Song. Review of *The Destruction of the Medieval Chinese Aristocracy* by Nicolas Tackett. *HJAS* 75.1 (2015): 233–43.

Clark, Hugh R. "Quanzhou (Fujian) during the Tang-Song Interregnum, 879–978." *T'oung Pao* 67 (1982): 132–49.

———. "Scoundrels, Rogues, and Refugees: The Founders of the Ten Kingdoms in the Late Ninth Century." In *Five Dynasties and Ten Kingdoms*, ed. Peter Lorge, 47–78. Hong Kong: Chinese University Press, 2011.

Cole, Alan. *Fathering Your Father: The Zen of Fabrication in Tang Buddhism*. Berkeley: University of California Press, 2009.

Copp, Paul. "Anointing Phrases and Narrative Power: A Tang Buddhist Poetics of Incantation." *History of Religions* 52.2 (2012): 142–72.

———. *The Body Incantatory: Spells and the Ritual Imagination in Medieval Chinese Buddhism*. New York: Columbia University Press, 2014.

———. "Notes on the Term 'Dhāraṇī' in Medieval Chinese Buddhist Thought." *Bulletin of the School of Oriental and African Studies* 71.3 (2008): 493–508.

Dai Weihua 戴偉華. *Tangdai shifu yu wenxue yanjiu* 唐代使府與文學研究. Guilin: Guangxi shifan daxue chubanshe, 1998.

Davis, Timothy M. *Entombed Epigraphy and Commemorative Culture in Early Medieval China: A History of Early Muzhiming*. Leiden: Brill, 2015.

DeBlasi, Anthony. *Reform in the Balance: The Defense of Literary Culture in Mid-Tang China*. Albany: State University of New York Press, 2002.

De Meyer, Jan. *Wu Yun's Way: Life and Works of an Eighth-Century Daoist Master*. Leiden: Brill, 2006.

Ditter, Alexei. "Civil Examinations and Cover Letters in the Mid-Tang: Dugu Yu's (776-815) 'Letter Submitted to Attendant Gentleman Quan of the Ministry of Rites.'" In *A History of Chinese Letters and Epistolary Culture*, ed. Antje Richter, 643-74. Leiden: Brill, 2015.

Du Songbo 杜松柏. *Chanxue yu Tang-Song shixue* 禪學與唐宋詩學. Taipei: Xinwenfeng chuban gongsi, 2008.

Duan Shuangxi 段雙喜. *Tangmo Wudai Jiangnan xidao shige yanjiu* 唐末五代江南西道詩歌研究. SHGJ, 2010.

Durrant, Stephen, Wai-yee Li, and David Schaberg. *Zuo Tradition: Zuozhuan* 左傳, *Commentary on the "Spring and Autumn Annals."* Seattle: University of Washington Press, 2016.

Dykstra, Yoshiko Kurata. *Miraculous Tales of the Lotus Sutra from Ancient Japan: The* Dainihonkoku hokekyōkenki *of Priest Chingen*. Osaka: Intercultural Research Institute, Kansai University of Foreign Studies, 1983.

Easley, David, and Jon Kleinberg. *Networks, Crowds, and Markets: Reasoning about a Highly Connected World*. Cambridge: Cambridge University Press, 2010.

Egan, Ronald C. *The Literary Works of Ou-yang Hsiu (1007–72)*. Cambridge: Cambridge University Press, 1984.

———. "Poet, Mind, and World: A Reconsideration of the 'Shensi' Chapter of *Wenxin diaolong*." In *A Chinese Literary Mind: Culture, Creativity, and Rhetoric in Wenxin diaolong*, ed. Zong-qi Cai, 101-26. Stanford: Stanford University Press, 2000.

Eide, Elling. "On Li Po." In Wright and Twitchett, *Perspectives on the T'ang*, 376-404.

Eubanks, Charlotte D. *Miracles of Book and Body: Buddhist Textual Culture and Medieval Japan*. Berkeley: University of California Press, 2011.

Fang Rui 房銳. *Sun Guangxian yu* Beimeng suoyan *yanjiu* 孫光憲與《北夢瑣言》研究. ZHSJ, 2006.

Feng, Linda Rui. *City of Marvel and Transformation: Chang'an and Narratives of Experience in Tang Dynasty China*. Honolulu: University of Hawaii Press, 2015.

Feng Zhihong 馮志弘. *Bei-Song guwen yundong de xingcheng* 北宋古文運動的形成. SHGJ, 2009.

Fincher-Kiefer, Rebecca. *How the Body Shapes Knowledge: Empirical Support for Embodied Cognition*. Washington, D.C.: American Psychological Association, 2019.

Fong, Wen. "Five Hundred Lohans at Daitokuji." PhD diss., Princeton University, 1958.

Formisano, Marco. "Towards an Aesthetic Paradigm of Late Antiquity." *Antiquité tardive* 15 (2007): 277-84.

Foulk, T. Griffith. "Chan Literature." In *Brill's Encyclopedia of Buddhism*, ed. Jonathan Silk, 693-722. Leiden: Brill, 2015.

———. "The Ch'an *Tsung* in Medieval China: School, Lineage, or What?" *Pacific World* n.s., 8 (1992): 18–31.

———. "Myth, Ritual, and Monastic Practice in Sung Ch'an Buddhism." In *Religion and Society in T'ang and Sung China*, ed. Patricia Ebrey and Peter Gregory, 147–208. Honolulu: University of Hawaii Press, 1993.

———. "The Spread of Chan (Zen) Buddhism." In *The Spread of Buddhism*, ed. Ann Heirman and Stephan Peter Bumbacher, 433–56. Leiden: Brill, 2007.

Foulk, T. Griffith and Robert Sharf, "On the Ritual Use of Ch'an Portraiture in Medieval China." *Cahiers d'Extrême-Asie* 7 (1993): 149–219.

Frye, Northrop. *Anatomy of Criticism: Four Essays*. Princeton: Princeton University Press, 1957.

Fu Xuancong 傅璇琮, ed. *Tang caizi zhuan jiaojian* 唐才子傳校箋. 5 vols. ZHSJ, 1987–1995.

———, ed. *Tang Wudai wenxue biannian shi* 唐五代文學編年史. 4 vols. Shenyang: Liaohai chubanshe, 1998.

———. *Tangdai keju yu wenxue* 唐代科舉與文學. Xi'an: Shanxi renmin chubanshe, 1986.

Fukui Fumimasa 福井文雅. *Hannya shingyō no rekishiteki kenkyū* 般若心経の歴史的研究. Tokyo: Shunjūsha, 1987.

Fuller, Michael A. *Drifting among Rivers and Lakes: Southern Song Dynasty Poetry and the Problem of Literary History*. Cambridge, Mass.: Harvard University Asia Center, 2013.

———. "Sung Dynasty *Shih* Poetry." In *The Columbia History of Chinese Literature*, ed. Mair, 337–69.

Galambos, Imre. "Composite Manuscripts in Medieval China: The Case of Scroll P. 3720 from Dunhuang." In *One-Volume Libraries: Composite and Multiple-Text Manuscripts*, ed. Michael Friedrich and Cosima Schwarke, 355–78. Berlin: De Gruyter, 2016.

———. "Confucian Education in a Buddhist Environment: Medieval Manuscripts and Imprints of the *Mengqiu*." *Studies in Chinese Religions* 1.3 (2015): 269–88.

Gernet, Jacques. *Buddhism in Chinese Society: An Economic History from the Fifth to the Tenth Centuries*. Translated by Franciscus Verellen. New York: Columbia University Press, 1995.

Gimello, Robert M. "Apophatic and Kataphatic Discourse in Mahāyāna: A Chinese View." *Philosophy East and West* 26.2 (1976): 117–36.

———. "Chih-yen (智儼, 602–668) and the Foundations of Hua-yen (華嚴) Buddhism." PhD diss., Columbia University, 1976.

Goble, Geoffrey C. *Chinese Esoteric Buddhism: Amoghavajra, the Ruling Elite, and the Emergence of a Tradition*. New York: Columbia University Press, 2019.

Goh, Meow Hui. *Sound and Sight: Poetry and Courtier Culture in the Yongming Era (483–493)*. Stanford: Stanford University Press, 2010.

Goodman, Amanda K. "The *Ritual Instructions for Altar Methods* (*Tanfa yize*): Prolegomenon to the Study of a Chinese Esoteric Buddhist Ritual Compendium from Late-Medieval Dunhuang." PhD diss., University of California, Berkeley, 2013.

Graf, Fritz. *Magic in the Ancient World*. Translated by Franklin Philip. Cambridge, Mass.: Harvard University Press, 1997.

Graham, A. C., trans. *The Book of Lieh-tzŭ: A Classic of Tao*. New York: Columbia University Press, 1960.
Grant, Beata. *Mount Lu Revisited: Buddhism in the Life and Writings of Su Shi*. Honolulu: University of Hawaii Press, 1994.
Greene, Eric M. *Chan before Chan: Meditation, Repentance, and Visionary Experience in Chinese Buddhism*. Honolulu: University of Hawai'i Press, 2021.
Gu Licheng 顧立誠. *Zouxiang nanfang: Tang-Song zhi ji zi bei xiang nan de yimin yu qi yingxiang* 走向南方—唐宋之際自北向南的移民與其影響. Taipei: Guoli Taiwan daxue wenxueyuan, 2004.
Guillén, Claudio. *Literature as System: Essays toward the Theory of Literary History*. Princeton: Princeton University Press, 1971.
Haeri, Niloofar. *Say What Your Longing Heart Desires: Women, Prayer, and Poetry in Iran*. Stanford: Stanford University Press, 2021.
Hakeda, Yoshito S., trans. *The Awakening of Faith, Attributed to Aśvagoṣa*. New York: Columbia University Press, 1967.
——, trans. *Kūkai: Major Works*. New York: Columbia University Press, 1972.
Halperin, Mark. "Heroes, Rogues, and Religion in a Tenth-Century Chinese Miscellany." *JAOS* 129.3 (2009): 413-30.
Hamill, Sam, and J. P. Seaton. *The Poetry of Zen*. Boston: Shambhala, 2004.
Hao Chunwen 郝春文. "Guanyu Dunhuang xieben zhaiwen de jige wenti" 關於敦煌寫本齋文的幾個問題. *Shoudu shifan daxue xuebao (shehuikexue ban)* 首都師範大學學報（社會科學版） 109 (1996): 64-71.
——. *Tang houqi Wudai Songchu Dunhuang sengni de shehui shenghuo* 唐後期五代宋初敦煌僧尼的社會生活. Beijing: Zhongguo shehuikexue chubanshe, 1998.
Hare, Thomas Blenman. "Reading Writing and Cooking: Kūkai's Interpretive Strategies." *Journal of Asian Studies* 49.2 (1990): 253-73.
Hargett, James M. "會稽: Guaiji? Guiji? Huiji? Kuaiji? Some Remarks on an Ancient Chinese Place-Name." *Sino-Platonic Papers* 214 (2013): 1-32.
Harper, Donald. "A Chinese Demonography of the Third Century BC." *HJAS* 45.2 (1985): 459-98.
Hartman, Charles. *Han Yü and the T'ang Search for Unity*. Princeton: Princeton University Press, 1986.
——. "The *Yinchuang zalu* 吟窗雜錄, *Miscellaneous Notes from the Singing Window*: A Song Dynasty Primer of Poetic Composition." In *Recarving the Dragon: Understanding Chinese Poetics*, ed. Olga Lomová, 205-239. Prague: Karolinum Press, 2003.
Hartwell, Robert M. "Demographic, Political, and Social Transformations of China, 750-1550." *HJAS* 42.2 (1982): 365-442.
Hawkes, David. *Songs of the South: An Anthology of Ancient Chinese Poems by Qu Yuan and Other Poets*. Harmondsworth: Penguin, 1985.
Hay, John. "Values and History in Chinese Painting, I: Hsieh Ho Revisited." *Res* 6 (1983): 72-111.
——. "Values and History in Chinese Painting, II: The Hierarchical Evolution of Structure." *Res* 7/8 (1984): 102-36.
Hesla, David H. "Religion and Literature: The Second Stage." *Journal of the American Academy of Religion* 46.2 (1978): 181-92.

Hinton, David. *Awakened Cosmos: The Mind of Classical Chinese Poetry.* Boston: Shambhala, 2019.

Hirano Kenshō 平野顕照. "Kōsen Hōnen hō–Tōdai shisō den" 広宣上人考–唐代詩僧伝. Part 1: *Ōtani gakuhō* 大谷学報 56 (1977): 22-35. Part 2: *Ōtani gakuhō* 大谷学報 57 (1978): 31-46.

Hobsbawm, Eric. "Introduction: Inventing Traditions." In *The Invention of Tradition,* ed. Hobsbawm and Terence Ranger, 1-14. Cambridge: Cambridge University Press, 1983.

Holzman, Donald. "A Dialogue with the Ancients: Tao Qian's Interrogation of Confucius." In *Culture and Power in the Reconstitution of the Chinese Realm, 200-600,* ed. Scott Pearce, Audrey Spiro, and Patricia Ebrey, 75-98. Cambridge: Cambridge University Press, 2001.

——. "Les Premiers vers pentasyllabiques datés dans la poésie chinoise." In *Mélange de sinologie offerts à Monsieur Paul Demiéville,* II, 77-115. Paris: Bibliothèque de l'Institute des Hautes Etudes Chinoises, 1974.

Hori, Victor. *Zen Sand: The Book of Capping Phrases for Kōan Practice.* Honolulu: University of Hawaii Press, 2003.

Hsiao Li-hua 蕭麗華. "Wan-Tang shiseng Qiji de shichan shijie" 晚唐詩僧齊己的詩禪世界. *Foxue yanjiu zhongxin xuebao* 佛學研究中心學報 2 (1997): 157-78.

——. *"Wenzi chan" shixue de fazhan guiji* 「文字禪」詩學的發展軌跡. Taipei: Xinwenfeng chuban gongsi, 2012.

Hsieh, Ding-Hwa. "Poetry and Chan 'Gong'an': From Xuedou Chongxian (980-1052) to Wumen Huikai (1183-1260)." *Journal of Song-Yuan Studies* 40 (2010): 39-70.

Hsieh, Shu-wei 謝世維. *Dafan milou: zhonggu shiqi daojiao jingdianzhong de fojiao* 大梵彌羅：中古時期道教經典中的佛教. Taipei: Taiwan shangwu yinshuguan, 2013.

——. "Writing from Heaven: Celestial Writing in Six Dynasties Daoism." PhD diss., Indiana University, 2005.

Hsu, Eileen Hsiang-ling. *Monks in Glaze: Patronage, Kiln Origin, and Iconography of the Yixian Luohans.* Leiden: Brill, 2017.

Hu Kexian 胡可先 and Yu Yuexi 虞越溪. "You 'Wuzhen shoudie ji Liangjie Dade zengdashi hechao' lun Guiyijun jianli chuqi yu Tang zhongyang de zongjiao jiaowang" 由《悟真受牒及兩街大德贈答詩合鈔》論歸義軍建立初期與唐中央的宗教交往. *Dunhuang xue jikan* 敦煌學輯刊, 2020.3: 62-70.

Hu Shi 胡適. *Baihua wenxue shi* 白話文學史. SHGJ, 1999 [1928].

Huang Yangxing 黃陽興. "Lüelun Tang-Song shidai de 'Suiqiu' xinyang (shang)" 略論唐宋時代的「隨求」信仰（上）. *Pumen xuebao* 普門學報 34 (2006): 125-54.

——. "Lüelun Tang-Song shidai de 'Suiqiu' xinyang (xia)" 略論唐宋時代的「隨求」信仰（下）. *Pumen xuebao* 普門學報 35 (2006): 1-15.

Hucker, Charles O. *A Dictionary of Official Titles in Imperial China.* Stanford: Stanford University Press, 1985.

Hureau, Sylvie. "Les commentaires de *sūtra* bouddhiques." In *La fabrique du lisible: la mise en texte des manuscrits de la Chine ancienne et médiévale,* ed. Jean-Pierre Drège and Constantino Moretti, 239-46. Paris: Collège de France, 2014.

Hurvitz, Leon. *Scripture of the Lotus Blossom of the Fine Dharma (The Lotus Sūtra)*. Rev ed. New York: Columbia University Press, 2009.

Ichihara Kōkichi 市原亨吉. "Chū-Tō shoki ni okeru Kōsa no shisō ni tsuite" 中唐初期における江左の詩僧について. *Tōhō gakuhō* 東方學報 28 (1958): 219–48.

Jao Tsong-yi 饒宗頤 and Paul Demiéville. *Airs de Touen-Houang (Touen-houang k'iu* 煌敦曲*): Textes à chanter des VIIIe-Xe siècles*. Paris: Éditions du Centre national de la Recherche scientifique, 1971.

Jasper, David. *The Study of Literature and Religion: An Introduction*. Basingstoke: Macmillan, 1989.

Jia Jinhua 賈晉華. "*Baolin zhuan* zhuzhe ji bianzhuan mudi kaoshu"《寶林傳》著者及編撰目的考述. *Wenxian* 文献 2011.2: 131–39.

—. "The Hongzhou School of Chan Buddhism and the Tang Literati." PhD diss., University of Colorado, 1999.

—. *The Hongzhou School of Chan Buddhism in Eighth- through Tenth-century China*. Albany: State University of New York Press, 2006.

—. *Jiaoran nianpu* 皎然年譜. Xiamen: Xiamen daxue chubanshe, 1992.

—. *Tangdai jihui zongji yu shirenqun yanjiu* 唐代集會總集與詩人群研究. 2nd ed. Beijing: Beijing daxue chubanshe, 2015.

—. "Translation and Interaction: A New Examination of the Controversy over the Translation and Authenticity of the *Śūraṃgama-sūtra*." *Religions* 13.474 (2022): 1–21.

Jiang, Tao. "The Problematic of Whole-Part and the Horizon of the Enlightened in Huayan Buddhism." *Journal of Chinese Philosophy* 28.4 (2001): 457–75.

Jiang Yin 蔣寅. *Dali shiren yanjiu* 大歷詩人研究. ZHSJ, 1995.

—. *Gudian shixue de xiandai quanshi* 古典詩學的現代詮釋. ZHSJ, 2003.

Jing Xiadong 景遐東. *Jiangnan wenhua yu Tangdai wenxue yanjiu* 江南文化與唐代文學研究. Beijing: Renmin wenxue chubanshe, 2005.

Johnson, Mark. *Embodied Mind, Meaning, and Reason: How Our Bodies Give Rise to Understanding*. Chicago: University of Chicago Press, 2017.

Jones, Nicholaos. "The Metaphysics of Identity in Fazang's *Huayan Wujiao Zhang*: The Inexhaustible Freedom of Dependent Origination." In *Dao Companion to Chinese Buddhist Philosophy*, ed. Youru Wang and Sandra A. Wawrytko, 295–323. Dordrecht: Springer, 2018.

Jorgensen, John. "The 'Imperial' Lineage of Ch'an Buddhism: The Role of Confucian Ritual and Ancestor Worship in Ch'an's Search for Legitimation in the Mid-T'ang Dynasty." *Papers on Far Eastern History* 35 (1987): 89–133.

—. *Inventing Hui-neng, the Sixth Patriarch: Hagiography and Biography in Early Ch'an*. Leiden: Brill, 2005.

—. "The Sensibility of the Insensible: The Genealogy of a Ch'an Aesthetic and the Passionate Dream of Poetic Creation." PhD diss., Australian National University, 1989.

Jorgensen, John, Dan Lusthaus, John Makeham, and Mark Strange, ed. and trans. *Treatise on Awakening Mahāyāna Faith*. Oxford: Oxford University Press, 2019.

Kahlos, Maijastina. "The Early Church." In *The Cambridge History of Magic and Witchcraft in the West: From Antiquity to Present*, ed. David J. Collins, 148–82. Cambridge: Cambridge University Press, 2015.

Kao Yu-ting 高于婷. "Guanxiu ji qi *Chanyue ji* zhi yanjiu" 貫休及其《禪月集》之研究. *Gudian shige yanjiu huikan* 古典詩歌研究彙刊, 12.8-9 (2012): 1-357.

Kawachi Shōen 河內昭圓. "'Tetsu shōnin bunshū jo' kanki: shisō Reitetsu no shōgai" 「澈上人文集序」管窺−詩僧靈澈の生涯. *Ōtani daigaku kenkyū nenpō* 大谷大學研究年報 26 (1974): 79-134.

Kent, Richard K. "Depictions of the Guardians of the Law: Lohan Painting in China." In *Latter Days of the Law: Images of Chinese Buddhism, 850–1850*, ed. Marsha Weidner, 183-213. Lawrence: Spencer Museum of Art, University of Kansas, 1994.

Kern, Martin. "*Shi jing* Songs as Performance Texts: A Case Study of 'Chu ci' (Thorny Caltrop)." *Early China* 25 (2000): 49-111.

Kieschnick, John. "Buddhist Monasticism." In *Early Chinese Religion, Part Two: The Period of Division*, ed. John Lagerwey and Lü Pengzhi, 1:545-74. 2 vols. Leiden: Brill, 2010.

——. *The Eminent Monk: Buddhist Ideals in Medieval Chinese Hagiography*. Honolulu: University of Hawaii Press, 1997.

Kieschnick, John, and Meir Shahar. Introduction to *India in the Chinese Imagination: Myth, Religion, and Thought*, 1-9. Philadelphia: University of Pennsylvania Press, 2014.

Kimura, Kiyotaka. "Huayan and Chan." In *Reflecting Mirrors: Perspectives on Huayan Buddhism*, ed. Imre Harar, 211-20. Wiesbaden: Harrassowitz Verlag, 2007.

Knechtges, David R., trans. *Wen Xuan, or, Selections of Refined Literature*. 3 vols. Princeton: Princeton University Press, 1982-1996.

Knechtges, David R., and Taiping Chang. *Ancient and Early Medieval Chinese Literature: A Reference Guide*. 4 vols. Leiden: Brill, 2010-2014.

Knight, Mark. *An Introduction to Religion and Literature*. London: Continuum, 2009.

——, ed. *The Routledge Companion to Literature and Religion*. Abingdon: Routledge, 2016.

Kobayashi Enshō 小林圓照. "Tonkō shahon *Shittan shō* rui no tokuisei−*Zenmon Shittan shō* no tekisuto kenkyū" 敦煌写本<悉曇章>類の特異性-『禅門悉談章』のテキスト研究. *Indōgaku bukkyōgaku kenkyū* 印度学仏教学研究 59.2 (2011): 36-44.

Kobayashi Taichirō 小林太市郎. "Tōdai no Daihi Kannon" 唐代の大悲觀音. In *Kannon shinkō* 觀音信仰, ed. Hayami Tasuku 速水侑. 39-136. Tokyo: Yūzankaku shuppansha, 1982.

——. *Zengetsu Daishi no shōgai to geijutsu* 禪月大師の生涯と藝術. Tokyo: Sōgensha, 1947.

Kojō Teikichi. *Shina bungaku shi* 支那文学史. Tokyo: Keisei zasshisha, 1897.

Kroll, Paul W. "Anthologies in the Tang." In *The Oxford Handbook of Classical Chinese Literature (1000 BCE–900 CE)*, ed. Wiebke Denecke, Wai-Yee Li, and Xiaofei Tian, 303-15. Oxford: Oxford University Press, 2017.

——. "Daoist Verse and the Quest for the Divine." In *Early Chinese Religion, Part Two: The Period of Division (220–589 AD)*, ed. John Lagerwey and Lü Pengzhi, 2:953-85. 2 vols. Leiden: Brill, 2010.

—. *Dharma Bell and Dhāraṇī Pillar: Li Po's Buddhist Inscriptions*. Kyoto: Scuola Italiana di Studi sull'Asia Orientale, 2001.

—. "Lexical Landscapes and Textual Mountains in the High T'ang." *T'oung Pao* 84 (1998): 62–101.

—. "Li Po's Purple Haze." *Daoist Resources* 7.2 (1997): 21–37.

—. "Li Po's Transcendent Diction." *JAOS* 106.1 (1986): 99–117.

—. "The Poetry of the T'ang Dynasty." In *The Columbia History of Chinese Literature*, ed. Mair, 274–313.

Kroll, Paul W., et al. *A Student's Dictionary of Early and Medieval Chinese*. 3rd ed. Leiden: Brill, 2022.

Kuo, Liying [郭麗英]. "Mandala et rituel de confession à Dunhuang." *Bulletin de l'Ecole française d'Extrême-Orient* 85.1 (1998): 227–56.

—. "Sur les apocryphes bouddhiques chinois." *Bulletin de l'Ecole française d'Extrême-Orient* 87.2 (2000): 677–705.

LaFleur, William. *The Karma of Words: Buddhism and the Literary Arts in Medieval Japan*. Berkeley: University of California Press, 1983.

Lanham, Richard. *A Handlist of Rhetorical Terms*. 2nd ed. Berkeley: University of California Press, 1991.

Lee Chien-k'un 李建崑. *Zhong-Wan Tang kuyin shiren yanjiu* 中晚唐苦吟詩人研究. Taipei: Xiuwei zixun keji gufen youxian gongsi, 2005.

Legge, James, trans. *Li Chi, Book of Rites: An Encyclopedia of Ancient Ceremonial Usages, Religious Creeds, and Social Institutions*. Ed. Ch'u Chai and Winberg Chai. 2 vols. New Hyde Park, New York: University Books, 1967.

—, trans. *A Record of Buddhistic Kingdoms, Being an Account by the Chinese Monk Fâ-hien of His Travels in India and Ceylon (A.D. 399–414) in Search of the Buddhist Books of Discipline*. Oxford: Clarendon Press, 1886.

Leys, Simon. *The Analects of Confucius*. New York: Norton, 1997.

Li Congjun 李從軍. *Tangdai wenxue yanbian shi* 唐代文學演變史. Beijing: Renmin wenxue chubanshe, 2006.

Li Dingguang 李定廣. *Tangmo Wudai luanshi wenxue yanjiu* 唐末五代亂世文學研究. Beijing: Zhongguo shehui kexue chubanshe, 2006.

Li Jiangfeng 李江峰. *Wan Tang-Wudai shige yanjiu* 晚唐五代詩格研究. Beijing: Renmin chubanshe, 2017.

Li Ling 李翎. "Dasuiqiu tuoluoni zhoujing de liuxing yu tuxiang" 大隨求陀羅尼咒經的流行與圖像. *Pumen xuebao* 普門學報 45 (2008): 127–67.

Li Xiaorong 李小榮. *Jin-Tang Fojiao wenxue shi* 晉唐佛教文學史. Beijing: Renmin chubanshe, 2017.

Li, Xiaorong. *The Poetics and Politics of Sensuality in China: The "Fragrant and Bedazzling" Movement (1600–1930)*. Amherst, N.Y.: Cambria Press, 2019.

Li Yinghui 李映輝. *Tangdao fojiao dili yanjiu* 唐代佛教地理研究. Changsha: Hunan daxue chubanshe, 2004.

Liao Chao-heng 廖肇亨. "Wan-Ming sengren 'Shanjushi' lunxi—yi Hanyue Fazang wei zhongxin" 晚明僧人《山居詩》論析―以漢月法藏為中心. In *Disijie tongsu wenxue yu yazheng wenxue yantaohui lunwenji* 第四屆通俗文學與雅正文學研討會論文集, ed. Guoli Zhongxing daxue Zhongguo wenxue xi 國立中興大學中國文學系, 49–74. Taichung: Xingda Zhongwenxi, 2003.

Lin Pei-ying. "A Comparative Approach to Śubhakarasiṃha's (637–735) *Essentials of Meditation*: Meditation and Precepts in Eighth-Century China." In Bentor and Shahar, *Chinese and Tibetan Esoteric Buddhism*, 136–39.

Lin Yun-jo 林韻柔. "Tangdai 'Foding zunsheng tuoluoni jing' de yichuan yu xinyang" 唐代《佛頂尊勝陀羅尼經》的譯傳與信仰. *Fagu foxue xuebao* 法鼓佛學學報 3 (2008): 145–93.

Liu Chao-lin 劉昭麟 et al. "*Quan Tangshi* de fenxi, tankan yu yingyong—fengge, duizhang, shehui wanglu yu duilian" 《全唐詩》的分析、探勘與應用—風格、對仗、社會網路與對聯. *The 2015 Conference on Computational Linguistics and Speech Processing* (2015): 43–57.

Liu Chao-lin, Thomas J. Mazanec, and Jeffrey R. Tharsen. "Exploring Chinese Poetry with Digital Assistance: Examples from Linguistic, Literary, and Historical Viewpoints." *Journal of Chinese Literature and Culture* 5.2 (2018): 276–313.

Liu Luming 劉鹿鳴. "Wei-Yangzong Chanfa gangzong chutan" 溈仰宗禪法綱宗初探. *Foxue yanjiu* 佛學研究 2010: 259–71.

Liu Ning 劉寧. *Tang-Song zhi ji shige yanbian yanjiu* 唐宋之際詩歌演變研究. Beijing: Beijing shifan daxue chubanshe, 2002.

Liu Shufen 劉淑芬. *Miezui yu duwang: Foding zunsheng tuoluoni jingchuang zhi yanjiu* 滅罪與度亡：佛頂尊勝陀羅尼經經幢之研究. SHGJ, 2008.

Liu Xinguang 劉新光. "Tang-Song Jiangnan diyu kongjian de fenhua yu zhenghe" 唐宋江南地域空間的分化與整合. *Tang yanjiu* 唐研究 11 (2005): 559–93.

Liu, Xinru. *Ancient India and Ancient China: Trade and Religious Exchanges, AD 1–600*. Oxford: Oxford University Press, 1988.

Loehr, Max. *The Great Painters of China*. New York: Harper & Row, 1980.

Long, Hoyt. *The Value in Numbers: Reading Japanese Literature in a Global Information Age*. New York: Columbia University Press, 2021.

Lowe, Bryan. *Ritualized Writing: Buddhist Practice and Scriptural Cultures in Ancient Japan*. Honolulu: University of Hawaii Press, 2017.

Lu, Hui-Wen [盧慧紋]. "Wild Cursive Calligraphy, Poetry, and Chan Monks in the Tenth Century." In *Tenth-Century China and Beyond: Art and Visual Culture in a Multi-centered Age*, ed. Wu Hung, 364–90. Chicago: Center for the Art of East Asia, University of Chicago, 2012.

Lu Qinli 逯欽立. "Hanshi bielu" 漢詩別錄. In *Han Wei Liuchao wenxue lunji* 漢魏六朝文學論集, 1–108. Xi'an: Shaanxi renmin chubanshe, 1984.

Ludwig, Theodore M. "Incantation." In *Encyclopedia of Religion*, 2nd ed., ed. Lindsay Jones, 4406–10. Detroit: Macmillan Reference, 2005.

Luo Shijin 羅時進. *Tangshi yanjin lun* 唐詩演進論. Nanjing: Jiangsu guji chubanshe, 2001.

Lynn, Richard John. "Orthodoxy and Enlightenment: Wang Shih-chen's Theory of Poetry and Its Antecedents." In *The Unfolding of Neo-Confucianism*, ed. William Theodore de Bary, 217–69. New York: Columbia University Press, 1975.

——. "The Sudden and the Gradual in Chinese Poetry Criticism: An Examination of the Ch'an-Poetry Analogy." In *Sudden and Gradual: Approaches to*

Enlightenment in Chinese Thought, ed. Peter N. Gregory, 381–427. Honolulu: University of Hawaii Press, 1987.
Mair, Victor H. *The Columbia Anthology of Traditional Chinese Literature*. New York: Columbia University Press, 1994.
———, ed. *The Columbia History of Chinese Literature*. New York: Columbia University Press, 2001.
———. "*The Heart Sutra* and *The Journey to the West*." In *Sino-Asiatica: Papers dedicated to Professor Liu Ts'un-yan on the Occasion of his Eighty-Fifth Birthday*, ed. Wang Gungwu et al., 120–49. Canberra: Faculty of Asian Studies, Australian National University, 2002.
———. "Scroll Presentation in the T'ang Dynasty." *HJAS* 38.1 (1978): 35–60.
———. *Wandering on the Way: Early Taoist Tales and Parables of Chuang Tzu*. New York: Bantam, 1994.
Mather, Richard B. "The Landscape Buddhism of the Fifth-Century Poet Hsieh Ling-yün." *Journal of Asian Studies* 18.1 (1958): 67–79.
Matsuura Tomohisa 松浦友久. *Kōchū Tōshi kaishaku jiten* 校注唐詩解釈辞典. Tokyo: Taishūkan shoten, 1987.
Mazanec, Thomas J. "Guanxiu's 'Mountain-Dwelling Poems': A Translation." *Tang Studies* 34.1 (2016): 99–124.
———. "How Poetry Became Meditation in Late-Ninth-Century China." *Asia Major*, 3rd ser., 32.2 (2019): 113–51.
———. "Literary Debts in Tang China: On the Exchange of Money, Merit, and Meter." *Monumenta Serica* 71.1 (2023): 21–41, https://doi.org/10.1080/02549948.2023.2198396.
———. "The Medieval Chinese *Gāthā* and Its Relationship to Poetry." *T'oung Pao* 103 (2017): 94–154.
———. "Networks of Exchange Poetry in Late Medieval China: Notes toward a Dynamic History of Tang Literature." *Journal of Chinese Literature and Culture* 5.2 (2018): 322–59.
———. "Of Admonition and Address: Right-Hand Inscriptions (*Zuoyouming*) from Cui Yuan to Guanxiu." *Tang Studies* 38 (2020): 28–56.
———. "Righting, Riting, and Rewriting the *Book of Odes* (*Shijing*): On 'Filling out the Missing Odes' by Shu Xi." *Chinese Literature: Essays, Articles, Reviews* 40 (2018): 5–32.
Mazanec, Thomas J., and Jason Protass. "Buddhist Poetry of China." *Oxford Bibliographies* in "China Studies," ed. Tim Wright. New York: Oxford University Press, 2023. https://www.oxfordbibliographies.com/view/document/obo-9780199920082/obo-9780199920082-0202.xml.
McBride, Richard D. "Dhāraṇī and Spells in Medieval Sinitic Buddhism." *JIABS* 28.1 (2005): 85–114.
McGill, Scott. "Latin Poetry." In *The Oxford Handbook of Late Antiquity*, ed. Scott Fitzgerald Johnson, 335–60. Oxford: Oxford University Press, 2012.
McMullen, David. "Historical and Literary Theory in the Mid-Eighth Century." In Wright and Twitchett, *Perspectives on the T'ang*, 307–42.
———. *State and Scholars in T'ang China*. Cambridge: Cambridge University Press, 1988.

McNair, Amy. *The Upright Brush: Yan Zhenqing's Calligraphy and Song Literati Politics.* Honolulu: University of Hawaii Press, 1998.

McRae, John R. "Ch'an Commentaries on the *Heart Sūtra*: Preliminary Inferences on the Permutation of Chinese Buddhism." *JIABS* 11.2 (1988): 85–115.

———. *The Northern School and the Formation of Early Ch'an Buddhism.* Honolulu: University of Hawaii Press, 1986.

———. "The Story of Early Ch'an." In *Zen: Tradition and Transition*, ed. Kenneth Kraft, 125–39. New York: Grove Press, 1988.

———. *Seeing through Zen: Encounter, Transformation, and Genealogy.* Berkeley: University of California Press, 2003.

———. *The Vimalakīrti Sutra.* In Diana Y. Paul and John R. McRae, *The Sutra of Queen Śrīmālā of the Lion's Roar and the Vimalakīrti Sutra*, 59–179. BDK English Tripitaka. Berkeley: Numata Center, 2004.

Miyazaki Noriko 宮崎法子. "Sōdai butsugashi ni okeru Seiryō-ji jūroku rakanzō no ichi" 宋代仏画史に於ける清涼寺十六羅漢像の位置. *Tōhōgakuhō* 東方学報 58 (1986): 209–74.

Mollier, Christine. *Buddhism and Taoism Face to Face: Scripture, Ritual, and Iconographic Exchange in Medieval China.* Honolulu: University of Hawaii Press, 2008.

Moore, Oliver. *Rituals of Recruitment in Tang China: Reading an Annual Programme in the* Collected Statements *by Wang Dingbao (870–940).* Leiden: Brill, 2004.

Morrison, Elizabeth. *The Power of Patriarchs: Qisong and Lineage in Chinese Buddhism.* Leiden: Brill, 2010.

Muzhai 木齋. *Gushi shijiushou yu Jian'an shige yanjiu* 古詩十九首與建安詩歌研究. Beijing: Renmin chubanshe, 2009.

Nanamoli, Bhikkhu, and Bhikkhu Bodhi, trans. *The Middle Length Discourses of the Buddha: A Translation of the Majjhima Nikaya.* Somerville, Mass.: Wisdom Publications, 1995.

Nattier, Jan. "The *Heart Sūtra*: A Chinese Apocryphal Text?" *JIABS* 15.2 (1992): 153–223.

Newman, M. E. J. *Networks: An Introduction.* Oxford: Oxford University Press, 2010.

Ni, Zhange. *The Pagan Writes Back: When World Religion Meets World Literature.* Charlottesville: University of Virginia Press, 2015.

Nie Shiqiao 聶石樵. *Tangdai wenxue shi* 唐代文學史. ZHSJ, 2007.

Nielson, Thomas P. *The T'ang Poet-Monk Chiao-jan.* Tempe: Center for Asian Studies, Arizona State University, 1972.

Nishiguchi Yoshio 西口芳男. "Kankyū 'Sankyoshi' shiyakuchū (jō)" 貫休「山居詩」試譯註（上）. *Zen bunka kenkyūjo kiyō* 禅文化研究所紀要 26 (2002): 399–428.

Nugent, Christopher M. B. *Manifest in Words, Written on Paper: Producing and Circulating Poetry in Tang Dynasty China.* Cambridge, Mass.: Harvard University Asia Center, 2010.

Nylan, Michael. *The Five "Confucian" Classics.* New Haven: Yale University Press, 2001.

Ogawa Tamaki 小川環樹. *Tōshi gaisetsu* 唐詩概説. Tokyo: Iwanami shoten, 1958.

Ogunnaike, Oludamini. *Poetry in Praise of Prophetic Perfection: A Study of West African Madīḥ Poetry and Its Predecessors*. Cambridge: Islamic Texts Society, 2020.

Orzech, Charles D. "After Amoghavajra: Esoteric Buddhism in the Late Tang." In *Esoteric Buddhism and the Tantras in East Asia*, ed. Charles D. Orzech, Henrik H. Sørensen, and Richard K. Payne, 315-35. Leiden: Brill, 2010.

Owen, Stephen. "The Cultural Tang (650-1020)." In *The Cambridge History of Chinese Literature*, vol. 1, ed. Kang-i Sun Chang and Stephen Owen, 286-380. 2 vols. Cambridge: Cambridge University Press, 2010.

——. *The Great Age of Chinese Poetry: The High T'ang*. New Haven: Yale University Press, 1981.

——. "How Did Buddhism Matter in Tang Poetry?" *T'oung Pao* 103 (2017): 388-406.

——. *The Late Tang: Chinese Poetry of the Mid-Ninth Century (827–860)*. Cambridge, Mass.: Harvard University Asia Center, 2006.

——. *The Making of Early Chinese Classical Poetry*. Cambridge, Mass.: Harvard University Asia Center, 2006.

——. "Periodization and Major Inflection Points." In *The Oxford Handbook of Classical Chinese Literature (1000 BCE–900 CE)*, ed. Wiebke Denecke, Wai-Yee Li, and Xiaofei Tian, 13-23. Oxford: Oxford University Press, 2017.

——. *The Poetry of Du Fu*. Edited by Paul Kroll and Ding Xiang Warner. 6 vols. Berlin: De Gruyter, 2016.

——. *The Poetry of Meng Chiao and Han Yü*. New Haven: Yale University Press, 1975.

——. *Readings in Chinese Literary Thought*. Cambridge, Mass.: Council on East Asian Studies, 1992.

——. "Spending Time on Poetry: The Poetics of Taking Pains." In *Recarving the Dragon: Understanding Chinese Poetics*, ed. Olga Lomova, 157-78. Prague: Karolinum Press, 2003.

Pearce, Nick. "Images of Guanxiu's Sixteen Luohan in Eighteenth-Century China." *Apollo* 158.500 (2003): 25-31.

Peng Wanlong 彭萬隆. "Wudai shige yanjiu" 五代詩歌研究. In *Tang Wudai shi kaolun* 唐五代詩考論, 387-443. Hangzhou: Zhejiang daxue chubanshe, 2006.

Peng Yaling 彭雅玲. "Tangdai shiseng de chuangzuolun yanjiu: shige yu Fojiao de zonghe fenxi." *Gudian shige yanjiu huikan* 古典詩歌研究彙刊 6.9 (2009): 1-263.

Penkower, Linda. "In the Beginning . . . Guanding 灌頂 (561-632) and the Creation of Early Tiantai." *JIABS* 23.2 (2000): 245-96.

——. "T'ien-t'ai during the T'ang Dynasty: Chan-jan and the Sinification of Buddhism." PhD diss., Columbia University, 1993.

Poceski, Mario. *Ordinary Mind as the Way: The Hongzhou School and the Growth of Chan Buddhism*. Oxford: Oxford University Press, 2007.

Pollock, Sheldon. "The Cosmopolitan Vernacular." *Journal of Asian Studies* 57.1 (1998): 6-37.

Poo, Mu-chou. "Images and Ritual Treatment of Dangerous Spirits." In *Early Chinese Religion, Part Two: The Period of Division (220–589 AD)*, ed. John Lagerwey and Lü Pengzhi, 2: 1076-94. 2 vols. Leiden: Brill, 2010.

———. "Ritual and Ritual Texts in Early China." In *Early Chinese Religion, Part One: Shang through Han (1250 BC–220 AD)*, ed. John Lagerwey and Marc Kalinowski, 281–314. Leiden: Brill, 2009.
Pregadio, Fabrizio, ed. *The Encyclopedia of Taoism*. 2 vols. London: Routledge, 2008.
Prickett, Stephen. *Modernity and the Reinvention of the Tradition: Backing into the Future*. Cambridge: Cambridge University Press, 2009.
Priest, Graham. "The Logic of the *Catuskoti*." *Comparative Philosophy* 1.2 (2010): 24–54.
Protass, Jason Avi. "Buddhist Monks and Chinese Poems: Song Dynasty Monastic Literary Culture." PhD diss., Stanford University, 2016.
———. "The Flavors of Monks' Poetry: On a Witty Disparagement and Its Influences." *JAOS* 141.1 (2021): 125–50.
———. *The Poetry Demon: Song Dynasty Monks on Poetry and the Way*. Honolulu: University of Hawaii Press, 2021.
Qi Wei 祁偉. *Fojiao shanjushi yanjiu* 佛教山居詩研究. Beijing: Shangwu yinshuguan, 2014.
Qian Zhongshu 錢鍾書. *Tanyi lu (budingben)* 談藝錄（補訂本）. ZHSJ, 1993.
Rao, Xiao. "Tales of Wit and Enlightenment: Laughter and Humor in Northern Song (960–1127) China." PhD diss., Stanford University, 2019.
Red Pine. *The Mountain Poems of Stonehouse*. Port Townsend, Wash.: Copper Canyon Press, 2014.
Reiter, Florian C. "The 'Investigation Commissioner of the Nine Heavens' and the Beginning of His Cult in Northern Chiang-hsi in 731 A.D." *Oriens* 31 (1988): 266–89.
Robson, James. *Power of Place: The Religious Landscape of the Southern Sacred Peak (Nanyue* 南嶽*) in Medieval China*. Cambridge, Mass.: Harvard University Asia Center, 2009.
———. "Signs of Power: Talismanic Writing in Chinese Buddhism." *History of Religions* 48.2 (2008): 130–69.
Roth, Harold D. "Evidence for Stages of Meditation in Early Taoism." *Bulletin of the School of Oriental and African Studies* 60.2 (1997): 295–314.
Rouzer, Paul. "Early Buddhist *Kanshi*: Court, Country, and Kūkai." *Monumenta Nipponica* 59.4 (2004): 431–61.
———. *On Cold Mountain: A Buddhist Reading of the Hanshan Poems*. Seattle: University of Washington Press, 2016.
Ruegg, D. Seyfort. "The Uses of the Four Positions of the *Catuṣkoṭi* and the Problem of the Description of Reality in Mahāyāna Buddhism." *Journal of Indian Philosophy* 3.1/2 (1977): 1–71.
Ryan, Yann C., and Sebastian Ahnert. "The Measure of the Archive: Robustness of Network Analysis in Early Modern Correspondence." *Journal of Cultural Analytics* 7 (2021): 57–88.
Sasaki, Ruther Fuller. *The Record of Linji*. Edited by Thomas Yūhō Kirchner. Honolulu: University of Hawaii Press, 2009.
Schafer, Edward H. "The Last Years of Ch'ang-an." *Oriens Extremus* 10.2 (1963): 133–79.

———. "Mineral Imagery in the Paradise Poems of Kuan-hsiu." *Asia Major* n.s., 10 (1963): 73–102.

Schlütter, Morten. *How Zen Became Zen: The Dispute over Enlightenment and the Formation of Chan Buddhism in Song-Dynasty China*. Honolulu: University of Hawaii Press, 2008.

Schmidt, J. D. "Ch'an, Illusion, and Sudden Enlightenment in the Poetry of Yang Wan-li." *T'oung Pao* 60 (1974): 230–81

Schottenhammer, Angela. "Local Politico-Economic Particulars of the Quanzhou Region During the Tenth Century." *Journal of Song-Yuan Studies* 29 (1999): 1–41.

Sen, Tansen. *Buddhism, Diplomacy, and Trade: The Realignment of Sino-Indian Relations, 600–1400*. Honolulu: University of Hawaii Press, 2003.

Shang Wei. "Prisoner and Creator: The Self-Image of the Poet in Han Yu and Meng Jiao." *Chinese Literature: Essays, Articles, Reviews* 16 (1994): 19–40.

Shanzer, Danuta. "Literature, History, Periodization, and the Pleasures of the Latin Literary History of Late Antiquity." *History Compass* 7.3 (2009): 917–54.

Sharf, Robert. "Buddhist Veda and the Rise of Chan." In Bentor and Shahar, *Chinese and Tibetan Esoteric Buddhism*, 85–120.

———. *Coming to Terms with Chinese Buddhism: A Reading of the* Treasure Store Treatise. Honolulu: University of Hawaii Press, 2002.

———. "The Idolization of Enlightenment: On the Mummification of Ch'an Masters in Medieval China." *History of Religions* 32.1 (1992): 1–31.

Shi, Longdu. "Buddhism and the State in Medieval China: Case Studies of Three Persecutions of Buddhism, 444–846." PhD diss., School of Oriental and African Studies, University of London, 2016.

Shields, Anna M. *Crafting a Collection: The Cultural Contexts and Poetic Practice of the* Huajian ji *(Collection among the Flowers)*. Cambridge, Mass.: Harvard University Asia Center, 2006.

Shinohara, Koichi. *Spells, Images, and Maṇḍalas: Tracing the Evolution of Esoteric Buddhist Rituals*. New York: Columbia University Press, 2014.

———. "Stories of Miraculous Images and Paying Respect to the Three Treasures: A Discourse on Image Worship in Seventh-Century China." In *Images in Asian Religions: Texts and Contexts*, ed. Phyllis Granoff and Koichi Shinohara, 180–222. Vancouver: University of British Columbia Press, 2004.

———. "Taking a Meal at a Lay Supporter's Residence: The Evolution of the Practice in Chinese *Vinaya* Commentaries." In *Buddhist Monasticism in East Asia: Places of Practice*, ed. James A. Benn, Lori Meeks, and James Robson, 18–42. London: Routledge, 2010.

———. "Two Sources of Chinese Buddhist Biographies: Stupa Inscriptions and Miracle Stories." In *Monks and Magicians: Religious Biographies in Asia*, ed. Phyllis Granoff and Koichi Shinohara, 119–228. Oakville, Ontario: Mosaic Press, 1988.

Skar, Lowell. "Lineages." In *Encyclopedia of Taoism*, ed. Pregadio, 1:10–13.

Skonicki, Douglas. "Viewing the Two Teachings as Distinct yet Complementary: Gushan Zhiyuan's Use of Parallelisms to Demonstrate the Compatibility

of Buddhism and Ancient-Style Learning." *Journal of Chinese Religions* 38.1 (2010): 1-35.
Smith, Jonathan Z. "Religion, Religions, Religious." In *Critical Terms for Religious Studies*, ed. Mark C. Taylor, 269-84. Chicago: University of Chicago Press, 1998.
Sokolova, Anna. "Master Shanghong (738?-815 CE) and the Formation of Regional Vinaya Traditions in Tang Buddhism." *T'oung Pao* 105 (2019): 315-56.
Soliman, Tamer M. et al. "It's Not 'All in Your Head': Understanding Religion from an Embodied Cognition Perspective." *Perspectives on Psychological Science* 10.6 (2015): 852-64.
Sørensen, Henrik H. "Central Divinities in the Esoteric Buddhist Pantheon in China." In *Esoteric Buddhism and the Tantras in East Asia*, ed. Charles D. Orzech, Henrik H. Sørensen, and Richard K. Payne, 90-132. Leiden: Brill, 2010.
——. "Dunhuang Buddhist Texts in Transition: A Note on the Chan Buddhist Material in P. 2104." *BuddhistRoad Paper* 7.3 (2022): 3-22.
——. "The Meeting and Conflation of Chán and Esoteric Buddhism during the Táng." In Anderl and Wittern, *Chán Buddhism*, 329-62.
——. "The Presence of Esoteric Buddhist Elements in Chinese Buddhism during the Tang." In *Esoteric Buddhism and the Tantras in East Asia*, ed. Charles D. Orzech, Henrik H. Sørensen, and Richard K. Payne. 294-303. Leiden: Brill, 2010.
——. "The Spell of the Great, Golden Peacock Queen: The Origin, Practices, and Lore of an Early Esoteric Buddhist Tradition in China." *Pacific World*, 3rd ser., 8 (2006): 89-123.
Soymié, Michel, ed. *Catalogue des manuscrits chinois de Touen-houang (Fonds Pelliot chinois), vol. 3.* Paris: Fondation Singer-Polignac, 1983.
Stainton, Hamsa. *Poetry as Prayer in the Sanskrit Hymns of Kashmir.* Oxford: Oxford University Press, 2019.
Steavu, Dominic. "Cosmogony and the Origin of Inequality: A Utopian Perspective from Taoist Sources." *Medieval History Journal* 17.2 (2014): 295-335.
Stevenson, Daniel B. "Buddhist Practice and the *Lotus Sūtra* in China." In *Readings of the Lotus Sūtra*, ed. Stephen F. Teiser and Jacqueline I. Stone, 132-50. New York: Columbia University Press, 2009.
——. "Tales of the Lotus Sūtra." In *Buddhism in Practice: Abridged Edition*, ed. Donald S. Lopez, Jr., 311-35. Princeton: Princeton University Press, 2007.
Stimson, Hugh M. "The Sound of a Tarng Poem: 'Grieving about Greenslope,' by Duh-Fuu." *JAOS* 89.1 (1969): 59-67.
Strickmann, Michel. *Chinese Magical Medicine.* Edited by Bernard Faure. Stanford: Stanford University Press, 2002.
——. *Mantras et mandarins: le bouddhisme tantrique en Chine.* Paris: Gallimard, 1996.
——. "On the Alchemy of T'ao Hung-ching." In *Facets of Taoism: Essays in Chinese Religion*, ed. Holmes Welch and Anna Siedel, 123-92. New Haven: Yale University Press, 1979.

Strong, John S. "The Legend of the Lion-Roarer: A Study of the Buddhist Arhat Piṇḍola Bhāradvāja." *Numen* 26.1 (1979): 50–88.

Stryk, Lucien, ed. *World of the Buddha: An Introduction to Buddhist Literature*. New York: Grove Press, 1982 [1968].

Su Xuelin 蘇雪林. *Tangshi gailun* 唐詩概論. Taipei: Taiwan shangwu yinshuguan, 1958.

Sun Changwu 孫昌武. *Chansi yu shiqing (zengdingben)* 禪思與詩情（增訂本）. ZHSJ, 2006.

Sun, Jingtao [孫景濤]. "Reduplication in Old Chinese." PhD diss., University of British Columbia, 1999.

Suzuki, D. T. *Essays in Zen Buddhism: First Series*. New York: Grove Press, 1961.

Swartz, Wendy. *Reading Tao Yuanming: Shifting Paradigms of Historical Perception (427–1900)*. Cambridge, Mass.: Harvard University Press, 2008.

Tackett, Nicolas. *The Destruction of the Medieval Chinese Aristocracy*. Cambridge, Mass.: Harvard University Asia Center, 2014.

Takise Shōjun 瀧瀨尚純. "Jōkaku hasen ni giserareru futatsu no *Shittan shō*" 淨覺派撰に擬せられる二つの『悉曇章』. *Rinzai-shū Myōshin-ji ha kyōgaku kenkyū kiyō* 臨済宗妙心寺派教学研究紀要 8 (2010): 77-99.

Tanahashi, Kazuaki. *The Heart Sutra: A Comprehensive Guide to the Classic of Mahayana Buddhism*. Boston: Shambhala, 2014.

Tanaka Ryōshō 田中良昭. "Relations between the Buddhist Sects in the T'ang Dynasty through the Ms. P. 3913." *Journal Asiatique* 269.1-2 (1981): 163-69.

———. *Tonkō Zenshū Bunken no kenkyū* 敦煌禅宗文献の研究. Tokyo: Daitō shuppansha, 1983.

Tang Yiming 唐翼明. *Wei Jin qingtan* 魏晉清談. 2nd ed. Chengdu: Tiandi chubanshe, 2018.

Tao Qingmei 陶慶梅. "Tangmo shige gainian de xinbian" 唐末詩歌概念的新變. *Tang yanjiu* 唐研究 11 (2005): 205-32.

Teiser, Stephen F. "The Literary Style of Dunhuang Healing Liturgies (患文)." *Dunhuang Tulufan yanjiu* 敦煌吐魯番研究 14 (2014): 355-77.

———. "Ornamenting the Departed: Notes on the Language of Chinese Buddhist Ritual Texts." *Asia Major*, 3rd ser., 22.1 (2009): 201-37.

Tian Gengyu 田耕宇. *Tangyin yuyun: Wan-Tang shi yanjiu* 唐詩餘韻：晚唐詩研究. Chengdu: Ba-Shu shushe, 2001.

Tian, Xiaofei. *Beacon Fire and Shooting Star: The Literary Culture of the Liang (502–557)*. Cambridge, Mass.: Harvard University Asia Center, 2007.

———. *The Halberd at Red Cliff: Jian'an and the Three Kingdoms*. Cambridge, Mass.: Harvard University Asia Center, 2018.

———. "Illusion and Illumination: A New Poetics of Seeing in Liang Dynasty Court Culture." *HJAS* 65.1 (2005): 7–56.

———. "Seeing with the Mind's Eye: The Eastern Jin Discourse of Visualization and Imagination." *Asia Major*, 3rd ser., 18.2 (2005): 67–102.

Tolkien, J. R. R. "On Fairy-Stories." In Dorothy Sayers et al., *Essays Presented to Charles Williams*. Grand Rapids, Mich.: Eerdmans, 1947.

Tosaki Tetsuhiko 戶崎哲彥. "*Hōrinden* no josha Reitetsu to shisō Reitetsu" 寶林傳の序者靈徹と詩僧靈澈. *Bukkyōshigaku kenkyū* 佛教史學研究 30.2 (1987): 28-55.

Twitchett, Denis. "Hsüan-tsung (reign 712–56)." In *The Cambridge History of China, Volume 3: Sui and T'ang China, 589–906*, 333–463. Cambridge: Cambridge University Press, 1979.

—. "The Seamy Side of Late T'ang Political Life: Yü Ti and His Family." *Asia Major*, 3rd ser., 1.2 (1988): 29–63.

US Bureau of Labor Statistics. "Employment and Earnings Online." January 2011, March 2011. http://www.bls.gov/opub/ee/home.htm; http://www.bls.gov/cps/home.htm.

US Census Bureau. "Households and Families: 2010." 2010 Census Briefs, April 2012.

Van Gulik, Robert. *Siddham: An Essay on the History of Sanskrit Studies in China and Japan*. Nagpur: International Academy of Indian Culture, 1956.

Van Zoeren, Steven. *Poetry and Personality: Readings, Exegesis, and Hermeneutics in Traditional China*. Stanford: Stanford University Press, 1991.

Verellen, Franciscus. *Du Guangting (850–933), taoïste de cour a la fin de la Chine médiévale*. Paris: De Boccard, 1989.

—. *Imperiled Destinies: The Daoist Quest for Deliverance in Medieval China*. Cambridge, Mass.: Harvard University Asia Center, 2019.

Versnel, H. S. "The Poetics of the Magical Charm: An Essay in the Power of Words." In *Magic and Ritual in the Ancient World*, ed. Paul Mirecki and Marvin Meyer, 105–58. Leiden: Brill, 2002.

Wagner, Marsha. *The Lotus Boat: The Origins of Chinese Tz'u Poetry in T'ang Popular Culture*. New York: Columbia University Press, 1984.

Wah, Wong Yoon. *Ssu-K'ung Tu: A Poet-Critic of the T'ang*. Hong Kong: Chinese University of Hong Kong, 1976.

Wang, Ao. *Spatial Imaginaries in Mid-Tang China: Geography, Cartography, and Literature*. Amherst, N.Y.: Cambria Press, 2018.

Wang, Eugene. *Shaping the Lotus Sutra: Buddhist Visual Culture in Medieval China*. Seattle: University of Washington Press, 2005.

Wang, Hongjie. *Power and Politics in Tenth-Century China: The Former Shu Regime*. Amherst, N.Y.: Cambria Press, 2011.

Wang Li 王力. *Hanyu shilüxue* 漢語詩律學. In *Wang Li quanji* 王力全集, vol. 17. ZHSJ, 2015.

Wang Xiaodun 王小盾. "'Xinglunan' yu Wei-Jin Nanbeichao de shuochang yishu" 《行路難》與魏晉南北朝說唱藝術. *Qinghua daxue xuebao (shehui kexue ban)* 清华大學學报 (社會科學版) 17 (2002): 9–13.

Wang Xiulin 王秀林. *Wan-Tang Wudai shiseng qunti yanjiu* 晚唐五代詩僧群體研究. ZHSJ, 2008.

Wang, Youru. "Philosophical Interpretations of Hongzhou Chan Buddhist Thought." In *Dao Companion to Chinese Buddhist Philosophy*, ed. Youru Wang and Sandra A. Wawrytko, 369–98. Dordrecht: Springer, 2018.

Wang Yuanjun 王元軍. *Tangdai shufa yu wenhua* 唐代書法與文化. Beijing: Zhongguo dabaike quanshu chubanshe, 2008.

—. *Tangren shufa yu wenhua* 唐人書法與文化. Taipei: Dongda tushu gongsi, 2008.

Wang, Yugen. "*Shige*: The Popular Poetics of Regulated Verse." *T'ang Studies* 22 (2004): 81–125.

Wang Zaojuan 王早娟. *Tangdai Chang'an fojiao wenxue* 唐代長安佛教文學. Beijing: Shangwu yinshuguan, 2013.

Wang Zhaopeng and Qiao Junjun. "Geographic Distribution and Change in Tang Poetry: Analysis from the 'Chronological Map of Tang-Song Literature.'" Translated by Thomas J. Mazanec. *Journal of Chinese Literature and Culture* 5.2 (2018): 360–74.

Watson, Burton. "Buddhism in the Poetry of Po Chü-i." *Eastern Buddhist* 21.1 (1988): 1–22.

—. "Buddhist Poet-Priests of the T'ang." *Eastern Buddhist*, n.s., 25.2 (1992): 30–58.

—. *The Columbia Book of Chinese Poetry: From Early Times to the Thirteenth Century*. New York: Columbia University Press, 1984.

Wei Daoru 魏道儒. *Zhongguo Huayanzong tongshi* 中國華嚴宗通史. Nanjing: Jiangsu guji chubanshe, 1998.

Weinstein, Stanley. *Buddhism under the T'ang*. Cambridge: Cambridge University Press, 1987.

Welsh, Andrew. *Roots of Lyric: Primitive Poetry and Modern Poetics*. Princeton: Princeton University Press, 1978.

Welter, Albert. *Monks, Rulers, and Literati: The Political Ascendancy of Chan Buddhism*. Oxford: Oxford University Press, 2006.

Wen Yiduo 聞一多. *Tangshi zalun* 唐詩雜論. ZHSJ, 2009.

Williams, Nicholas Morrow. "Beyond Arbitrariness: Kūkai's Theory of Languages and Scripts." *Journal of the Pacific Association for the Continental Tradition* 4 (2021): 77–94.

—. "A Conversation in Poems: Xie Lingyun, Xie Huilian, and Jiang Yan." *JAOS* 127.4 (2007): 491–506.

—. *Imitations of the Self: Jiang Yan and Chinese Poetics*. Leiden: Brill, 2015.

—. "The Metaphysical Lyric of the Six Dynasties." *T'oung Pao* 98 (2012): 65–112.

—. "Quasi-Phantasmal Flowers: An Aspect of Wang Wei's Mahāyāna Poetics." *Chinese Literature: Essays, Articles, Reviews* 39 (2017): 27–54.

—. "The Taste of the Ocean: Jiaoran's Theory of Poetry." *Tang Studies* 31 (2013): 1–27.

Witzling, Catherine Anne. "The Poetry of Chia Tao (779–843): A Re-examination of Critical Stereotypes." PhD diss., Stanford University, 1980.

Wolf, Mark J. P. *Building Imaginary Worlds: The Theory and History of Subcreation*. New York: Routledge, 2012.

Wong, Kwok-yiu [王國堯]. "The Mid-Tang Scholar-Monk Shenqing and His *Beishan lu*." *Monumenta Serica* 63.1 (2015): 32–78.

Worthy, Edmund H., Jr. "Diplomacy for Survival: Domestic and Foreign Relations of Wu Yüeh, 907–978." In *China among Equals: The Middle Kingdom and Its Neighbors, 10th–14th Centuries*, ed. Morris Rossabi, 17–44. Berkeley: University of California Press, 1983.

Wright, Arthur F., and Denis Twitchett, eds. *Perspectives on the T'ang*. New Haven: Yale University Press, 1973

Wu, Chi-yu [吳其昱]. "Trois poèmes inédits de Kouan-hieou." *Journal Asiatique* 247 (1959): 349–78.

Wu, Fusheng. *The Poetics of Decadence: Chinese Poetry of the Southern Dynasties and Late Tang Periods*. Albany: State University of New York Press, 1998.

Wu Hung. "Buddhist Elements in Early Chinese Art (2nd and 3rd Centuries A.D.)." *Artibus Asiae* 47.3/4 (1986): 263-352.

Wu Xianlin 伍先林. "Wei-Yangzong de Chanxue sixiang" 溈仰宗的禪學思想. *Shijie zongjiao yanjiu* 世界宗教研究 2014, no. 3: 52-60.

Wu Yansheng [吳言生]. *The Power of Enlightenment: Chinese Zen Poems*. Translated by Tony Blishen. New York: Better Link Press, 2014.

Wu Zaiqing 吳在慶. "Lüelun Tangdai de kuyin shifeng" 略論唐代的苦吟詩風. *Wenxue yichan* 文學遺產 2002, no. 4: 29-40.

Xiang Chu 項楚. *Dunhuang geci zongbian huibu* 敦煌歌辭總編匡補. Taipei: Xinwenfeng chuban gongsi, 1995.

Xiao Chi 蕭馳. *Fofa yu shijing* 佛法與詩境. ZHSJ, 2005.

Xiong, Victor Cunrui. *Sui-Tang Chang'an: A Study in the Urban History of Medieval China*. Ann Arbor: Center for Chinese Studies, 2000.

Xu Lejun 徐樂軍. *Wan-Tang wenren shijin xintai yanjiu* 晚唐文人仕進心態研究. Beijing: Shehuikexue wenxian chubanshe, 2014.

Xu Zong 許總. *Tang shi shi* 唐詩史. 2 vols. Nanjing: Jiangsu jiaoyu chubanshe, 1994.

Xue Tianwei 薛天緯. *Tangdai gexing lun* 唐代歌行論. Beijing: Renmin wenxue chubanshe, 2006.

Yamamoto, Kōshō. *The Mahayana Mahaparinirvana Sutra*. Edited by Tony Page. New York: Nirvana Publications, 2007.

Yampolsky, Philip, trans. *The Platform Sutra of the Sixth Patriarch: The Text of the Tunhuang Manuscript*. New York: Columbia University Press, 1967.

Yanagida Seizan 柳田聖山. *Shoki zenshū shisho no kenkyū* 初期禅宗史書の研究, Kyoto: Hōzōkan, 1967. Reprinted in *Yanagida Seizan shū* 柳田聖山集 vol. 6, Kyoto: Hōzōkan, 2000.

Yang Fenxia 楊芬霞. *Zhong Tang shiseng yanjiu* 中唐詩僧研究. Beijing: Zhongguo shehui kexue chubanshe, 2019.

Yang Jidong. "Zhang Yichao and Dunhuang in the 9th Century." *Journal of Asian History* 32.2 (1998): 97-144.

Yang, Jingqing. *The Chan Interpretations of Wang Wei's Poetry: A Critical Review*. Hong Kong: Chinese University of Hong Kong Press, 2007.

Yang, Shao-yun. *The Way of the Barbarians: Redrawing Ethnic Boundaries in Tang and Song China*. Seattle: University of Washington Press, 2019.

Yang, Xiaoshan. *Wang Anshi and Song Poetic Culture*. Cambridge, Mass.: Harvard University Asia Center, 2021.

Yang Xin 楊新. *Wudai Guanxiu luohan tu* 五代貫休羅漢圖. Beijing: Wenwu chubanshe, 2008.

Yang Zhifei 楊志飛. *Song gaoseng zhuan yanjiu* 宋高僧傳研究. Chengdu: Ba-Shu shushe, 2016.

Yates, Robin D. S. *Washing Silk: The Life and Selected Poetry of Wei Chuang (834?-910)*. Cambridge, Mass.: Council on East Asian Studies, 1988.

Yifa. *The Origins of Buddhist Monastic Codes in China: An Annotated Translation and Study of the* Chanyuan Qinggui. Honolulu: University of Hawaii Press, 2002.

Yin Chubin 尹楚彬. "Hu-Xiang shiseng Qiji yu Wei-Yangzong" 湖湘詩僧齊己與溈仰宗. *Hunan daxue xuebao (Shehui kexue ban)* 湖南大學學報（社會科學版）15.4 (2001): 22–27.

Yoshikawa Kōjirō 吉川幸次郎. *Chūgoku bungakushi* 中國文學史. Tokyo: Iwanami shoten, 1974.

Yoshimura Shūki 芳村修基. "Chōshin kōronan zankan kō" 徵心行路難殘卷考. In *Seiki bunka kenkyū: Tonkō Bukkyō shiryō* 西域文化研究第一：敦煌佛教資料, 187–196. Kyoto: Hozōkan, 1958.

Yu, Anthony C. *Comparative Journeys: Essays on Literature and Religion East and West*. New York: Columbia University Press, 2009.

Yü, Chun-fang. *Kuan-yin: The Chinese Transformation of Avalokiteśvara*. New York: Columbia University Press, 2001.

Zach, Erwin von. *Han Yu's Poetische Werke*. Cambridge, Mass.: Harvard University Press, 1952.

Zha Minghao 查明昊. *Zhuanxingzhong de Tang Wudai shiseng qunti* 轉型中的唐五代詩僧群體. Shanghai: Huadong shifan daxue chubanshe, 2008.

Zhang Bowei 張伯偉. *Chan yu shixue (zengdingben)* 禪與詩學（增訂本）. Beijing: Renmin wenxue chubanshe, 2008.

Zhang Chengdong 張承東. "Shilun Dunhuang xieben zhaiwen de pianwen tese" 試論敦煌寫本齋文的駢文特色. *Dunhuangxue jikan* 敦煌學輯刊 2003, no. 1: 92–102.

Zhang Jing 張晶. "Jiaoran shilun yu Fojiao de Zhongdao guan" 皎然詩論與佛教的中道觀. *Wenxue yichan* 6 (2007): 107–16.

Zhang Peifeng 張培鋒. *Fojiao yu chuantong yinchang de wenhuaxue kaocha* 佛教與傳統吟唱的文化學考察. Tianjin: Tianjin jiaoyu chubanshe, 2016.

Zhang Peiheng 章培恒 and Luo Yuming 駱玉明. *Zhongguo wenxue shi xinzhu* 中國文學史新著. 3 vols. Shanghai: Fudan daxue chubanshe, 2007.

Zhang Xingwu 張興武. *Wudai zuojia de renge yu shige* 五代作家的人格與詩格. Beijing: Renmin wenxue chubanshe, 2000.

Zhang Xingwu and Wang Xiaolan 王小蘭. *Tang-Song shiwen yishu de jianbian yu zhuanxing* 唐宋詩文藝術的漸變與轉型. Beijing: Zhongguo shehui kexue chubanshe, 2014.

Zhang Yong 張勇. *Beiye yu yanghua: Zhongguo Chanxue de shixing jingshen* 貝葉與楊花：中國禪學的詩性精神. ZHSJ, 2016.

Zhang Zhenying 张震英. *Hanshi de diyin: Jia Dao shige yishu xintan* 寒士的低吟—賈島詩歌藝術新探. Beijing: Zhongguo shehuikexue chubanshe, 2006.

Zhao Changping 趙昌平. *Zhao Changping zixuanji* 趙昌平自選集. Guilin: Guangxi shifan daxue chubanshe, 1997.

Zheng Acai 鄭阿財. *Dunhuang Fojiao wenxian yu wenxue yanjiu* 敦煌佛教文獻與文學研究. SHGJ, 2011.

Zhou Guangrong 周廣榮. "Dunhuang *Xitanzhang* geci yuanliu kaolüe" 敦煌《悉昙章》歌辭源流考略. *Dunhuang yanjiu* 敦煌研究 67 (2001): 141–50.

Zhou Xunchu 周勛初, Mo Lifeng 莫礪鋒, and Yan Jie 嚴傑. *Tangshi dacidian* 唐詩大辭典. Nanjing: Fenghuang chubanshe, 2003.

Zhou Yukai 周裕鍇. "Jia Dao ge shige yu Chanzong guanxi zhi yanjiu" 賈島格詩歌與禪宗關係之研究. In *Shibian yu chuanghua: Han-Tang, Tang-Song*

zhuanhuanqi zhi wenyi xianxiang 世變與創化: 漢唐, 唐宋轉換期之文藝現象, ed. Lo-fen I 衣若芬 and Liu Yuanru 劉苑如, 425-58. Taipei: Zhongyang yanjiuyuan Zhongguo wenzhe yanjiusuo choubeichu, 2000.
—. *Wenzi chan yu Songdai shixue* 文字禪與宋代詩學. Beijing: Gaodeng jiaoyu chubanshe, 1998.
—. *Zhongguo Chanzong yu shige* 中國禪宗與詩歌. Shanghai: Shanghai renmin chubanshe, 1992.
Zhu Gang 朱剛. *Tang–Song "guwen yundong" yu shidafu wenxue* 唐宋「古文運動」與士大夫文學. Shanghai: Fudan daxue chubanshe, 2013.
Zhu Zihui 朱子輝. *Tangshi yuyanxue piping yanjiu* 唐詩語言學批評研究. Guilin: Guangxi shifan daxue chubanshe, 2016.
Zieme, Peter. "The Old Uighur Translation of the *Siddhaṃ Songs*." In Anderl and Wittern, *Chán Buddhism*, 143-93.
Ziporyn, Brook. *Zhuangzi: The Essential Writings*. Indianapolis: Hackett, 2009.
Zürcher, Erik. "Buddhism and Education in Tang Times." In *Neo-Confucian Education: The Formative Stage*, ed. William Theodore de Bary et al., 19-56. Berkeley: University of California Press, 1989.
—. *The Buddhist Conquest of China: The Spread and Adaptation of Buddhism in Early Medieval China*. 3rd ed. Leiden: Brill, 2007.

Index

absorption, ideal of, 197-199, 205-206
Accounts of Propagation and Praise of the Lotus Sūtra (*Hongzan fahua zhuan*; Huixiang), 262n7
Accounts on the Transmission of the Lotus Sūtra (*Fahua jing zhuanji*; Sengxiang), 262n7
"After 'Ballad of the Bitter Cold'" (*Ni kuhan xing*; Guanxiu), 124-126, 259n35
Āgamas, 131
alliterative binom parallelism, 117, 134-135
allusions, aversion to, 196
Amitābha Buddha, 23
Amoghavajra, 164, 178
An Lushan Rebellion, 23, 24, 25, 50, 56, 108
An Shigao, 278n26
anadiplosis, 124, 126, 141
anadiplotic retriplication, 121, 124-126
anapasati, 278n26
anātman, 128
Anderl, Christoph, 269n91
apophasis/apophatic approach, 114, 128, 129, 130-132, 135, 139, 142, 214
arcane studies (*xuanxue*), 6, 23
arhat paintings, 170-172, 171*fig*, 184
Aśvagoṣa, 104
Autumn Light of Recent-Style Poetry (*Jinti qiuyang*), 221
Awakening of Mahāyāna Faith (*Dasheng qixin lun*; Aśvagoṣa), 104, 105, 107, 174, 192

Bai Juyi, 9, 28, 74-76, 79, 91, 98, 99, 116, 129-130, 232n34
Baizhang Huaihai, 282n88
Bao Ji, 42, 64-65
Bao Zhao, 71
Baoyue, 5-6, 22, 66, 67, 104

Baozhi, 116
Barrett, T. H., 234n53
Beimeng suoyan (Sun Guangxian), 98
Bender, Lucas, 232n36
Benjing, 148
betweenness, 40-42, 41*t*
biographical texts, 49-52
Biographies of Eminent Monks (*Gaoseng zhuan*; Huijiao), 262n6
blandness, 240-241n81
Book of Odes (*Shijing*)
  anadiplotic retriplication and, 124
  AXAY pattern in, 257n17
  double drafting (*shuangni*) and, 119
  Elegantiae and, 161
  "Great Preface" to, 201
  Hymns of Zhou and, 210-211
  light imagery in, 252n44
  Lotus Sūtra contrasted with, 143
  moral purity of, 206
  poetic perfection and, 204
  reduplication and, 117
  shi and, 48
  Way of poetry and, 97
  zouyu in, 89
Book of Rites (*Liji*), 57, 282n86
borderline letters (*jiepan zi*), 167
Borges, Jorge Luis, 207
Bourdieu, Pierre, 232n38
Brāhmī script, 164, 168, 184
Brose, Benjamin, 250n20
Buddhists/Buddhism
  Chan, 22-23, 55-56, 64, 102-103, 185, 213, 216-217
  double drafting (*shuangni*) and, 119
  Guanxiu and, 163
  Han Yu on, 69-70
  in Jiangnan, 23-24
  Jiaoran on, 61-62
  negation and, 130-131
  persecution and, 85-86

INDEX

Buddhists/Buddhism (*continued*)
  poetry of, 4–6
  reception of poet-monks and, 73–77, 215–219
  restoration of, 90
  retriplication and, 116–117
  Right Man (*Zhengren*) and, 2–3
  scriptures and, 143–144
  spells and, 143
  spread of, 21–22
Bunkyō hifuron (Kūkai), 153–155, 198–199

caesura violation, 142, 156
Cai Jing, 101
calligraphy, 272–273n134
Company, Robert, 13
Canglang shihua (Yan Yu), 220, 249n6
Cao Pi, 287n24
catuṣkoṭi (*siju*), 131, 133–134, 135–137, 138–139, 142
centrality, measures of, 40–42, 41t
Chan Buddhism, 22–23, 55–56, 64, 102–103, 185, 213, 216–217
Chan Interpretations of Wang Wei's Poetry (Yang Jingqing), 234n54
Chang'an, 28–30, 82, 108
Chau, Adam Yuet, 12
Chen Lin, 126
Chen Shidao, 224–225
Chen Tao, 88–89, 90, 101
Chengdu, 29, 34
"Cherishing Intoning" (*Ai yin*; Qiji), 194–195
chin couplet (*hanlian*), 131–132
Chumo, 105
ci poetry, 34
Collected Poetry of Three Eminent Monks of the Tang, The (*Tang san gaoseng shiji*), 220
Collection among the Flowers (*Huajian ji*), 34
Collection of Ministerial Spirit from the Restoration (*Zhongxing jianqi ji*; Gao Zhongwu), 49, 53–55
Collection of Tang Monks' Extensive Flowers (*Tangseng hongxiu ji*), 220
Columbia Book of Chinese Poetry (Watson), 230n12
Columbia History of Chinese Literature, 7
complex retriplication, 121, 122–124, 126, 127
Confidential Matters of the Way of Elegantiae (*Yadao jiyao*; Xu Yin), 187, 257n17
Confucian classicism, 2–3

Confucians, 69–71, 91
Confucius, 51–52
creation/creator, 57–58, 78, 79–80
cross-regulation, 160, 162
Cui Rong, 117
Cui Tu, 192

Dai Shulun, 242n19
Dao'an, 65, 71
Daobao, 74
Daodejing, 128
Daoism, 2–3, 6, 24, 32, 128
Daoqian, 6, 224–225
Daozong, 74–76, 80
decentralization of power, 108
devotion to poetry, 191–192, 197
dhāraṇī, 152, 157, 159, 173–174, 183, 184
dhāraṇī pillars, 143, 152–153
Dhāraṇī Sūtra of the Great Protectress (*Dasuiqiu tuoluoni jing*), 157, 159
Dhāraṇī Sūtra of the Jeweled Pavilion (*Baolouge jing*), 157, 159
Dharmatara-dhyāna sūtra (*Damoduoluo chan jing*), 285n111
Dianlun lunwen (Cao Pi), 287n24
"Digest of the Essentials of Meditation" (*Chanmen biyao jue*), 148
digital tools, 9
Dinghui, 164
doctrinal esoterica, 161
Donglin monastery, 23, 95–96, 169
double drafting (*shuangni*), 117, 119, 129, 138, 176
Du Fu, 232n36, 253n59
Du Guangting, 34, 257n10
Du Mu, 8
Du Songbo, 277n6
Du Xunhe, 191–192, 257n18
Duan Shuangxi, 119, 232n34, 257n18
Dugu Ji, 42, 49–53, 55, 56, 85, 93
Dunhuang manuscripts, 4, 116, 139–141, 144, 178, 215
Dushun, 107, 261n71

Elegantiae (*Ya*), 161
elite poetry (*shi*), 5, 9, 12, 37, 48, 69
emptiness, nature of/śūnyata, 128, 130, 131
End of Tang (*Tangmo*), 7–8, 26, 34
enlightenment, 22, 87, 107, 143, 167, 186, 190, 193, 201–202, 206, 211, 212
Ennin, 161
"Essay on Seeing Off the Venerable Lingche Back to Wozhou from

INDEX   319

Mount Lu" (Song Lingche shangren Lushan huigui Wozhou xu; Quan Deyu), 66–68
"Essay on the Occasion of Seeing off Canliao" (Song Canliao xu; Chen Shidao), 225
Essential Forms of Poetry (Fengsao yaoshi; Xu Yan), 229n4
Essential Stories of the Old Masters, Continued (Xu gu zunsu yuyao), 217
exchange poetry, 36–42, 37–38t, 39fig, 40fig, 41t, 45fig, 64, 90
Exemplary Models of Poetry (Fengsao zhige; Qiji), 119, 187, 229n4
"Explaining Intoning" (Yu yin; Qiji), 203–204

Fachong, 173–174
"Facing the Moon on the Fifteenth Night of the Gengwu Year [March 4, 910]" (Gengwu nian shiwu ye dui yue; Qiji), 221–222
Fan Tai, 77, 248n83
Fang Gan, 119, 120
Fangguang bore jing, 258n34
Fangji, 71–72, 74, 80
Fashen, 50
Faxian, 164
Fazang, 107
Fazhen, 78
field of production, 232n38
Five Dynasties and Ten Kingdoms (Wudai shiguo), 7–8, 26, 34
foreignness, 144–145, 162–172
Foulk, T. Griffith, 235n9
four alternative positions/fourfold negation, 131, 133–134, 135–137, 138–139, 142
Foyin Liaoyuan, 218–219
"Preface to the Venerable Shangyan's Literary Collection" (Yan shangren ji xu; Li Tong), 93–94
"Preface to the Venerable Shangyan's Literary Collection" (Yan shangren ji xu; Yan Rao), 90–92
Frye, Northrop, 151–152
Fu Xuancong, 26
Fuller, Michael, 233n49
Fuzhou, 34–35

Gao Zhongwu, 49, 53–55
gate metaphor, 205
gāthā (ji), 77, 148

"Gāthās on the Nature of the Way" (Daoqing ji; Guanxiu), 134–135
"Given to an Itinerant Monk" (Zeng xingjiao seng; Dai Shulun), 242n19
"Given to Master Guangxuan" (Zeng Xuan dashi; Li Yi), 86–87
"Given to the Lotus Sūtra-Minding Monk" (Zeng nian Fahuajing seng; Qiji), 179–184
"Given to Tripiṭaka Zhiman" (Zeng Zhiman sanzang; Qiji), 155–156
gold, daily consumption of, 178–179
Goodman, Amanda, 275n163, 275n164
"Great Elegantiae" (Daya), 229n4
Great Sūtra on Minding Inhalation and Exhalation (Da anban shouyi jing), 278n26
Great Wisdom Śāstra (Da zhidu lun), 236n14, 247n70
Gu Kuang, 42
Gu Yanwu, 265n42
Gu Yun, 253n59
Guanding, 135–137
Guangbai, 10
Guangxuan, 28, 29, 86–87, 89
Guanxiu
    in anthologies, 220
    arhat paintings of, 170–172, 171fig, 184
    double drafting (shuangni) and, 119, 129
    exchange poetry and, 36, 38, 40, 41, 42
    foreignness and, 162–165, 168–172
    growth in number of poet-monks and, 33
    identity of poet-monks and, 103–105
    imitation of, 215
    incantation and, 144
    influence of, 10–11
    innovation of, 8
    kuyin aesthetic and, 193–194
    Lotus Sūtra and, 145–148, 150, 152, 176–179
    meditation and, 186
    mobility and, 44, 46
    negation and, 128–129, 130, 134–135, 137–139
    old-style poetry and, 12
    productivity of, 4
    Qiji on, 196
    reception and, 217, 218–219
    repetition and, 114–116, 120, 121, 141
    reputation of, 222–226

INDEX

Guanxiu (*continued*)
   retriplication and, 121–122, 124–126
   Sanskrit words and, 156–157
   on sense of the divine, 3
   spells and, 149*fig*, 157–162
   Sun Guangxian on, 201
   tradition of poet-monks and, 97–102, 108
   use of "poet-monk" by, 82–83
   Wang Jian and, 34
Guillén, Claudio, 232n38
Guiren, 278n36
Gushan Zhiyuan, 286n12
guwen movement, 219–220, 225

Han Yu, 24, 58, 69–70, 83, 145, 194, 279n48
Handmirror of Streams and Categories (*Liulei shoujian*; Xuzhong), 187
Hangzhou, 34
Hanlin Academy, 24
Hanshan, 4, 9, 230n15
hardship, 207
He Chang, 222–223
"Hearing that the True Body has been Received" (*Wen ying zhenshen*; Guanxiu), 156–157
Heart Sūtra, 129–130
High and Mid-Tang, 26
Hongju, 200
Hongren, 95–96, 192–193, 208
Hongshi, 160–162
Hongyan, 89
Hongyi, 159
Hongzhi Zhengjue, 36
Hongzhou, 29, 34–35, 201–202, 213
Hongzhou lineage, 25
Hsiao Li-hua, 277n9
Hu Zhenheng, 286n6
Hu Zi, 222
Huaichu, 96
Huainanzi, 259n37
Huaipu, 154–155
Huaisu, 254n74
Huang Chao Rebellion, 26, 30, 32, 35, 94, 109, 114–115
Huangfu Ran, 42, 54
Huangfu Zeng, 42
Huanzhong, 164
Huayan teachings, 107
Huibao, 216
Huida, 56
Huiguo, 152, 153
Huihong, 6, 216
Huijiao, 262n6

Huilin, 72–73, 74
Huineng, 95–96, 135, 242n19
Huixian, 202
Huixiang, 262n7
Huixiu, 5–6, 71, 72–73, 74, 76, 77, 79, 231n21
Huiyuan, 5, 6, 22, 23, 65, 66, 67, 71
Huiyue, 77
Huzhou, 56
Hymns of Zhou (*Zhou song*), 210–211

"I Watered My Horse by the Great Wall Caves" (*Yin ma changcheng ku xing*; Chen Lin), 126
i-graph, 168, 170, 184
"In Exile in Tingzhou" (*Zhe Tingzhou*; Lingche), 78
"In Praise of the *Lotus Sūtra*-Reciting Monk" (*Zan nian Fahuajing seng*; Guanxiu), 145–148, 150, 152
incantation
   characteristics of, 144
   defined, 144
   efficacy of, 150
   foreignness and, 114, 162–172
   impact of, 214
   introduction to, 143–145
   Lotus Sūtra and, 172–184
   sonority and, 114, 151–162
   spells and scripture and, 145–151
"independent enlightenment" (*duwu*), 242n24
India, 162–164, 170, 183, 184
ingested spells, 273n137
inner and outer meanings, 133
"Inscribed on the Temple of Reverend Hongshi and Shown to Commissioned Lord Du" (*Ti Hongshi heshang yuan jian cheng Du shijun*; Guanxiu), 160–162
"Inscription for the Pagoda of the Former Yinaya Master Lingyi of Qingyun Monastery in Yangzhou of the Tang (with preface)" (*Tang gu Yangzhou Qingyun si lüshi Yi gong taming bing xu*; Dugu Ji), 49–53, 55
"Inscription on Seated Meditation" (*Zuochan ming*), 148
Introduction to the Methods of Contemplation (*Siwei lüeyaofa*), 254n68

Japanese Esoteric Buddhism (Shingon), 153
Ji Yun, 221
Jia Dao

absorption and, 89–90
Guanxiu on, 193–194
kuyin aesthetic and, 83–84, 96, 186–187, 189–190, 192, 212, 213, 219
as monk, 38, 152
Yao He and, 199–200
Zhou He and, 104
Jia Dao's Secret Exemplars of Poetry Standards (Jia Dao shige mizhi), 277n14
Jia Jinhua, 55–56, 242n24
Jianfu monastery, 43
Jiang Yan, 50, 51, 76, 231n21
Jiangnan, 23–24, 26–28, 30, 32
Jiaoran
  in anthologies, 220
  attention due to, 4
  first generation of poet-monks' reception and, 48
  Guanxiu on, 103–104, 255n83
  hardship and, 207
  Lingche and, 78
  main discussion of, 55–66
  meditation and, 186
  number of poems written by, 10–11
  "outside the lines" (*fangwai*) and, 52
  Qiji and, 197
  reputation of, 28, 42, 69, 79–80
  Sun Guangxian on, 98–99
  use of "poet-monk" by, 20–21
  Wu Yun and, 24
  Xie Lingyun and, 239n62
jing (poem-world), 99
Jingde Lamp Transmission Records (Jingde chuandenglu), 102
Jorgensen, John, 277n7
Judun, 148

Kant, Immanuel, 233n49
karmic connection (*yeyuan*), 98–99
karmic traces, literary activity and, 62–63
Kepeng, 216
Kōchū Tōshi kaishaku jiten (Matsuura), 230n12
Kūkai, 116, 152, 153–154, 198–199, 262n78, 266n62
Kumārajīva, 167, 259n41
"Kuyin" (Du Xunhe), 191–192
kuyin aesthetic, 83–84, 89, 96, 104, 121, 186–197, 199–200, 202–203, 205–209, 212–213, 219–220, 223

Lai Peng, 249n14
Lalitavistara Sūtra (*Puyao jing*), 164

lamp-transmission records (*chuandeng lu*), 102
landscape descriptions, 55, 58–60, 138
landscape poetry, 22
language instruction, 153–154
Laṅkāvatāra Sūtra (*Lengqie jing*), 165
Late Tang (*Wan Tang*), 26
Late Tang, The (Owen), 7
lettered Chan (*wenzi Chan*), 6
Li Bai, 98, 101, 219, 253n59, 263n11
Li Dingguang, 257n11
Li Dong, 38, 187
Li Gong, 220
Li He, 97, 101, 219–220
Li Hong, 247n72
Li Jiangfeng, 232n36, 260n59
Li Qunyu, 42
Li Shangyin, 8, 28, 153, 254n71
Li Shu, 42, 62–63
Li Tong, 92–94
Li Xianyong, 100–102, 105
Li Yi, 86–87
Li Zhao, 28, 69
Liezi, 251n36
lineage transmission, 94–97
Lingche, 28, 42, 48, 64–69, 77–78, 80, 84, 93, 119, 200
Lingye, 56
Lingyi, 28, 42, 48, 49–55, 56, 69, 79, 80, 93, 98–99
Lingyou, 107, 282n88
linked verses (*lianju*), 56
literal versus symbolic meaning, 133
literary history, overview of Chinese, 6–11
literati readers, 219–226
literature
  defined, 12
  religion and, 11–14
  renewed attention to, 24
Liu Bang, 138
Liu Deren, 119, 153, 188–189, 193–194, 279n49, 279n50
Liu Ning, 255n75
Liu Shaoyu, 191
Liu Ying, 231n18
Liu Yuxi, 42, 77–79, 91, 95, 98, 105, 200–201, 220, 280n56
Liu Zongyuan, 69, 71–72, 73, 74, 79, 91
Liu-Song dynasty, 73
Liying Kuo, 275n164
localization, 26
Longhua ji (Tanyu), 255n88
"Looking for the Venerable Tripiṭ aka" (*Xun sanzang shangren*; Wu Yuanheng), 266n56

"Looking over the Poetry Collections of Jiaoran and Nanqing" (*Lan Jiaoran Nanqing ji*; Guanxiu), 103–104
Lotus Sūtra (*Miaofa lianhua jing*), 104, 143–144, 145–148, 150, 152, 157, 172–184, 254n68
"Lotuses at Yuanxin Monastery" (*Furong Yuanxin si*; Lingche), 78
Lü Dongbin, 257n9, 262n79
Lu, Hui-Wen, 272–273n134
Lu Ji, 93, 198, 199, 204, 212, 213, 245n54
Lü Shang, 85
Lu Tong, 221
Lü Wen, 70
Lu You, 7
Luo Binwang, 257n9
Luo Yin, 44

Ma Yi, 221
"Mad Inscriptions" (*Kuang ti*, Sikong Tu), 32–33
Madhyamaka, 56
Mahāparinirvāṇa Sūtra (*Niepan jing*), 133–134, 135, 150–151, 168
Mahāprajñāpāramitā Sūtra (*Da bore boluomiduo jing*), 261n76
Mahāyāna teachings, 56, 87, 107, 131, 165
Maitreya, 274n149
maṇḍala rites, 178–179
Mañjuśrī, 163
mantra, 152
Mao Jin, 220
Māra, 195
Matsuura Tomohisa, 230n12
Mazu Daoyi, 29, 55, 107–108, 193, 202, 269n94
meditation, 58–60, 63, 76, 114, 185–213, 214
"Meeting a Poet-Monk" (*Feng shiseng*; Qiji), 208–209
Mei Shengyu, 224
melopoeia, 144
Mencius, 252n46
Meng Jiao, 187–188, 189, 192
"Merits of the Dharma Preacher, The" (*Fashi gongde*), 174
Miaoxi Monastery, 56
"Middle Way" (*Zhongdao*), 131
miracle tales, 143–144
Mirror of Sources for the Sea of Rimes (*Yunhai jingyuan*; Yan Zhenqing), 56

Miu Duyi, 279n47
moderation, 72
Mohe bore boluomiduo xinjing. see *Heart Sūtra*
"Moral Hero" type, 52. *see also* recluses/reclusion
morel pearl, 135
Mount Heng, 31, 35–36
Mount Lu, 23, 24, 28–29, 31, 35–36, 66, 96
Mount Shishuang, 217–218
Mount Wutai, 163
"Mountain-Dwelling" series (*Shanju shi*; Guanxiu), 124, 215
mundane versus ultimate, 106–108, 129, 138, 161, 169, 202, 210, 211, 226
Museum of the Imperial Collection in Tokyo, 171

Nāgārjuna, 131
names, teaching of, 153–154
Nattier, Jan, 259n41
nature, connection to, 51–52, 58–60, 154
negation, 128–142
New Tang History (*Xin Tangshu*), 189
nirvāna, 128, 135
non-cultivation, 202, 208
North Mountain Record (*Beishan lu*; Shenqing), 22, 216
Northern School of Chan, 165
"Notes on Venerable Lingche's Literary Collection" (*Che shangren wenji ji*; Liu Yuxi), 77–78
Nugent, Christopher, 144

Old History of the Tang (*Jiu Tangshu*), 287n26
old-style *shi* (*guti shi*), 12, 117, 167
"On a Fan" (*Yong shan*), 133
"On Literary Meaning" (*Lun wenyi*; Wang Changling), 154
"On the Chin Couplet" (*Lun hanlian*; Shenyu), 131–133
"On the Goose" (*Yong e*; Luo Binwang), 257n9
"On the Meanings of Sound, Script, and Reality" (*Shōji jissō gi*, Kūkai), 154
Origins of the Vinaya School (*Lüzong yinyuan*; Lingche), 65
Ornamental Rafters of Brush and Tablet (*Bizha hualiang*; Shangguan Yi), 117
ornate speech, 22

INDEX

"outside the lines" (*fangwai*), 51–52, 53, 67–68, 80, 85, 91
Ouyang Jiong, 171
Ouyang Xiu, 219, 223–224, 240–241n81, 248–249n5
Owen, Stephen, 7–8, 53, 83, 186, 230n15, 241n82, 283n94

Pan Dingwu, 266n60
Pan Yue, 50, 51
Pañcaviṃśati-sāhasrikā-prajñāpāramitā sūtra (*Fangguan bore jing*), 258n34
Parable of the Burning House, 274n148
Parable of the Jewel in the Robe, 274n151
parallelism, 117, 119, 134–135, 208
"Parting with Master Haochu at Haiyang Lake" (*Haiyang hu bie Haochu shi*; Liu Yuxi), 248n85
Patriarch's Hall Collection (*Zutang ji*), 102
patronage, 36
patterned language, 12
Pei Yue, 32, 200, 202
perfect interfusion of principle and phenomenon, 107
"Perfect Man" type of recluse, 52. *see also* recluses/reclusion
Perfected Lord of Inspection (*Caifang zhenjun*), 24
performative speech, 145
phenomena, 174, 202
physical toll of writing poetry, 191, 197, 208
Piṇḍola Bhāradvāja, 171
Platform Sūtra of the Sixth Patriarch (*Liuzu tanjing*), 96
Poems of the Masters (*Qianjia shi*), 230n12
poem-worlds (*jing*), 99
poetic orthodoxy, 53
Poetic Paradigms (*Shishi*; Jiaoran), 57–58, 63–64, 207, 243n25, 280n57
poet-monks (*shiseng*)
  defined, 237n34
  expansion of usage of, 84–85
  fame of, 82
  first generation of, 48–81
  formation of tradition of, 82–109
  as general term, 81
  geography of, 25–36, 27fig, 29fig, 30fig, 31fig
  growth in number of, 33
  history of, 19–25
  mobility and, 44, 46

networks and, 42–43
reception of, 214–219
as respectable, 94
self-awareness among, 102
sociality of, 36–46
spread of term of, 69
stages of development of, 35–36, 46–47
see also individual poet-monks; individual works
"poetry demon" (*shimo*), 195
Poetry Manual of the Literary Grove (*Wenyuan shige*), 99
practical esotericae (*shimi*), 161
Prajñā-pāramitā Heart Sūtra. see *Heart Sūtra*
prajñāpāramitā scriptures, 130
"Prayer Summons" (*Qizhao*), 161, 267n69
"Preface to *Poetic Paradigms*" (*Shishi xu*; Jiaoran), 57, 63
"Preface to the Collection of Chan Sources" (*Chanyuan zhuquan ji duxu*; Zongmi), 284n97
"Presented to Master Gu" (*Shang Gu dafu*), 263n17
"Presented to the Reverend of Donglin Monastery" (*Shang donglin heshang*; Guanxiu), 168–170
"Presented to Vice Director Cui on Taking the Examinations" (*Shengshi ri shang Cui shilang*; Liu Deren), 189
principle (*li*), 174, 202
pure conversation (*qingtan*), 6, 231n24
purity aesthetic (*qing*), 196

Qian Liu, 44
Qian Qi, 42
Qian Zhongshu, 185
Qibai, 40, 43–44, 45fig, 88
Qichan, 3, 210–211
Qiji
  in anthologies, 220
  attention due to, 4
  double drafting (*shuangni*) and, 119
  exchange poetry and, 36, 38, 40, 41
  incantation and, 144
  influence of, 10–11
  on Jia Dao, 187
  in Jiangnan, 34
  kuyin aesthetic and, 193, 194–197
  Lotus Sūtra and, 176, 179–184
  meditation and, 186, 201–213
  preface to works of, 98
  prominence of, 8, 105–108

Qiji (*continued*)
  reception and, 217, 218–219
  repetition and, 121
  reputation of, 221–222, 225–226
  retriplication and, 123
  Right Man and, 1–2, 3
  spells and, 155–157, 162
  Tanyu and, 255n88
  use of "poet-monk" by, 82–83
  White Lotus Society and, 23
Qinggu, 106
Qingjiang, 78, 174
Qinglong Monastery, 152, 153
Qisong, 216
Qiyi, 130
Qu Yuan, 138
Quan Deyu, 42, 52, 62, 64, 66–68, 85, 93
Quan Tang shi, 10, 33, 116, 119

"Reading a Compilation of the Venerable Xiumu's Songs" (*Du Xiumu shangren ge pian*; Li Xianyong), 100–102
"Reading the Poetry Collections of Liu Deren and Jia Dao" (*Du Liu Deren Jia Dao ji*; Guanxiu), 193–194
"Reading the Venerable Qiji's Collection" (*Du Qiji shangren ji*; Qichan), 210–211
recent-style *shi* (*jinti shi*), 12
reception of poet-monks, 214–219
recluses/reclusion, 51–53, 68, 80, 85
Record of Buddhist States (*Foguo ji*; Faxian), 164
Record of Conversations (*Yinhua lu*; Zhao Lin), 27–28
Record of Famous Painters of Yizhou (*Yizhou minghua lu*), 170
Record of Linji (*Linji lu*), 178
Record of Signs from the Unseen Realm, A (*Mingxiang ji*; Wang Yan), 262n6, 262n79
Record of Yunmen (*Yunmen guanglu*), 102
records of sayings, 102
Records of the Grand Historian (*Shiji*; Sima Qian), 85
reduplication, 117, 118*fig*, 141
religion
  defined, 11–12
  literature and, 11–14, 226–227
  as set of practices, 13–14
  see also Buddhists/Buddhism
Ren Bantang, 269n91
repetition, 113–142, 214
"Replying to Editor Yu's 'On a Winter Night'" (*Da Yu jiaoshu dongye*; Jiaoran), 59–60, 63

"Replying to the Venerable Guang" (*Chou Guang shangren*; Qiji), 202–203
"Replying to Vice Director Wei Yingwu of Suzhou" (*Da Suzhou Wei Yingwu langzhong*; Jiaoran), 60–61
"Replying to Zheng Fanghui" (*Da Zheng Fanghui*; Jiaoran), 245n46
"Respectfully Given to Dharma Master Zhen of Hexi" (*Fengzeng Hexi Zhen fashi*; Qibai), 43–44
retriplication, 114–117, 121–127, 127*fig*, 139, 142, 182
Return to Allegiance Army (*Guiyi jun*), 43
"Rhapsody on Literature" (*Wen fu*; Lu Ji), 93, 198, 199, 204, 212
rhyming binom parallelism, 117
Right Man (*Zhengren*), 2–3
"Rising from an Illness" (*Bing qi*; Lai Peng), 249n14
Ritual Instructions for Altar Records (*Tanfa yize*), 178, 179
Robson, James, 273n135
Roth, Harold D., 259n37
Ruan Ji, 50, 51, 115, 122
Ruichuan, 152
Rules of Purity for Gardens of Chan (*Chanyuan qinggui*), 216, 217
"Running into an Indian Monk Going to Mount Wutai" (*Yu Wutian seng ru Wutai*; Guanxiu), 163–164

Śākyamuni, 195
samādhi, 258n34
Saṃgha Rectifier (*Sengzheng*), 31, 34, 106
saṃsāra, 135
Sanskrit, 156–157, 162–163, 164, 165, 167, 173–174
scriptures, 143–144, 145–151
Secret Exemplars of the Two "Souths" (*Ernan mizhi*; Jia Dao), 187
"Sending Thoughts of Sengda, the Old Meditator of Jiangxi" (*Ji huai Jiangxi Sengda chanweng*; Qiji), 196–197
Sengda, 197
Sengxiang, 262n7
"Sent to a Poet-Monk" (*Zeng shiseng*; Wuke), 84
"Sent to Clergyman Yuanfu" (*Ji Yuanfu daoren*; Chen Tao), 88–89
"Sent to Director Zheng Gu" (*Ji Zheng Gu langzhong*; Qiji), 204–207
"Sent to Qinggu of Xuzhou" (*Ji Xuzhou Qinggu*; Qiji), 106–108
"Sent to the Poet-Monk Wenxiu" (*Ji ti shiseng Wenxiu*; Zheng Gu), 95–97

INDEX 325

"Sent to the Venerable Wuke" (*Ji Wuke shangren;* Yao He), 84
"Sent to the Venerable Zhongyi of Tianxiang Monastery and Recluse Sun of Fuchun" (*Ji Tianshang si Zhongyi shangren Fuchun Sun chushi;* Xu Hun), 84–85
Shangguan Yi, 117, 119
Shangyan, 41–42, 90–94, 239n62
Shaowei, 20–21
Sharf, Robert, 235n9, 265n40, 275n163
Shegong, 242n19
Shen Yue, 248n83
Shenqing, 22, 72–73, 74, 216, 236n14
Shenxiu, 95–96
Shenyu, 119–121, 131–133
Shidi yishu, 264n26
Shige (Shenyu), 131–133
shi-poetry, 5, 9, 12, 37, 48, 69. *see also* elite verse
Shishuang Qingzhu, 217–218, 225
Shouzhi, 284n101
Shu (geographic region), 34
Shu Wei, 4
Shuowen jiezi, 255n88
Siddham, 164, 168
"Siddham Stanzas for the Meditation Gate of the *Laṅkāvatāra Sūtra* Spoken by the Buddha" (*Foshuo lengqiejing chanmen xitan zhang,* Dinghui), 164–168
Sikong Tu, 9, 32–33, 116
Siku quanshu, 221–222
silence, 208
simple retriplication, 121–122, 126, 182
"single breath" (*yi qi*), 2
"Sitting in Stillness" (*Jingzuo;* Qiji), 207–208
Song Biographies of Eminent Monks (*Song gaoseng zhuan;* Zanning), 105, 172, 236–237n19, 252n50, 254n73, 263n16
Song dynasty, 26, 34, 215–220
"Song of Bright Spring" (*Yangchun qu;* Guanxiu), 114–116, 121–122
"Song of Sun after Sun" (*Riri qu;* Qiji), 123
"Song of the Realization of the Way" (*Zhengdao ge*), 148, 178
"Song on Listening to the Venerable Jian and Zheng Recite the *Lotus Sūtra* in Huaizhou, with Master Qingjiang on a Moonlit Night, A" (*Tong Qingjiang shi yueye ting Jian Zheng er shangren wei Huaizhou zhuan Fahua jing ge;* Zhu Wan), 174–176
"Song on Looking at Huaisu's Cursive Calligraphy" (*Huaisu caoshu ge;* Guanxiu), 223
Song Yu, 256n6
Songs of Chu (*Chuci*), 21, 138, 198, 254n70
song-style poetry (*gexing*), 9, 101, 165, 219–220
sonority, 144–145, 151–162, 174, 176
Sørensen, Henrik, 265n40, 269n91, 275n163
"Sorrows of Parting" (*Bie yuan;* Huixiu), 77, 231n21
"South" (*Nan;* section of *Bunkyō hifuron*), 154
"Spell for Contemplating the Three Paths" (*Ruo nian sandao zhou*), 148
"Spell for Distributing Food" (*Sanshi zhou*), 148
"Spell for Release from Purgatory" (*Diyu cuisui zhou*), 148
"Spell of Great Compassion" (*Dabei zhou*), 152–153
Spells, 143, 145–151, 149fig. *see also dhāraṇī*
"Spring" (*Chun;* Guanxiu), 128–129, 130
"Staying at Lingdong Abbey" (*Su Lingong guan;* Lingyi), 54–55
"Stirred at Night, Dispelling My Sorrow" (*Yegan ziqian;* Meng Jiao), 187–188
"Stirred by a Whim in Mid-Spring" (*Zhongchun ganxing;* Qiji), 1–2
Su Shi, 222, 225
sub-creation, theory of, 63
"suchness" (*zhenru*), 2
Sun Chuo, 5
Sun Guangxian, 98–99, 201, 211
śūnyatā/emptiness, nature of, 128, 130, 131
Supplement to the History of Our State (*Guoshi bu,* Li Zhao), 28, 69
Śūraṃgama Sūtra (*Shoulengyan jing*), 157, 211
"*Sūtra*-Upholding Monk, The" (*Changchijing seng;* Guanxiu), 177–179
system, idea of literature as, 232n38

Taizong, Emperor, 24–25
"Taking Backroads to My Hometown during the Chaos" (*Luanzhong tou lu ru guxiang;* Pei Yue), 32
Talks on Poetry (*Liuyi shihua;* Ouyang Xiu), 224
Tanaka Ryōshō, 275n163

Tang Poetry, Sorted (*Tangshi gui*), 220
Tanyu, 10, 97, 104–105, 255n88
Tao Qian, 52
"Ten Rhymes Inscribed for the Venerable Daozong" (*Ti Daozong shangren shiyun*; Bai Juyi), 74–76
"Text for the Transfer of Merit after the Transfer of Scriptures" (*Zhuanjing hou huixiangwen*), 148
Three Hundred Tang Poems (*Tangshi sanbai shou*), 230n12
Tian Qiuzi, 254n71
Transmission of the Baolin Monastery (*Baolin zhuan*), 64, 102
"Traveling's Hard" (*Xinglu nan*; anonymous), 139–141
"Traveling's Hard" (*Xinglu nan*; Baoyue), 104
Treatise on Perfect Illumination (*Yuanming lun*), 282n79
Treatise on the Essentials of Gurading the Mind (*Shouxin yaolun*; Hongren), 192–193
Treatise on the Men and Dharma of Laṇkāvatāra (*Lengqie ren fa zhi*), 165
Tripiṭaka (title), 155, 157
Tripiṭaka Zhiman, 155–156
true and false, metacognition of, 137
truth, two levels of, 107, 129
two Esotericae, 161–162

ultimate, mundane versus, 106–108, 129, 138, 161, 169, 202, 210, 211, 226
Uruvilvā Kāśyapa, 242n19
Uṣṇīṣavijayā-dhāraṇī Sūtra (*Foding zunsheng tuoluoni jing*), 152

versatility, praise of, 78, 80
Vinaya, 22–23, 50, 55, 64

Wang Anshi, 257n11
Wang Changling, 99, 154, 198
Wang Dao, 23, 247n73
Wang Fanzhi, 4, 230n15
Wang Jian, 34, 44
Wang Li, 230n12
Wang Mao, 286n15
Wang Wei, 25, 230n15, 234n54
Wang Xiulin, 266n60
Wang Xizhi, 71
Watson, Burton, 230n12, 234n1
Way, the (*Dao*), 2, 13, 169
Way of poetry, 97–98
Wei Yingwu, 42, 60–61
Wei Zhuang, 32, 34, 44

Weijin, 107
Wei-Yang lineage, 107, 201
Wen of Zhou, King, 85
Wen Tingyun, 8, 153
Wenchang, 69–71, 73
Wenxin diaolong, 281n65
Wenxiu, 95–97, 105
Wenxuan, 76, 143, 198, 231n21
Wenxuan commentary (Li Shan), 254n71
White Lotus Collection, The (*Bailian ji*; Qiji), 23
White Lotus Society, 23, 96
"White Snow in Bright Spring" (*Yangchun baixue*; Song Yu), 256n6
Williams, Nicholas Morrow, 56, 234n54
"Written Offhand, Having Thought of a Clergyman in the Mountains" (*Ouzuo yin huai shanzhong daolü*; Guanxiu), 137–138
"Written on the Temple of Tripiṭaka Hongyi" (*Ti Hongyi sanzang yuan*; Guanxiu), 157–160, 263n17
Wu Ke, 7
Wu Rong, 42, 97–98, 102, 104, 105
Wu Yuanheng, 266n56
Wu Yun, 24
Wu Zetian, Emperor, 139
Wuben, 83
Wuke, 36, 38, 40, 83, 84, 89, 96, 152, 162
Wunengzi, 32
Wuzhen, 43–44, 45*fig*
Wuzong, Emperor, 35, 86

Xi Zuochi, 71
Xiang Yu, 138
Xiao Gang, 89
Xie An, 71
Xie Lingyun, 5, 23, 50, 51, 71, 164, 239n62
Xiufeng, 78
Xiongnu, 44
Xitanzi ji (Zhiguang), 164
Xiumu, 31, 100–102
Xu Dong, 240–241n81
Xu Hun, 84–85
Xu Yan, 229n4
Xu Yin, 187, 257n17
Xuantai, 217
Xuanyuan Ji, 44
Xuanzang, 129–130, 155
Xuanzong, Emperor, 24, 43, 86
Xue clan, 90–91, 239n62
Xue Neng, 90–92

INDEX

Xue Tianwei, 255n75
Xunzi, 137, 138, 252n46
Xuzhong, 187

Yan Rao, 90–92
Yan Wei, 42
Yan Yu, 220, 249n6, 276n2
Yan Zhenqing, 24, 56, 104
Yang Jingqing, 234n54
Yang Juyuan, 199
Yang Xiaoshan, 257n11
Yao He, 42, 83, 84, 104, 199–200, 221
Yellow Emperor, 251n36
yi (idea), 99, 132–133
Yongjia Xuanjue, 148
Yu Di, 52, 58, 245n48
Yu Xuanji, 232n28
Yuan Zhen, 28, 232n34
Yuanfu, 88–89
Yuchi Gong, 287n26
yuefu, 12, 100, 102, 104, 115, 124, 139
Yunxian zaji, 278n28

Zanning, 236–237n19, 247n72
Zha Minghao, 237n35
Zhang Biaochen, 287n19
Zhang Bowei, 258n20

Zhang Daoling, 259n37
Zhang Hu, 249n10
Zhang Shu, 253n59
Zhang Yu, 256n2
Zhang Zhuo, 217–218
Zhao Lin, 27–28
Zheng Gu, 95–96, 204–207, 257n18
Zhenguan, 10
Zhi Dun, 5, 6, 22, 71
Zhiguang, 164, 167
Zhixuan, 28, 29, 88, 152–153
Zhiyi, 135, 137
Zhong Xing, 220, 221
Zhou, 269n91
Zhou He, 38, 40, 96, 103–104, 187
Zhou Yukai, 277n9
Zhu Wan, 174–177, 184
Zhu Yun, 116
Zhuangzi, 3, 51–52, 135, 229n3
Zhuanxingzhong de Tang Wudai shiseng (Zha), 237n35
Zigong, 51–52
Zong Bing, 23
Zongmi, 284n97
Zongyuan, 105–106
zouyu (mythical beast), 89
Zuozhuan, 161

www.ingramcontent.com/pod-product-compliance
Lightning Source LLC
Chambersburg PA
CBHW021149230426
43667CB00006B/316